I0605049

HATED BY ALL THE RIGHT PEOPLE

HATED BY ALL THE RIGHT PEOPLE

Tucker Carlson and the Unraveling of the Conservative Mind

JASON ZENGERLE

Crooked Media Reads
A zando IMPRINT
NEW YORK

Crooked Media Reads is an imprint of Zando.
zandoprojects.com

First Edition: January 2026

Text design by Neuwirth & Associates, Inc.
Cover design by Zevvy Smith-Danford

Library of Congress Control Number: 2025939089

978-1-63893-293-2 (Hardcover)
978-1-63893-294-9 (ebook)

10 9 8 7 6 5 4 3 2 1
Manufactured in the United States of America
LBK

For Claire

We are what we pretend to be.

—Kurt Vonnegut

It is autumn and my camouflage is dying.

—David Berman

PROLOGUE

ON THE FIRST SATURDAY OF March in 2020, Tucker Carlson embarked on a secret mission to Mar-a-Lago. He was hoping to scare Donald Trump straight about the coronavirus.

Carlson was one of the forty-fifth president's biggest media boosters. His prime-time Fox News show, *Tucker Carlson Tonight*, was the most-watched cable-news program in America. Among the four million or so people who regularly tuned in were Trump and his top aides. As Jared Kushner, Trump's son-in-law and a senior adviser to the president, admonished one new hire, "You can't work in this White House and not watch Tucker Carlson."

And yet Carlson had conflicted, complicated feelings about the Big Orange, as he liked to refer to the president behind his back. On the one hand, Carlson admired what he viewed as Trump's political courage and pugnaciousness, and he agreed with many of Trump's policies, especially his restrictionist immigration ones. But, in Carlson's mind, Trump's good traits were in constant tension with his destructive ones. He was repulsed by Trump's solipsism, his thin skin, his emotional immaturity, and his work ethic (or lack thereof)—all of which threatened an ideological project that Carlson deeply believed in. When

Trump would sometimes call Carlson after he'd signed off from *Tucker Carlson Tonight*, Carlson wasn't flattered so much as disturbed; he was incredulous that the leader of the free world had nothing better to do than watch cable news and then gossip about what he'd just seen. Unlike his Fox brethren Sean Hannity and Lou Dobbs, who reveled in their access to the president, Carlson maintained a wary, personal and professional distance. He didn't want to get too close to Trump, concluding that everyone who did, like his and Trump's mutual friend Roger Stone—who'd been convicted of seven felony counts for trying to obstruct a federal investigation into Trump's 2016 campaign—was ultimately destroyed by the association.

But on that Saturday in March, it was Carlson who was seeking an audience with Trump. For weeks, he had been watching with growing alarm as the coronavirus spread from China to Europe to the United States. While the other Fox prime-time hosts, Hannity and Laura Ingraham, ignored COVID-19—or, when they did address it, dismissed the virus as a liberal hoax—Carlson had devoted several segments to it on his show, even inviting Anthony Fauci on as a guest. But Trump never called to talk after *those* episodes. Carlson knew that the president was not taking the threat of the pandemic seriously. He was loath to ask Trump for any favors. In fact, when Trump would call Carlson, Carlson tried to keep his side of the conversation to a polite minimum. But now, facing the prospect of a global pandemic, he believed he had a moral obligation to try to get Trump to do something about it. Carlson's wife, Susie, told him that it was his duty as an Episcopalian.

Carlson—who spends his winters in Florida, where he owns a home on the exclusive Gasparilla Island—drove 180 miles across the state to Palm Beach. He'd never been to Mar-a-Lago, and he did not want anyone to know that he was going now, so he arranged with the Secret Service to slip into the club through a little-used entrance, away from the bustling lobby. Then he was hustled to Trump's private quarters, where the president was expecting him. For the next two hours, Carlson tried to put all the persuasive skills he'd honed as a TV pundit to the task of convincing the president that COVID-19 was not a joke. He told Trump about a personal friend—someone he'd just seen a month and a half before for dinner—who caught the virus and was now in the ICU with double pneumonia and fighting for his life. He explained the concept of community transmission and offered dire predictions about a lack of ventilators. He argued as passionately as he could that the pandemic posed an existential threat to the United States—and, in case that didn't resonate with his intended audience, to Trump's reelection too. Trump heard Carlson out. At one point, the president even got Mike Pence to sit in on the meeting so he could listen, as well. But when the conversation was over, Carlson could tell that he hadn't gotten through to the president. His influence, seemingly, could only go so far.

To add insult to injury, as Carlson was leaving Mar-a-Lago, he stumbled upon the lavish fifty-first birthday party for Kimberly Guilfoyle, Carlson's former colleague at Fox News and Donald Trump Jr.'s then girlfriend. A who's who of the MAGA universe had descended on the private club to celebrate. It included Jared and Ivanka, Rudy Giuliani and Matt Gaetz, Pence and Lindsey Graham. One of the revelers spotted Carlson. Before he could escape, he was ushered into the Mar-a-Lago ballroom, where the party's emcee shouted his name over the PA system and he was promptly seated at the head table—his reluctant presence at Mar-a-Lago no longer a secret.

In the following months, Carlson's feelings about Trump became less conflicted—and the distance he put between himself and the president grew greater, not just behind the scenes but also on-air. As Trump continued to bungle the COVID response,

Carlson warned his viewers, "People you trust, people you probably voted for, have spent weeks minimizing what is clearly a very serious problem." In the wake of George Floyd's murder in May, Carlson lambasted Trump for not cracking down harder on Black Lives Matter protesters in Washington and elsewhere. "If you can't keep a Fox News correspondent from getting attacked directly across from your house, how can you protect my family?" Carlson rhetorically asked the president on his show. "How are you going to protect the country? How hard are you trying?" And in the days after Trump lost to Joe Biden in November, Carlson was the rare Fox host who publicly refused to countenance Trump's claims that the election had been stolen. Speaking of Sidney Powell, a Trump lawyer who'd been making the rounds on Fox and other conservative outlets to allege a vast conspiracy that "communist" interests had hacked into voting machines to delete votes for Trump, Carlson told his viewers in an incredulous tone, "What Powell was describing would amount to the single greatest crime in American history. Millions of votes stolen in a day. Democracy destroyed. The end of our centuries-old system of government." When he invited Powell on his show to make her case—offering her the full hour, even the entire week, during which, he promised, he would have "listened quietly the whole time at rapt attention"—she demurred. "She never sent us any evidence, despite a lot of requests, polite requests," Carlson said. "When we kept pressing, she got angry and told us to stop contacting her." In a text exchange with Ingraham, Carlson complained that Trump had refused to rein in Powell. "They said nothing in public. Pretty disgusting. And now Trump, I learned this morning, is sitting back and letting them lose the senate. He doesn't care. I care."

After Trump's supporters stormed the US Capitol on January 6, in an unsuccessful effort to prevent Congress from certifying Biden's election, Carlson had seemingly had enough.

In a text message to one of his producers, Alex Pfeiffer, he raged against Trump: "He's a demonic force, a destroyer. But he's not going to destroy us. I've been thinking about this every day for four years." In another text to Pfeiffer, Carlson relished the prospect of finally getting out from under the Big Orange cloud. "We are very, very close to being able to ignore Trump most nights," he wrote. "I truly can't wait."

Almost four years later, Carlson again found himself at Mar-a-Lago, but in a very different headspace, attending Trump's election-night party on November 5, 2024. In the days to come, the supplicants seeking forgiveness for having opposed Trump—Joe Scarborough and Mika Brzezinski, Jeff Bezos and Mark Zuckerberg, and a host of other media and business titans—would troop to his Florida estate to engage in ritual acts of self-abasement. "Everyone wants to be my friend," Trump would marvel. But on this evening, in the anxious and hopeful hours before he completed the greatest comeback in American political history, Trump wanted to be surrounded by his most loyal and valued supporters, those who had already bent the knee.

The party's guest list was, again, a who's who of the MAGA universe. It included Eric and Donald Trump Jr., Elon Musk and Dana White, and Robert F. Kennedy Jr. and Marjorie Taylor Greene. They gathered in a gilded ballroom, where they ate beef Wellington and sushi and sipped champagne while watching the election results on giant television screens. And then, when their appointed time came, they headed, one by one, to Mar-a-Lago's billiard room, just off the ballroom floor, where Carlson was waiting for them.

Carlson was also on Trump's guest list, as loyal and as valued as anyone at Mar-a-Lago that evening. In the months leading up to the election, he had, for all intents and purposes, become part of the Trump campaign. Behind the scenes, Carlson was a crucial voice in Trump's ear urging him to pick JD Vance as his running mate; in June, after Carlson got wind that Trump was leaning toward Marco Rubio or Doug Burgum, he called Trump from Australia, where he was on a speaking tour, to warn that Rubio and Burgum were neoconservative ideologues who supported military adventurism overseas—and, more ominous, that if Trump made either one his vice president, US intelligence agencies would try to assassinate him. (In July, two days after Trump survived an assassination attempt in Butler, Pennsylvania, he announced Vance as his vice presidential choice.)

In front of the cameras and crowds, Carlson stumped for Trump—including in prime time at the Republican National Convention in July and at Trump's Madison Square Garden rally in October. During Carlson's own sixteen-city speaking tour that fall, which played to sold-out arenas across the country, he had Vance and Trump join him as his special guests in the crucial battleground states of Pennsylvania and Arizona respectively. There was no one better, save for the candidate himself, at cutting through the noise. Speaking at a Trump rally in Georgia in October, Carlson bizarrely but memorably compared the United States to a misbehaving "hormone-addled 15-year-old girl" and Trump to an angry "dad" who comes home to give her "a vigorous spanking." At Madison Square Garden, he racistly mocked Kamala Harris as a "Samoan Malaysian, low-IQ former California prosecutor."

Carlson seemed as intent on inflaming Trump's opponents as firing up his supporters; he recognized that in an age defined by populism, tribalism, polarization, and negative partisanship, the true measure of a person's political worth is determined by the number—and nature—of his enemies. As Carlson once complimented Viktor Orbán, the Hungarian prime minister whose autocratic ways have made him anathema to Western liberals but a hero to America's New Right, "You're truly hated by all the right people."

Carlson had spent the early part of election night in Mar-a-Lago's ballroom with Trump himself, enjoying his front-row seat to history. Recalling later how he had watched Trump make fun of one of his wealthiest donors, he gushed, "I don't think anyone has spoken to this billionaire that way ever." But at 7:00 p.m., when the first polls closed, Carlson ducked out of the party; he had to get to work. He was hosting an election-night show that was streaming on YouTube and X—and, with Trump's permission and encouragement, he was broadcasting live from Mar-a-Lago.

Wearing his standard 2024 campaign uniform of blue blazer, khakis, and blue-and-gold rep tie, Carlson sat at a small, marble-topped table beneath a giant oil painting of a young, sun-dappled Trump in tennis togs; over the next three hours, in between swigs of Perrier and the occasional popping of a nicotine pouch, he bantered with fellow members of Trump's inner circle. When they weren't offering fulsome praise of Trump for his intelligence, his sense of humor, and his work ethic—"an absolute beast," according to White; "Shouldn't scientists study him?" Carlson asked—they were congratulating one another on the roles they played in Trump's victory, which was drawing ever closer by the minute. "I appreciate what you've done, Tucker," Kennedy told Carlson. "You just went more all in than I've ever seen anybody ever go," Carlson told Musk.

When it was time to sign off for the evening, Carlson could barely contain his glee. "I've never seen anything like this in my life. . . . Amazing," he told the millions of viewers who were watching his live stream. "We're going to see Trump—and join the celebration!" He headed back into the ballroom.

The personal and professional distance Carlson traveled in the nearly four years between those two Mar-a-Lago visits is dotted with failure and success, principle and compromise, insight and delusion—but it is defined by unshakable confidence, unswerving ambition, and unbending will. In all of that, it is a synecdoche of Carlson's longer journey through American media and American politics over the last three decades.

THE FIRST TIME I MET Tucker Carlson was in 1997, when I was an intern at *The New Republic* and he was a hotshot young writer for *The Weekly Standard*. Back then, Carlson had a standing lunch date with *TNR* writer Stephen Glass, his fellow tyro, and every so often he would swing through our Washington offices.

Carlson and Glass were just a few calendar years older than I was, but their careers were already light-years ahead of my own. Only in their mid-twenties, they were regularly churning out rollicking, must-read stories for Washington's two most prestigious political magazines—the conservative *Standard* and the progressive *TNR*—about oddball characters like the Orthodox rabbi working for Pat Buchanan's presidential campaign or the group of evangelicals who, believing George H. W. Bush was the messiah, founded the Church of George Herbert Walker Christ.

Occasionally, the bow-tied Carlson would hang out and make small talk with the *TNR* interns, offering tidbits of Capitol Hill gossip or dropping hints about his next big story. He had a wicked sense of humor and a strong contrarian streak. I remember him describing the conservative éminence grise Grover Norquist as a "comb sniffer." As we picked at our sad desk salads or Styrofoam containers from the nearby Greek deli, we were captivated. Carlson seemed so much older, wiser, and worldlier than we were. Then Glass would emerge from his office, Carlson would bid us adieu, and together they would head to the Palm or the Tabard Inn to discuss what we could only assume were far weightier and dishier matters.

It was, of course, a very different world from the world of

today, both in politics and in media. Bill Clinton was in his second term in the White House and squarely in the crosshairs of Newt Gingrich and what Hillary Clinton famously described as the vast right-wing conspiracy. The year before, the federal government had shut down because of a budget battle. A year later, Clinton would be impeached. And yet, for all the partisan rancor, the stakes were impossibly low. The Cold War was over, and the economy was booming. Looking back on it now, there was a LARPing quality to all of the political fighting. In print, writers at *TNR* and *The Standard* were waging ideological war. In real life, they were meeting for lunch.

Which was yet another sign of how different those times were. Cable news was still in its infancy. CNN was not long removed from its breakthrough coverage of the Gulf War, and both the Fox News Channel and MSNBC were just a year old. The Internet was brand-new. Print publications were just beginning to launch rudimentary websites. The sinkhole of social media was unimaginable—and still more than a decade away from swallowing us all. The great stories, and the consequential debates they sparked, were still found in the periodicals that came out weekly and monthly. *Time*, *Newsweek*, *New York Magazine*, *The Atlantic*, *Esquire*, *GQ*, *Vanity Fair*. On Mondays, I'd arrive at the *TNR* offices early and go to the mail room, where stacks of the new issues of *The New Yorker* had been hand delivered. Pilfering copies that were intended for more senior staff, I'd flip to the table of contents and look for the bylines of Remnick, Lemann, Frazier, and the other legendary magazine writers. It seemed foreordained that Carlson and Glass would eventually join their storied ranks.

That didn't happen. In May 1998, about eight months after I arrived at *TNR*, Glass was unmasked as the perpetrator of perhaps the most sustained and elaborate fraud in journalistic history. Practically all the unforgettable characters who populated his stories were figments of his imagination. All told, he fabricated people or scenes in more than three dozen stories. As an intern, I'd fact-checked several of them, and while I wish I could say I was the one who busted Glass, I was fooled like everyone else. In the end, it was Adam Penenberg, a *Forbes Digital Tool* reporter, who called bullshit. The moment Penenberg published his story exposing Glass's perfidy, Glass's journalism career came to a sudden and shocking end. Today, he works for a personal injury law firm in Beverly Hills—not as a lawyer but as a paralegal; although Glass graduated from law school, the California Supreme Court rejected his admission to the state bar on the grounds of his lack of moral fitness to practice law.

Although Glass's downfall prompted some whispers that perhaps Carlson, too, had fabulist tendencies—after all, the characters and scenes in his stories were as colorful as those in his now-erstwhile friend's—that speculation quickly subsided, and his magazine career continued on its same ineluctably upward trajectory. In 1999, the former *Vanity Fair* and *New Yorker* editor Tina Brown signed him up as a political reporter for her splashy new magazine *Talk*; his profile of George W. Bush in the inaugural issue—portraying the then Texas governor as stubborn, callow, and profane—was a characterological X-ray revealing precisely the flaws that would make Bush such a disastrous president. Two years later, *New York Magazine* tapped Carlson to write its prestigious National Affairs column; after 9/11, he reported from Pakistan, just a few months before *The Wall Street Journal*'s Daniel Pearl was kidnapped and killed there. In 2003, Carlson's *Esquire* story about his trip to Africa with Al Sharpton, Cornel West, and a group of other Black leaders trying to end a civil war in Liberia was deemed a "low-grade miracle, a masterpiece of absurdity" by *The Washington Post* and was a finalist for a National Magazine Award. Carlson's byline now had the effect afforded only few journalists.

Still, for all his success in print, Carlson was increasingly drawn to the bright lights and cold studios of cable news. For the longest time, only the most seasoned and celebrated scribblers were afforded the opportunity to go on TV. But the advent of cable news led to an exponential increase in airtime that needed to be filled. By the mid-nineties, it seemed like every political writer in Washington, even *TNR* interns, was being asked to do dayside hits. Ever mindful of Gore Vidal's famous dictum—"never miss a chance to have sex or appear on television"—we all leaped at the opportunity.

Vidal, indeed, was a pioneer in this respect. His acrimonious debates with William F. Buckley during ABC's coverage of the 1968 Democratic and Republican conventions doubled the network's ratings and gave birth to the age of TV punditry. Needless to say, very few of us flooding the cable airwaves in the nineties were heirs to Vidal or Buckley. But Carlson turned out to be a natural talking head. With his preppy haircut and ever-present bow tie—the latter an affectation he picked up as a teenager from watching George Will on *This Week with David Brinkley*—he popped on-screen. Meanwhile, his glib self-assurance enabled him to speak with confidence about whatever that day's news required—whether it was Bob Dole or O. J. Simpson or Slobodan Milošević. Before long, Carlson was a regular on CNN, with a fifty-thousand-dollar-a-year contributor contract that almost doubled his *Weekly Standard* salary.

When Christopher Hitchens and other writer friends warned Carlson that television punditry was a waste of his prodigious journalistic talents, he reassured them that he shared their dim view of cable news. He knew the work wasn't serious. He recognized that TV people had "low IQs." His interest in television, he explained, was purely mercenary. He'd married his prep school girlfriend just a few months after both had finished college, and they already had two children (on their way to four).

He had a family to take care of, and TV was one way to ensure that he could.

But Carlson's professed fears of future penury belied his fascination with cable news—and his recognition of its growing political and cultural capital. While he still idolized George Plimpton, Hunter S. Thompson, and the other writers featured in Tom Wolfe's *The New Journalism* anthology that he kept in his *Weekly Standard* office, he recognized that their careers were no longer possible. Or, rather, that the fame, power, and influence they enjoyed as a result of their writing were no longer possible. Carlson intuited, more acutely than many of his ilk, that the brass ring we were all reaching for—the column in *Time*, the staff job at *The New Yorker*, the book contract with a major publisher—would be worth a whole lot less by the time any of us grasped it. Television, on the other hand, offered the surest path to what he sought. Whether he was being honest with his writer friends about how he viewed cable news, one thing was certain: Carlson was not one to temper his ambitions, and the winds of opportunity were changing.

And so Carlson largely put writing to the side and concentrated on television. The focus he once brought to dissecting Joan Didion's sentences he now spent on studying Ricki Lake's interview technique. In 2000, CNN bumped him up from a contributor to a bona fide host, giving him and the liberal commentator Bill Press their own talk show, *The Spin Room*. A year later, the cable network installed him in the "on the right" chair on its venerable political debate show *Crossfire*. At the age of thirty-two, he occupied perhaps the most prestigious perch in cable-news punditry. His decision to ignore his writer friends' advice appeared to be the right one.

But Carlson's early television success would prove illusory.

He became a national punchline in 2004 when Jon Stewart went on *Crossfire* and accused the show of "hurting America," while making fun of Carlson's bow tie and calling him a "dick"—all to the laughter and applause of the studio audience. A few months later CNN put *Crossfire* on hiatus. Carlson decamped to MSNBC to host a prime-time show, but after three time slots and two names, his program was canceled before it reached its third anniversary. A weekly public affairs show he hosted on PBS, *Tucker Carlson: Unfiltered*, had an even shorter run, lasting just a year. Meanwhile, Carlson's attempts to build a television career beyond the realms of news and politics were busts. The game show pilot he taped for CBS wasn't picked up. His stint as a contestant on the third season of ABC's *Dancing with the Stars* ended after just one episode when he was the first contestant eliminated. To his friends and admirers, his was a sad and cautionary tale—of a smart and talented journalist who'd been seduced and ultimately ruined by TV.

At his lowest point, he became a political analyst at the only cable-news network he'd yet to work at, Fox News—or, as he'd once described it, "a mean, sick group of people." It was quite a comedown from his CNN and MSNBC days. Prime-time appearances, much less his own show, were distant dreams. He was relegated to the bottom of Fox's on-air-talent depth chart—doing the dayside hits the more esteemed pundits passed on and spending his Saturdays and Sundays in New York, away from his wife and kids in Washington, to host cooking segments on Fox's weekend morning show. Such is the lot of the cable-news journeyman, which was what Carlson had become. But he continued to pay his dues, hoping for his big break.

And then it arrived in 2016 in the unlikely form of Donald J. Trump. It's hard to imagine now, but in the early days of Trump's first White House run, Fox News—and the conservative commentariat in general—was skeptical of, if not outright hostile to, the thrice-married, formerly pro-choice Hillary Clinton campaign donor. Carlson was the rare exception. He didn't necessarily support Trump, but he didn't dismiss him, either. He'd always loved rogues, and his contrarian streak had morphed into a populist one in recent years; long before most conservative pundits, he recognized the anger Trump was tapping into. As Trump dominated cable coverage, Fox was desperate for talking heads who were at least Trump agnostic, not for political reasons but for programming ones, and Carlson began to get more airtime. And as Trump gained steam, Carlson began to speak more forcefully in favor of him, embracing him as an avatar of the right-wing populism Carlson had come to embrace. In November, six days after Trump's victory, Fox premiered Carlson's own evening show, *Tucker Carlson Tonight*, which soon became the highest-rated show in the history of cable news. It also became a platform for some of the most extreme, inflammatory, and racist content to ever appear on cable television. But that only seemed to make the show, and Carlson, more consequential.

Even after Carlson was fired from Fox in the spring of 2023—a move that, to this day, remains shrouded in mystery—he managed to maintain his grip on both the conservative movement and the nation's attention. Six weeks after leaving Fox News, he debuted a new show on the social media platform then known as Twitter, and in December 2023, he launched—with the support of Musk and a handful of other reactionary billionaires—his own media company, the Tucker Carlson Network, and continued to do his show online. He used his new platform to lend a crucial hand to Trump—first when it seemed as if the former president might face a real challenge in the 2024 Republican presidential primaries from Florida governor Ron DeSantis, and then in the general election against Harris—and a sympathetic ear to Vladimir Putin, who picked Carlson to conduct his first interview with a Western journalist since Russia's invasion of

Ukraine in 2022. Indeed, Carlson's departure from Fox turned out to be a blessing in disguise for him, as it freed him from the albatross of declining cable-news viewership and launched him into the brave new world of new media and social media. With Trump now back in the White House, and the media landscape being remade by the day, Carlson has achieved a level of power and influence that not even he could have imagined when he was promoted to Fox's prime-time lineup nine years ago, much less three decades ago when he embarked on his career in political journalism at *The Weekly Standard*.

I can't claim to have been friends with Carlson. He never treated me to lunch at his regular table at the Metropolitan Club. Before he stopped drinking, we didn't shut down campaign trail bars in Manchester and Des Moines. But he was the subject of—and, more frequently, a source for—a decent amount of my reporting over the last twenty-five years. He was an eager interview. Rare was the phone call or text that he didn't return within minutes. Some of this, of course, was the usual Washington game of self-preservation and reputation management. As Carlson's *Crossfire* colleague (and nemesis) Robert Novak used to say, you're either a source or a target. But with Carlson, it seemed to be more than that. He functioned as a collaborator of sorts. He was unusually, even gratifyingly interested in whatever story I happened to be working on. He still had the muscle memory of a great magazine writer—the eye for detail, the proclivity to psychoanalyze—and he often provided the color and the insight that I didn't even realize I needed until he'd given it to me. I genuinely enjoyed talking to him as part of my job, and I looked for opportunities to do so, even when he may have been only tangentially related to the story I was working on.

All of which is to say, I understand why Carlson is an object of fascination—and a source of tsuris—for so many of my fellow journalists. Here is someone who once did work they could respect, even if they disagreed with it, who was once their friend—who was at their wedding, who was in their wedding *party*—but who has now come to stand for everything that is deplorable in media and in politics. If you get more than three political reporters in a room these days, it's a pretty good bet that the conversation will eventually turn to Carlson. *Did he think the things he now says when we were friends a dozen years ago? Does he really believe the things he's saying today? What the hell happened to Tucker?*

In this book, I set out to answer some of these questions. Although Carlson became suddenly reticent when I told him I was writing a book about him—first explaining that Fox News wouldn't allow him to talk to me, and then, after being fired from Fox, refusing to respond to my entreaties—I spoke to more than a hundred people who have known or worked with him over the years. But, ultimately, I'm not sure if those questions are answerable—or if the answers are that important. Whether Carlson really believes the awful things that he says these days matters less than that he says them at all, and that millions of people—members of Congress, titans of industry, the president, and just everyday Americans—listen to and take their cues from him. What matters is that by saying these things, Carlson has finally achieved the fame, power, and influence that for so long eluded him. The story of what happened to Tucker Carlson between the gifted young writer I encountered as a *New Republic* intern in the late 1990s and the noxious talking head we all see today is the larger story of conservative politics and conservative media over the last thirty years. It is also the story of the United States during that period. In telling the story of Tucker Carlson, I hope to answer the question of what the hell happened to us.

■

HATED BY ALL THE RIGHT PEOPLE

ONE

ONE SUMMER DAY IN 1995, Tucker Carlson walked into the American Enterprise Institute building in Washington, DC. Showered and blue-blazered and wearing his favorite bow tie, he was there for a job interview with Bill Kristol. It was, at that point, the most important meeting of his life.

Carlson was twenty-six and had recently quit his first job in journalism at the *Arkansas Democrat-Gazette*. He'd worked on the newspaper's editorial page for nearly two years, writing about local crime and various goings-on in the state capitol. His boss at the paper, Paul Greenberg, who won a Pulitzer Prize for editorials he wrote about civil rights in 1968, was enamored with Carlson and believed that his young protégé might one day follow in his own footsteps as a crusading Southern newsman. But Carlson always viewed his time in Little Rock as an apprenticeship. Now, after slumming it in the sticks, he believed he was ready to move up to the big leagues in DC.

Kristol, who was in his early forties, had scant journalism experience. What he did have was the reputation of being one of the shrewdest operators—and one of the most relentless self-promoters—in both Republican politics and the conservative intellectual world. A political-philosophy PhD, he'd left academia for jobs in the Reagan and Bush administrations, serving in the latter as the vice president's chief of staff, which earned him the nickname "Dan Quayle's brain." In 1993, he founded a think tank called the Project for the Republican Future, where he created a new political art form—the blast-fax strategy memo. These memos, which were soon dubbed Kristolgrams, were addressed to Republican members of Congress and offered policy advice on how to deal with the Clinton administration. But rather than send the memos only to elected officials, Kristol, in a genius stroke, faxed them to reporters and editorial writers, as well—influencing not just Republican politicians' actions, but also the media's coverage of them. The Kristolgrams about health care reform, which urged Republicans to refuse to compromise with Clinton on the issue for fear of giving Democrats a legislative victory, were instrumental in killing Hillarycare and, as a result, delivering the GOP control of Congress in the 1994 midterms. Even Bill Clinton himself said so, complaining to an audience in Iowa, "Mr. Kristol—you've probably never heard of him, but he's the fellow that tells them what to think up in Washington."

More than anyone not named Newt Gingrich, Kristol was responsible for the Republican Revolution (and the hyperpartisanship and polarization that came in its wake). Now, with Clinton looking like a one-term president and the prophesied dawning of a new conservative era on the horizon, Kristol was seeking to extend his influence—and cement his status—by venturing into journalism. He was creating a new political magazine that, from its inaugural issue in the fall of 1995, would be the preeminent publication in American conservatism. He called it *The Standard*.

Kristol hatched the idea for *The Standard* shortly before the 1994 midterms at the Utopia coffee shop on New York's Upper West Side during a breakfast with John Podhoretz, a former

Reagan and Bush White House speechwriter who was a columnist and editor at *The Washington Times*. Both men were princes of the conservative intellectual world. Podhoretz's father, Norman, was the longtime editor of *Commentary*. Kristol's father, Irving, was the brilliant polemicist who was commonly known as "the godfather of neoconservatism." (Their mothers were formidable conservative intellectual figures in their own rights: Podhoretz's, Midge Decter, was a leading anti-feminist writer; Kristol's, Gertrude Himmelfarb, was a prominent historian of Victorian England.)

But while their fathers had grown up as poor, Depression-era Brooklyn kids who spent their college years and early adulthoods, in the 1940s and '50s, as socialists before veering right in the '60s—"a neoconservative," Irving famously joked, "is a liberal who has been mugged by reality"—Kristol and Podhoretz were to the manner, and to their ideology, born. Both cradle conservatives raised on the Upper West Side, they had comfortable childhoods and went to fancy private high schools, where they pointedly abstained from the libertine pleasures of sex and drugs embraced by so many of their classmates. At Harvard in the early '70s, Kristol provoked his fellow students by wearing a Spiro Agnew T-shirt. At the University of Chicago in the late '70s, Podhoretz started a conservative campus newspaper that cheered on Ronald Reagan.

Their parents, and their parents' cohort of conservative intellectuals, had labored to create the quarterly journals, editorial pages, and think tanks that ultimately cohered into what the liberal political journalist Sidney Blumenthal called the counterestablisment. Kristol and Podhoretz blithely assumed their prized places in that counterestablishment as if they were birthrights. "He takes things for granted," Decter once said of her son, "that we had to struggle our way to intellectually."

Yet it could be frustrating to toil in their parents' shadows. Kristol's boss in the Reagan administration, secretary of education Bill Bennett, liked to tell people that he hired Kristol because he knew "his DNA pretty well." At *The Washington Times*, Podhoretz's colleagues snickeringly referred to him as "John P. Normanson" because the paper's editor so frequently introduced him as "John Podhoretz, Norman's son." They revered their parents, believed they were following in their footsteps, and gladly described themselves as neocons—but their critics called them "mini-cons." For all their successes, both men forever felt they had something to prove.

At Utopia, Kristol and Podhoretz sketched their vision for a magazine that would not just build on the work of their parents but would reorient and even surpass it. Where the previous generation of neocons had, through their writings in *Commentary* and *The National Interest* and *The Wall Street Journal* editorial page, laid the intellectual groundwork for the Reagan Revolution, *The Standard* would do the same for the new era of conservative governance that the 1994 midterms seemed to herald. Unlike *National Review* and *Commentary*, which were based in New York and published biweekly and monthly—thereby operating at a certain remove from the rapidly accelerating political news cycle—*The Standard* would be headquartered in Washington and come out every week. Advance copies of the magazine would be hand delivered to about two hundred Washington movers and shakers on Sunday mornings, a day before it appeared on newsstands.

The Kristolgrams, setting out a strategic course for the GOP, would be refashioned into a weekly editorial at the front of *The Standard*. (Kristol would hire David Tell, the Project for the Republican Future employee who actually wrote most of the Kristolgrams, to be *The Standard*'s opinion editor.) Following the editorial would be a lively mix of wonky essays and take-no-prisoners reportage that tackled the knottiest political issues of the day—and that wasn't afraid to skewer ideological allies when necessary. In fact, *The Standard*'s model wouldn't even be a conservative magazine but a liberal one: *The New Republic*, which in the 1980s became the most important publication in American politics by challenging Democratic Party orthodoxies and, in the process, helping to reshape the party. Not long after their meeting at Utopia, Kristol and Podhoretz recruited Fred Barnes, a well-sourced conservative reporter at *The New Republic*, to their venture, and the trio began looking for a financial backer.

A few months later, Rupert Murdoch, who'd been briefed about their project, invited Kristol, Podhoretz, Barnes, and Tell to his Beverly Hills mansion. The billionaire mogul, who was in his mid-sixties, oversaw media empires on three continents. In his native Australia and Britain, Murdoch's media properties didn't just bring him fabulous financial wealth but also unrivaled political power; he was in the habit of using his newspapers and television stations to help elect his preferred conservative prime ministers, including Margaret Thatcher. But that sort of political influence had eluded Murdoch in the United States, where he'd become a citizen a decade earlier. While the 20th Century Fox film studio and Fox TV network gave him cultural cachet in the form of products like *Broadcast News* and *The Simpsons*, and the *New York Post* provided him with a serious say in that city's municipal affairs, he had no real presence in national politics. He could only read *National Review* and *The Wall Street Journal* editorial page with envy.

Over dinner, Kristol pitched Murdoch on why he should subsidize *The Standard*—which, like all political magazines, would never be profitable. He flattered Murdoch with high-minded talk about the importance of conservative ideas and robust political debate, and he appealed to the billionaire's self-image as someone who was, at heart, still an ink-stained wretch. (Murdoch's global multimedia empire began with a single small-circulation Australian newspaper that he inherited from his father.) But it was the subtext of Kristol's pitch that most resonated with Murdoch. In 1995, the Fox News Channel was barely a gleam in Murdoch's eye (he wouldn't meet with Roger Ailes to discuss creating a conservative cable news network until that fall and it wouldn't launch until September 1996), and *The Wall Street Journal* was not for sale (Murdoch wouldn't buy it until 2007). If Murdoch wanted to be a real player in American politics, Kristol suggested, he needed to establish a beachhead in Washington. *The Standard* would allow him to do just that. When dinner was over, Kristol and his partners had secured Murdoch's commitment to bankroll the magazine at three million dollars a year for a minimum of three years. "Let's try to make sure we don't lose too much money on this," Murdoch told one of his business advisers.

With Murdoch's cash in hand, and a Labor Day launch date, Kristol set out to build a stable of writers. Some of them were familiar, like the esteemed columnist Charles Krauthammer, whom he lured away from *The New Republic*, and the veteran humorist P. J. O'Rourke. Other hires required a more discerning eye for talent. He signed up a thirtysomething *Wall Street Journal* editor and writer (who'd briefly been the paper's film critic) named David Brooks and Andy Ferguson, a former Bush White House speechwriter who was profiling politicians for *Washingtonian*. He poached two young reporters from *The American Spectator*—Christopher Caldwell and Matt Labash—and tapped Robert Kagan, a former Reagan State Department functionary, to write about foreign policy. David Frum, a former *Wall Street Journal* editorial writer and the author of a recent book savaging the Reagan and Bush administrations for straying from their conservative roots, was brought on to keep the new Republican Congress honest.

By the summer, *The Standard*'s masthead was mostly filled, save for a spot toward the very bottom for a junior writer. Sitting in the magazine's new offices in the American Enterprise Institute building—five floors below the office Irving, an AEI fellow, now kept—Kristol flipped through piles of clips and résumés. Eventually, he pulled Tucker Carlson's from the stack. Liking what he saw, he invited him in for an interview.

CARLSON WAS ALSO THE SON of a conservative personage. His father, Dick, ran the Voice of America for Ronald Reagan and was George H. W. Bush's ambassador to the Seychelles. In 1992, the Corporation for Public Broadcasting (CPB) made him its president and CEO in the hope that he might appease Congressional Republicans who were vociferously complaining about the liberal bias of PBS and NPR—and the fact that the federal government was subsidizing both. At the very moment Tucker was trying to gain a toehold in Washington political journalism, Dick was tangling with Newt Gingrich as the new House Speaker sought to "zero fund" CPB.

Dick's road to that confrontation was an unlikely and uneven one. Born to teenage parents outside of Boston, he was placed in an orphanage called the New England Home for Little Wanderers and, at the age of two, was adopted by a childless couple, the Carlsons, from Norwood, Massachusetts. When Dick was twelve, his adopted father died of a heart attack, and Dick spent his teenage years as something of a juvenile delinquent. After being expelled from his high school, he enlisted in the Marines and later attended the University of Mississippi on an ROTC scholarship. He worked a series of Runyonesque jobs—a cop in Ocean City, Maryland; a legman for the Hollywood gossip columnist Louella Parsons; a private eye in San Francisco—before eventually settling into a career in the early seventies as a local television newsman in Southern California.

At KABC in Los Angeles, he was a muckraking investigative reporter who excelled at delivering tabloid-y scoops. His biggest story was a 1975 investigation into the Twentieth Century Motor Car Corporation and its CEO Liz Carmichael. In the midst of the oil embargo, Carmichael and her company made headlines—and millions of dollars from investors and potential customers—by promising to produce the Dale, a three-wheeled car that got seventy miles per gallon; standing six feet tall and weighing two hundred pounds, Carmichael cast herself as a feminist business visionary who was going to take down the Big Three. But Dick didn't buy the hype. In a twenty-eight-part series, which later won a Peabody Award, he discovered that the Dale wasn't just a dud but a scam (the car didn't work) and that Twentieth Century was bilking consumers and investors. He also revealed that Carmichael was, in the parlance of the times, a "transsexual" who, before transitioning, was a fugitive con man who'd been on the run from the FBI for over a decade.

Shortly thereafter, Dick went to work at KFMB, the CBS affiliate in San Diego. There, he made national news when he reported that Renée Richards, a local ophthalmologist who had won a women's tennis tournament at the La Jolla tennis club, had once been Richard Raskind, a New York City ophthalmologist and nationally ranked over-thirty-five men's tennis player. When Dick confronted Richards with his discovery, she pleaded with him to spike the story, arguing that she was a private citizen and that the news would harm her four-year-old son. Dick told her she'd forfeited her privacy when she'd entered a public tennis tournament and that he wouldn't be doing his job as a journalist if he didn't report the facts.

Even when he wasn't outing transgender women, Dick carried himself with a macho swagger. Wearing a trench coat or a station-logo-branded blazer, he'd venture with a cameraman into race riots and red-light districts, thrusting his microphone in the faces of cops and pimps. He liked to drink and was known to occasionally do the news after having a few. Once during what he thought was a commercial break, he sat in the anchor chair, took a drag on his Pall Mall, and said to no one in particular, "God, I can't wait till this fucking show is over"—only to discover that he was still on the air. Decades later, when the movie *Anchorman* was released with Will Ferrell starring as Ron Burgundy—a seventies-era, polyester-suit-wearing, scotch-swilling, buffoonish San Diego newscaster—a number of Dick's friends surmised that Ferrell had modeled Burgundy on Dick. (Adam McKay, who cowrote *Anchorman* with Ferrell, said the model for Burgundy was, in fact, the Detroit newscaster Mort Crim.)

Dick became a San Diego civic icon. In 1984, after a stint as a banker, he ran for mayor. His opponent was the incumbent, a fellow Republican named Roger Hedgecock, who'd been indicted on felony perjury charges for taking illegal campaign contributions in his previous race. Dick attacked Hedgecock for giving San Diego "a black eye" and cast himself as a reformer. With the help of his second wife, Patricia, who was an heiress to the Swanson frozen food fortune, he lent his campaign nearly five hundred thousand dollars and outspent Hedgecock by an almost two-to-one margin.

But it wasn't enough, as Dick learned the hard way that media celebrity didn't necessarily translate to political power. Hedgecock trounced him by sixteen points, or fifty-five thousand votes. Eleven months later, Hedgecock was convicted on twelve counts of perjury and one count of conspiracy related to illegal campaign contributions and resigned as mayor. (The California Supreme Court later reversed twelve of those counts and the thirteenth was reduced to a misdemeanor.) By the time

Hedgecock resigned, Dick had alighted to Washington, DC, where some California Republican friends and Patricia—whose wealthy family included former Arkansas senator and DC power broker William Fulbright—helped him land a position in the Reagan administration.

Patricia wasn't just Dick's second wife. She was his second *heiress* wife. His first wife was Lisa McNear Lombardi, who belonged to one of California's most prominent and wealthiest families. She was a descendant of Henry Miller, a German émigré who became a California cattle baron and who, at one point in the late nineteenth century, was believed to be the largest landowner in the United States. ("I thought once that I would own the whole State of California," Miller said a few years before his death in 1916.)

Lisa grew up as a member of the San Francisco aristocracy. As a teenager, she had her debutante ball at the Palace Hotel. She attended Cal Berkeley and joined Kappa Kappa Gamma, the university's oldest and most exclusive sorority. She seemed to be headed down the same cosseted path as her mother—a house on Russian Hill, volunteer work at the Golden Gate Park botanical garden during the day, and charity galas at night.

But Lisa nursed a rebellious streak, which became increasingly more pronounced during her Berkeley years. While her sorority sisters studied English literature and art history, she majored in architecture. And instead of dating well-bred fraternity boys from Sigma Chi or Deke, she preferred the company of older, rougher-edged men. Like Dick Carlson, an orphan who didn't even graduate from Ole Miss and who was then on the overnight news crew for the San Francisco TV station KGO—or, as he called it, "Killings, Guts & Orgies." Dick would pull up on his Triumph motorcycle in front of the Kappa house on

Piedmont Avenue, Lisa would hop on the back, and together they would ride off into the night.

In 1967, Lisa and Dick eloped in Reno, Nevada. Their marriage came as a surprise to Lisa's mother, who was traveling in Europe with her second husband at the time. "Family members have been unable to locate them to reveal the nuptials," the *San Francisco Examiner*'s gossip columnist reported. In 1969, one day after her and Dick's second anniversary, Lisa gave birth to Tucker McNear Carlson. Twenty-one months after that, Buckley Peck Carlson was born.

The family settled in Los Angeles, where Dick emerged as a star at KABC, but his and Lisa's marriage grew troubled. Some of the tensions were small. Dick, an autodidact who'd eventually assemble a personal library of more than ten thousand books, looked down on Lisa for only reading magazines, criticizing her for her lack of self-discipline. Other problems were weightier. Living in Laurel Canyon, where band members of the Eagles were next-door neighbors, Lisa seemed to take her rebellious streak even further and soon fell in with a crowd of artists and musicians. Dick, who was becoming increasingly conservative in his tastes and his politics (their second child was named after William F. Buckley), had a difficult time abiding his wife's new friends—and their hedonistic lifestyle. When Dick moved to San Diego in 1975 to take the KFMB job there, Tucker and Buckley went with him, while Lisa stayed in Los Angeles. On weekends, the family reunited in Los Angeles or San Diego.

It was supposed to be a temporary arrangement while Dick and Lisa worked out their differences. But after just a few months, Dick filed for divorce. In the legal battle that ensued, Lisa petitioned for sole custody of Tucker and Buckley; she argued in a court filing that if Dick was awarded custody, the children "would in fact be raised by hired help" and that only she "can devote the necessary time and attention to their well-being." Dick countered that he feared for his sons' safety if they were raised by Lisa. In his own court filing, he alleged that during their marriage Lisa "had repeated difficulties with abuse of alcohol, marijuana, cocaine and amphetamines"; that she had put the boys on a plane from Los Angeles to San Diego "shoeless" after one of their visits to her; and that Lisa's own mother, stepfather, cousin, and grandmother had all beseeched him not to leave Tucker and Buckley alone with her. So concerned was Dick about Lisa getting custody of their children that he contemplated fleeing the country and taking Tucker and Buckley with him.

Such desperate measures turned out to be unnecessary. In 1977, just a week after Tucker's eighth birthday, a California Superior Court judge awarded full custody of Tucker and Buckley to Dick. Lisa did not even attend the hearing. According to court records, she had left the country. Indeed, Lisa would spend much of the rest of her life abroad. For a time, she lived in Los Angeles, where she married—and created fanciful sculptures with—Mo McDermott, David Hockney's longtime assistant. After McDermott drank himself to death in 1988, Lisa began a relationship with Michael Vaughan, another British artist in Hockney's circle, and the couple eventually moved to France, where they settled in a rural village called Cazac.

In 2011, a relative contacted Carlson with some news about his mother, whom he hadn't seen since she'd lost the custody battle more than three decades earlier. "I got this call, like, 'She's dying in this weird little town on a farm she lived on in southwestern France,'" Carlson later recalled. The relative urged him to go visit her. "And so I called my brother, and he was like, 'What?! No! You know, my son's got a soccer game,'" Carlson said. "And I said, 'I feel the same way. I don't know this person.' And actually this sounds cold or whatever, but I had already made my peace with this over many decades, over thirty-five years, and I didn't fall apart, at all. I went out to dinner. I mean, I felt sad for her, I guess. . . . But she wasn't part of my life, and I wasn't part of hers." In her will, Lisa left Tucker and Buckley one dollar each.

BUT IF LISA WAS ABSENT from Tucker's life, Dick was decidedly—at times overwhelmingly—present. Single fathers were still relatively rare in the 1970s and Dick tried to make the necessary adaptations to his new, unusual role. He traded in his classic Mercedes-Benz for a late-model Ford Country Squire station wagon. He packed Tucker and Buckley brown-bag lunches every morning before school, including handwritten quotes or riddles, and hired a nanny to help care for the boys when they came home. And although he was the parent who'd had the hardscrabble upbringing, he tried to instill in his sons an aristocratic temperament—lecturing them on the importance of good manners and meticulously proofreading the thank-you notes he made them write for excessive use of the first person, lest they read like "a swim in Lake Me."

At the same time, Dick wasn't about to turn himself—or Tucker and Buckley—into a beta male. If he had to drive his boys around in a station wagon, then at least he would occasionally let them ride on the roof as he gunned the land yacht's V-8 engine and careened down a dirt road; "Who dares, wins," he told them. In addition to making his sons brown-bag lunches in the mornings, for breakfast he'd feed them Cap'n Crunch—which, given the warm climate of San Diego, was often infested with bugs; when they complained, he ate the insect-laden cereal himself, admonishing them, "The fact that a few bugs bother you is just pathetic." The nannies he hired were usually men—including a former Korean intelligence officer whom Tucker and Buckley addressed as Colonel Kwon and who instructed the boys on how to disembowel someone. Dick's etiquette advice didn't just include the proper way to write thank-you notes, but also about how, in prison, "the cigarette pack is your friend."

Years later, Tucker Carlson would claim that his conservative politics were formed during his childhood—specifically in reaction to the weird, wild, and woolly hyperliberalism of 1970s California, as exemplified by the twin cultural capitals of Los Angeles and San Francisco, where the parties in Laurel Canyon lasted all night and the Summer of Love went on all year. "Liberals were everywhere," he recalled. "They smelled like patchouli. They showed up late to everything. They talked incessantly about solar power, humpback whales, and the Hopi Indians. They annoyed the hell out of me."

In fact, after leaving Los Angeles and the influence of his mother at the age of six, Carlson spent his childhood largely insulated from the excesses of the California left. San Diego in the 1970s, Dick's landing spot for himself and his two sons, was a conservative military town. Its thrice-elected mayor was Pete Wilson, a Republican up-and-comer who, two decades later as California's governor, successfully campaigned for the Proposition 187 ballot initiative that denied public services to undocumented immigrants (and served as a precursor for Donald Trump's nativist policies). And La Jolla, the affluent seaside village a dozen miles north of downtown San Diego where Dick and his boys lived, was a zone of aggressive, hidebound traditionalism— "full of tired old men and tired old money," as Raymond Chandler, who spent his final years there after departing Los Angeles, once wrote. There was scant discussion of the Hopi and the humpbacks when Wilson and *San Diego Union-Tribune* editor Jerry Warren, a former White House press secretary for Richard Nixon, visited Chez Carlson as regular dinner guests. The scent of patchouli was well-nigh indetectable over the pool at the La Jolla Beach & Tennis Club, where Carlson lounged during his summer vacations.

Carlson attended the La Jolla Country Day School, a twenty-four-acre oasis inside an oasis that had educated the sons and daughters of San Diego's political, business, and military elite for half a century. By the mid-seventies, the joke among some LJCDS teachers was that their students were like "good milkshakes: thick and rich." But Carlson was a notable exception. While he was a middling student in terms of grades, showing little enthusiasm for homework or tests, he possessed an obvious native intelligence. Egged on by his father, he read widely outside of class—*Animal Farm*, *War and Peace*—and liked to discuss the books, as well as current events, with his teachers. He treated them less as authority figures than quasi peers. After his sixth-grade teacher moved him from the back of the classroom to the front, in an attempt to cut down on his disruptiveness, Carlson showed up to class with an umbrella. "If you're going to make me sit in the front row, I need to protect myself," he told the teacher. "You're spitting all over me."

To his peers, he was a natural ringleader. His backyard boasted a clubhouse, where he and his friends—after consulting a copy of *The Anarchist Cookbook*, pilfered from Dick's library—fashioned flamethrowers out of cans of WD-40 and throwing stars out of circular saw blades. Venturing further afield (in other words, the golf course near Carlson's house), they conducted commando missions, lobbing improvised hand grenades made with hydrochloric acid purchased at the local hardware store at unsuspecting duffers. No one was safe.

DICK MARRIED PATRICIA IN 1979, when Tucker was ten; she soon adopted him and Buckley (they both would later add Swanson as a second middle name) and began to play a role in their parenting. She didn't wield too heavy a hand on some matters. Before Carlson was even a teenager, he was smoking cigarettes and drinking alcohol; when he was fourteen, he lost his virginity on a visit—arranged by Dick—to a Nevada brothel. For all of his talk today about the sordid, broken world that was California in the 1970s, people who knew Carlson in La Jolla remember him being much edgier and far more debauched than any of his peers.

Patricia did have strong opinions about education. When it was time for Carlson to begin high school, she insisted he go away to boarding school. Initially, he attended Collège du Léman, a Swiss school on Lake Geneva that catered to international students, but his stay there was brief; he later claimed he was "kicked out." Things went better for him at St. George's, a boarding school in Rhode Island, where he started as a tenth grader in 1984.

Among the elite New England prep schools, St. George's was considered second tier—the sort of place that educated the nouveau riche and the offspring of lesser branches of America's prominent families. (George W. Bush, the son of a future president and a future president himself, went to Andover; his cousin Billy, whose father was a banker and who would go on to become an entertainment reporter, attended St. George's.) But with its Gothic and Tudor campus designed by Frederick Law Olmsted that sits on a promontory overlooking the Atlantic Ocean, and annual tuition of thirteen thousand dollars at the time, these sorts of distinctions might be lost on a casual observer.

Coming from a broken home in California—with an absent heiress mother, an orphan father, and a new adoptive heiress mother—they might have been lost on Carlson, as well. While his classmates grudgingly abided by the coat-and-tie dress code, he embraced it, sporting natty Brooks Brothers blazers and an impressive collection of bow ties. Brash and outspoken, he quickly established a reputation as both a conservative and a contrarian. In his room in Auchincloss Dormitory, he hung an elephant poster; after class, he taunted liberal teachers about Walter Mondale. He seldom passed up an opportunity to impress his classmates and teachers with his wit and intelligence.

That fall, one of St. George's few Black students, a senior, gave a speech to an all-school assembly about Eleanor Bumpurs, an elderly Black woman in the Bronx who had recently been shot to death by New York City police officers while she resisted being evicted from her public housing unit. "Does anyone think that woman deserved to die?" the Black student asked, presumably rhetorically. Carlson raised his hand. Today, it's tempting to view that raised hand as a racist gesture, a foreshadowing of the sort of inflammatory rhetoric Carlson would traffic in on television, online, and onstage. But at the time, it was viewed less as racist than puckish—at least by the people at St. George's. "Tucker had a lot of attitude and a big mouth for someone that age," Ian Toll, who was two years ahead of Carlson, recalled. "St. George's was a very hierarchical and deferential place, and Tucker immediately made an impression that he was not going to defer."

And yet Carlson's greatest renown at St. George's may have come from being Susie Andrews's boyfriend. The couple met as new students and began dating that September. "She was the cutest 10th grader in America," Carlson later said. But what made Susie's romantic life of particular interest to St. George's students, and even faculty, was her father—George Andrews, the school's new headmaster. Gaining entry to a female student's dorm room at St. George's could be difficult enough for the boys there, but Carlson became something of a campus legend for his ability to sneak into Susie's room on the second floor of the Memorial Schoolhouse, where the headmaster and his family lived.

St. George's was an Episcopal school, so in addition to being a headmaster, George Andrews was also a priest. As the older of Reverend Andrews's two daughters, Susie herself was quite devout. Carlson was not. But Susie's religiosity began to rub off on him. He not only attended chapel on Tuesday and Thursday, as all St. George's students were required to do; he began going to optional chapel services as well, always sitting in a pew next to Susie, and joined an interdenominational ministry organization called FOCUS.

The brand of Episcopalianism practiced at St. George's, and by the Andrews family, was an orthodox one—and a redoubt against the liberal trends that were then growing inside the denomination in the United States. It embraced traditional gender roles, opposed abortion and the ordination of gay priests, and rejected the concept of pastoral theology, in which priests were viewed more as social workers and therapeutic counselors than religious leaders. Its inherent conservatism appealed to Carlson; what began as a sop to a girl he liked blossomed into deep conviction. He soon became a member of the Episcopal Church—an affiliation and identity that would be central to his life, and his politics, for the next four decades, especially as he grew increasingly alienated from the ever more liberal official church itself.

Although Carlson found religion, he didn't suddenly forsake all earthly pleasures. He continued to drink and smoke and began doing drugs, resolving to duplicate the pharmaceutical regimen of his literary hero, Hunter S. Thompson—marijuana, acid, cocaine, even ether, the latter of which he obtained from a head shop in Manhattan during a break from St. George's. Like many prep school boys in the eighties, he was a devotee of the Grateful Dead and traveled around the Northeast to their shows; unlike other members of this cohort, he was lucky enough to have a father who arranged for him to get his picture taken with Jerry Garcia when Garcia visited the Voice of America offices in Washington, DC.

At St. George's, Carlson inhabited two different worlds—and two different personas. With Susie—who did not drink, smoke, or do drugs—he was the doting, chapel-attending boyfriend who seemed to value the stability offered by her and her family, a stability sorely lacking in his own family. But when that stability became stifling, he returned to his group of male friends to play Hacky Sack, listen to the Dead, and smoke pot and drink Kool-Aid mixed with vodka. Indeed, Carlson almost seemed to suffer from a double consciousness. St. George's was a small place—with fewer than one hundred students in each class—but Carlson tried to keep his two worlds as separate as possible. In the St. George's yearbook from 1987, Carlson's senior year, there's a photo of him talking to a classmate with a look of concern on his face. "What do you mean you told Susie?" reads the caption.

St. George's wasn't Exeter or Andover, but it still sent a smattering of its graduates each year to Harvard, Princeton, and Yale. Carlson believed he should be one of them. But his grades and test scores were nowhere near good enough. His failure to gain entrée to the Ivy League gnawed at him and would, decades later, serve as a touchstone for his populist ideology. On his Fox show, Carlson was fond of listing the people he deems intellectual inferiors—Chris Cuomo, Dante de Blasio, Al Gore's four children—who nonetheless attended Harvard or Yale. "If you want to get into a top American college, it's best to have a parent who's a well-known Democratic politician," he told his viewers during one segment. "That's the most effective credential of all."

In any event, Carlson's academic record at St. George's was sufficiently poor that he had a difficult time gaining admission to any prestigious universities, not just those in the Ivy League. Finally, Reverend Andrews intervened and greased the wheels to secure his daughter's boyfriend a spot in the freshman class at Trinity College, his alma mater.

Trinity was in Hartford, Connecticut, just a forty-five-minute drive away from New Haven and Yale, but the academic distance was vast. Much like St. George's, Trinity was viewed as second tier—the kind of place rich kids went when they couldn't get into an Ivy (or an Amherst or a Williams) and their parents couldn't deal with the stigma of sending them to a state school.

On his first day at Trinity, Carlson met Neil Patel—the son of Indian physicians, who was born in Scotland but grew up in Worcester, Massachusetts—and the two of them got drunk on beer and bonded over their mutual love of the Dead. After they sobered up, they realized they also shared an interest in conservative politics; before long, they were debating the finer points of the latest column by George Will (Trinity class of 1962) and swapping copies of *The American Spectator* and *National Review*.

Trinity in the late 1980s was a largely apolitical campus, devoid of the anti-apartheid protests and AIDS-awareness rallies that roiled other colleges and universities at the time. But in the spring of Carlson and Patel's freshman year, a handful of liberal students shook off their apathy long enough to raise a stink about a recruiting event the Central Intelligence Agency was hosting at the school. As those students protested on the quad, Carlson and Patel painted a bedsheet with the message "WELCOME CIA" and hung it from Carlson's dorm-room window.

A crowd gathered, including members of Trinity's football team, who decided to mount an impromptu counterprotest in favor of the CIA. Someone suggested the two sides debate each other. The lefties were game, but none of the football players wanted to speak. Noticing the banner hanging from Carlson's dorm window, they invited him to represent the pro-CIA side.

When it was Carlson's turn to address the crowd, he stood silent for a moment before pointing an accusatory finger at the liberals and the jocks. "I think you're all a bunch of greasy chicken fuckers," he said. Then he walked off the quad.

The episode no doubt displayed Carlson's contrarian streak, but it also captured his dilettantism. He and Patel developed a small circle of like-minded friends, and for their sophomore year, five of them moved off campus to a dilapidated triple-decker in a working-class Hartford neighborhood. There, the group mainlined coverage of the 1988 presidential election and celebrated with cases of Carling Black Label beer when George H. W. Bush trounced Michael Dukakis in November. It was a heady moment, in a heady decade, for young conservatives—the Reagan Revolution was continuing, the United States was on the verge of winning the Cold War, the end of history was in sight—and Carlson and his friends began cooking up ideas about how they might seize the moment for themselves.

At other colleges and universities, conservative students were experiencing great success starting their own newspapers and magazines, often with the financial support of conservative foundations like Irving Kristol's Institute for Educational Affairs. The most famous—or infamous, depending on your perspective—of these publications was *The Dartmouth Review*. Founded in 1980 with an initial ten-thousand-dollar grant from IEA, *The Review* didn't merely anathematize campus liberalism but went out of its way to offend liberal sensibilities. It once ran a satirical article defending affirmative action that was written from the supposed perspective of a Black Dartmouth student in that Black student's supposed dialect. ("Dem white mo-fo be sayin' 'firmative action ain't no good fo' us, cause it be puttin' down ac-demic standards," read one representative sentence.) In another instance, a *Review* reporter surreptitiously recorded a meeting of Dartmouth's Gay Students Association and then published excerpts, branding the group "cheerleaders for latent campus sodomites."

The Review was subject to campus protests, a libel lawsuit from a Dartmouth professor, and an investigation by the New Hampshire attorney general—among other things. And yet, despite—or, perhaps, because of—all the opprobrium and controversy, *Review* alums were graduating from Dartmouth and immediately going on to plum positions in conservative media and politics in Washington and New York; a couple of former *Review* editors named Dinesh D'Souza and Laura Ingraham even worked in the Reagan White House.

Back at Trinity, Carlson and his friends took notice. In their off-campus apartment, they drew up plans for their own conservative campus publication. They'd call it the *Trinity Review*, and like their ideological comrades at Dartmouth and elsewhere, they'd use it to argue with, provoke, and offend their liberal classmates and professors—and, hopefully, make names for themselves in the larger world of conservatism. But, in the end, the *Trinity Review* never made it past the talk stage; starting a magazine, they concluded, was too big of a commitment.

Instead, Carlson resorted to the lazy man's version of political journalism—letters to the editor. In epistles to the weekly student newspaper, the *Trinity Tripod*, he struck a combative, wounded, reactionary tone that he'd perfect in the years to come. In one, he objected to an op-ed by a female classmate that decried sexism at Trinity. "The truth is that due to angry and confused activists such as Ms. Levin, the gap between genders has grown wider in recent years," he wrote. "And how could it not, with the phantom of discrimination lurking behind every ambiguously worded statement and the intent of every badly planned seating arrangement." In another, he attacked a history professor for her own previous letter to the editor complaining about the "racism, sexism, homophobia, and other prejudices" expressed in the pages of the newspaper. "Professor Greenberg does not, or will not, recognize the values of certain contributions because she doesn't agree with them," he wrote. "With all respect to the Professor, it seems like she is more interested in force-feeding her opinions to others than in genuine intellectual freedom." In a third, he complained about the *Tripod*'s coverage of an inaugural anti-homophobia rally held on campus. "I am offended by the idea that everyone who objects to homosexuality is a homophobe," Carlson wrote. "I for one think that sex between two people of the same gender is unnatural and unhealthy. No amount of education or consideration has changed my view. Still, I don't hate gay people at all; some are friends of mine." The letters invariably ended: "Sincerely, T.S.M. Carlson."

Throughout his time at Trinity, Carlson maintained a long-distance romantic relationship with Susie, whose academic performance at St. George's had been strong enough to get her into Vanderbilt University in Nashville, Tennessee. During their senior year, Carlson went to Susie's father and asked for permission to marry his daughter. Reverend Andrews granted it, and Carlson and Susie were wed in August 1991 in the St. George's chapel. They honeymooned in Bermuda before moving to Washington, DC, where Carlson's father had helped him land a fourteen-thousand-dollar-a-year internship fact-checking a quarterly journal at the Heritage Foundation.

Their wedding was supposed to come after Carlson's graduation from Trinity, but that was not to be. If Carlson had been a poor student at St. George's, he was an abysmal one at Trinity. With no need to keep up appearances for Susie, who was hundreds of miles away in Nashville, studying took a back seat to brewing beer with Patel—one of their concoctions, Coal Porter, took first prize at a New England home-brewing competition—and repairing and riding vintage motorcycles with his friends. They thought of themselves as a biker gang. "That's the terrible secret of college: It's sort of boring," Carlson later confessed. "I often think I would have been far better off if I'd spent four years making furniture or working in a coal mine or collating page proofs at a newspaper—anything, really, but sitting around drinking beer and waiting for real life to happen."

By Carlson's senior year, he and some of his friends simply stopped showing up to classes altogether. Right before midterm exams, the economics professor for one of those friends, Bill, informed him that, no matter what he scored on the test, he would fail the class due to his poor attendance. With Carlson's help, Bill forged a letter to the professor from a fictitious Maryland psychologist informing the professor that Bill suffered from "acute neurotic depression." The letter went on to say that through "a combination of antidepressant and anti-anxiety drugs," plus regular attendance at Alcoholics Anonymous meetings, Bill's recovery prospects were good, but that the "road to wellness is a long one" and that "of paramount importance are instances in which he can meet success in tangible ways." The letter ended by asking the professor to show Bill "the sensitivity that his full recovery requires."

Carlson and Bill sent off the letter and kept their fingers crossed. But it actually worked too well. Upon receipt of the letter, the professor informed the dean of students, who summoned Bill to his office. Trinity was kicking him out of school—not for forgery but because administrators considered him a suicide risk. "We just don't have the facilities to meet your needs," the dean of students told him.

Perhaps that's why Carlson took a different approach when Janice Farnham, a Catholic nun and church historian who taught a religion seminar Carlson took the second semester of his senior year, sent him a message that she was going to fail him because of his attendance problems. He immediately paid a visit to her office. "He said, 'Please don't take this personally,

Professor Farnham,'" Farnham recalled. "I said, 'It's not about me. It's about you. When you leave here and you have a job, if you don't show up, you're going to lose your job. They're going to fire you. This is about you and your responsibilities.'" Carlson said he understood. But he didn't return to Farnham's class—and she failed him.

That June, when Patel and most of Carlson's other friends received their Trinity diplomas, Carlson was not among them. His 1.9 GPA was deemed too low. He would never graduate from college.

SUCH WAS THE LIFE EXPERIENCE—AND the résumé—Carlson carried with him into his *Standard* job interview with Bill Kristol in the summer of 1995.

As he tried to break into the political-journalism big leagues, he would have jumped at the opportunity to work at a mainstream-media organ like *The New York Times*, *The Washington Post*, *Time*, or *Newsweek*. But he knew that wasn't in the cards. Part of the problem, he recognized, was that pesky résumé: Even if he had managed to graduate, Trinity still didn't carry any cachet in the Ivy-heavy newsrooms of those publications. Indeed, George Will, Trinity's most esteemed journalistic alumnus, seemed to distance himself from his undergraduate alma mater; when he went jogging in his Chevy Chase neighborhood, Will wore a sweatshirt bearing the insignia of Princeton, where he did his doctoral work.

But even if Carlson had attended, much less graduated from, the right school, he was convinced that wouldn't have helped him. By the 1990s, mainstream media, he believed, was no country for white men. The newspaper industry was trying to bring more racial diversity to newsrooms: In 1985, journalists of color held 5.76 percent of newspaper jobs; by 1993, their representation had nearly doubled to 10.25 percent. Of course, that meant that newsrooms were still almost 90 percent white, but Carlson griped that the fancy internships and coveted entry-level reporting jobs were all going to minority applicants. If you were a white woman, maybe you could land one. But a preppy white boy like him? Carlson didn't think he had a chance.

So he looked for an opportunity in conservative media, which still was willing to give a white guy a fair shake. It had to be the right opportunity, however. Carlson had been reading *National Review* and *The American Spectator* for years, but he had qualms about both. He thought *National Review* was too stuffy. As for *The Spectator*, he'd always appreciated its independence and rollicking tone, but lately, he felt the magazine had gone around the bend in its coverage—and hatred—of Bill Clinton; he was especially skeptical of *The Spectator*'s hotshot young investigative reporter, David Brock, who—while Carlson had been covering local crime and the state capitol in Little Rock—had been crisscrossing Arkansas digging up dirt on Clinton's sex life. Carlson later confessed that he feared he'd "be written off as a wing nut" if he took a job at *The Spectator*.

Although *The Standard* wouldn't put out its first issue for a few more months, that was where he wanted to work. Over the next three decades, the people who were there at *The Standard*'s beginning—Bill Kristol and Rupert Murdoch, Andy Ferguson and David Brooks, Matt Labash and David Frum—would serve as Carlson's patrons and mentors, collaborators and allies, foils and enemies. For different periods of time, the same person would often assume diametrically opposite roles. But Carlson, of course, had no way of knowing any of that then. What he did know, courtesy of a finely tuned political and professional radar that would serve him exquisitely well through the years, was that *The Standard* would be at the center of conservative media and politics. He also had the preternatural self-confidence, even as a twentysomething who'd attended but not graduated from a second-tier college, to believe that's where he belonged.

"I called everyone I ever met and begged each one of them to beg Kristol to hire me," Carlson later recalled. Kristol agreed to interview him. He was in the habit of taking most potential hires to the American Enterprise Institute's wood-paneled top-floor dining room for lunch, but Carlson was low enough on the totem pole that he decided to see the applicant in his spartan office. He had Fred Barnes join him.

Carlson may have desperately wanted to work at *The Standard*, but he didn't necessarily give that impression to Kristol and Barnes. When they asked him for story ideas, he proffered merely three and stumbled on their other questions. His natural charm was no match for his typical lack of preparation. He bombed the interview. When it was over, Kristol and Barnes were in easy agreement. *The Standard* would not be hiring Tucker Carlson.

TWO

IT'S NOT HARD TO IMAGINE *The Standard*'s rejection sending a young Tucker Carlson into a tailspin. It was easy enough for him to slough off the judgment of the liberal pointy-heads in the Yale admissions and Trinity provost offices. But if Bill Kristol didn't want Carlson for the all-star team of conservative writers and reporters he was assembling at *The Standard*? Then maybe Carlson would be forced to conclude that he wasn't cut out for political journalism in Washington, after all.

Of course, we'll never know—because Carlson's rejection by *The Standard* was only temporary.

It was Carlson's good fortune that, at the same time Kristol was standing up *The Standard*, a recent Williams College graduate named Mark Gerson was working on a book about neoconservative intellectuals, including (and especially) Kristol's father, Irving. That meant that in the summer of 1995 Gerson, who was heading off to Yale Law School in the fall, was a frequent presence at the American Enterprise Institute building, where both Irving and Bill had their offices.

Gerson was Carlson's polar opposite: Jewish rather than Episcopalian; Williams (where he edited the conservative newspaper) instead of Trinity; a try hard, not a slacker. But this dichotomy had actually brought the two into contact with each other several years earlier. That was when a post-Trinity Carlson was holding down the Heritage Foundation internship his father had helped him secure, and Gerson, assiduously building his résumé, was spending the summer between his sophomore and junior years of college as a Heritage intern. Two years younger than Carlson, Gerson was essentially the intern's intern, and he developed a deep and abiding admiration for his boss. He was enamored with Carlson's sense of humor, his writing chops, his intellectual curiosity, even his relationship with Susie. "I remember thinking, 'Wow, this is what a young marriage should be like,'" Gerson said, recalling that Carlson called Susie multiple times each day to profess his love. "I learned so much from him that summer."

On the day of Carlson's *Standard* interview, Gerson parked himself outside of Kristol's office. When the interview was over and Carlson had left, Gerson immediately asked Kristol what he thought of his friend. "He was terrible," Kristol told him. Gerson was stunned. When Carlson called Gerson later that day, Gerson gave him the bad news. "You're not going to get the job," Gerson told his friend.

But then Gerson decided to try an intervention. He went to Kristol and asked him to give Carlson a second chance. "You really shouldn't reject him on the basis of one interview," Gerson said. "He's the best. Give him a second interview." Kristol agreed.

It was also Carlson's good fortune that, prior to quitting her job to be a stay-at-home mom, Susie had been a religious-school teacher for some of Fred Barnes's children at the Falls Church, a historical Episcopal congregation in suburban Virginia. (A dozen years later, Barnes and a majority of the Falls Church congregation would vote to leave the Episcopal Church to protest the ordination of a gay bishop.) Barnes's kids were upset that "Mrs. Carlson's husband" might not get a job at their dad's new magazine. So Barnes reached out to Susie and suggested that Carlson come to his second interview with more than the three story ideas he brought to his first.

Carlson did just that, bringing a dozen story ideas, and the second interview went much better. Afterward, Kristol offered him the job. Gerson, who went on to found a financial-information-services firm and today is a wealthy philanthropist, viewed the episode as an example of Kristol's broad-mindedness. "How many people of Bill's stature would have said to me, a twenty-two-year-old, 'Okay, I'll give him a second interview'?" Gerson said. "Most people would have said, 'It's nice enough I gave him a first interview.' But that wasn't Bill at all."

Kristol awarded himself far less credit for listening to Gerson about Carlson. "It's pretty cost free to hire twenty-three- or twenty-four-year-olds," he said. "It's cheap—and you can always fire them in a year or two."

ON SEPTEMBER 11, 1995, THE inaugural issue of *The Weekly Standard* hit newsstands. (Kristol ultimately decided his new magazine needed a reminder of its publication schedule in its name; he had considered giving it a geographic marker and calling it *The American Standard*, until he realized that was also the name of a toilet manufacturer.) The cover featured a cartoon of a bandolier-wearing Newt Gingrich swinging from a rope and firing an Uzi under the headline "Permanent Offense."

Inside, Barnes wrote a typically credulous story about Gingrich's bold plans "to replace, not merely reform, the welfare state and the status quo in Washington" in a mere six to ten years. A few pages later, a former *Wall Street Journal* reporter delivered an access-driven, laudatory account of Gingrich's first nine months as Speaker of the House that contained such gems as, after a scene in which Gingrich has a screaming argument with a Republican committee chairman over a 30 percent cut to the committee's operating budget: "'This is not the pleasant part of being Speaker,' Gingrich says. The pleasant part of being Speaker occurs that evening when the House, with Gingrich presiding, approves a bill limiting certain lawsuits."

Staying true to its mission of being a *New Republic* for the right, *The Weekly Standard*'s inaugural issue wasn't all cheerleading for the home team. Charles Krauthammer panned Gingrich's book *To Renew America* and its techno-utopian vision of conservatism, admonishing that "it is not the business of conservatives to offer utopias." Kristol, ever the shit stirrer, argued that Colin Powell, not the anointed Bob Dole, should be the 1996 Republican presidential nominee. "I hope it's a little unpredictable," Kristol told *The New York Times* in its article about *The Standard*'s launch.

Carlson's contribution to the inaugural issue was a short article about Mumia Abu-Jamal and his celebrity supporters. Abu-Jamal was a former Black Panther and radio reporter who was sentenced to death for the 1981 murder of a Philadelphia police officer and who, by the mid-nineties, had become the face of the anti-death-penalty movement in the United States. More than one hundred actors, writers, and intellectuals had recently signed an open letter in *The New York Times* demanding a new trial for him. Carlson interviewed some of the signatories to test their knowledge of the case.

Molly Ivins complained that Abu-Jamal didn't receive a fair trial but was unable to recall the specifics of unfairness. "Anybody who remembered them would reach the same conclusion," she told Carlson. Gloria Steinem drew a similar blank. Ben Cohen, of Ben & Jerry's fame, said he supported Abu-Jamal because Amnesty International and Human Rights Watch had declared him to be "a political prisoner"—something, it turned out, neither group had ever said. As Carlson noted, Abu-Jamal had "become more famous than many of the Big Names who have worked to get him off death row."

"One hears the same refrain from [Abu-]Jamal's celebrity supporters," Carlson wrote. "The judge—or the cops, or the press, or the country generally—was (or were, or are) racist. Therefore Mumia Abu-Jamal did not shoot a policeman in 1981. There are a number of advantages to using this line of argument, the main one being it requires only feelings."

The story was a hit with his new colleagues. A few weeks before the magazine's launch, John Podhoretz, the only one of *The Standard*'s three founding editors with any real editing experience, stopped by Andy Ferguson's office holding an early draft of Carlson's story. "This kid was born knowing how to write a magazine article," Podhoretz told Ferguson. After reading it for himself, Ferguson, who was considered the best writer on staff, concurred. "I thought, 'Jesus, it's like it's come out of the womb full grown,'" Ferguson recalled. "He needed no grooming or tutoring or anything. He was just ready to go out of the box."

Like many of his future *Standard* articles, Carlson's Abu-Jamal story was off the news—a (relatively speaking) light and frothy culture-war distraction from the heavier political and policy articles about Gingrich and entitlement reform and the coming presidential race. Although Abu-Jamal's death sentence would ultimately be reduced to a life one in 2011, owing to an appeals court ruling that jurors had potentially received improper instructions during his original trial, the case for his innocence was always weak, and Carlson was correct to criticize his supporters for their unquestioning embrace of it. Nearly three decades later, the story holds up.

Yet parts of Carlson's first *Standard* article make for discomfiting reading today. Like his effortless ability to make asses out of liberals—noting that Ivins was "reached at a hotel on Martha's

Vineyard." And the dexterity with which he picked at racial scabs—describing Abu-Jamal as "the incarcerated 'journalist' . . . whose last regular job was driving a cab." Indeed, the story is a foreshadowing of some of the topics and tactics Carlson would exploit and employ to such malign effect in the years to come.

BEFITTING A CONSERVATIVE MAGAZINE, *THE Standard*'s office environment in 1995 was a throwback to an earlier era—a predominately male domain where writers and editors smoked at their desks and stashed bottles of booze in their drawers. Matt Labash later likened it to "*Mad Men* without the sexual harassment and good tailoring."

Carlson's office at the magazine was even more of a time capsule. Although he, like all *Standard* staffers, wrote and filed his articles on a computer, he kept an IBM Selectric typewriter on his desk, which he used for his personal correspondence. His nicotine addiction was sufficiently severe that he slaked it with both cigarettes and chewing tobacco, repurposing a Waterford crystal vase, a wedding present, as a spit receptacle.

The office down the hall from Carlson's belonged to Labash, his fellow junior writer. An air force brat who graduated from the University of New Mexico, Labash did not know many people named Tucker—much less Tuckers who wore bow ties and needlepoint belts and who "looked like some WASP from the Lost Tribe of Whit Stillman," as Labash later recalled. Based on name and appearance, plus the natural competitive pressures felt by colleagues sharing the bottom rung of the masthead, Labash expected to hate Carlson. But within minutes of their first meeting at the *Standard* offices that summer, Carlson invited Labash to lunch at a nearby day-drinking bar called Sign of the Whale. A couple of hours and several beers later, the two were fast friends. For the next two decades, not a day would go by when Carlson and Labash did not talk, text, or email—until, one day, they did not.

The Standard's writers each brought their own unique literary influences and styles to the magazine's pages. Kristol was a disciple of the conservative philosopher Leo Strauss and advocated for a politics of "guided populism," by which elites, like himself, would steer and harness the passions of the masses. Barnes emulated the punchy, ideologically slanted reportage of his mentor, Robert Novak. David Brooks attempted to follow in the "sociological journalism" footsteps of William H. Whyte, author of *The Organization Man*. Carlson and Labash, meanwhile, worshipped at the New Journalism altars of Hunter S. Thompson, Tom Wolfe, and P. J. O'Rourke. After Carlson introduced Labash to Joseph Mitchell's *Up in the Old Hotel*, the old *New Yorker* entered their shared pantheon.

Most *Standard* writers sought to influence the direction of the GOP or impact government policy. Their goal, Barnes said, was to "affect the game, which is what the political community in Washington is working out every day." But Carlson and Labash put a premium on good stories and good writing—and having a good time doing their jobs. If Podhoretz's vision for *The Standard* was to be a high-low mix of *Foreign Affairs* and *Mad* magazine, Carlson and Labash definitely tilted toward the *Mad* end of the spectrum. Brooks referred to the pair as "merry pranksters."

The result was, more often than not, some excellent and entertaining journalism. Profiling James Carville, the mastermind of Bill Clinton's first presidential campaign, Carlson documented Carville's "difficulty balancing economy-class rhetoric with an Admiral's Club lifestyle" as he cashed in on his newfound fame with corporate speaking gigs and a ghostwritten book. Carville boasted to Carlson that when the Hotel Employees and Restaurant Employees Union went on strike at the Palm, his (and Carlson's) favorite DC steak house, "I never crossed any picket lines." Carlson reported this was true, but only because "Carville simply called ahead. When the picketers left, he showed up for steak."

In another story, Carlson diagnosed the paranoia and conspiratorial thinking that plagued not just Ross Perot but Perot's entire political movement. "One of the major tenets of the Perot faith holds that the media intentionally distort coverage of 'Ross,'" he wrote. "For Perot's followers, it is a natural conclusion. Perot, they believe, is a threat to the cabal they call 'The Establishment,' of which the mainstream press is a central conspirator." The Perot campaign was a cult of personality, Carlson concluded, comprised of "Perot's true believers, for whom nothing Perot does or says, no matter how strange, seems amiss—or, if necessary, goes undefended." Interviewing one of the true believers, a Texas man who ran phone banks at Perot's headquarters, Carlson wondered "why one of the richest men in the world would rely on the free labor of lower-income people like him to achieve a vain personal ambition."

His coverage of other political heavyweights of the 1990s was consistently insightful—and frequently withering. Describing Jack Kemp's awkward courtship of Black voters at a campaign stop in Chicago, Carlson showed Kemp "giving a soul handshake to a man in the crowd, adding a slight urban lilt to his voice, and generally doing his best to sound like just another black Republican supply-sider who happens to be white. At one point he referred to his wife, Joanne, as his son's 'mama.'" Quoting the already ubiquitous GOP consultant Frank Luntz singing the praises of the Louisiana congressman Billy Tauzin, Carlson offered the disclaimer: "Luntz is legendary for flattering his clients, both current and potential, but when he talks about Tauzin, the praise sounds almost genuine." Of Al Gore's dullness, he wrote, "Gore cultivates this image, aware that there is advantage in being considered too bland to be calculating, and that stiffness is easily mistaken for principle."

Carlson's journalism was fearless. Sometimes too fearless for his bosses at *The Standard*. In 1997, he set his sights on Grover Norquist. At the time, Norquist was the most powerful conservative operative in Washington. A former executive director of the College Republicans and a strident anti-communist who as a twentysomething took a LARPing expedition to Angola to embed with Jonas Savimbi's freedom fighters, Norquist was the founder of Americans for Tax Reform (ATR). In that role, he wrote what came to be known as the Taxpayer Protection Pledge—a promise not to raise taxes that pretty much every Republican politician had signed since he first introduced it in 1986 and that had become a central tenet of the modern GOP. More important, in the early days of the Clinton administration Norquist began hosting a weekly Wednesday-morning meeting in the ATR offices near Dupont Circle of what he called the Leave Us Alone Coalition—a rotating group of nearly one hundred Republican members of Congress, their aides, conservative think tankers, and ideologically simpatico journalists—to plot strategy. Norquist was "the Grand Central Station" of conservatism, as *The Wall Street Journal* editorial writer John Fund, a regular Wednesday meeting attendee, put it. "All the trains run through his office."

Carlson suspected that Norquist was also a typical Washington sleazeball. Ever since Republicans had taken the House and his friend Gingrich had become Speaker, Norquist was selling his access to the Republican Revolutionaries to the highest bidder. He was an activist *and* a lobbyist. Carlson wanted to do an exposé on Norquist's influence peddling. But when he pitched the story to *The Standard*, Podhoretz shot him down.

The reason Podhoretz gave Carlson was Gingrich. *The Standard* had become increasingly critical of the man it had portrayed as Rambo on the cover of its inaugural issue. The dream of "permanent offense" had given way to a desperate desire not to get run off the court, as the magazine repeatedly attacked Gingrich for fecklessness, timidity, and above all, routinely getting outmaneuvered by—and ultimately caving to—Clinton. In March, *The Standard* cover carried a caricature of a disintegrating Gingrich under the headline "Newt Melts" and inside featured an article by Peter King, a Republican congressman from New York, declaring Gingrich "roadkill on the highway of American politics" and calling on him to step aside. Podhoretz told Carlson that he was worried a critical piece about Norquist would be interpreted as excessive piling on against Gingrich. Of course, *The Standard* didn't relent in its harsh coverage of Gingrich. That it wouldn't run a critical story about Norquist spoke to the relative standing of both men at that moment in the conservative movement.

So Carlson, with the tacit approval of his bosses at *The Standard*, took his Norquist story to *The New Republic*, which had absolutely no qualms about getting on the bad side of the conservative power broker. The article, titled "What I Sold at the Revolution," ran in June and immediately became the talk of Washington. Carlson portrayed Norquist as a "cash-addled, morally malleable lobbyist" who, for the right price, would take the pet issues of "Third World" leftists and Fortune 500 companies and present them as conservative causes.

Carlson's story revealed that despite having spent his political life crusading to shrink the size of government—"to get it down to the size where we can drown it in the bathtub," as he later put it—Norquist lobbied against a proposal to close the American embassy in the Seychelles, whose government happened to be paying him ten thousand dollars a month. Similarly, Norquist told participants in the Wednesday meeting that they should be against the Communications Decency Act—a bill to regulate online pornography—because it violated conservative principles. This came as a surprise to some Wednesday-meeting regulars, especially the Christian conservative ones, but it turned out that Microsoft, which vehemently opposed the CDA, also had Norquist on a ten-thousand-dollar-a-month retainer.

Norquist wasn't just a sleazeball, according to Carlson; he was a weird sleazeball—one who "eschew[ed] bourgeois conventions like a wife and family, table manners, even personal relationships" and who "has lived with roommates in the same shabby rented house for years." A popular Washington rumor at the time was that Norquist was gay, and Carlson's story seemed designed to amplify those whispers. (In 2004, Norquist would marry a Muslim woman, which sparked a new round of rumors—heavily circulated by *Breitbart*, Glenn Beck, and others on the far right—that ATR was an Islamist front group.)

Norquist was furious about the story. He accused Carlson of having an undisclosed conflict of interest, claiming that Carlson nursed a grudge against him because he had once clashed with Carlson's father, Dick, in Dick's roles as ambassador to the Seychelles and head of the Corporation for Public Broadcasting. "His father and I were on opposite sides of the fight for democracy in the Seychelles, and we were on opposite sides of the right to defund PBS, and we gave him an Enemy of the Taxpayer Award," Norquist complained. "When Tucker interviewed me, he clearly knew the history with his father. When I mentioned his father, he looked embarrassed." Carlson, for his part, accused Norquist of "concocting an utterly ridiculous conspiracy theory" while Dick maintained that his relationship with Norquist had been "perfectly amicable. . . . If he said we had run-ins, he's a little liar."

Of course, Norquist's real beef with Carlson wasn't his loyalty to his family; it was his disloyalty to the conservative movement, which Norquist believed he himself personified. Norquist was accustomed to conservative journalists following his marching orders. As one Wednesday-meeting attendee told Carlson, the gatherings were useful to attend "if you want to know what *The Washington Times* and *National Review* will be writing about next week." On those rare occasions when a conservative journalist didn't toe the party line, he or she was harshly dealt with.

The previous fall, Laura Ingraham, a former Reagan White House aide and Clarence Thomas clerk who'd left her law firm job to embark on a career as a conservative pundit, wrote a *New York Times* op-ed urging Gingrich to appoint someone other than Indiana congressman Dan Burton as the chairman of the House Oversight Committee, which would play a crucial role in investigating the Clinton administration. Ingraham's argument was both well-reasoned and, from a Republican perspective, well-intentioned. She presented a convincing bill of goods that Burton was a conspiratorial nutjob—including his belief that the Clinton White House lawyer Vince Foster hadn't died by suicide but in fact had been murdered by Clinton's henchmen, a belief he once tried to prove by reenacting Foster's shooting in his backyard with a .38-caliber pistol and a pumpkin—and made the case that, if Burton was chair of the Oversight Committee, "it would be easier than ever for the White House to tar" the committee's work as "pure partisanship."

Ingraham's article proved prescient. Burton's chairmanship was a disaster: He was caught doctoring transcripts of taped jailhouse conversations between a former Clinton aide and his wife to make them seem more incriminating of Clinton than they were, and he undercut his and his fellow Republicans' perceived objectivity when he publicly called Clinton "a scumbag." ("If Bill Clinton didn't have Rep. Dan Burton (R-Ind.) in the House, he would have to invent him," the Democratic political analyst Bob Beckel later wrote in the *Los Angeles Times*.) But not only was Ingraham's advice ignored; she was punished for offering it. Robert Novak sneeringly identified Ingraham in his column as "a supposedly conservative activist who until recently was a law firm associate of Clinton attorney Robert Bennett." Soon thereafter, Norquist confronted Ingraham at an end-of-year conservative gathering she helped organize called the Dark Ages Weekend—a self-consciously reactionary analogue to the Clintons' famed New Agey Renaissance Weekend—and told her that she would need to decide "whether to be with us or against us." He then disinvited her from future Wednesday meetings for good measure.

Norquist used similar pressure tactics against Carlson—some of them even before he'd written the article. The day after Carlson's first interview with Norquist, during which he pressed Norquist about his work for the Seychelles, Norquist ambushed him during lunch at the Palm. Sitting down uninvited at Carlson's table, his hands shaking, Norquist accused Carlson of being part of a conspiracy to destroy him and, by extension, to "destroy the Speaker." His and Gingrich's enemies, Norquist continued, were using Carlson to "get a Movement conservative to attack Movement conservatives." Carlson's questions about the Seychelles were "not helpful to the Movement."

After the article came out, Norquist and his allies stepped up the pressure. Carlson was bombarded with angry phone calls from conservative machers castigating him for his apostasy. "No one who believes what we believe should be attacking Grover," Michael Ledeen, the neoconservative foreign policy guru, scolded Carlson. Even though *The Standard* had passed on Carlson's story, it didn't escape the blowback. Norquist demanded that Kristol fire Carlson. At the same time, he lobbied Murdoch to pull his funding from the magazine.

Kristol refused to sack Carlson, and Murdoch continued to pour money into *The Standard*. That seemed to embolden

Carlson, who ratcheted up the feud. Writing in *Slate*, he called Norquist "a mean-spirited, humorless, dishonest little creep." Working through back channels, he fed tips about Norquist to other reporters. Ben Domenech, a precocious homeschooled fifteen-year-old from suburban Virginia who was interning at the conservative newspaper *Human Events*, had called Carlson to congratulate him on the story. Not realizing his admirer's age, Carlson invited Domenech to drinks at the Mayflower Hotel bar, where he pitched Domenech on an investigative project. "I took a notebook and I wrote down four or five pages of Tucker ranting about Grover," Domenech recalled. "He was wanting me to follow his leads on some stuff and do another negative piece about Grover."

Things came to a head in November at *The American Spectator*'s thirtieth-anniversary gala. About a thousand conservative politicians, operatives, and journalists gathered in the Sheraton Washington Hotel's ballroom to celebrate the magazine (as well as Robert Bork and Rush Limbaugh, who were receiving awards). Both Carlson and Norquist were among those in attendance. During the cocktail hour, after several drinks, Carlson noticed Norquist standing near the dais. Borrowing Labash's Bloody Mary, Carlson mounted the dais and feigned extreme interest in the lectern. When Norquist came within range beneath it, Carlson dumped the Bloody Mary on his head. "The celery stuck behind Grover's ear, making him look like a conservative Carmen Miranda," one witness said. Carlson claimed that the spill was an accident and offered to pay Norquist's dry-cleaning bill, but no one, least of all Norquist, believed him. Later that evening, a woman who worked for Norquist tracked down Carlson and threw a glass of white wine in his face.

THE NORQUIST STORY AND ITS aftermath helped establish Carlson's reputation in Washington as a different kind of conservative journalist.

Yes, he would sometimes write with an eye toward advancing an ideological agenda. This was particularly true when it came to abortion, which, largely as a result of Susie's influence, he was adamantly against.

In one *Standard* article, written in the summer of 1996, he methodically attacked pro-choice Republicans for staking out a position—in which they were personally opposed to abortion but were against government restrictions on the procedure—that was "difficult, maybe impossible, to defend as a species of logic." The only explanations for their stance, Carlson concluded, were "simply a political calculation" or, more sinister, "the belief that since abortion rates are highest in inner cities, legal abortion results in fewer indolent ghetto dwellers whose presence drains the country's economy."

In another *Standard* piece later that year, Carlson lamented how improvements in prenatal testing had led to an increase in the number of pregnancies that were being terminated because the fetus had been diagnosed with Down syndrome—a development, he argued, that was evidence of "the eugenic utility of abortion." He wrote: "It is one of the triumphs of modern society that the life of the average person with Down Syndrome has become strikingly normal. Except that, unlike normal people, people with Down Syndrome have been targeted for elimination."

Carlson was similarly willing to stake out a position on immigration. In October 1997, he wrote an op-ed for *The Wall Street Journal* criticizing the Federation for American Immigration Reform (FAIR), America's leading anti-immigration group. Headlined "The Intellectual Roots of Nativism," the article argued that FAIR's advocacy for "tighter national borders" was motivated by Malthusian fears about overpopulation and theories of racial superiority.

Carlson quoted FAIR founder John Tanton fretting that unless the United States sealed its borders, it would be overrun by people "defecating and creating garbage and looking for jobs." And he revealed that FAIR had once received a six-hundred-thousand-dollar donation from the Pioneer Fund, which was established in the 1930s to support "research in heredity and eugenics." Noting that a number of conservatives—including *National Review* editor John O'Sullivan and the activist Paul Weyrich—had recently embraced FAIR and its calls for a more restrictive immigration policy, he asked whether they "know all they should about the object of their affections."

One FAIR board member later complained that Carlson was "a combative journalist writing for the Open Border editorial page of the *Wall Street Journal*" whose "technique was the standard guilt-by-association lynching in print, Joe McCarthy style."

More often than not, though, Carlson actively avoided opining. Shortly after he was hired by *The Standard*, Mitch Horowitz, an editor at the Free Press, signed Carlson to a book deal. (Horowitz was Mark Gerson's book editor, and Gerson had recommended Carlson to him.) At the time, the conservative sociologist James Q. Wilson's "broken windows" theory of law enforcement—which held that cracking down on small crime, like graffiti and subway-turnstile jumping, led to a decrease in violent crime—was in vogue; most notably New York mayor Rudy Giuliani seemed to be using it to great effect in his city. The book, as Carlson and Horowitz envisioned it, would build on this conservative approach to police reform, arguing that police should be given even more freedom to fight crime.

But as Carlson sat down to write the book, he encountered a problem. "I had this crisis when I realized I didn't agree with the essential thesis of the book," he explained. "I decided my thesis was repugnant." By then, he and Susie had had their second child, and he was feeling financial discomfort, but the pressure of committing to an argument he didn't believe was even more uncomfortable. "He sent me a handwritten letter saying, 'Look, I'm sorry, I just cannot complete this book,' and he included a personal check, made out to my publishing company, for his advance of ten thousand dollars," Horowitz said. "It was the first and last time anything like that happened."

All around Carlson, the hallways and conference room of *The Standard*'s offices, to say nothing of its pages, thrummed with ideological combat. Brooks stumped for a domestic policy he dubbed "national greatness conservatism" that promoted "great projects"—compulsory national service, a mission to Mars, anything that might "physically and spiritually unify the nation." As he and Kristol explained in a subsequent *Wall Street Journal* op-ed: "Wishing to be left alone isn't a governing doctrine." (It was a far more direct, and yet far more subtle, rebuke of Norquist than the one Carlson had delivered.) Kristol and Robert Kagan advocated for a maximalist vision of American foreign policy—with a bigger defense budget and a greater willingness to take on, and take out, rogue regimes around the world. In November 1997, the pair coauthored a cover story with the straightforward headline "Saddam Must Go." At editorial meetings, over lunch, and during after-work happy hours, *Standard* writers debated and discussed their various ideological projects.

But Carlson stayed out of the fray. "Tucker was always less ideologically defined than a lot of the rest of us," Brooks said. "When we had arguments about public issues at meetings, I don't recall him being vocal on those things or taking an ideological stand one way or the other. He was way more a storyteller than an arguer."

After Matt Drudge revealed in January 1998 that *Newsweek* had spiked a story about Clinton's affair with a White House intern, Monica Lewinsky, *The Standard* became a full-throated advocate for Clinton's impeachment. That August, in an editorial titled "Clinton Must Go," David Tell wrote: "Every time Bill Clinton appears in public to perform the work that only a president can, he represents a walking, brutal rebuke to the spirit of our constitutional order." Numerous (and similar) anti-Clinton editorials followed.

Carlson was skeptical that a president's sexual peccadillos warranted removing him from office. He was not the only *Standard* writer who held that view. But rather than make that case in editorial meetings or even in print, as Christopher Caldwell and Andy Ferguson did, Carlson stayed mum. Instead, he devoted his energies toward reporting out the Clinton-Lewinsky scandal.

Jonah Goldberg, whose mother, Lucianne, possessed tapes of Linda Tripp talking to Lewinsky about the affair with Clinton, worked in the AEI building as a producer on AEI fellow Ben Wattenberg's PBS show and was a casual acquaintance of Carlson's. Carlson tried to persuade Goldberg to give him the tapes. "He was very schmoozy and friendly about it in a way that wasn't the hard sell," Goldberg said. "It didn't come across as insincere the way other reporters did." Still, Carlson struck out; Goldberg ended up handing over the tapes to a US Marshal working for the independent counsel Ken Starr.

Carlson had better luck with a friend who participated in a morning conference call among Democratic strategists to formulate and coordinate talking points defending Clinton against Starr. The friend gave Carlson the phone number and passcode to the call so that he could eavesdrop. The friend made Carlson promise not to write about or quote from the call. But just listening proved to be a boon to Carlson's reporting, and he produced a series of stories on the White House's efforts to combat Starr and beat back impeachment.

His most entertaining scoop was early in the scandal, when Clinton's defenders were trying out the defense that Lewinsky's confessions to Tripp about her affair with the president were the product of her overactive imagination. Carlson tracked down Irene Kassorla, a Hollywood psychologist who had treated Lewinsky. "She would have to be very sick to fantasize to that degree," Kassorla told Carlson. She also told Carlson that, while she wouldn't disclose what Lewinsky had confided to her, the notion that her patient had had an affair with the president was totally plausible. Lewinsky's first day as a White House intern, Kassorla said, was

> like your first day of kindergarten. Can you imagine being this little kid in kindergarten and there's this nice daddy there? Your mommy has left you, she's gone home and told you to be brave. There are 250 of you in the class, and all of a sudden the biggest daddy in the place takes you by the hand and shows you how to color, and shows you how to play with the clay, and shows you how to get on the tricycle, and when you fall he picks you up. I mean, it's pretty nice.

Yet, while Carlson wasn't terribly interested in advancing ideological arguments, he was very focused on advancing his career. Unlike his friend Labash, who so enjoyed the freedom (and the generous expenses budget) *The Standard* offered him to pursue whatever stories struck his fancy that he turned down freelance assignments and lunches with editors from mainstream media outlets, Carlson was not content spending his career at a small-circulation conservative magazine.

The IBM Selectric typewriter he kept in his office wasn't just for decoration. He used it to write short notes on *Weekly Standard* letterhead to other, more established journalists—like *The New York Times*'s R. W. Apple or *Slate*'s Michael Kinsley—complimenting them on their stories. When Andy Ferguson would spy the pile of cards in *The Standard*'s outgoing mail pile, he'd rib Carlson. "You're not trying to get a job at *The New York Times*, are you?" Ferguson teased his colleague.

"I always thought it was kind of a sign of his ambition," Ferguson said. "He knew how the game was played."

In 1999, Carlson got the opportunity he'd been angling for. It wasn't *The Times*, but, at that moment, it seemed even better.

Tina Brown wanted him to write for her.

Brown was considered by many to be the greatest magazine editor of her generation. In the 1980s she resurrected *Vanity Fair* by chronicling—and, often, celebrating—the excesses of Decade of Greed–era Hollywood and Wall Street; in the '90s she revivified *The New Yorker* by bringing a heady mix of high and low culture to its ossified pages. Now, at the dawn of a new century, she wanted to "create a new form for a magazine without the institutional history of any publication before me, or my mind," she said. With the financial backing of Harvey Weinstein and his film studio, Miramax, she was launching a new monthly magazine called *Talk*.

Brown's singular talent as an editor was her knack for both assessing and creating buzz; the highest praise she offered writers was when she returned their drafts with the note "hot" or, even better, "v. hot." In her estimation, Carlson was, like Martin Amis and Paul Theroux and all the other contributing editors she recruited to *Talk*, v. hot—a "gadfly scamp," she said, who "had an almost Evelyn Waugh–ish ability to skewer people and make it really funny."

Carlson's first assignment for *Talk*, for its inaugural issue that September, was a profile of George W. Bush. The then Texas governor was the front-runner for the Republican presidential nomination in 2000 and a natural subject for both *Talk* and Carlson, whose conservative-media bona fides, Brown knew, would afford him unique access to GOP politicians. (It was a source-greasing tactic Brown had employed since her days at *Vanity Fair*, when she secured Ronald and Nancy Reagan's participation in a cover story by assigning the piece to William F. Buckley.) Over the course of several months, Carlson visited with Bush in Austin, traveled with Bush to California, and at one point even hitched a ride with Bush after bumping into the governor at church.

The story that resulted wasn't an obvious skewering. Like most political reporters who covered him during the campaign, Carlson was impressed by Bush's towel-snapping, nickname-bequeathing, f-bomb-dropping bonhomie. (It's instructive that Frank Bruni, who covered the Bush campaign for *The New York Times*, titled his book about the experience *Ambling into History*.) Carlson relayed a scene from a campaign event outside of Austin in which Bush encounters "a sullen-looking man of about 25 with a wispy goatee and a biker T-shirt" who, with a beer in his hand, "is hanging back, as if he wandered into the event and is now looking for a way to leave." Bush, Carlson wrote,

> takes hold of one of his arms, which are pasty white and covered from shoulder to wrist with tattoos. "Where'd you get 'em done?" Bush asks, sounding genuinely impressed by the quality of the snakes, flames, and death's-heads. "Here and there," the man mumbles. Bush nods. "Good," he says. For a moment the man looks confused—is the

> governor being serious?—then relaxes and smiles. He has been disarmed.

Carlson was disarmed, too. "You get the sense that if Bush had chosen his own campaign slogan he would have printed bumper stickers that read GEORGE W. BUSH: SO SECURE, HE DOESN'T CARE WHAT YOU THINK OF HIM," he wrote. "Above all, Bush wants to let voters know that he's not desperate for their approval—that unlike Bill Clinton he doesn't have a compelling psychological need to be elected."

But, unlike so many of his Fourth Estate colleagues, Carlson didn't stop his analysis there. Just because Bush was, in Carlson's estimation, a "weirdly compelling" person didn't mean he was fit for the White House. There was the matter of his poor work ethic. "Bush isn't ashamed to admit he's not a detail man," Carlson wrote. "As governor, Bush became famous for cutting meetings short, refusing to read memos longer than two pages, and making unusually quick decisions based on instinct and a few simple principles." There was his thin skin. Despite his claims that he was "comfortable in [his] soul," Carlson noted that "it's still pretty easy to get a rise out of Bush."

Which Carlson proved when, during a car ride, he asked Bush about Karla Faye Tucker, a double murderer who was executed in Texas the year before. Carlson wanted to know if Bush had met with any of the protesters who traveled to Austin seeking clemency for her.

"Bush whips around and stares at me," Carlson wrote.

> "No, I didn't meet with any of them," he snaps, as though I've just asked the dumbest, most offensive question ever posed. "I didn't meet with Larry King either when he came down for it. I watched his interview with [Tucker], though.

He asked her real difficult questions, like 'What would you say to Governor Bush?'"

"What was her answer?" I wonder.

"'Please,'" Bush whimpers, his lips pursed in mock desperation, "'don't kill me.'"

In subtle but unmistakable fashion, Carlson painted a portrait of Bush—stubborn, profane, callow—that should have told voters everything they needed to know about why he would be such a terrible president. It was a masterful takedown, for anyone who read it carefully.

The Bush campaign certainly did. It viewed the story as a great betrayal. "You fucked us!" Jack Oliver, Bush's deputy campaign chairman, fumed to Carlson on a phone call. Bush himself complained about Carlson's portrayal of him mocking Karla Faye Tucker. "Mr. Carlson misread, mischaracterized me," Bush told the Associated Press. "He's a good reporter, he just misunderstood about how serious that was. I take the death penalty very seriously. I take each case seriously. I just felt he misjudged me. I think he misinterpreted my feelings. I know he did." Karen Hughes, Bush's communications director, went further, insinuating to George Will that Carlson had made up some of Bush's more inflammatory and profane quotes. "I don't remember those words being used," she said. In off-the-record conversations with other journalists, Hughes didn't just insinuate; she flat-out told them that Carlson had made up the quotes.

Talk and Carlson stood by the story. Carlson even confronted Hughes in a phone call, he later recalled, "to demand that she stop slandering me." But among some people, questions about the story persisted—or eventually resurfaced.

David Frum, who was friendly with Carlson through *The Standard*, initially assumed the Bush campaign's complaints were bogus. "Tucker Carlson was a journalist for a magazine and the magazine was presumably fact-checked and Bush was a politician," Frum said, "so everyone in the press believed that the story was true." But then, after Frum went to work in the Bush White House as a speechwriter—where, in 2002, he would come up with the phrase "axis of evil" that Bush infamously used to describe North Korea, Iran, and Iraq—he began to have his doubts. "I got to know Bush, not well but a little, and the story really bothered me because it was just harder and harder for me to reconcile it with the Bush I knew," Frum said. "Not that Bush couldn't say flippant things, but he did take the ultimate questions of life and death incredibly seriously."

Frum's doubts only grew in subsequent years, as he and Carlson drifted apart politically and personally and then, after Trump's election, became fierce ideological antagonists. (During a Fox News segment in 2021, Carlson described Frum as a "dopey middle-aged Canadian Twitter celebrity whose life goal is to force America into yet another unwinnable pointless war.") "This guy lies a lot and lies in ways that injure others and aggrandize himself," Frum said. "I think it would be an interesting thing to go back and find out, was that story fact-checked? And did the fact-checkers hear a tape?"

According to former *Talk* editors, the story was indeed fact-checked, as were all stories at the magazine. Tina Brown had sought to re-create *The New Yorker*'s vaunted fact-checking department at her new magazine. But if there was a tape of Carlson's interview with Bush, or if Carlson simply handed the fact-checkers his notes, no one who worked on the story can remember. And no one, save for Carlson's current-day critics, harbors real doubts about the story.

BACK AT *THE WEEKLY STANDARD*, Carlson's bosses stood behind him, as well. "He's great at digging up stuff and great at getting people to confide in him and tell him things they later wish they hadn't," Kristol told *The Washington Post*. "Some Republicans and conservatives think he's a fellow conservative and he'll give them a break. Tucker, to his credit, reports it like it is."

The 2000 presidential election was setting up to be a major moment for *The Standard*. While the then-four-year-old Fox News Channel looked at the race as a chance to boost its ratings, and publications like *The American Spectator* and *National Review* viewed it as a chance to finally be rid of Democratic rule, Kristol and *The Standard* had something bigger in mind. The new conservative majority that he and *The Standard*'s other founders hoped to shape with the magazine's launch in 1995 had, as a result of Gingrich's spectacular implosion, not come to pass; the 1996 campaign was destined to be decided in Bill Clinton's favor no matter whom the GOP nominated. So the 2000 Republican primaries to determine which candidate would face a Clinton-scandal-hobbled Al Gore were *The Standard*'s first real chance to throw its weight around in a presidential race. Moreover, if the Republicans did win back the White House, its new occupant would have the opportunity to usher in that new era of conservative governance, just a few years later than originally planned. Who the Republicans nominated mattered—and *The Standard* wanted to make sure the party got it right.

The Standard was quite clear about who it *didn't* want to win the Republican nomination: Pat Buchanan. *The Standard*'s opposition to Buchanan was practically foundational, with the magazine spilling copious amounts of ink in its first few months of existence to repeatedly inveigh against the pundit turned politician's 1996 presidential campaign. Buchanan, who referred to his supporters as "peasants with pitchforks," represented a brand of paleoconservative populism that was anathema to the neocons. "In an increasingly conservative America, one political figure defiantly resists the historical tide," Frum wrote in one of *The Standard*'s many anti-Buchanan jeremiads during its early days.

> This man still denounces big banks and multinational corporations. Still unabashedly puts the interests of the American factory worker ahead of those of the so-called international trading system. Still refuses even to contemplate any cuts in the generosity of big middle-class spending programs like Medicare and Social Security. This man is Patrick J. Buchanan, America's last leftist.

David Brooks recalled that the day after Buchanan scored an upset victory in the 1996 New Hampshire primary, Buchanan's sister, Kathleen, who worked as an executive assistant at *The Standard*, reassured the magazine's writers, "Don't worry. I'll protect you guys when the pitchforks come."

Four years later, Buchanan was running for president again, and *The Standard* was, if anything, even more hostile toward him and his candidacy. Since his last campaign, Buchanan had written a book, *A Republic, Not an Empire*, in which he attempted to rehabilitate Charles Lindbergh's "America First" foreign policy and argued that the United States should not have gone to war against Hitler's Germany. Buchanan was no longer just America's last leftist. *The Standard* now proclaimed him to be both anti-Semitic and anti-American—a "Blame-America-Firster" in Kristol's formulation. When Buchanan threatened to bolt the GOP for Perot's Reform Party, and prominent Republicans including George W. Bush were beseeching him to stay lest he cut into the GOP presidential nominee's support in November, *The Standard* editorialized that he shouldn't let the door hit him on the way out. "If the Republican party can't stand up to Pat Buchanan, and it can't explain why it rejects his view of America," Kristol wrote, "is it a party worthy of governing?" Buchanan, for his part, was just as contemptuous of *The Standard*. Appearing on *Today* in the midst of the fracas, he complained to Katie Couric, "Let me tell you about Mr. Kristol. He runs that dinky little magazine that's subsidized by Rupert Murdoch that pretends to be conservative."

Carlson's contributions to the anti-Buchanan effort consisted of a couple of snarky *Standard* articles reporting on dysfunction in Buchanan's campaign, plus a *Talk* story about the Washington political-media class's continued high regard for Buchanan. ("We're not used to people with such extreme political views being so charming," Charles Krauthammer told Carlson. "I don't think Himmler had such a sense of humor.") But it was clear he subscribed to *The Standard*'s broader critique. A month before Buchanan ultimately followed through on his threat to leave the GOP, Carlson appeared on C-SPAN's *Washington Journal*, the no-frills cable channel's no-frills public affairs show, on which print reporters sat at a newspaper-and-magazine-cluttered table and fielded questions from Brian Lamb and viewers who called in. One caller demanded of Carlson, "You work for Bill Kristol, correct?" Carlson replied, "I do, happily." The caller went on, "That guy, he's not a Republican. He's a disgrace," adding, "We don't need Republicans like you and Bill Kristol. We need Republicans and conservatives like Pat Buchanan." Carlson chuckled and said that Buchanan's supporters were essentially brainwashed; he mimicked Buchanan's claims that "'the tiny cabal that controls American politics doesn't like me because I speak truth to power . . . that I offend the plutocracy, that I'm a wanted man by the inside-the-Beltway people.'" Buchanan, Carlson said, "in every sense casts himself as a victim who is sort of a Karen Silkwood of politics, someone who's so truthful that he's being hunted down by the conspiracy that runs Washington.

It's all a bit much. Maybe Pat Buchanan says things that are kind of kooky, and that's why he's being criticized."

Carlson believed that Buchanan would soon be as disreputable as the political writer Joseph Sobran. Sobran was Buchanan's fellow paleocon and good friend who'd once been William F. Buckley's protégé at *National Review* but was fired from the magazine in the early 1990s for his anti-Israel and anti-Semitic views, leading to his eventual banishment from the conservative movement. Carlson had a running joke those days in which he told people that he'd just bumped into Sobran at a suburban Denny's. He reported that Sobran—who by then had been reduced to writing screeds about the "Jewish Establishment" in his self-published newsletter—was disheveled, with long, dirty fingernails, and was sitting alone in a booth, talking to himself, holding court to no one. To Carlson, it seemed as if it was only a matter of time before Buchanan suffered the same fate.

While *The Standard*'s writers and editors were unanimous in their opposition to Buchanan, they—much like Republican voters themselves—were split over which 2000 presidential candidate to support. One group lined up behind Bush. The other championed John McCain. The Bush backers were led by Fred Barnes. In addition to being naturally deferential to the GOP establishment's pick (Barnes's big *Standard* cover story on Bush was titled "The Anointed One"), they believed that Bush's compassionate conservative agenda of education reform and poverty reduction was a smart bit of lip service that would ultimately pave the way for what they truly cared about: upper-income tax cuts. McCain's most enthusiastic supporters, meanwhile, were Kristol and Brooks. They saw in the Arizona senator—with his wartime heroism, calls to service, and heterodox views on campaign-finance reform (for it) and upper-income tax cuts (against them)—a standard-bearer for their national greatness conservatism, which they believed would give the GOP a much-needed makeover.

"Either by accident or by design," Kristol and Brooks wrote of McCain, "he has become an agent of creative destruction."

Carlson threw in with Kristol and Brooks—and McCain. McCain's 2000 bid garnered the most positive press of arguably any presidential campaign in American history, with reporters (and the occasional moonlighting novelist, like David Foster Wallace, who filed for *Rolling Stone*) seemingly competing among themselves to produce the most fawning coverage. Even so, Carlson's *Standard* stories about McCain stood out for how in the tank he was. McCain, in Carlson's telling, was "about the coolest guy who ever ran for president"; "a happy warrior, maybe the only real one in American politics"; and a candidate who was "determined to run the most amusing and least conventional campaign possible." The gushing wasn't just for McCain but also for those in McCain's circle, like Lindsey Graham, then a South Carolina congressman and McCain's campaign trail sidekick, about whom Carlson wrote: "In television interviews, Graham can sometimes seem simple. He's not. On stage, Graham is a compelling speaker, inspiring and cuttingly witty."

The good feelings were mutual. McCain tended to like all reporters, referring to the media, only partly in jest, as "my base." But he had favorites—and Carlson was one of them. Along with *Salon*'s Jake Tapper and *Time*'s John Dickerson, Carlson not only had a regular (and coveted) seat in the salon at the back of McCain's Straight Talk Express campaign bus but was also invited to watch election results with the candidate in his hotel suite and even in his family's living room. "Each of them had a sense of humor and McCain liked going back and forth with them," Mark Salter, a longtime aide to and confidant of McCain, recalled. "He enjoyed Tucker's company." (And the reporters enjoyed each others'. Six years later, Carlson would be honored at Tapper's wedding as one of the four people present when Tapper met his future wife in an Iowa bar.)

When McCain ultimately lost the nomination to Bush, Carlson portrayed the defeat as "proof that everything [McCain] has been saying for the past year is true: That money is the decisive factor in politics. That the system is rigged to exclude outsiders and mavericks. That the Establishment felt so threatened by his honesty that it mobilized to crush him." In the end, Carlson wrote, McCain "lost because he would not do anything to win."

CARLSON'S FELLOW MCCAIN BACKERS AT *The Standard* were similarly bitter, treating Bush's general election matchup with Gore as a contest between the lesser of two evils, or, as Kristol and Brooks called it, "a bidding war more worthy of a campaign for city council." Even after the Supreme Court decided the election in Bush's favor and he entered the White House, a good portion of *The Standard*'s writers were critical of him and his administration.

In April 2001, a US Navy reconnaissance plane collided with a Chinese interceptor jet over international waters and made an emergency landing on China's Hainan Island. The twenty-four Navy crewmen on board the US plane were taken into custody by the People's Liberation Army and were released ten days later only after the US ambassador to China delivered a letter to the Chinese foreign minister saying that the United States was "very sorry" for what happened. Kristol and Robert Kagan complained about the "profound national humiliation that President Bush has brought upon the United States." A few months later, after Bush released his 2002 Pentagon budget, Kristol and Kagan lamented "the impending evisceration of the American military" and recommended that secretary of defense Donald Rumsfeld and his deputy Paul Wolfowitz, "two old friends," resign.

But then came 9/11. The terrorist attacks on New York City and Washington, DC, boosted Bush's popularity not just among voters (who gave him an approval rating of 90 percent) but in the media too. Writing in *The New Yorker*, David Remnick hailed Bush's post-9/11 speech to Congress—in which Bush declared, "Either you are with us, or you are with the terrorists"—for being "simple and direct, with an unhackneyed vigor of language" that "went some distance in reassuring those who feared his response to this crisis would be a primitive spasm of vengeful violence." *Vanity Fair* went so far as to have Annie Leibovitz photograph Bush, Dick Cheney, and Colin Powell for the magazine's cover and assigned the accompanying article, "War and Destiny: The White House in Wartime," to William F. Buckley's son, Christopher, who compared Bush to Reagan, Teddy Roosevelt, and Harry Truman.

The Standard's writers and editors rallied around Bush not just out of patriotic fervor. They rallied to his side because, after 9/11, he began to take theirs. In October, the same month Bush launched Operation Enduring Freedom in Afghanistan, *The Standard* published "The Case for American Empire" by Max Boot. Hauling out the title of Buchanan's book *A Republic, Not an Empire* for yet another flogging, Boot wrote, "In fact this analysis is exactly backward: The September 11 attack was a result of insufficient American involvement and ambition; the solution is to be more expansive in our goals and more assertive in their implementation." That meant, Boot went on to argue, the United States should go to war not just in Afghanistan but in Iraq, as well. Later that month, Kristol and Kagan declared that war in Iraq was necessary even if the United States had to go it alone. "The wider conflict ahead will have to be fought with or without the approval of every single member state of the United Nations, or every tribe and clan of every ethnically divided nation in Central Asia and the Middle East," they wrote.

"Colin Powell's grand coalition will have to give way to a narrower coalition of the willing, the capable, and the committed—committed, that is, to the security of the West."

Bush was obviously listening. In the coming years, *The Standard* would achieve a level of political influence that exceeded even its founders' wildest dreams, as the Bush administration's foreign policy seemed to come directly from the magazine's pages. (It was not a coincidence that Cheney dispatched a staffer to *The Standard*'s offices every Monday to pick up thirty copies of the new issue.) "I'm a little amused, but pleased and happy that the bus has become more crowded and that it is heading in the right direction," Kristol said in 2003, shortly before the United States invaded Iraq. "I admire what the president has done so far and am happy that we are in agreement." He later boasted, "It's probably fair to say that we were for the 'Bush Doctrine' before there was a 'Bush Doctrine.'"

The influence of *The Standard*—and of neoconservatives, more generally—on the Bush administration did not go unnoticed. Among those opposed to the Iraq War, on both the left and the right, there was dark, often anti-Semitic talk about how Kristol and his allies had hypnotized Bush into doing their bidding. Writing in *The American Conservative*, the magazine he cofounded in 2002 to try to wrest the conservative movement back from the neocons whom he believed had hijacked it, Buchanan issued a cri de coeur on behalf of his fellow paleocons:

> We charge that a cabal of polemicists and public officials seeks to ensnare our country in a series of wars that are not in America's interests. We charge them with colluding with Israel to ignite those wars and destroy the Oslo Accords. We charge them with deliberately damaging U.S. relations with every state in the Arab world that defies

> Israel or supports the Palestinian people's right to a homeland of their own. We charge that they have alienated friends and allies all over the Islamic and Western world through their arrogance, hubris, and bellicosity.

But to those at and allied with *The Standard*, Buchanan's charges were just so much noise—the sounds of a movement, and its leader, in their death throes. The paleocons, Frum wrote at the start of the Iraq War, "began by hating the neoconservatives. They came to hate their party and this president. They have finished by hating their country." The neocons, by contrast, were now firmly in control. In Bush—who, John Podhoretz wrote in his 2004 book, *Bush Country: How Dubya Became a Great President While Driving Liberals Insane*, "constructed one of the most consequential presidencies in the nation's history"—the neocons had found an unlikely standard-bearer to helm the new era of conservative governance they'd been anticipating and planning for since Podhoretz and Kristol met at the Utopia coffee shop a decade earlier.

The neocons were so giddy about their success, so certain of their triumph that they almost seemed to welcome their critics' calumnies. In 2005, at a Harvard Kennedy School symposium commemorating *The Standard*'s tenth anniversary, Fred Barnes was asked what impact the magazine had had on the American political debate. "Oh, I think we've played a big role," he replied, failing to suppress a smile. "We started a war in Iraq, we got tax cuts, we reelected Bush. We've had great influence."

But by then, Carlson had not just left *The Standard* and print journalism; he'd begun his political migration away from the neocons, as well.

THREE

On an August evening in 1999, Tucker Carlson took a ferry from Lower Manhattan to Liberty Island, where he found himself in glittering company. Gathered at the base of the Statue of Liberty were eight hundred or so members of America's political, entertainment, business, and media elite: Robert De Niro and Joan Didion, Jerry Seinfeld and Al Sharpton, Henry Kissinger and Madonna. They were there for a party celebrating the launch of *Talk*. "This one is for you, Salman," George Plimpton said into a microphone, addressing his fellow guest Salman Rushdie. "It's banned in Iran." Then Plimpton, Rushdie, Carlson, and the rest of the partygoers took in a twenty-minute fireworks display over New York Harbor, the Twin Towers looming in the background. Years later, after 9/11 and the Great Recession and the collapse of the magazine industry (of which *Talk* was an early casualty, shuttering in 2002) and the general malaise that came to hover over American media and politics, *Talk*'s launch party took on an elegiac, near-mythic status. "It was the end of something extraordinary," Tina Brown said, "but none of us knew it at the time."

In fact, Carlson did have an inkling that the media business, at least, was about to undergo a tumultuous shake-up. Ever since he was twelve and picked up a copy of *Fear and Loathing in Las Vegas* that a family friend had left behind on the nightstand in the Carlsons' guest room, he'd wanted to follow in Hunter S. Thompson's footsteps and be a journalist—specifically a magazine writer. While his father may have disparaged his mother for reading magazines instead of books, Carlson didn't share his disdain. "Magazine buyers are people who've chosen reading over watching television or going to the mall or playing video games as a form of entertainment," he wrote in 1999. "This is a relatively small group of people, presumably more literate—or at least interested in becoming more literate—than the average person."

That Carlson had made it to the top of the magazine profession by the age of thirty, his reporting abilities and writing chops the envy of his colleagues and competitors, was a source of tremendous pride, even self-aggrandizement. "I do think that without the purifying influence of the press, the United States would devolve into a totalitarian police state within about 20 minutes," he wrote that same year, before going on to acknowledge his hyperbole.

> If I tend to get overwrought on the subject, it's only because there's so much noise coming from the other side. I couldn't be sicker of hearing how Ordinary People, Folks Outside the Beltway, Average Working Americans (insert your favorite euphemism for the Great Unread here) have contempt for journalists. (My gut response, seldom voiced, is: Good, now we're even.) The problem is particularly acute in some conservative circles, where belief in the liberal media conspiracy is part of the catechism. Polls I keep reading about claim to indicate that most people consider journalists inaccurate and arrogant, if not simply evil. This bugs me, and not just because it's me they're talking about. I don't like the perception mainly because it isn't true.

And yet, Carlson was antsy. If he'd been born a few decades earlier, a long and distinguished career in print journalism like those of his idols—Thompson and Plimpton, A. J. Liebling and Joseph Mitchell—would have been possible. "His highest journalism ideal," Matt Labash said, "would have been to become a war correspondent for *The New York Times*, or to write some twenty-thousand-word McPhee-style piece on the New Jersey Turnpike for *The New Yorker*." By the time Carlson ascended to the upper reaches of the magazine world in the late 1990s, however, the view from the top was no longer so rosy. The Internet was still in its infancy, but he surmised that it was about to profoundly change, or even eliminate, the types of plum print jobs he'd once hoped to hold. He confided as much to—and sought the advice of—older colleagues whom he admired, including Andy Ferguson. In addition to his job at *The Standard*, Ferguson also wrote a column for *Time*—a job Carlson once considered "the ultimate." "He wanted to know, 'Where do I go next?'" Ferguson recalled. "He said, 'If I get to do something like a column for *Time*, then what's the next step?' He was anticipating that he was going to get to the top part of the print-journalism business and then wouldn't have anywhere else to go. And I think his answer to himself was: 'I go to television.'"

His timing couldn't have been better. For one, cable television was in the process of completely revolutionizing TV news. By 1992, more than 60 percent of US households had cable—and a host of new cable-news channels were springing up to take advantage of this new audience. Most significant, in the span of three months in 1996, General Electric (the corporate owner of NBC) and Microsoft teamed up to launch MSNBC while Rupert Murdoch's News Corporation started the Fox News Channel. CNN was no longer the only cable-news game in town, and now there was three times as much cable-news airtime to fill.

The challenge was how to fill all of it. Since its launch in 1980, CNN had adhered to its founder Ted Turner's mantra that "the news is the star." The network programmed its twenty-four hours with what was essentially a rolling newscast—a couple of anchors sitting behind a desk in Atlanta who would introduce reports from the network's far-flung correspondents in Washington, New York, London, Moscow, Mogadishu, or wherever news was happening. But neither Fox News nor MSNBC had CNN's extensive—not to mention expensive—news-gathering operation. They would need to broadcast something else.

Dating back to the 1950s, TV news had a long tradition of public affairs programming—staid shows, usually broadcast on Sunday mornings, on which journalists interviewed politicians and then soberly discussed the issues of the day. In 1982, *The McLaughlin Group* debuted and livened up (or dumbed down, depending on your point of view) the public affairs show, as John McLaughlin, a former Jesuit priest and Nixon White House aide, and four other journalists engaged in a weekly shouting match about politics. *The McLaughlin Group* soon spawned imitators, including on CNN, which created its own pundit shows, *Crossfire* and *Capital Gang*. But these shows were discrete, self-contained half-hour islands in CNN's ocean of straight-news programming. The news was still very much the star.

The innovation that would be pioneered by Fox News and MSNBC is that the news would take a back seat to the punditry. Fox's executives conceived of their network as "news talk-radio with video." At MSNBC, the network went so far as to use a health care staffing model, scheduling its talking heads to be on call in its Fort Lee, New Jersey, studios for three-hour shifts—ready to be summoned to the set at a moment's notice to offer up takes on whatever news events might arise during their duty hours.

The second thing that made the timing of Carlson's turn toward television so propitious is that conservative talking heads were in especially high demand. Mainstream-media executives had been caught flat-footed by the 1994 midterms, when Republicans won fifty-two seats in the Senate and gained control of the House for the first time in forty years, and they scrambled to find people who could help them make sense of this new political landscape. "Suddenly we were hot, and they wanted us," John Podhoretz recalled. Like "every young journalist on the right in the world," he was invited to New Jersey for an audition to become one of what MSNBC executives called "The Friends"—a cast of twenty or so young, hip (for pundits, at least) political journalists who could gab with one another about politics the way the twenty- and thirtysomething characters on NBC's top-rated sitcom at the time talked to one another about their love lives; the MSNBC set was even designed to be reminiscent of the coffee shop where the sitcom characters hung out. It was almost as if MSNBC executives had read Neil Postman's 1986 book *Amusing Ourselves to Death*—in which he argued that television was "transforming our culture into one vast arena for show business" where "serious conversation becomes a form of baby-talk" and "a people become an audience and their public business a vaudeville act"—and treated it as a how-to rather than a lament.

Podhoretz didn't make the cut for MSNBC's Friends, but a number of his real-life friends from Washington's circle of young conservatives did, including Ann Coulter and Laura Ingraham. Although Coulter was soon fired from MSNBC after telling a disabled Vietnam vet that it was "people like you [who] caused us to lose that war," Ingraham was a hit and, during the Clinton impeachment, was given her own daily show called *Watch It!* Her rapid ascent raised hackles among older, more established, predominantly male TV pundits, many of whom suspected she was being promoted because of her good looks. "When Laura Ingraham was still a lawyer, she went to see Robert Novak for career advice," Fred Barnes told *The New York Times Magazine* in 1997.

> He told her, "I started in Omaha, Neb., as an A.P. reporter," then recited the litany of his reporting career for 30 years before he started going on "McLaughlin," before he came up with "The Capital Gang." She didn't listen. That's not what she wanted to do, or needed to do, when on television her opinion is valued as much as mine.

Ingraham was uncowed. "Those old white males don't speak to a lot of America," she said. "What does Fred Barnes know about my world?"

Carlson may have been a white male, but he was notably young and green when he got his start as a talking head. In the fall of 1995, shortly after *The Weekly Standard*'s launch, a booker for Dan Rather called the magazine's offices looking for a conservative journalist to go on CBS's prime-time news show, *48 Hours*, that night to talk about the cultural significance of the O. J. Simpson trial. Carlson was the only *Standard* reporter who happened to be in the office—everyone else was at lunch—so, despite knowing nothing about the Simpson case, he drew the assignment. He got a quick crash course from some colleagues about how to do TV—sit on your coattails so your jacket's not rumpled; decide on a spiel and say it no matter what the question is—and then headed to New York. His appearance on *48 Hours* went fine. It was unremarkable and utterly forgettable. What mattered was that he appeared. "The world of talk show guests is like a closed union: You can't join unless you're already a member," Carlson later explained. "Bookers resist booking people they've never seen on television. Conversely, once you've been booked you're bookable. The process is self-authenticating." Indeed, the next day, he was invited to appear on CBS's morning show to talk some more about Simpson.

Carlson had entered the TV bloodstream. While MSNBC did not cast him as a Friend, CNN took a shine to him. (Fox, in its infancy, had an aversion to younger talking heads; its only contributor under the age of thirty-five for its first few years was Monica Crowley, a former research assistant to Richard Nixon who, after his death, wrote two tell-all books about him.) Soon he would be in high demand. The Lewinsky scandal, in particular, was a boon to the nascent cable-news networks. CNN's and MSNBC's ratings grew 40 and 53 percent respectively, while Fox News's ratings went up 400 percent in prime time. "Monica was a news channel's dream come true," John Moody, Fox News's executive editor, later said.

The insatiable demand for Lewinsky content meant that pretty much any telegenic political journalist who wanted airtime could get it. Norah O'Donnell, who was the anchor of the *CBS Evening News* from 2019 to 2025, got her start in television when, as a recent Georgetown graduate working for the Capitol Hill–focused *Roll Call* newspaper, she'd regularly appear on cable news to "report" on what her "sources" were telling her about the Lewinsky investigation—reporting that almost invariably seemed to track with whatever *The Washington Post* or *The New York Times* had published that morning.

Carlson was never quite that shameless. His Lewinsky commentary largely consisted of glib pontificating—"I wouldn't be surprised if six months from now polls show that your average American thinks that it was Newt Gingrich who went after his intern," he said after Gingrich appointed himself the GOP's spokesman on the scandal—with the occasional dollop of empathy for Lewinsky herself, who, after all, was only a few years younger than him. As he discovered during the O. J. Simpson trial, it almost didn't matter what he actually said—just so long as he was willing to go on camera and say it. Six months into the Lewinsky scandal, *The Hotline*, a daily political newsletter, tallied up the number of TV appearances for the twenty or so most ubiquitous pundits. Carlson ranked just behind David Gergen and ahead of James Carville.

The amount of television Carlson was doing became a source of both bemusement and amusement at *The Weekly Standard*. It wasn't like the magazine's writers and editors were strangers to the capital's greenrooms. Barnes and Kristol, in particular, were regular talking heads; they believed that the magazine, and its ideological project, benefited from their TV work. Still, they were picky about when and where they did their televised talking. Barnes preferred *The McLaughlin Group*, on which he appeared for a decade before, in 1998, going to Fox News to cohost his own show, while Kristol largely confined his television appearances to ABC's Sunday show *This Week* before also signing with Fox. The idea of blowing a hole in the middle of your day—taking a town car to the studio, sitting in makeup, cooling your heels during the two preceding segments—all to do a five-minute hit on dayside cable was anathema to them. In their view, Carlson was wasting his time.

In the spring of 2000, not long after John McCain ended his presidential campaign, the Arizona senator returned to Vietnam, where he'd been a POW three decades earlier. Accompanying him on the trip were a handful of his favorite reporters, including Jay Carney, Jake Tapper, and Carlson. McCain and his personal press corps toured the lake where his navy fighter jet crash-landed and the prison where he was held captive for five years. It was a reunion of sorts and a balm, for both the politician and the reporters, after the bitter end of McCain's presidential bid. "McCain in Vietnam turned out to be a lot like McCain in Des Moines or Manchester or Dearborn," Carlson later recalled. But when the group prepared to return to the United States, there was a problem. Carlson had failed to get an entry stamp on his passport when he'd arrived in Vietnam, and now immigration authorities wouldn't let him leave, under the Kafkaesque logic that, since he'd never officially entered the country, he wasn't legally permitted to depart. McCain tried to argue on Carlson's behalf, to no avail. The senator, Carney, Tapper, and the other reporters boarded their flight, while Carlson was forced to stay behind. He was detained for a few hours in an airport holding room, but after the American embassy intervened, Carlson was able to spend the night at a five-star Saigon hotel and then board a flight back to the United States the next day.

Though brief, Carlson's ordeal made headlines back in the United States; "Vietnam Detains Journalist on McCain Trip," read one in *The Washington Post*. It also provided fodder for his *Standard* colleagues. In every issue of the magazine, the last page carried a parody of a news story; David Brooks, who frequently wrote the parody, decided to use it, and Carlson's Vietnam misadventure, to mock Carlson's abiding love of television. Titled "Faith of My Producers: A Prisoner's Memoir"—a play on McCain's best-selling book, *Faith of My Fathers: A Family Memoir*—Brooks, pretending to be Carlson, recounted the episode in purplish prose. "I was alone in a hostile land. Captive. Memories of home flooded my brain: the red light of the TV light when you're on-air, the blue of Larry King's veins, the white skin of the hosts of *Crossfire*. I didn't realize how much I loved America's News Leader until I was deprived of her," Brooks-as-Carlson wrote. "It'd been hours since pancake make-up had been applied to my face, and I began to feel the first withdrawal tremors."

Carlson, who didn't see the parody before it went to press, was not amused. Some of his *Standard* colleagues couldn't blame him. Andy Ferguson told Brooks that if he'd done that to him, he would have quit the magazine. "That sobered me up," Brooks said. "I thought it was in the spirit of the way we made fun of each other in the office, but I probably shouldn't have put it out in public. It was not the right thing to do to parody your own colleague." He went, hat in hand, to Carlson's office. "I apologized, and he accepted extremely graciously," Brooks recalled. "I'll always remember it as a moment of Tucker showing a very, very generous spirit."

Indeed, Carlson was almost always conciliatory—even apologetic—about his television work, at least when discussing it with fellow writers. With Ferguson, he would joke about the television truism that "good writing is key," noting that the kind of writing that works on television actually looks ridiculous on the page. "He was amused by the pomposity of television people," Ferguson said. "He agreed with me that TV was basically a joke and sort of a lower form of human endeavor." With Brooks, who was then becoming a regular on *PBS NewsHour*—a gig he'd hold down for the next two and a half decades—Carlson commiserated. "When you're on TV, you can give yourself the illusion that you're performing an act of journalism," he told Brooks, "but it's not really journalism." The only reason he debased himself by going on television, he told his fellow scribes, was that he needed the money.

But Carlson had other reasons for his interest in television—reasons he didn't share with his writer friends. One was that he found writing very, very difficult. Although his colleagues at *The Standard* marveled at his natural ability to, as Labash put it, "knock out colorful, effortless copy," it wasn't so effortless. Carlson was a terrible procrastinator and seized on any excuse to avoid facing the blank computer screen: playing with his dogs, alphabetizing his books, calling readers who'd left him angry voicemails. To write his stories, he typically pulled all-nighters on the eve of, or sometimes after, his deadlines, typing away on a converted porch in his house while Susie and his kids slept. "I have a lot of trouble writing or doing anything unless the pressure is on," he explained. The pressure contributed to his drinking, which was becoming a problem. Three-martini lunches at the Palm were turning into four- or five-martini affairs. On one occasion Carlson got so loaded that he accidentally boarded a flight to Cleveland when he was supposed to be going to Dallas. He liked to joke that he'd know his drinking had gotten out of hand when he started adding Wild Turkey to his bowl of Cap'n Crunch. And yet he was starting more and more of his days with double screwdrivers for breakfast.

What's more, Carlson discovered that the tossed-off asides he was offering on TV oftentimes drew as much of a response, sometimes even a greater response, than the magazine stories he was sweating and stressing over. He could feel his profile rising. One time, after making some critical comments about the Environmental Protection Agency during an appearance on *The McLaughlin Group*, he received a phone call from Carol Browner, the EPA head, to dispute his remarks. Browner was "acting like what I said is important," he marveled. "I was just shocked." He wasn't about to admit it to his colleagues who still toiled in print, but television had its benefits.

Carlson also recognized that, while his natural glibness gave him a leg up when it came to talking on TV, to be truly good at it wasn't effortless—maybe not as difficult as writing, but difficult nonetheless. He may have gone along with their jokes, but he disagreed with his *Standard* colleagues who mocked television talking as brainless. Unlike a magazine feature, you didn't have seven thousand words to make your point. Concision was key. He likened being an effective talking head to composing haiku. "Wordloaf doesn't work on television," he said. He began to study its leading practitioners. Just as he'd once hoovered up the stories of Joseph Mitchell and Hunter S. Thompson, now he consumed videotape of John McLaughlin and Chris Matthews; he tried to glean tips about interview technique from watching Ricki Lake. A piece of unsolicited advice about how to succeed in television that he received from Larry King at the Democratic National Convention in 2000 took on profound meaning. "The trick is to care, but not too much," King said. "Give a shit—but not really." (Carlson later made King's quote the epigraph of his 2003 book *Politicians, Partisans, and Parasites*.)

His responsibilities—and airtime—at CNN grew. He was bequeathed a regular spot on CNN's Sunday-morning show, *Late Edition*, and had a weekly segment with the liberal *Time* writer Margaret Carlson called "Squabbling Carlsons." Although, in truth, there wasn't that much squabbling. "The disappointment to CNN is we don't disagree as much as we could because we have a lot of common ground," Margaret Carlson said. "He's very conservative, but he's not conservative in that doctrinaire way. He crosses over. You can be surprised." CNN signed him to a fifty-thousand-dollar annual contract—which was almost double what he was making at *The Standard*.

Kristol and Barnes feared they were losing Carlson to television and made him an offer: They'd reduce his writing responsibilities at *The Standard* by half so he could do more television. The important thing was that he'd remain at the magazine. "Keep your day job," Barnes advised Carlson. "Print is what matters most. TV is great. You can make money on the speaking circuit. It's fun. People recognize you. But at the end of the day, it's kind of a weird business. You don't want to be at the mercy of some TV types."

Carlson was considering *The Standard*'s offer when, on the eve of the 2000 election, CNN made a counteroffer: How would Carlson like to cohost his own show? It would debut after the first and only vice presidential debate between Dick Cheney and Joe Lieberman, and in a nod to its lead-in, it would be called *The Spin Room*. (After debates, there's something called the "spin room" where staffers and surrogates for the candidates try to spin reporters on who won.) Carlson's cohost would be Bill Press, a wizened liberal talking head who often occupied the "on the left" chair on *Crossfire*. The time slot wasn't exactly auspicious—*The Spin Room* would air at midnight—but a late-night show of his own seemed (not to mention paid) better than dayside guest hits. What's more, the CNN executives informed Carlson, he would be the "youngest anchor in the history of CNN." He accepted the offer. He loved CNN and all that it stood for—especially in contrast to its cable-news rivals. Fox News and MSNBC, which were still a distant second and third in the ratings, were parochial, focusing on American politics and not even really covering American politics, merely opining on them. CNN, by contrast, covered not just the United States but the world. Talking about his television employer a few years later, Carlson gushed: "I'm always struck that if you're in Gambia, as I was this summer, or if you're in Peshawar, they're not watching Fox News Channel, they're watching CNN. I know it sounds trite, but I love the fact that CNN is engaged with the world."

Still, Carlson hoped to hold on to his day job at *The Standard*, at least symbolically. He asked if he could keep an office there and a place on the masthead and contribute the occasional story. Kristol and Barnes were amenable, but Rupert Murdoch was not. It was one thing for a *Standard* writer to appear as a regular guest on a Fox News competitor; hosting his own show on a Fox rival was something else entirely. If he was going to be a CNN anchor, News Corp ruled, he could no longer be a *Weekly Standard* staff writer. "It was CNN or us," a former

Standard editor recalled. "It couldn't be both." Carlson cleaned out his *Standard* office, sorting through five years' worth of detritus—a necktie Steve Forbes once gave him, a manuscript of Donald Trump's self-published autobiography that Trump had sent him. In a final story for *The Standard*, he lamented, "I'm not a magazine writer anymore."

IN JANUARY 2001, A FEW months into Carlson's new full-time job at CNN, *New York Magazine* sent its media columnist Michael Wolff to the Palm in Washington to have lunch with the youngest anchor in the cable network's history. He came away smitten. "Tucker isn't tainted by Republican rage," Wolff, who'd go on to enjoy a decades-long relationship with Carlson as a source, wrote after their first meeting. "He's a genuinely likable conservative. He's jocular. He's optimistic. He's cool, even." Wolff's prediction that Carlson would "be the first star of the new Bush administration" turned out to be premature; it would be another sixteen years before Carlson became the breakout hit of a new Republican White House. But he was spot-on with his observation that "the thing about conservative pundits is that they all seem to have found their calling in grammar school." In fact, Wolff was even more correct than he realized.

When Carlson was in the sixth grade at the La Jolla Country Day School, Jimmy Carter and Ronald Reagan were facing off in the 1980 presidential election. Carlson had established himself as the class's most outspoken conservative; his best friend, a boy named Russell, had earned the reputation as the class's most eloquent liberal. Their teacher, Bobby Garon, thought it would be an educational exercise to have the two politically precocious sixth graders conduct a mock presidential debate before their classmates voted in a mock presidential election.

But there was a catch: Garon assigned the role of Reagan to the liberal Russell, while the conservative Carlson would play Carter. On the day of the debate, both candidates made opening statements. Russell went first. He'd clearly done his homework as he delivered a concise summary of Reagan's platform: lower taxes, higher defense spending, a promise to "Make America Great Again." Then it was Carlson's turn. If he'd bothered to research Carter's positions, he didn't show it. Instead, he attacked his opponent. "Ronald Reagan is like Lassie," Carlson told his classmates. "He's a trained dog. They just put words in his mouth and he says them. He might as well be a border collie." When the LCDS sixth graders voted, Carter won in a landslide. "Tucker's heart wasn't in it to be a Carter supporter," Garon recalled. "But clearly he rose above it to accomplish the goal." He also learned a lesson that would serve him well in his future endeavors: Making a strong argument against someone can be far more effective than a strong argument for.

Such rhetorical ruthlessness wasn't really necessary for *The Spin Room*. Although it was technically a debate show, Carlson and Press achieved a détente early in their partnership. "There were some issues, gay rights and abortion in particular, that we would not debate," Press said. Other issues that would later divide left and right simply weren't salient. When the conservative commentator Linda Chavez withdrew as George W. Bush's nominee to become secretary of labor after it was revealed that she'd once employed an undocumented immigrant as a live-in housekeeper, both men were nonplussed. Press accused Bush of treating her "shabbily." Carlson concurred. "She has an illegal alien live in her house for a while. It's a very minor crime," he said. "Linda Chavez essentially did nothing wrong. No big deal, she shouldn't have been penalized." As Press later recalled, "Tucker was much more of a libertarian. He wasn't an extreme-right conservative, so he and I actually agreed on some issues."

The Spin Room was less concerned about arguing the issues than highlighting the absurdities of politics. "We would just keep track of dumb things, or outrageous things that people had said during the day, and figure out what we wanted to poke fun at that night," Press said. While the talking heads on the left and right bickered with one another on *Crossfire* or *Hardball* during the Florida recount, Carlson and Press found common cause in mocking Florida secretary of state Katherine Harris with a heavily made-up Katherine Harris puppet. At the top of every show, Carlson or Press would give out a 1-800 number and an email address so that they could take live phone calls from viewers and read out their missives on the air—especially the nasty ones, which they commemorated in a nightly segment called "Hate Mail Moment." Responding to a viewer email that deemed *The Spin Room* to be "probably the dumbest idea in TV to date," Carlson marveled, "There's something majestic about that. In fact, this isn't hate. This is a sort of compliment."

Carlson's favorite *Spin Room* guest was Jim Traficant, a backbench Democratic congressman from Youngstown, Ohio. Traficant was an avowed populist. He opposed NAFTA and wanted to deploy the US military to the border with Mexico. He was also boorish and corrupt. On one of his visits to *The Spin Room* set, he groped a CNN makeup artist; he later went to prison for taking bribes from business executives and demanding kickbacks from his staff. What Carlson liked about Traficant, though, was that he was entertaining. Sporting denim suits and a toupee that made it look as if a small rodent had taken up residence atop his head, he was a master of the one-minute House floor speech, bloviating on everything from the perfidy of the IRS to the magnificence of the brassiere, always ending with the exclamation, "Beam me up!"

When Traficant appeared on *The Spin Room*, he was usually drunk and spent most of his time interrupting and insulting the show's cohosts. "I once thought that CNN should be hired and we should have fired the CIA, but since you guys, I'm not so sure about that," he told Carlson and Press during one visit. "I don't know what you make, but you're probably overpaid." Carlson ate it up. During one show, he announced the creation of the Jim Traficant Legal Defense Fund, on the grounds that it would be a tragedy to have such a great TV guest behind bars and away from the cameras. In many ways, Traficant—with his populist politics, outlandish statements, and sleazy personal behavior—presaged Donald Trump. But in the American politics of the early aughts, that combination of qualities added up to make him a marginal, mostly harmless figure (unless, of course, you were a makeup artist or his staffer). After he was convicted on federal corruption charges in 2002, the House voted 420 to 1 to expel Traficant, and his political career came to an end.

The end of *The Spin Room* came even sooner. In May 2001, after eight months and multiple late-night time slots, CNN executives pulled the plug on the show due to poor reviews and poor ratings. Sid Bedingfield, CNN's general manager, broke the news to Carlson over dinner at a Capitol Hill restaurant. As Carlson slugged a martini to steady his nerves, Bedingfield told him that the move was for his own good. CNN was giving up on *The Spin Room*, but it wasn't giving up on Carlson. In fact, the network was giving him a promotion. Mary Matalin, one of the two conservative cohosts of *Crossfire*, had recently departed CNN to join George W. Bush's White House. Bedingfield told Carlson that CNN wanted him to fill Matalin's chair "on the right."

Crossfire was CNN's oldest and most venerated political show. Its cohosts were considered a cut above the usual cable-news talkers. For years the show was anchored by Pat Buchanan or Robert Novak on the right, and Tom Braden, a former CIA official and newspaper columnist, or *New Republic* editor Michael

Kinsley on the left. *Crossfire* wasn't exactly the Oxford Union, but it managed to be both entertaining and smart television—the sort of program where, one night, Novak would debate Frank Zappa about censoring rock lyrics and, another night, Kinsley would spar with an up-and-coming talk radio host named Rush Limbaugh about flag burning. After the initial fear that his television career was over before it even got started, Carlson was thrilled to be included in such esteemed company.

But others were less pleased. When CNN announced Carlson's new *Crossfire* gig, some prominent Republicans argued that Carlson was insufficiently conservative to represent the right on the show. A spokeswoman for Tom DeLay, the archconservative Texas congressman, complained to the *New York Post* that Carlson was "not a real Republican." Even worse, the caustic and curmudgeonly Novak—who would alternate with Carlson as the show's conservative cohost—shared this view. He had respected Carlson's reportage for *The Standard* (where his son-in-law, Christopher Caldwell, was a writer), but he deemed Carlson "an unreconstructed McCainiac who did not like Bush" and considered his previous television work on *The Spin Room* to be "fatuous." Carlson tried to win over his new colleague during a long breakfast at the Army and Navy Club, ingratiatingly asking for Novak's advice on what it took to succeed on *Crossfire*. Novak told him it was essential for the conservative host on *Crossfire* to be conservative. Carlson replied that Novak couldn't imagine how conservative Carlson really was. But Novak—of whom Kinsley once said, "Underneath the asshole is a nice guy, but underneath the nice guy is another asshole"—was unmoved. He lobbied CNN executives to dump Carlson in favor of Pat Buchanan's sister Bay.

The question of Carlson's conservative bona fides was particularly acute because of Fox News. For the first few years of Fox's existence, CNN had easily maintained its ratings dominance,

But after the sugar high of the Lewinsky scandal wore off, CNN's ratings quickly returned to Earth, falling about 30 percent from its Monica peak in 1999. Fox's ratings, by contrast, kept going up, rising another 11 percent. In October 2000, Fox beat CNN in prime time for the first time, as Bill O'Reilly supplanted Larry King as the most-watched cable-news host. Thanks to his relentless shilling for it on *The O'Reilly Factor*, his book of the same name soon topped the bestseller list. It turned out that the "talk-radio with video" approach was a hit with viewers.

Fox News CEO Roger Ailes publicly insisted that his network abided by its slogan of "Fair and Balanced," but the channel's conservative tilt was an undeniable reason for its ratings success. As Charles Krauthammer once joked, "The genius of Rupert Murdoch and Roger Ailes was to have discovered a niche market in American broadcasting—half the American people." Even *Hannity & Colmes*, Fox's *Crossfire* rip-off, was rigged so that the liberal always lost. Sean Hannity, the show's conservative cohost, was not only a better debater than his liberal foil, the milquetoast Alan Colmes, whom the media critic Bob Garfield memorably dubbed "the human straw man"; he was handsomer. "We grew up watching *Crossfire*, and who's the conservative? It's Robert Novak, whose nickname was Satan or something," Ken LaCorte, a former Fox News executive, said. "Hannity was the only left-right guy where the guy on the right looked better than the guy on the left." Just to further stack the deck, off air, the show's producers let Hannity pick the show's debate topics and ignored Colmes's requests. "Sean basically served as executive producer of the show," one of them later confessed to the writer Gabriel Sherman for his Ailes biography *The Loudest Voice in the Room*. (When Colmes eventually left Fox in 2009 and the show was renamed *Hannity*, his absence barely registered.)

Personally, Carlson took a dim, condescending view of Fox News. When *Newsweek* profiled O'Reilly in February 2001—"He is Everyman on a barstool, mad as hell, but with a wink," the magazine gushed—Carlson provided a lonely dissenting opinion. "Only masochists would go on his show—or watch it," Carlson told *Newsweek*. "I hate to say it because it sounds snobby, but I don't know anyone who's read his book." Elsewhere, he dismissed Fox's biggest star as "a thin-skinned blowhard" and "a humorless phony." As for the rest of Fox, Carlson deemed them a "a mean, sick group of people." He didn't believe Fox's approach to the news was admirable—or sustainable. "I don't like partisanship because it abets lying," Carlson said of Fox. "And I think you burn out fast when you demagogue." After Bob Woodward reported that Ailes wrote a private memo to Karl Rove in the days after 9/11 suggesting policies for President Bush—"The only thing America won't forgive you for is under-reaching," Ailes advised the president—Carlson lambasted the Fox News CEO for a violation of journalistic ethics. "Roger Ailes is the editorial chief of Fox News, and this gives the appearance of partisanship," he complained. "This makes it look like Roger Ailes is sucking up to power."

Still, Carlson knew—and, more important, he knew that CNN executives knew—that Fox's approach was working with viewers. He recognized that doubts about whether he was a real conservative, about whether he'd be a reliable Republican voice, were a problem. "Being called a secret liberal was a serious charge," he later confessed. "It made me sound like a poseur, or at the very least a lightweight who didn't know what he believed. It provided more ammunition to those who claimed that CNN skewed to the left. I felt smeared." He fantasized about "punching out" DeLay. But he recognized that violence would be self-defeating. So Carlson did the next best thing and went in the opposite direction. He became a partisan shill.

Granted, a certain degree of party line toeing was a job requirement for a *Crossfire* host. As Carlson explained a few years into his gig,

> One benefit of hosting a talk show is that it forces you to learn about, and take a position on, virtually everything that happens in the news. That's also the downside. The more you learn about the subject, the more complicated it becomes, and so, inevitably, do your views on it. From "complicated," it's a short trip to "nuanced." Nuance, needless to say, is the enemy of clear debate.

Before going on the air, *Crossfire*'s producer Sam Feist would give Carlson pep talks—encouraging him to get all the nuance out of his system; Carlson likened Feist to "the corner man in a boxing match" whose job it was to whip him "into a controlled frenzy."

Occasionally Carlson was able to ditch nuance without completely abandoning his principles. Of the Confederate flag being displayed outside the South Carolina statehouse, for instance, he was not a fan. "For one thing, the Confederates were traitors who fought a war against their own country," he wrote in 2003.

> For another, the flag offends black people. Maybe it shouldn't, but it does. Many black people do think of segregation when they see the Confederate flag. Why should a black person have to be confronted with a symbol he finds deeply offensive every time he walks into a public building that he helps pay for with his tax dollars? I don't want to see a portrait of Louis Farrakhan every time I go to my statehouse. The average black South Carolinian shouldn't have to see the Confederate flag every time he goes to his.

The problem for Carlson was that it was Democrats, not Republicans, who were protesting the flag. He couldn't sit comfortably in *Crossfire*'s chair on the right and say that he agreed with the Democrats. Still, he was loath to defend the Confederate flag. So when the issue was in the news in January 2003 because John Edwards, a Democratic candidate for president, stayed in the private homes of his supporters when he visited South Carolina to abide by the NAACP's tourism boycott of the state, Carlson found a third way to debate it. Ticking off the "terrifying and depressing statistics" about the number of African American children born out of wedlock and the percentage of African American families living below the poverty line, Carlson attacked Edwards for moral preening. "Edwards, who has articulated no plan at all to strengthen black families, believes the flag issue is so important he is boycotting South Carolina hotels, thereby depriving the black employees of income," Carlson argued. "And I must say, I don't want to be misunderstood here. I don't support the Confederate flag at all. I just think it takes a deeply unserious person to think that's the central issue facing black America."

More often than not, though, Carlson was unable to weasel his way out of saying things on *Crossfire* that seemed to contradict his personal views. His job required him to praise Republicans and criticize Democrats—and he did so with gusto. In fact, he frequently seemed to overcompensate with his partisan hackery, lest anyone continue to accuse him of being insufficiently conservative. He didn't just fall in line behind George W. Bush, the man he not so long ago had filleted in *Talk*; he was fawning in his praise. Bush, Carlson told *Crossfire* viewers, was "a genius politically" and "the perfect man" for the presidency. "I just want to remind us how lucky we are to have President Bush in the White House," he declaimed.

When his old political crush John McCain, who remained Bush's and the GOP establishment's bête noire, came on the show in April 2002, Carlson assailed the Arizona senator for the heterodoxies he only two years earlier had celebrated. "Senator McCain, it's not as if you have taken exception to a couple of parts of the Republican agenda," Carlson lectured him.

> I want to read you a partial list of the issues on which you've diverged from your party: campaign finance reform, tobacco, Bush's tax cut, drilling in ANWR, patients' bill of rights, prescription drugs, airport security, the Kyoto Treaty, emission standards, gun control. My hand got tired so I stopped, but I could probably go on. You have had more problems with your party than Jim Jeffords did, and he switched.

Carlson paused and then went in for the kill. "Why are you still there?" he asked. McCain replied that he regretted not using his influence to make sure the Vietnamese had kept Carlson in detention.

Carlson even had kind words for Tom DeLay. Privately, he may have wanted to punch the Texas congressman, but for public consumption, he hailed DeLay's ascension to House Majority Leader. "I think people will like Tom DeLay the more they get to know him," he predicted. "It is hard to beat up on people when they are on television every day. And hopefully Tom DeLay will be, and people will begin to see the more complicated and interesting side of him. And there is one." Sucking up to power could take many forms.

Carlson's most difficult balancing act on *Crossfire*—between staying true to his beliefs and being a good team player, between advancing ideas and creating a persona—involved the Bush administration's foreign policy.

He was, literally, a Cold War kid. His father, Dick, was both a supporter and a sexton of Reagan's long, twilight struggle against the Soviet Union. As the head of the Voice of America, Dick created and hosted a weekly radio show, *On the Line*, that was devoted to explaining and justifying the Reagan administration's foreign policy positions to a global audience. Perhaps more important, he played a constant cat and mouse game with the Soviet Union as Voice of America evaded the Soviets' jamming transmitters to broadcast its Russian-language radio service into the communist country. The goal of the broadcasts, he explained, was "putting pressure on the Soviet Union in an indirect way by reminding, offering up as a reminder what life was like in the West." Later, as the US ambassador to the Seychelles, Dick's primary responsibility was protecting a sophisticated US Air Force tracking station that monitored Soviet satellites. The defeat of the Soviet Union and revolutionary communism was a fundamental tenet of his political identity. "The continuing conflict between the United States and the Soviet Union is in some respects not necessarily about land or about power, which are the historical areas of conflict," he said in a 1988 speech. "It is about in many ways perceptions about the character and the purpose of life itself."

(Dick's résumé has led some of his son's current critics on both the left and the right to surmise that he was a CIA operative. He was undoubtedly a "CIA fanboy," as one former VOA colleague described him, who was thrilled when the VOA's agency liaison would come to the office, a briefcase handcuffed to his wrist, to read Dick the transcripts of intercepted conversations between Cuban officials complaining about something they'd heard on Radio Martí. But it seems unlikely that Dick, who died in 2025 at the age of 84, actually worked for the agency, given his well-deserved reputation for being incorrigibly indiscreet. A favorite parlor game among VOA employees during his tenure was for staffers to walk into Carlson's office first thing in the morning and tell him a piece of gossip, then track how far into the day he could get before summoning them back to his office "to hear some incredible news" and repeat to them the bit of gossip they had told him.)

Carlson idolized Dick, and so it was only natural that he'd inherit his father's foreign policy views—at least initially. In 1988, during the summer break after his freshman year at Trinity, he and his best friend at the college, Neil Patel, decided to go to Nicaragua. At the time, the Central American country was a Cold War hot spot, as the Contras, a US-backed right-wing rebel group, were fighting to overthrow Nicaragua's communist Sandinista government. It was not uncommon for liberal American college students to travel to Nicaragua to demonstrate their solidarity with the Sandinistas; it was practically unheard-of for conservative American college students to go there to support the Contras. But Carlson and Patel prevailed upon Dick to use his Voice of America contacts to get them internships at *La Prensa*, an opposition newspaper in Managua. "We are both extremely political and we felt that getting to know the country and some of its citizens would give us better perspective on the situation," Carlson later told the *Trinity Tripod*.

In their Birkenstocks and khaki shorts—the wardrobe they'd sport to classes and Grateful Dead concerts—Carlson and Patel didn't look all that different from the *sandalistas*, as the lefty Americans and Europeans who flocked to Nicaragua were known. But, of course, they were their polar opposites. Indeed, once the pair realized that Nicaraguans were mistaking them for leftists, they began wearing long pants and close-toed shoes. Their internship at *La Prensa* was a nothingburger; Patel spoke only a little Spanish and Carlson none at all, and the newspaper had little use for a couple of unskilled nineteen-year-old Americans. The Contras, with whom Carlson and Patel hoped to embed, were similarly uninterested; the two Americans never got close to the front lines. Mostly, the two college kids consumed a lot of beer and developed an appreciation for Nicaragua's lax drunk driving laws.

But Carlson and Patel made some valuable contacts, and two years later, when *La Prensa*'s editor Violeta Chamorro ran for president against Daniel Ortega, the pair, along with two of their Trinity housemates, returned to Nicaragua. Using their US driver's licenses, the four college students bluffed their way into the foreign-press center in Managua. There, they encountered a small group of conservative American journalists who'd come to cover the election, one of whom was P. J. O'Rourke. Carlson was in the habit of devouring every word O'Rourke wrote for *The American Spectator*; he loved—and later sought to emulate—O'Rourke's preppy, glib libertarian humor. Slightly starstruck, Carlson introduced himself and his friends. O'Rourke was flattered—and tickled that a bunch of conservative college kids had made the trek to Nicaragua. He invited them to tag along with him and his fellow "*wing-tipistas*"—as he called the conservative American journalists in Nicaragua—for the final days of the campaign. Carlson and his pals attended political rallies, visited polling places, and ultimately celebrated Chamorro's upset win over Ortega at her victory party. Carlson returned to Connecticut more convinced than ever about the righteousness of anti-communism and Reaganite foreign policy.

At *The Weekly Standard* in the 1990s, Carlson's remit was domestic politics, but he evinced no discomfort with the magazine's hawkish foreign policy positions; he frequently grabbed lunch with staffers from the Project for the New American Century, the foreign policy think tank that Kristol and Robert Kagan founded, which shared office space with *The Standard* and which published an open letter to Bill Clinton in 1998 calling on the United States to unilaterally remove Saddam Hussein from power. (Dick Cheney, Donald Rumsfeld, and Paul Wolfowitz were among the letter's signatories.) He liked to describe himself as "an Episcopalian neo-con," elaborating: "I'm supportive of a vigorous foreign policy. I like Israel." After 9/11, Carlson, like pretty much every pundit to the right of Susan Sontag, enthusiastically backed the US military campaign against Afghanistan. "Call this self-serving, if you will, but it's essentially true: We are not an imperialist power; we're not seeking to take over Afghanistan for its mineral resources, for instance," he said on *Crossfire* about two weeks after the launch of Operation Enduring Freedom. "I'm still confused as to why exactly people don't like us." When liberals criticized Bush as irresponsibly bellicose for labeling Iran, Iraq, and North Korea as an "axis of evil" in his 2002 State of the Union address, Carlson continued to be befuddled. "All three are evil and all three of them are a threat to the United States," he said on *Crossfire*. "What's wrong saying so?"

But as it became increasingly clear that the Bush administration sought not just a rhetorical war against Iraq but a real one, Carlson began to harbor doubts. He was friendly with Christopher Hitchens—who'd once selected a *Weekly Standard* story by Carlson for an anthology of the best political writing from the 1990s—and he occasionally attended salons at Hitchens's Kalorama apartment. Hitchens was a man of the left, but after 9/11, he became a sworn enemy of what he called "Islamofascism" and a strong supporter of the Bush administration's war on terrorism; he was an especially fervent advocate for going to war in Iraq. The gatherings at Hitchens's apartment frequently drew his fellow Iraq hawks, including Wolfowitz, who by then was deputy secretary of defense, and the Iraqi exile leader Ahmed Chalabi. At the salons, Hitchens and the other hawks would argue with liberal congressmen and lefty journalists about the wisdom of invading Iraq. Carlson often found himself agreeing with the latter and would say as much during the gatherings.

He was more circumspect publicly, but sometimes his skepticism shone through. The case the administration and its allies were making for preemptively attacking Iraq, he said on *Crossfire* in January 2003, a little more than two months before the invasion, was "not a clear they-bombed-Pearl-Harbor kind of argument" but rather "a very abstract type argument" that he found unconvincing. "I have not been very enthusiastic about it," he said about the prospect of the invasion. "I'm still not."

That lack of enthusiasm for a war in Iraq, however, would be impossible for Carlson to sustain. One reason was Patel, his old college roommate and the godfather to his first child. (Carlson was also godfather to Patel's first child.) Since graduating from Trinity—unlike Carlson, he received his degree—Patel had become a player in Republican national-security circles. At the outset of the Bush administration, Lewis "Scooter" Libby, Cheney's chief of staff and national-security adviser, tapped Patel to serve as Cheney's staff secretary. If Libby was known around Washington as "Cheney's Dick Cheney" because of his close relationship with the vice president, then Patel was Libby's Scooter Libby. He was intimately involved in the administration's war planning, much of which was run out of Cheney's office. And just as CIA director George Tenet infamously told Bush that it was a "slam dunk" that Saddam had weapons of mass destruction, Patel repeatedly and privately assured Carlson that the intelligence propping up the administration's case for war was solid.

Of course, Carlson sought Patel's assurances because his skepticism was becoming increasingly untenable. If he were still a magazine writer, he could have given voice to his doubts.

Even at *The Weekly Standard*, which provided so much of the intellectual architecture for the war, Labash, Ferguson, and Caldwell wrote pieces that dissented from the neocon line on Iraq. "Freedom matters, and Bill [Kristol] was a freedom lover," Labash recalled. "Not just for the people of Iraq, but for his writers." But that sort of laissez-faire attitude didn't exist in the world of cable news. As the conservative cohost of *Crossfire*, it was Carlson's professional duty to take the Bush administration's side and make the case for the war in Iraq. The debate show didn't work otherwise. And so, in early 2003, as the inevitability of the war became clear, Carlson transformed from an occasional skeptic into a reliable cheerleader.

He offered any and every justification he could think of for toppling Saddam, from Iraq's 1993 attempt to assassinate George H. W. Bush ("When you try and kill an American president, even a recently retired one, that's not acceptable and you should not continue as a head of state") to Iraq's supposed links to al-Qaeda ("Those claims are uncontested") to the distant threat of a nuclear attack ("Wouldn't the president be irresponsible not to address it directly and quickly?"). He dismissed the American allies that opposed the invasion—France and Germany—as "elderly, increasingly irrelevant nations" and referred to the countries as "old Europe," adopting Rumsfeld's insult for them. And he accused those who opposed the war of racism. Interviewing the liberal national-security wonk Joseph Cirincione on a February *Crossfire*, Carlson lectured:

> Joe, at the end of World War II, as you know, American forces occupied Japan, and General MacArthur ran the country for a relatively short time. American forces left; Japan was a constitutional democracy. And yet when Paul Wolfowitz or the president of the United States suggests that a similar scenario could unfold in Iraq, we could turn

> it into a democracy, people scoff and say, "That's outrageous," as if Arabs don't have the capacity for self-governance. Isn't that the message?

Cirincione replied, "That's not the message at all," adding: "I'm all for bringing democracy to the Arab world, to the Muslim world, to help them do this. But you can't bring democracy at the point of bayonets. You don't invade and kill a country to bring them democracy." Carlson blustered, "We dropped an atom bomb in Japan!"

Off air, Carlson acknowledged his qualms—if not about the war itself then about the way it was debated on *Crossfire*. Participating in an online chat on *The Washington Post*'s website in March, about a week before the United States launched its invasion, he fielded a question from a reader in New York who wrote,

> I like your answers in this forum a lot more than the ones given (from both sides) on Crossfire. Here, you seem to be a bit more balanced, a lot more open-minded and even have some nice things to say about the Democrats. I guess my question is more a complaint, though, and it's why can't you guys debate the issues thoughtfully, as opposed to radically, on the air?

Carlson wrote back: "I agree. This is something I've thought about a lot and tried to correct. Partly it's the venue—Crossfire exists to highlight clear arguments—partly it's the medium: television isn't conducive to nuance."

After Baghdad fell to US forces just twenty-one days into the fighting, conservative pundits took their own victory lap—and took their shots at the war's opponents. "No day will come when the enemies of this endeavor turn around and say, 'We were wrong. Bush was right,'" Brooks wrote in *The Standard*. Carlson joined in the gloating. "You said a moment ago that we shouldn't rub the French noses in our victory—rather large French noses—we should be magnanimous in victory and we should make up with France," Carlson complained to one *Crossfire* guest. "My question is why? Why should we?" As for the looting and civil unrest that followed Saddam's overthrow, he struck a cavalier tone. "Transitions are difficult, things get lost," he said. "Remember when the Clintons left the White House?"

But as the war dragged on, Carlson's on-air enthusiasm, not to mention glibness, waned. In December, about nine months after the first bombs fell on Baghdad, his doubts had become so profound that he decided he needed to leave Washington, and the *Crossfire* studio, and see the war firsthand. He drew up a will, wrote open-only-if-I-die letters to his wife and children, and flew to Kuwait. There, he met up with a group of security contractors, one of whom was also a terrorism talking head for CNN and a frequent *Crossfire* guest and who agreed to let Carlson tag along with the group as the contractors crossed into Iraq and drove to Baghdad. That's how Carlson found himself holding an AK-47 and sitting in the back seat of an SUV as it sped at 120 miles per hour through the Iraqi desert dodging carjackers and IEDs. Once in Baghdad, Carlson spent a week with the contractors as they tried to secure a neighborhood around a couple of hotels that housed American policemen. Then he and the contractors made the white-knuckle drive back to Kuwait. During the week he was in Iraq, the only time he didn't hear explosions or gunfire was when he had lunch with a Pentagon official at the empty Baghdad airport. "If the goal is to control the country, there are not enough American forces in Iraq," Carlson wrote a few months later in *Esquire*. "If the goal is to rebuild it, there could never be enough."

In 2004, with the violence in Iraq getting worse and the reality setting in that the prime rationale for the US invasion, that Saddam possessed WMDs, was not, in fact, true, most of the war's cheerleaders in the conservative commentariat still refused to admit defeat—or error. "We have no second thoughts about the justice and necessity of the war," Kristol told *The Washington Post*. Writing in *The Weekly Standard*, Fred Barnes lamented that Iraqis were "sullen and suspicious and conspiracy-minded"; nevertheless, he hailed "the impressive momentum" of the US reconstruction effort, deeming it "the greatest act of benevolence one country has ever done for another." Meanwhile, Stephen Hayes, a young *Standard* reporter who was hired shortly after Carlson's departure, churned out a series of credulous articles, based on dubious leaks from the Bush administration, that Saddam and Osama bin Laden enjoyed, as Hayes wrote, "an operational relationship from the early 1990s to 2003 that involved training in explosives and weapons of mass destruction, logistical support for terrorist attacks, al-Qaeda training camps and safe haven in Iraq, and Iraqi financial support for al-Qaeda." Vice President Cheney cited one of Hayes's articles as the "best source of information" about the supposed al-Qaeda–Iraq connection, but both the CIA and the Pentagon refuted Hayes's findings. (Cheney later tapped Hayes to write his authorized biography.)

For a time, Carlson tried to be a good soldier. While he refrained from outright praising the war on *Crossfire* after he returned from Iraq, he didn't explicitly criticize it, either. Rather, he attacked Democrats for attempting "to politicize the war" and claimed that ties between bin Laden and Saddam were "a completely open question," hailing Hayes as "one of the great, enterprising, and responsible writers around." Misdirection and deflection were his preferred debating tactics whenever Iraq came up on the show.

Finally, Carlson could no longer maintain the pretense of agnosticism. In June, he fessed up. “I am embarrassed that I supported the war in Iraq,” he told *The Washington Post*. In another interview with the journalist Joe Hagan, he said, “I think it’s a total nightmare and disaster, and I’m ashamed that I went against my own instincts in supporting it. It’s something I’ll never do again. Never.” He blamed his mistake on Patel, and their relationship became strained. “I got convinced by a friend of mine who’s smarter than I am, and I shouldn’t have done that,” he told Hagan. During a tense beach vacation with his family and Patel’s, he raged at his friend, “You’re the asshole who made me do this!”

Carlson was one of the first—and, for many years, only—conservative pundits to recant his support for the Iraq War. But he didn’t stop at just the war. He began to reevaluate his other priors, as well. Although he singled him out, Patel wasn’t his only friend or colleague or person he’d admired who’d been wrong about Iraq. There were Kristol and McCain and even his father, who now served as the vice chairman of the neoconservative foreign policy think tank the Foundation for Defense of Democracies. Carlson started to wonder what else these people were wrong about.

And he started to wonder what the people he held in low regard might be right about. Like Pat Buchanan. “Buchanan is a perfect example of somebody who’s been name-called into oblivion,” Carlson told Hagan. “And I did some of that. I definitely called Pat a lot of names. And I feel bad about that. I think he deserved some of those names. On the other hand, calling people names is a way of ignoring what they’re saying. It’s actually an outrage, and I actually feel really bad about my role in that.” He felt so bad that he even called Buchanan to personally apologize for the two stories he wrote calling him an anti-Semite. "While he may be an anti-Semite, I would say, in Buchanan's case, not all his ideas are crazy," Carlson explained.

He added, in what at the time seemed like a jokey attempt at self-deprecation: "I'm getting more paleo every day."

FOUR

THERE WERE FEW PROFESSIONAL OR personal repercussions for the pundits who supported the Iraq War. Some of them even seemed to be rewarded for their blunder. David Brooks ascended from *The Weekly Standard* to his columnist's perch at *The New York Times* six months after the US invasion. Jeffrey Goldberg, who wrote an influential article for *The New Yorker* about Saddam's supposed ties to al-Qaeda, was lured to *The Atlantic* after the magazine's owner offered him a hefty signing bonus and sent ponies to his house to entertain his children.

Carlson joined them in appearing to escape any opprobrium for his support of the war. While his mistake may have prompted a bout of personal introspection and a reevaluation of his political beliefs, it did not cause any of his friends and colleagues to reconsider their opinion, or think less, of him. If anything, his stature in the clubby confines of Washington political journalism actually grew. In the summer of 2004, PBS tapped him to host a weekly magazine-style show, *Tucker Carlson: Unfiltered*.

Crossfire remained Carlson's primary gig and the foundation of his stature. Not long after he was named a *Crossfire* host in 2001, the show was given a radical makeover. Its time slot was doubled, from thirty minutes to an hour, and it moved from its cramped, bare-bones studio at CNN's Capitol Hill offices to a new, elaborate set that accommodated a live audience of two hundred people at George Washington University. The biggest change was in its liberal hosts. Bill Press, Carlson's old sparring partner on *The Spin Room*, was toast; now sitting on the left would be the two former Bill Clinton advisers Paul Begala and James Carville. Begala and Carville weren't left-leaning journalists, like previous liberal *Crossfire* hosts, but Democratic activists; they were guaranteed to toe the party line—and to do so aggressively. CNN executives, looking nervously over their shoulders at Fox News gaining on them in the ratings, hoped that Carville and Begala squaring off against Carlson and Novak in front of a hooting crowd of college students and tourists would lead to fireworks. The show's new opening credits featured pictures of the hosts wearing boxing gloves and satin robes and gave them fight-card nicknames. Carville's and Novak's were "the Ragin' Cajun" and "the Prince of Darkness." Begala's was "the Lone Star Lefty." Carlson's was, naturally, "the Bowtie Brawler."

The strategy worked as intended. On the air, Carlson and Novak belittled Democrats as feckless and weak, while Begala and Carville railed against Republicans for being dumb and evil. The show often devolved into schoolyard taunting.

"Look me right in the eyes and tell me truthfully you're not embarrassed by what you just saw Madeleine Albright get up there and, off the top of her head, rambling on about this administration isn't as great as hers was," Carlson demanded of Begala after playing a video of Bill Clinton's secretary of state criticizing Bush's foreign policy.

"No, I'm embarrassed every time I see our president speaking," Begala shot back, "and I want to hide under the covers, because it's incoherent the way he tries to define how the world works. That's what embarrasses me."

"The new *Crossfire*," Novak later lamented, "was louder, shriller, and less substantive."

But off the air, Carlson got along swimmingly with his new liberal colleagues. In fact, while he and Novak remained chilly toward each other, Begala and Carville became some of his best friends. After shows, he'd go with Carville to the Foggy Bottom restaurant Carville owned; the Ragin' Cajun, who liked to tell Carlson about his sexual fantasies during commercial breaks, was "one of my favorite people," Carlson later recalled, while Carville pronounced himself "crazy about" Carlson. Begala, meanwhile, introduced Carlson to the paid lecture circuit, where the pair could pocket five-figure checks for putting on right-left debates for colleges and trade associations. When Carlson's town car, on the way back to Washington from a gig in Pennsylvania, swerved to avoid one deer only to strike another one, Begala's town car stopped and gave him a lift the rest of the way home. "I'm afraid the deer was not long for this world," Begala reported. "But as we were inspecting damage, I thought I heard the deer yelling from the woods, 'Your show sucks!'"

The goodwill and bonhomie extended to the politicians who appeared on *Crossfire*. When the US House relaxed its ethics rules so that lobbyists could cater meals for congressional offices and reimburse travel expenses for congressmen, Carlson defended the move. "Members of Congress don't make enough money. They're actually more pinched financially than most people recognize," he said on CNN. "There's a certain sort of person who thinks Washington is deeply corrupt. It's not deeply corrupt." Carlson wasn't being insincere when, at the end of a spirited *Crossfire* segment, he enthused: "Congressman Pete King of New York, Congressman Rahm Emanuel of Illinois, two of our favorite guests, thank you very much!"

Even Hillary Clinton got in on the fun. On the air, Carlson loved to take shots at her. "First envisioned as an explanation of how she could have put up with a husband like that, the book reportedly will be spice-free," he told viewers in 2003 on the eve of the publication of the first of Clinton's (so far) four memoirs, *Living History*. "In the absence of steamy details, Senator Clinton will attempt to sell the book on the strength of her charisma and electrifying personality alone. And good luck." He pledged that if the book sold a million copies, and recouped its eight-million-dollar advance, "I will eat my shoes. I promise that right here." A couple of months later, after *Living History* turned out to be a runaway bestseller, Clinton surprised Carlson on the *Crossfire* set with a cake in the shape of a shoe. "I really want you to notice, Tucker, that this is a wingtip," she told him. "It's a right-wing wingtip." Carlson, Begala, and the studio audience all howled. "I'm actually shocked," Carlson gushed. "That is fantastic."

It seemed as if every day at *Crossfire* brought Carlson that sort of surprise and delight. He recognized that being a cable-news host afforded him the sort of prominence—and power—that he never could have achieved as a magazine writer. Combined with his newfound sobriety—he'd stopped drinking in August 2002, days before Susie gave birth to their fourth child—he was at a personal and professional pinnacle, and he was eager to share his good fortune. When he went on vacation, he unsuccessfully tried to convince Matt Labash to fill in for him as a substitute host—hoping that it might provide his old friend an off-ramp from the bleak future of print journalism. As far as Carson was concerned, *Crossfire* wasn't just a TV show; it was a members-only club, where the pundits and the politicians bickered with one another about various matters—elections, tax cuts, war—but were fundamentally secure in the knowledge that they were on the same team. In the cultural geography of the nation's capital, Carlson wasn't merely a pundit; he was the host of Washington's most exclusive cocktail party.

And then Jon Stewart came and crashed it. As the host of *The Daily Show*, a late-night satirical news show that aired on Comedy Central, Stewart had become the unlikely leader of the liberal resistance. While actual Democratic politicians like John Kerry, the party's 2004 presidential nominee, flailed impotently against Bush on the campaign trail, Stewart, a comedian masquerading as a news anchor, deftly skewered the administration on the war and torture and gay marriage from 11:00 p.m. to 11:30 five nights a week. The *Crossfire* bookers had desperately pursued him as a guest, even buttonholing him when he appeared on other CNN shows, only to be repeatedly rebuffed. As Stewart told those bookers, he hated their show, viewing it as sensationalistic, trivial, and stupid. But in October 2004, with the election a month away and (perhaps more important) a new book to flog, Stewart finally succumbed to *Crossfire*'s entreaties.

Novak was dead-set against having Stewart on the show. The only comedian who'd ever appeared on *Crossfire* was Mark Russell, the piano-playing satirist beloved by Washington's octogenarian set. Russell, in Novak's view, was "a good-natured tweaker of Republicans and Democrats"; Stewart, by contrast, "was a left-wing ideologue obsessed with demeaning President Bush." But, as it turned out, on the day Stewart was booked to appear on *Crossfire*, Novak was a few blocks away in the hospital, receiving a blood transfusion after breaking his hip in a fall, so his objection was moot. Begala, for his part, viewed Stewart as an ideological ally. Carlson, meanwhile, felt warmly toward Stewart from their shared smoke breaks outside CNN's Washington studios, when Stewart was appearing on Larry King and Carlson was waiting to host *The Spin Room*. He and Begala were excited to have such a high-profile guest. (*The Daily Show* averaged about 1 million viewers per episode, compared to *Crossfire*'s 615,000.) They planned to devote the entire episode to their interview with Stewart. They knew he did not like cable shout fests in general and *Crossfire* in particular—he'd frequently mocked both on *The Daily Show*—but that would make his appearance that much more interesting. They could debate. It would be fantastic.

Stewart had other ideas. "Both of us were excited to go, guns a blazin' and get some stuff off our chest that we had been stewing on for some time," Ben Karlin, the producer of *The Daily Show* who accompanied Stewart to his *Crossfire* appearance, recalled. "I think the strategy was as simple as: 'You know how we sit around the writer's room and make fun of this? You should do that, but directly to them.'" Karlin added, "We thought they knew their show was trash. Turned out they didn't."

After a glowing introduction from Begala—"He's either the funniest smart guy on TV or the smartest funnyman"—Stewart, who'd ditched his usual fake-anchorman attire of suit and tie for a V-neck sweater and T-shirt, as if to further differentiate himself from the *Crossfire* hosts, pushed past the niceties. "Can I say something very quickly? Why do we have to fight? The two of you?" he asked Carlson and Begala. "Why do you argue, the two of you?"

Carlson put a question to Stewart about whether John Kerry was the best the Democrats could do, but Stewart pivoted. "I made a special effort to come on the show today, because I have privately, amongst my friends and also in occasional newspapers and television shows, mentioned this show as being bad," he said to the laughter of the studio audience. "It's not so much that it's bad, as it's hurting America."

"But in its defense—" Carlson interjected, before Stewart cut him off.

"So I wanted to come here today and say, here's just what I wanted to tell you guys," Stewart continued "Stop. Stop, stop, stop, stop hurting America."

For the rest of the show, Begala, either out of shock or prudence, stayed mostly silent. But Carlson rose to Stewart's challenge, and he and his guest went at each other. Carlson accused Stewart of being Kerry's "butt boy" for having conducted a softball interview with the candidate. Stewart mocked Carlson for wearing a bow tie at the tender age of thirty-five.

In between the insults, Stewart continued to press his case. He argued that *Crossfire* both reduced and sensationalized political disagreements into simplistic partisan frames that made everyone involved dumber. To claim that *Crossfire* was a show about politics, he said, was "like saying pro wrestling is a show about athletic competition."

"You're doing theater, when you should be doing debate," he admonished Carlson. "What you do is not honest. What you do is partisan hackery."

"I think you're a good comedian. I think your lectures are boring," Carlson complained. "I do think you're more fun on your show."

"You know what's interesting, though?" Stewart fired back. "You're as big a dick on your show as you are on any show." The studio audience—which Carlson had once celebrated for bringing "energy and excitement" to *Crossfire* and for letting him know "that our thoughts are being heard and supported"—cheered.

When the episode was over, Stewart wanted to keep arguing. For another ninety minutes, he and Karlin hung around backstage, where they talked to Begala and *Crossfire*'s executive producer Sam Feist about all the ways in which their show was awful. But Carlson was nowhere to be found. He claimed that he had a dinner to get to and left the studio as soon as the floor manager yelled, "Clear."

Two decades later, Stewart's contention that *Crossfire* was "hurting America" seems naive and overwrought, if not wrong. Now that cable-news channels have become siloed, partisan echo chambers—in which toxic arguments go unrebutted and are instead amplified—it's hard not to feel a little nostalgic for a debate show that, by its very design, presented both sides of an issue and forced its hosts, guests, and (most important) viewers to confront contrasting points of view, even if those points of view were not always offered with total sincerity.

But at the time, Stewart's broadside against *Crossfire* resonated in ways that media criticism rarely does. The episode drew 867,000 viewers—about 250,000 more than usual. What's more, Stewart's *Crossfire* appearance had a second life online: It was downloaded nearly 670,000 times, becoming one of the first video clips to ever go viral. (Those download stats caught the eye of a twentysomething software engineer named Jawed Karim, who noted how kludgy video-sharing sites tended to be; a few months later, he and two friends created YouTube.) Thanks to Stewart and his Howard Beale moment, it was as if all the public's anger and frustration over the media's shortcomings in its coverage of the Iraq War had settled on a convenient target in *Crossfire*—and Carlson.

Worst of all for Carlson, Stewart's critique struck a chord with Jon Klein. A former CBS News executive who once oversaw *60 Minutes*, Klein was hired as CNN's president in November. One of his first orders of business was to figure out what to do with Carlson, whose contract with the network had expired in October and who was working on a month-to-month deal. Early in Klein's tenure, Carlson traveled to New York to try to win over his new boss.

CNN had recently moved its headquarters into the new Time Warner Center on Columbus Circle, which boasted some of New York's most acclaimed (and expensive) restaurants, but Klein felt no need to wine and dine Carlson. He suggested they meet for lunch in the employee cafeteria. There, Carlson told Klein that he had a job offer from MSNBC, but that he wanted to stay at CNN. While he recognized that, after Stewart, his days as a *Crossfire* host were likely numbered, he believed there were other things he could do for the network. He pitched Klein on hosting his own show in prime time. Klein agreed to give Carlson an audition of sorts by letting him fill in as the anchor of CNN's flagship ten o'clock newscast, *CNN NewsNight*, while Aaron Brown took a week off around Christmas.

It would make for a better story if Carlson had tanked on *NewsNight*—if he'd been like Albert Brooks's character in *Broadcast News*, an award-winning war correspondent who melts into a puddle of flop sweat when he finally gets a chance to sit in the anchor's chair. But Carlson actually did fine, smoothly delivering the latest news about the tsunami in South Asia and holiday travel delays in US airports. The problem for Carlson was that fine was not good enough. "He clearly wasn't going to be a game changer there," Klein recalled. When the audition was over, Klein told Carlson that he didn't see a role for Carlson at CNN and that Carlson should take the offer from MSNBC. "I was not particularly worried that he would somehow damage us in prime time," Klein said.

Before Carlson could announce his move to MSNBC, however, Klein had an announcement of his own. On the first workday of 2005, he sent out a press release with the news that not only was CNN not renewing Carlson's contract; the network was canceling *Crossfire*, ending its twenty-three-year run. Carlson was blindsided, learning about the release only when *The New York Times*'s media reporter called him for comment during his lunch at the Palm. "I don't know what CNN is saying," Carlson sputtered to *The Times*. "But I have no dispute with CNN." Klein, meanwhile, confidently declared that he wanted to move CNN away from "head-butting debate shows," boasting, "We report the news. Fox talks about the news." *Capital Gang* was on the chopping block, as well. As

Klein told *The Times*, "I agree wholeheartedly with Jon Stewart's overall premise."

WHEN *THE SITUATION WITH TUCKER Carlson* premiered at 9:00 p.m. on a Monday in June 2005, MSNBC was almost nine years old—and still lacking a clear identity. Fox News was conservative talk radio on television. CNN was a globe-spanning network devoted to reporting the news, especially now that it had gotten rid of its shouting-head shows. And MSNBC was . . . confused.

The Friends had come and gone; Laura Ingraham's show *Watch It!* was canceled after a couple of years, and she departed the network for actual talk radio. ("Radio is where I feel most like myself," she insisted.) For a time after 9/11, MSNBC tried to outflank Fox on the right with rah-rah, flag-waving commentary and the new slogan "America's News Channel." The next year, it brought Phil Donahue out of retirement to host an 8:00 p.m. talk show, which he turned into cable news's only anti-war outpost in the run-up to the US invasion of Iraq. After Donahue was fired a few weeks before the war started—because, as consultants hired by the network concluded, he was a "difficult public face for NBC in a time of war"—MSNBC retreated to a muddle of hard-news, tabloid, and opinion shows. Nothing clicked. The only constant was that MSNBC remained mired in a distant third place behind Fox and CNN in the cable-news-ratings race.

For Carlson—whose time at CNN was spent looking over his shoulder at Fox and then watching it pass his network in the ratings—landing at the third-place cable network did have one upside. "There's less pressure on our show to perform in the first three weeks than there would be on a show on another network," he said shortly before *The Situation with Tucker Carlson* launched. Which was crucial, since he knew his show was going to be a hard sell.

Carlson stubbornly refused to lend any credence to Stewart or his critique of *Crossfire*. He dismissed the comedian as "an angry, weird guy" and his argument as "banal"; the only reason Stewart was deemed the winner of their fight was "because he's more famous and popular" than Carlson was. And yet, Carlson knew from personal experience the limitations and malignancies of *Crossfire* and shows like it. Always having to toe a party line, he believed, made for bad politics—and bad television. He was determined not to do a *Crossfire*-type show at MSNBC. "Yelling, not yelling, who cares? That's not the point," he said. "The problem with that kind of TV is that it can be phony. It's inauthentic. It's people reading other people's lines."

One type of show that avoided the inauthenticity trap was what Carlson called the "Big Brother format." On a "Big Brother" show, as Carlson explained it, "you have one person whose opinion dominates the show and anyone who comes on the show either has to parrot that opinion; or is so much weaker and less articulate and less impressive—and less attractive, in many cases—that he is just overwhelmed by the host." The "Big Brother" format was best exemplified by the highest-rated show in cable news, Fox News's *The O'Reilly Factor*. Needless to say, Carlson did not want to emulate that thin-skinned blowhard.

Instead, the show Carlson envisioned for himself at MSNBC would feature his opinions—his real opinions, not ones he felt he had to voice in order to represent the GOP. But the show would also feature the opinions—the real opinions—of people who disagreed with its host. "I'm not interested in institutional positions. I'm interested in heartfelt passionate points of view," he said. "If you're an adult, you ought to say what you think. You ought to speak freely and not parrot some line that you've been handed by a higher-up." Just as important, the people voicing those heartfelt points of view wouldn't be "cut outs" or "straw men," as Carlson called them; they would be "smart" and "interesting" people who were Carlson's intellectual and television equals. He wanted the show to feel like a "dinner party conversation," one that might occur at Christopher Hitchens's apartment.

MSNBC hired Bill Wolff, a former Harvard water polo player who had helped create the hot take genre of sports debate shows at ESPN and then Fox Sports Net, as the executive producer of *The Situation with Tucker Carlson*. His and Carlson's first order of business was to find Carlson a regular liberal sparring partner. They knew they wouldn't be picking from the A-list. Carlson was considered damaged goods after the Stewart episode. ("When a man gets dissed on his own show by a fake journalist and a dog puppet, he packs up his bow tie and starts the slow work of rebuilding his dignity," read the description of his MSNBC show in *Entertainment Weekly*'s viewers guide. *The New York Times*'s review was headlined "Talk Show Washout Tries Again.") Even worse, his show would be broadcasting at nine o'clock from MSNBC's studios in Secaucus, New Jersey—a forty-five-minute drive from Midtown Manhattan. But the lure of a regular guest spot on cable news was powerful, and Carlson and Wolff had no shortage of audition tapes to sort through. The tape that Carlson kept returning to was that of a thirty-two-year-old liberal talk radio host named Rachel Maddow.

A nerdy, self-described butch lesbian with short brown hair and a prominent nose, Maddow didn't look like the typical blonde, rhinoplastied female cable-news talking head. She didn't sound like one, either, eschewing aggressive point making in favor of a cheerful, even tone. But Carlson liked her. He liked that she was smart (a Rhodes scholar) and interesting ("the first openly gay Rhodes scholar," according to her bio) and more of a progressive ideologue than a Democratic partisan (during the 2004 presidential race, she was just as withering about Kerry's opposition to gay marriage as she was about Bush's). Wolff liked her too. The problem was that Carlson's and Wolff's bosses at MSNBC didn't like her. The higher-ups told them to pick someone more conventional for Carlson's liberal foil.

But Carlson and Wolff held their ground, inviting Maddow to the show's rehearsals and beseeching their bosses to give her a chance. And when *The Situation with Tucker Carlson* debuted, there was Maddow on the premiere episode—arguing with Carlson about the big news of that particular day, the acquittal of Michael Jackson on child-molestation charges.

"I'll be honest with you," Carlson said. "I am baffled by this."

"He is innocent until proven guilty," Maddow said. "And we're all going to say that he should have been convicted, but we weren't there."

It was the first of countless on-air disagreements between the two, as Maddow became a regular on Carlson's show, debating him on everything from polygamy to foreign aid to assisted suicide to whether Tom Cruise's romance with Katie Holmes was real over the course of scores of appearances. Maddow frequently got the better of their exchanges. "You're smarter than what you're saying right now," she chided Carlson during one dispute about a survey that asked teenagers if they'd had a same-sex experience. "She was unbelievably prepared," Wolff later said. "And she just killed him."

But Carlson didn't mind. Off the air, the pair bonded over their shared love of fly-fishing and shooting guns. On the air, he and Maddow both seemed to delight in their disagreements—and each other. "What's the first thing, apart from nationalizing the railroads and passing the transgender amendment,

Democrats are going to do when they take power?" Carlson asked a laughing Maddow shortly before the 2006 midterms.

"I mean there is a lot to get to right away," Maddow replied, as Carlson struggled to keep a straight face. "We have to make everybody get gay married, and we have to ban the Bible, and we have to send you to Guantánamo."

Maddow wasn't Carlson's only discovery. Wolff had brought with him a handful of producers from Fox Sports, one of whom was Willie Geist. "From the first dinner I had with him, I thought he was one of the funniest people I had ever met," Carlson later recalled. He considered it a shame that Geist's humor was confined to production meetings. Though Geist had no on-air experience, Carlson decided to bring him out from behind the camera with a segment called "The Cutting Room Floor"; at the end of every episode, in a cable-news version of breaking the fourth wall, Geist would emerge from the control room, headset hanging around his neck, and run through the various news stories from that day that were deemed too frivolous or too trashy to be discussed earlier in the program, like the security camera video of a Nebraska man robbing a store even though his pants had fallen down or Donald Trump's feud with Rosie O'Donnell. ("The loathsome versus the loathsome," Carlson said of the latter.) "There were most nights where I thought it was the best thing on the whole show," Carlson said. MSNBC executives agreed; just as with Maddow, they began envisioning a bigger platform for Geist.

Unfortunately for Carlson, his star-making powers did not extend to himself. Despite his expectation of a grace period, abysmal ratings prompted MSNBC, after just two months, to move his show from nine o'clock to eleven o'clock (which, ironically, was the same time slot as Jon Stewart). Eleven months later, his show was shifted to six o'clock, then four o'clock, then back to six. Along the way, MSNBC changed the name of the show from *The Situation with Tucker Carlson* to *Tucker*, and Carlson abandoned the bow tie for a regular tie and, eventually, no tie at all. He was a cable-news journeyman on his own cable-news channel.

Nonetheless, despite the time, title, and wardrobe changes, Carlson mostly managed to achieve his original vision for the show. The debates and conversations were significantly smarter than typical cable-news fare—and not just because of Maddow. Carlson liked to book as guests his old colleagues from *The Standard*—including Ferguson, Frum, and O'Rourke—and writers from other small, serious magazines of politics and culture, like *The New Republic*'s Peter Beinart. But he cast a wider net, as well. One episode Carlson might interview Harvard professor Graham Allison about nuclear proliferation; in another he would talk to the atheist writer Sam Harris about Western liberals' attitudes toward radical Islam. Throw in the discussions of pop-culture detritus with Geist and, on some evenings, Carlson's show did indeed achieve the heady fun of a Christopher Hitchens dinner party—especially when Hitchens himself paid a visit, as he often did.

In the process, Carlson seemed to find his authentic voice as an ideologue. He continued to harangue Democrats, but he had no qualms about criticizing Republicans or President Bush, either—and not just about Iraq. The influence of Buchanan, who was a frequent guest on his show, now extended to domestic policy, particularly immigration; Carlson hadn't been joking when he said he was becoming a paleocon. He attacked Bush's plan to overhaul the nation's immigration laws by giving legal status to millions of undocumented workers in the United States as a scheme "to create or maintain a serf class that does work at lower wages than Americans are willing to do." The man who just a few years earlier pooh-poohed a cabinet nominee's hiring of an undocumented worker to clean her home as a "very minor crime" now complained that after petroleum sales "the single largest source of foreign currency in Mexico . . . is your housekeeper sending money home," adding, "That's not the behavior of someone who wants to be a part of this country in the long term." When, after the 2006 midterms, a *New Republic* writer appeared on Carlson's show and criticized a Republican congressman from Arizona for having run "breathtaking demagogic, xenophobic ads" about border security, Carlson shot back, "It's pretty easy to say that if you live, as I do, in Washington, but I'm telling you, if you live—people in Arizona and people in the border states are mad." He was now picking up a pitchfork on behalf of those he not so long ago had dismissed as the "Great Unread."

In fact, border security was a recurring topic on Carlson's show. On one episode in 2005, Maddow, after listening to Carlson and Buchanan both talk about the need for a two-thousand-mile-long "security fence" on the US-Mexico border, wryly remarked that their idea "sounds very nineteenth century at this point." Carlson replied, more heatedly than usual, "This is our country. That is their country. They have an interest in sending their unemployed here. We have an interest in keeping them out. A wall would solve that problem."

Carlson's increasingly strident political views, and his voicing of them on his show, didn't ruffle any feathers among MSNBC executives, at least not at first. "I honestly don't think anyone higher up at the network cared about our show," said one person who worked on it. "I think they didn't give a shit." Indeed, Carlson may well have been able to continue his peripatetic existence on MSNBC in perpetuity, bouncing from one time slot to the next, save for one new development: MSNBC, once described as a "no-man's-land" by one on-air personality, finally found an identity—an identity that ran counter to Carlson's.

The channel's identity formation began with Keith Olbermann. In 2003, MSNBC had hired Olbermann, an extremely talented but notoriously difficult broadcaster who rose to fame as an anchor on ESPN's *SportsCenter*, to host its eight o'clock show. MSNBC executives envisioned it as a "newscast of record," and Olbermann delivered that type of program for a time. But in 2005, he began taking his show in a different direction. Like Carlson, Olbermann harbored a deep contempt for Bill O'Reilly; unlike Carlson, he started to give full voice to that contempt on the air. He subjected O'Reilly, whom he referred to as "Bill-O," to almost nightly mockery, regularly featuring the "Fox Noise" host in his show's "The Worst Person in the World" segment. Before long, Olbermann baited O'Reilly to respond in kind, ushering in the era of cable-news hosts talking less about the news and more about one another. While their feud didn't do much for O'Reilly's ratings, which were already sky-high, it provided a boost to Olbermann's. "I really do owe him a percentage of my salary," Olbermann told *The New Yorker*. From O'Reilly, Olbermann moved on to bigger targets—like Cheney, Rumsfeld, and Bush—routinely excoriating them in an opening monologue, called "Special Comment," that oftentimes ran for more than ten minutes. His ratings continued to climb—by nearly 75 percent in 2006. It dawned on MSNBC executives that there was an audience for a liberal analogue to Fox News, and they went about remaking their network in Olbermann's braying, lefty image. "Keith Olbermann is our brand," Phil Griffin, MSNBC's president, said.

MSNBC's new liberal identity and its successful repositioning as a sort of mirror image of Fox didn't spell curtains for every conservative who worked there. Some, including Buchanan, kept their contributor contracts and stayed on as talking heads, if only to give the network's new liberal stars someone to argue with. Joe Scarborough even managed to continue hosting his own show. A former congressman from Florida who was once a foot soldier in Newt Gingrich's Republican

Revolution, Scarborough had held down a poorly rated prime-time program—an *O'Reilly Factor* knockoff called *Scarborough Country*—for nearly four years when, in the spring of 2007, MSNBC abruptly fired its morning-show host Don Imus. (Imus, a veteran shock jock who for decades had pushed the boundary of mainstream acceptability with racist and misogynistic humor, finally crossed it when he described the Rutgers University women's basketball team as "nappy-headed hos.") Scarborough lobbied MSNBC executives to let him fill the network's suddenly empty morning slot. Presenting them with a laminated page of bullet points, he pitched them on a three-hour show of hardcore but breezy political chat that featured him and, as sidekicks, Geist and an MSNBC newsreader named Mika Brzezinski. MSNBC executives gave him the green light, less because they believed in his vision than because they desperately needed to put something in Imus's place. Launched in the middle of a historic presidential campaign, *Morning Joe* quickly became a must-watch—and, soon, a must-visit—for political insiders and power brokers, Democrats and Republicans alike. Meanwhile, Scarborough, who sanded down his rough political edges with his move to the mornings and now likened himself to Obama, describing himself as "post-ideological," became the sort of unofficial mayor of the Acela Corridor.

It was a role that may have been even better suited for Carlson, an ingratiating gabber and inveterate gossip who was skilled in the art of early-morning discourse with members of the political and media elite after years of regular breakfasts at Washington's Metropolitan Club. Despite his increasingly paleo politics, he, like Buchanan, remained personally popular with establishment types. (As Garry Wills once wondered about Buchanan, "How can such a fanatic be so likable?") If only he'd thought of the idea for the show before Scarborough. But by then Carlson was focused on another escape route from MSNBC's conservative ghetto: Hollywood.

In the fall of 2006, Carlson traveled to California to compete on ABC's *Dancing with the Stars*. The reality TV show, which premiered the previous year, teamed celebrities with professional dancers and then had the couples compete in a single-elimination tournament. The term "star" in the title was relative—the celebrities were of the C-list variety, mostly washed-up actors and retired athletes—and Carlson's friends pleaded with him not to do the show, saying it was beneath him and that he'd look like a buffoon. Carlson countered that plenty of pundits did goofy things on TV. Robert Novak, a septuagenarian pundit no less, had recently jumped out of an airplane as a stupid pundit trick for a CNN show. Besides, Carlson insisted, it would be an interesting experience. "I want to have an interesting life," he told his friends. "That's my goal."

Usually left unsaid was Carlson's other goal: to jump-start a television career outside of political punditry. He knew he was on thin ice at MSNBC. Not only was Griffin looking to replace conservative hosts with liberals as he sought to capitalize on Olbermann's popularity and rebrand the network; Olbermann himself nursed a grudge against Carlson, viewing him and a handful of other conservatives at the network as a potential fifth column. Carlson was confident in his abilities as a broadcaster. He'd learned—and improved—a lot in the five years since he'd become a full-time TV guy. He believed it wasn't him that was holding him back; it was cable news. Ever since he'd appeared on *Jeopardy!* during a special "Power Players" episode in 2004—besting Peggy Noonan and Bob Woodward—he'd daydreamed about one day replacing Alex Trebek or, short of that, hosting another game show. He could stay involved in politics—*Wheel of Fortune* host Pat Sajak certainly wasn't shy about supporting conservative causes—but, according to a friend with whom he discussed his game show ambitions, "He thought that would just be an easier route to kind of have a fun, lighter career."

He hoped *Dancing with the Stars* would take him a step closer to that career—that, as Bill Wolff explained, it would provide "a chance for a big audience to see what a good sport and charming person Tucker is." Carlson soon discovered that he was a terrible dancer; he insisted that if he made it through the first episode without falling, he'd consider that a victory. But he took his preparations seriously, knowing that the further he went in the competition, the more opportunity he'd have to change people's perceptions of him.

In the month leading up to the show, he worked intensely with his partner, a Russian professional dancer named Elena Grinenko, sandwiching their practice sessions around the morning production meetings for his MSNBC show. He even had Grinenko join him and Susie and their four children in Maine on his family's summer vacation. When *Dancing with the Stars* finally arrived, though, all of Carlson's preparations were for naught. His and Grinenko's "Cha-Cha-Cha" on the show's first episode was a dud. "What an awful mess," one of the show's judges huffed. The viewing audience agreed. Carlson was the first competitor to be voted off the show; he lasted just one episode.

But Carlson's escape plan wasn't a total bust, at least not yet. Seven months after his *Dancing with the Stars* washout, he returned to Hollywood to tape a pilot for a prime-time game show for CBS. The show was called *Do You Trust Me?* and it was a combination of *Who Wants to Be a Millionaire* and the prisoner's dilemma, with two contestants playing as a team answering trivia questions to win one million dollars, all while wondering if one of them will betray the other and quit the game for a smaller payday. *Do You Trust Me?* was the brainchild of Phil Gurin, who'd recently created NBC's hit game show

Weakest Link and was in high demand. In fact, Gurin was shooting game show pilots for all three major networks that spring.

Over the course of several days, Gurin shot six episodes of *Do You Trust Me?* He and his team were happy with Carlson's performance as host. "He was very poised and very fluid and very conversational," Ray Giuliani, one of the executive producers, recalled. "News broadcasters make good game show hosts because they know how to think on their feet." They had high hopes for *Do You Trust Me?* But, in the end, CBS decided not to pick it up. The only Gurin game show pilot to make it to air that fall was NBC's *The Singing Bee*, a karaoke-style competition that was hosted by Joey Fatone, a former member of the boy band NSYNC.

Resigned, Carlson headed back to MSNBC. The channel was becoming Olbermann's network more and more by the day. "Phil thinks he's my boss," Olbermann said of MSNBC's president. Carlson tried to focus on the presidential race. Despite disagreeing on immigration with McCain, who supported a guest-worker program, he still had a soft spot for the Arizona senator. Back in 2005, when McCain appeared on one of the first episodes of his MSNBC show, Carlson had told him that he hoped he ran for president in 2008. Now that he was—and was on the verge of staging a remarkable comeback to capture the Republican nomination—Carlson was giddy. "You look at John McCain and you ask yourself, how would I feel if my son grew up to be John McCain?" he said on the eve of the New Hampshire primary in January. "And you would feel proud. I feel most people would feel proud about that. That's not something you can say about most candidates."

But the good feelings wouldn't last. In March, eight months before the election, Carlson was given the inevitable news. MSNBC was canceling his show. On the final episode of *Tucker*, the Clinton dead-ender Lanny Davis appeared to talk up

Hillary's by then nonexistent chances in her primary with Obama—and to pay tribute to Carlson. "I come on this show because unlike almost everybody else on television, you allow people to finish their answers," Davis told him. "Being able to disagree agreeably is what you stand for." Al Sharpton, who was there to defend Obama from racist remarks made by his preacher, Jeremiah Wright, told Carlson, "Thank you for all you've done to keep the dialogue alive." And Geist, now a star on *Morning Joe* and on his way to eventually hosting NBC's *Sunday Today* show, came on to thank for Carlson for launching his career: "Suffice it to say that I wouldn't be on this show, the six a.m. show, or any show without you, your friendship, and your advocacy." For his part, Carlson tried to put on a brave face. Although he later admitted that he was devastated and embarrassed by the show's cancellation, on that night he kept things light. "Well, that's it," he said as the hour wound down. "That's the end of our show. We *won't* be joining you on Monday."

Six months later, *The Rachel Maddow Show*, with Bill Wolff as its executive producer, premiered on MSNBC in Carlson's original time slot at 9:00 p.m. Within a few weeks, it surpassed Olbermann as MSNBC's top-rated show.

FIVE

On a Saturday evening in February 2009, Rush Limbaugh stood in the packed ballroom of Washington's Omni Shoreham Hotel and delivered the keynote address to the Conservative Political Action Conference. It was a bleak, anxious time for Republicans. A month earlier, Barack Obama had been sworn in as the forty-fourth president of the United States after beating John McCain in a landslide the previous November; eyeing the young and dynamic new president's sky-high approval ratings, many Republicans resigned themselves to the prospect of either compromising with Obama on his ambitious domestic agenda—universal health care, a second Troubled Asset Relief Program, a bailout of the Big Three automakers—or spending a generation in the political wilderness. Limbaugh did not hold this view and was eager to offer an alternative vision. In previous years, when David Keene, the chairman of the American Conservative Union, had invited Limbaugh to speak at CPAC, he'd turned Keene down after Keene refused his demands of a hefty honorarium and private air travel. This time, Limbaugh had approached Keene. He wanted to anoint himself the leader of the opposition, and he could think of no better place to do that than CPAC, the largest annual gathering of conservative activists from across the United States.

Speaking to the eighty-five hundred CPAC attendees, as well as the hundreds of thousands of people watching on Fox News and CNN—which were both carrying his speech live—Limbaugh, wearing a black suit and a black shirt that made him look like a bloated Johnny Cash, urged them to stand up to Obama and reject his calls for bipartisanship. "Where is the compromise between good and evil? Should Jesus have cut a different deal?" he demanded. Limbaugh had recently come under fire, from Democrats and Republicans, for saying on his radio show that he hoped Obama would fail, a sentiment that at the time was quaintly considered outside the bounds of acceptable political rhetoric; at CPAC, he doubled down. "What is so strange about being honest to say that I want Barack Obama to fail if his mission is to restructure and reform this country so that capitalism and individual liberty are not its foundation?" he asked. "Why would I want that to succeed?"

Limbaugh's speech set the tone for Republican politics in the Obama era. Where members of the opposition party were once expected to at least pay lip service to notions of bipartisanship, now any GOP official who was thinking about cooperating with the Democratic president quickly adopted a stance of massive resistance; merely greeting Obama when he visited your state, as Florida governor Charlie Crist discovered, spelled the end of your career in Republican politics. Years later Keene deemed Limbaugh's speech "the biggest speech at CPAC since Reagan's 'pale pastels' speech"—Ronald Reagan's 1975 oration that urged conservatives to eschew "pale pastels" in favor of "bold colors" and that signaled his intention to remake the GOP in his own uncompromising image.

Tucker Carlson also spoke at that year's CPAC. His speech came two days before Limbaugh's. It was delivered at a sparsely attended morning session and was not carried live by any of the cable-news channels. But Carlson was grateful just to have the platform.

If Republicans were feeling low after Obama's election, Carlson, he'd later confess, was at a professional and personal nadir. When he took the job at MSNBC in 2005, he moved Susie and their four kids from Washington, DC, to New Jersey, where he bought a nine-thousand-square-foot mansion in the ritzy town of Madison for $3.3 million. He ditched his 1987 Volvo and began driving a Hummer. He was a prime-time cable-news anchor now, and he was going to live like one—even if the cable-news channel was MSNBC. So when MSNBC canned him, he didn't just lose his job; he lost his lifestyle and his identity. "I looked around and I was like, 'Oh wow, I'm living this totally unsustainable life and I'm not making any money,'" Carlson later recalled. "It was a pretty low-grade disaster. I didn't lose a limb in war or get paralyzed in a car accident. But for me, who'd grown up in a pretty privileged world, it was distressing and a shock." He sold the New Jersey mansion out from under his family and returned to Washington. Pulling into his driveway at night, he thought he saw his neighbors averting their gaze. While he managed to avoid the temptation of going back to drinking, he dramatically upped his Nicorette consumption, buying it in bulk from a supplier in New Zealand. He couldn't shake the feeling, he said, that "everybody hated me." But the reality was actually worse: People didn't hate Carlson; they didn't think about him at all.

At CPAC, Carlson seemed to invite his audience's disapproval. Smirking and looking every bit the preppy know-it-all he used to play on TV (and that had once earned him the derisive nickname Chatsworth Osborne Jr. from Limbaugh), he informed the couple hundred people scattered around the hotel ballroom, "Most speakers hate to be interrupted, but I enjoy it, having spent about ten years in cable news getting interrupted and yelled at by a large bald man from Louisiana called James Carville." As the crowd tittered, he went on, "It actually makes me uncomfortable if people don't scream at me as I speak." Unlike Limbaugh and most of the other speakers at that year's CPAC, who reassured the hardcore conservatives in attendance that they were not to blame for the Republican Party's struggles and that they simply needed to remain strong in their convictions until the moderates and squishes bent to their will and the GOP's fortunes improved accordingly, Carlson called for a course correction. He argued that one of the reasons conservatives were struggling was because of conservative media, which "refused to put accuracy first" and instead prioritized bombast and opinion.

"This is the hard truth, and conservatives need to deal with it," Carlson continued. "If you create a news organization whose primary objective is not to deliver accurate news, you will fail." He paused before he repeated himself: "You will fail." Then Carlson delivered the words that he knew would make the CPAC audience scream. "*The New York Times* is a liberal paper," he said, "but it's also a paper that cares about whether they spell people's names right, by and large. It's a paper that cares about accuracy. Conservatives need to build institutions that mirror those institutions." The CPAC crowd began to boo. "*The New York Times* is twisted!" one woman shouted. "But I'm not saying they're not!" Carlson shot back. "I'm merely saying that at the core of their news-gathering operation is gathering news." Amid louder boos, Carlson pressed his case. "You can believe it or not!" he admonished the hecklers. "But conservatives need to mimic that in their own news organizations. They need to go out there and find what is happening, find actually what is going on, not just interpret things they hear in the mainstream media but gather the news themselves. That's expensive. It's difficult. And it is worth doing."

Carlson's words may have been unwelcome at CPAC, but they were hailed outside of the hardcore conservative bubble—even by liberals. "Tucker Carlson calls for the professionalization of conservative media—and is booed for it. Too bad. He's basically right," Ta-Nehisi Coates wrote in *The Atlantic*. Both responses, the jeering and the cheering, were precisely what Carlson was hoping for. Just like Bill Clinton had once attacked the rapper Sister Souljah in a speech to Jesse Jackson's Rainbow Coalition—prompting Jackson to attack Clinton, which bolstered Clinton's standing with white suburban swing voters—Carlson had waded into the fever swamps of CPAC fully intending to provoke his audience. Not only would the hostile response from the hard-right activists there gin up attention (most CPAC speeches were snoozes and went unnoticed outside the conference); it would earn Carlson plaudits from the people who looked down their noses at those hard-right activists—namely political journalists and mainstream conservatives. And Carlson needed all of that because he was already planning his next act: launching a conservative news organization that embodied the goals—reporting instead of opinion, accuracy rather than bombast—that he lauded at CPAC.

Shortly after the 2008 election, Carlson had dinner with Neil Patel at the Palm. They'd long since buried the hatchet over Iraq, and the old friends were both at a crossroads. Carlson, of course, had been fired by MSNBC; as for Patel, his time in the Bush administration was drawing to a close. (Although Patel's mentor, Scooter Libby, had resigned as Dick Cheney's chief of staff in 2005, after Libby was indicted for obstruction of justice and perjury, Patel continued to work for the vice president until the end of Cheney's term.) Political journalism seemed to be at a crossroads, as well. Coverage was migrating to the Internet, where scores of blogs and websites were popping up. In conservative media, *National Review* had launched a more freewheeling web operation called *National Review Online*, while *The Weekly Standard* had supplemented its print magazine with *The Daily Standard*; new websites like *FrumForum*, run by David Frum, tried to plot a course for the conservative movement. "Do we really want to delegitimize the best and brightest?" a young Yale Law student named James Hamel wrote on *FrumForum*, bemoaning the "victimologist propaganda" and "cynical political nihilism" of those conservatives who launched populist attacks on the "academics, intellectuals, and most of all, government officials." (A few years later, Hamel would change his last name, which he got from his mother's second ex-husband, to Vance, in honor of his grandparents; he'd also start formally going by his nickname, JD).

But the website that fascinated Carlson and Patel wasn't conservative at all. *The Huffington Post* was an "Internet newspaper" founded by Arianna Huffington that, after just three years in existence, was generating so many millions of page views that it was coming to be seen as a competitor of *The Washington Post* and *The New York Times*. Carlson's interest was largely political: *The Huffington Post*, which was stridently liberal, had played a major role in the bitter Democratic presidential primary between Obama and Hillary Clinton. Patel's interest was mostly financial: *The Huffington Post* had recently been valued at two hundred million dollars. Despite the growing number of conservative websites, there was no conservative analogue to *The Huffington Post*, and Carlson and Patel sensed an opportunity. Over their meal, they hashed out a plan to start one. "You'll know how to run the business side, and I can play the sort of Arianna role," Carlson told Patel. Nearly two decades after they'd tried and failed to launch a Trinity College version of *The Dartmouth Review,* they decided to found a conservative version of *The Huffington Post*.

One important order of business was coming up with a name for their new publication. Following *The Huffington Post* playbook quite literally, they briefly considered calling it *The Tucker Report* before thinking better of it. Patel was partial to *News Queue* because he thought it had an Internet-y feel to it, even going so far as to purchase the www.newsqueue.com URL; Carlson liked *Punji Stick*—after the bamboo spears the Vietcong used. Ultimately, though, Carlson wanted a name that was "suggestive of kind of a traditional newspaper," he later explained, to reflect the publication's commitment to the sort of traditional journalism he praised in his CPAC speech. The problem was, Patel later recalled, that it was "virtually impossible to find a domain name that includes words like *Times* or *Tribune* these days—unless you want to pay a lot of money for them."

That's when Patel remembered an episode from his time working for Cheney. After the vice president accidentally shot a friend in the face during a 2006 hunting trip in Texas, Patel came up with the controversial press strategy of disclosing the news to a local paper, the *Corpus Christi Caller-Times*, instead of alerting the White House press corps in the futile hope that the story would not gain any traction. Patel and Carlson had fond memories of the episode and thought the *Caller* had a nice, old-timey ring to it. They decided to name their new publication *The Daily Caller*.

Coming up with a name for Carlson and Patel's new publication was much easier than coming up with the three million dollars needed to get it off the ground. The US was in the midst of the Great Recession and, the success of *The Huffington Post* aside, the journalism industry was in especially dire straits. One of the first people Carlson and Patel approached was the billionaire Richard Mellon Scaife, a prodigious donor to conservative causes who had bankrolled *The American Spectator*'s infamous dirt digging into Bill Clinton's Arkansas dealings in the 1990s. In a meeting in Pittsburgh, Scaife told the pair that he would invest in the *Caller*, and they celebrated. But when Carlson and

Patel went to close the deal with Scaife's attorney, the attorney informed them that, whatever Scaife had told them, all of Scaife's money was tied up in his messy divorce from his second wife and that Scaife wouldn't be able to make good on his pledge.

Carlson and Patel hired the law firm DLA Piper, which had a robust start-up practice, to get them meetings with venture capital firms in Silicon Valley, New York, Boston, Toronto, and Washington, DC. Their road show ultimately netted an offer from Fairhaven in Boston. Unfortunately, neither of them understood how much control venture firms expect in exchange for their money and were dismayed when, in reviewing the term sheet, they discovered that the firm would control a majority of the seats on the *Caller*'s board of directors and would require an audit committee and a management committee to oversee the company. They told themselves that they would sign the term sheet if absolutely necessary, but they wanted to make one more attempt to find a deep-pocketed conservative benefactor.

Through a Cheney connection, Patel was able to get himself and Carlson a meeting with Foster Friess, a Wyoming businessman and Republican megadonor who was friendly with the former vice president. Over lunch at Friess's private club in Jackson Hole, Carlson and Patel made their pitch for the *Caller*; they explained that they had an offer from a venture capital firm but were reluctant to accept it because of its terms. Friess was a deeply eccentric man who loathed bureaucracy and embraced an unorthodox management style: His investment firm famously held its rare staff meetings in rooms without chairs to keep them as short as possible. Fifteen minutes into the meal, he'd heard enough. He told Carlson and Patel that he'd agree to invest the same amount of money into the *Caller* as the venture capital firm, except he didn't want any of the controls the firm had demanded; his only stipulation was that Carlson and Patel go hunting with him once a year. "I don't want to run your lives," he told the pair. He backed the *Caller*, he explained a few months later, because he believed that "Tucker and Neil present a huge opportunity to re-introduce civility to our political discourse. . . . They want to make a contribution to the dialogue that occurs in our country that has become too antagonistic, nasty and hostile."

Carlson and Patel left Jackson Hole with a three-million-dollar equity investment. Now, back in Washington, they just needed to hire a staff. Carlson's CPAC speech had piqued the interest of conservative journalists who were searching for a place where they could do good, substantive work that wasn't unduly influenced by the political or business considerations of their bosses. One of them was Jon Ward.

A *Washington Times* reporter in his early thirties, Ward was raised in the Maryland suburbs of Washington, DC, in an evangelical family and church community that was largely isolated from mainstream popular culture and politics, save for attending the annual antiabortion March for Life on the National Mall and listening to Rush Limbaugh during car rides. In his early twenties, after graduating from the University of Maryland and becoming a reporter, he grew apart from his church; while he remained a Christian (and a Republican), journalism—and its objective pursuit of truth—became, in some ways, his new faith. During his eight years at *The Washington Times*, Ward rose from an unpaid intern on the paper's metro desk (who moonlighted as a waiter at a Macaroni Grill) to White House correspondent, traveling the country and the world on Air Force One with Bush and Obama. But *The Washington Times* could be a hard place for a serious journalist, even a conservative one, to work. Its owner was the Korean cult leader and self-proclaimed messiah Sun Myung Moon, who boasted that his paper was "the instrument in spreading the truth about God to the world," and its editor was Wesley Pruden, who described Hillary Clinton as "everybody's candidate for bitch-in-chief."

Carlson was a fan of Ward's reporting. He was particularly impressed that, despite *The Washington Times*'s baggage, Ward was respected by his mainstream-media colleagues and the people he covered, including those in the Obama White House. Carlson believed that a reporter like Ward would lend legitimacy to a new conservative publication like the *Caller*, maybe even get the *Caller* a seat in the White House briefing room, and he began recruiting him. Carlson's pitch was essentially the same one he made at CPAC—that the *Caller* would demonstrate how conservatives could reform the media. He told Ward that he would leverage his own media celebrity to get Ward's stories—and Ward himself—more attention. To sweeten the pot further, he offered Ward ninety thousand dollars a year, which would make him the highest-paid *Caller* employee. Ward didn't need much more convincing than that. "It was going to be new media, it was going to be online, I was going to get paid more, and it was going to be legit," Ward recalled. "It was just a really good place to land."

The *Caller* continued to staff up in preparation for its January 2010 launch. Over breakfasts at the Metropolitan Club and lunches at the Hay-Adams, Carlson flattered, charmed, and cajoled a parade of mostly twentysomething reporters and editors from alternative papers, trade publications, and conservative think tanks to come work for him. And it wasn't just conservatives. Megan Mulligan, a well-regarded editor in the Washington bureau of *The Guardian*, the lefty British newspaper, succumbed to Carlson's entreaties and became the *Caller*'s executive editor.

Carlson turned to his impressive Rolodex for additional help. Matt Labash agreed to write the *Caller*'s advice column, and the notorious Republican dirty trickster (and notorious dandy) Roger

Stone signed up to be its fashion critic. After its launch, Ginni Thomas, the wife of Supreme Court justice Clarence Thomas, became a special correspondent for the *Caller*. Carlson even mended fences with Grover Norquist—going hat in hand to one of Norquist's Wednesday meetings to drum up interest in the *Caller* among members of the Leave Us Alone Coalition. "That was then," Carlson said of the time he poured a Bloody Mary on Norquist's head. "I'm not into having enemies." For advice on how to run a newsroom of twenty people, Carlson sought out the counsel of his old boss at *The Weekly Standard*. "I want to be like Bill Kristol in the way I manage people," Carlson said. "He's the perfect combination of supportive and smart, and is always throwing out interesting ideas, if you care to take him up on them, but also very much hands off. He's the best boss I've ever had."

As Carlson talked up the *Caller* in the months before its launch, he cast himself as a prodigal son. After a decade spent wasting his talents in cable news—spouting loud and glib opinions that, if they weren't actually hurting America, certainly weren't helping it—he was returning to the world of serious, substantive journalism, which was in dire straits. It was an all-hands-on-deck situation, and he wanted to help however he could. "We think that with the crisis in the news business, particularly with daily newspapers, there are fewer people covering really more stories," Carlson said, sounding like a program officer at a goo-goo nonprofit. "There's a lot to write about, a lot to probe, and fewer people to do it, so we're going to add some people to the mix." He promised "lots of original and, I hope, hard-nosed reporting. More facts." Seemingly cribbing from the mission statement his old protégé Rachel Maddow crafted for her now-thriving MSNBC show—"try to increase the amount of useful information in the world"—Carlson's goal for the *Caller* was to publish "stories that add to the sum total of known facts about politics and government."

The excitement for, and goodwill toward, the *Caller* that Carlson was able to generate among Washington's chattering class was considerable. On a Tuesday evening in January 2010, eleven months after Carlson was heckled by a sparse crowd at CPAC and one day after the *Caller*'s website went live, nearly three hundred people packed into a Kalorama mansion to fete Carlson and his new endeavor. The mansion belonged to Juleanna Glover, a Republican lobbyist and Washington's preeminent hostess ("You haven't made it in D.C. until hostess Juleanna Glover throws a party for you," *Politico* wrote). The tab was being picked up by the US Chamber of Commerce and a couple of trade groups. And the guest list included Paul Begala, David Frum, Savannah Guthrie, Stephen Hayes, Christopher Hitchens, Scooter Libby, Jake Tapper, and scores of other famous-for-DC types. As women in French-maid outfits passed hors d'oeuvres and a man dressed up as Napoleon poured vodka shots, Carlson, clutching a glass of ice water and looking happier than he had in years, greeted the throngs of well-wishers.

"It hasn't been a big month for sleeping," Carlson said in a toast. "The launch has been an adventure. Ten years from now, when virtually all news is delivered digitally online and there are hundreds of sites doing pretty much exactly what we do, I'm sure we'll have competitors. As of today, we have only friends." Then Carlson and Glover's dog, a brown-and-white terrier named Popper Popcorn, both let out long celebratory howls.

THE *CALLER*'S OFFICES WERE JUST a block from the White House in a building that, until recently, had been occupied by the back end of a bank. Leaning into the publication's online identity, Carlson and Patel tried to give the space the feel of a Silicon Valley start-up, outfitting it with the requisite Ping-Pong table and permitting employees to bring their pets to work. But the *Caller* ended up having more of "a frat house vibe," as one staffer described it. Carlson assured his charges, some of whom were underage interns from local colleges or conservative think tanks, that no one would be checking IDs at the office kegerator. He wanted to allow smoking on the premises, as well, until the landlords informed him it was prohibited. "As long as you do your work, and work as hard as you can," Carlson told *Caller* employees, "if you come to work wearing a chicken costume, it's not my business."

Befitting the *Animal House* atmosphere, Carlson was a big fan of pranks. Not long after the *Caller* launched, it purchased for four hundred dollars the domain keitholbermann.com and set up a keith@keitholbermann.com email address, splashing a big picture of Carlson's old MSNBC persecutor on its home page under the headline "WE OWN YOU." In a blog post, Carlson explained, "We plan to make *The Daily Caller* the one-stop online shop for Keith Olbermann commentary. . . . We will be THE Keith Olbermann superstore."

The prank might have petered out there, if not for the *Philadelphia Daily News* columnist Stu Bykofsky, who, after Olbermann was suspended by MSNBC president Phil Griffin for making campaign contributions to three Democratic candidates in the 2010 midterms, emailed Olbermann seeking comment. The heated response Bykofsky received read, in part: "I could have Phil Griffin fired tomorrow if I felt like it, trust me. And if he keeps yapping about me in public, I may. For the moment, however, keeping Phil around is like having a drunk chimp in the office—more amusing than threatening." Bykofsky gave the response to a Philadelphia gossip website, which reprinted it in full. It was only after Olbermann denied that he'd sent the emails to Bykofsky that Bykofsky's mistake was discovered. Apparently not a big reader of *The Daily Caller*, he'd emailed keith@keitholbermann.com. Carlson fessed up that he'd sent the response posing as Olbermann. "Could you resist?" he said. "It was just too funny. The flesh is weak."

Kegerator and pranks notwithstanding, the *Caller* in its early days was a pretty straightforward, even conventional, news site. Ward, who did in fact secure the *Caller* a seat in the White House briefing room, aggressively but fairly covered Obama, producing wonky stories about the administration falling short of its transparency pledges and its struggles to pass health care reform. Chris Moody, who'd previously worked at the libertarian Cato Institute, tackled Capitol Hill, writing about Congressional Budget Office reports on federal deficits and partisan squabbling over the defense-spending bill. And Alex Pappas, a recent Sewanee grad who came to the *Caller* from the *Mobile Register* in Alabama, went all in on reporting about the still new but rapidly growing Tea Party movement; Pappas was less reflexively hostile toward the conservative activists than reporters at, say, *The Washington Post* and *The New York Times*, but his stories were hardly puff pieces, as he shined a harsh light on the profiteering and grifting that plagued some Tea Party groups. Carlson helmed the 8:30 a.m. editorial meeting every morning, but overseeing the newsroom was Mulligan, an exacting editor who pressed her reporters to double and triple source their work. The *Caller* was delivering on Carlson's simple promise of "more facts."

The problem was, those facts weren't getting many readers. During the *Caller*'s launch, traffic was impressive, with the site receiving more visitors on its first day than it had predicted in its pitch to venture capital firms that it would receive in its first month. But that didn't continue. "There was this curiosity spike about 'what does Tucker Carlson's website look like?'" said Mike Riggs, who wrote the *Caller*'s morning newsletter. "And then within a week it fucking flatlined. And we weren't writing enough, and we weren't fast enough, and our copy wasn't engaging enough."

Carlson became fixated on one solution to the *Caller*'s traffic woes: getting links from Matt Drudge. The Drudge Report, of course, had become the preeminent political tip sheet twelve years earlier, when it revealed that *Newsweek* had spiked its story about Bill Clinton's affair with Monica Lewinsky. It drove more web traffic than Facebook and Twitter combined. Unfortunately for Carlson, Drudge apparently hated him. The source of Drudge's animus was a bit of a mystery. Some people speculated it was because Carlson once, in a cable-news aside, had made reference to the fact that Drudge, who was intensely private bordering on paranoid, lived in Miami; others thought it was because Drudge, who is assumed to be gay (although he has repeatedly denied it), was turned off by Carlson's homophobia. Whatever the reason, Drudge refused to link to any *Daily Caller* stories.

Caller reporters, and Carlson himself, flooded Drudge's AOL inbox with links to stories. No bites. Carlson asked Ann Coulter, a longtime Drudge friend, to arrange a sit-down between the two. She either wouldn't or couldn't. At one point, Carlson went to a Starbucks in suburban Virginia to meet with Joseph Curl, a former *Washington Times* reporter who was the Drudge Report's morning editor. There, Carlson proposed a business relationship—"non-publicized," he hastened to add—in which the *Caller* would pay the Drudge Report for links. "[Curl] looked at me like it was an FBI sting operation," Carlson later recalled to Moody, for a 2024 podcast about Drudge, "like I was trying to entrap him or something." Curl turned him down.

About three months after the *Caller*'s launch, Jonathan Strong wrote a story that Carlson hoped might finally tempt Drudge. Strong was a young journalist who'd arrived at the *Caller* from a trade publication that covered the EPA. He was a solid reporter, and after a few articles about some internal regulatory matters at the EPA that he was proud of but that left

Carlson cold, he had a scoop that both he and his boss agreed was a blockbuster. Digging through the Republican National Committee's federal filings for a story about the committee's spending, Strong came across an entry for an expenditure of nearly two thousand dollars at a West Hollywood business called Voyeur. "'Voyeur West Hollywood' is very intriguing as a reporter," Strong said. "I thought, 'What is that?'" A Google search told him it was a bondage-themed nightclub featuring topless female dancers. "I remember jumping up and down in my apartment," he said. "I was like, 'This is going to be gold.'"

The RNC's chairman at the time was Michael Steele. Steele, who is Black, got the job shortly after Obama's election with the promise to run an "off the hook" public relations campaign that would make the GOP more popular in "urban-suburban hip-hop settings." He was wildly unpopular with the Tea Party and conservative activists; Limbaugh attacked him as "gutless." Strong's article, which revealed that the RNC under Steele had spent money at Voyeur, as well as tens of thousands of dollars on private air travel, limousines, and "chic and costly hotels," gave Steele's critics additional ammunition. "You nailed him," Carlson told Strong. It also gave the *Caller* the most traffic it had had in its first three months. "I was writing for twenty people about the EPA's Office of Water, and then one of my stories was on all three cable channels," Strong marveled. But, much to his and Carlson's dismay, Drudge did not end up linking to the story.

Still, the episode made an impression on Carlson. He was constantly urging his reporters to be less afraid of writing stories that generated blowback. He told them, "If you're riling people up, while being accurate, you're doing something right." Moody went so far as to write those words down on a piece of paper and tape it to his computer. Strong needed no such reminders or encouragement. Steele and the RNC were furious over his story—especially the incorrect implication that Steele himself had gone to the bondage-themed nightclub; the excursion was made by underlings—and Carlson was impressed that Strong didn't seem bothered at all by their vitriol. That's why Carlson decided to enlist Strong to work on what, he hoped, would be an even splashier story.

One of the worst-kept secrets in political journalism in 2010 was an ostensibly secret email listserv called JournoList. Created three years earlier and run by Ezra Klein, who was then a young, liberal, and ambitious blogger for *The Washington Post*, JournoList was an invitation-only, off-the-record Google Groups forum comprised of more than four hundred primarily lefty reporters and columnists, as well as academics and think tankers, discussing politics and media. But it wasn't all liberals. In addition to the presence of a number of objective, nonideological journalists, JournoList even boasted a few closeted conservative members—including a *Daily Caller* reporter named Gautham Nagesh. Nagesh, who joined JournoList when he worked at the nonpartisan *Government Executive* magazine, frequently regaled the *Caller* newsroom with hints about the supposedly hair-raising things that were being discussed on the listserv and the vast left-wing media conspiracy they revealed. "He would not talk in detail about what was going on, but according to him, it was really bad," Strong said. "Like, 'If you guys only knew about what they were talking about, you'd be appalled.' He acted like it was a big scandal that was waiting to be uncovered."

Carlson was intrigued. He asked Nagesh for details—or, even better, to give him access to the listserv. Nagesh demurred. Carlson then approached Klein about becoming a member of JournoList. "Dear Ezra," Carlson wrote in an email, "I keep hearing about how smart the policy conversations on JournoList are, and am starting to feel like I'm missing out by not reading them. Could I join?" He encouraged Klein to ask around about him; he was sure people would vouch for him. Klein was inclined to grant Carlson's membership request—"We definitely have friends in common, and I'd have no worries about you joining," he replied—but he wanted to put the question to JournoList's other members. They voted it down. Klein broke the bad news to Carlson, asking if he'd be interested in working together to create a bipartisan list. Carlson never answered.

Perhaps that was because Carlson was already on to a different scheme. He recalled from his days in Little Rock a liberal Arkansas political reporter named Max Brantley, who'd developed a bit of a national following. Then, according to a former *Caller* staffer, Carlson created an email account, maxmbrantley@yahoo.com, and sent Klein a note. "Dear Ezra," the email read, "It's Max Brantley, editor of the Arkansas Times, the progressive weekly in Little Rock. Joe Klein"—the then-*Time* columnist who is not related to Ezra—"has piqued my interest in JournoList, and said you're the one to talk to about joining. I'd love to. Best, Max." Klein granted maxmbrantley@yahoo.com membership, giving Carlson access not just to current JournoList discussions, but the listserv's archives, as well.

Those archives contained tens of thousands of emails dating back to 2007. To comb through them, Carlson turned to Strong. He tasked the young reporter, still riding the high of his Steele story, to come up with an even bigger scoop. ("I don't want to take credit for it," Strong said of the *Caller*'s JournoList reporting. "Tucker is the one who secured the leak of it.") For the next week, Strong disappeared from the *Caller*'s offices. Working from his apartment, sometimes with the help of his wife, he put in twenty-hour days reading the JournoList archives, searching for evidence of a liberal-media conspiracy. It was relatively slim pickings. But amid the earnest and often tedious discussions about health care reform and the US troop surge in Afghanistan,

Strong did find a few things that tickled Carlson's fancy. First among them were a handful of emails from Dave Weigel, who blogged about the conservative movement for *The Washington Post*. In the emails, Weigel made nasty and untoward remarks about various prominent conservatives: Pat Buchanan was "an anti-Semite"; Newt Gingrich was "an amoral blowhard"; when Rush Limbaugh was hospitalized with chest pains, Weigel wrote, "I hope he fails. Too soon?"

In late June, the *Caller* published Strong's story about Weigel's JournoList contributions. Under the headline "E-mails reveal *Post* reporter savaging conservatives, rooting for Democrats," Strong wrote that the emails betrayed "a personal animus toward conservatives" by the person whom the *Post* had hired "to cover the conservative movement." Strong's article did not mention that most of Weigel's JournoList emails were written before he worked at the *Post*, nor did it mention that Weigel had once worked for the libertarian *Reason* magazine and cast a presidential vote for Ron Paul—two data points that don't suggest hatred of conservatives. But it was still a fairly clean, straightforward hit—Weigel wrote what he wrote—and the article became an instant sensation. Klein immediately disbanded JournoList, while Weigel apologized and resigned from the *Post*. (He was soon hired by *Slate* and, five years later, would be rehired by the *Post*. Today he writes for *Semafor* and is one of the best political reporters in the country.) The *Caller*'s scoop was covered not just by conservative media and Fox News, but by the other two cable networks and *The New York Times*, as well. Not surprisingly, the article broke the *Caller*'s traffic records.

Perhaps most important, Strong's Weigel scoop earned the *Caller* the first of what would eventually be hundreds of links from the Drudge Report, which sent so many readers to the JournoList story that the *Caller*'s website eventually crashed.

What finally moved Drudge to shine his beneficent light upon the *Caller* was unknowable; Drudge moves in mysterious ways. But it couldn't have hurt that, in his story, Strong had included a JournoList email from Weigel that read: "It's really a disgrace that an amoral shut-in like Drudge maintains the influence he does on the news cycle while gay-baiting, lying, and flubbing facts to this degree."

Shortly before the *Caller* pressed publish on Strong's Weigel story, Carlson summoned its staff to a meeting. The JournoList project had been a closely guarded secret inside the *Caller* offices; not even Mulligan knew about it (much less about the underhanded means by which Carlson had secured access). As Carlson told the staff about Strong's forthcoming article, he could barely contain his enthusiasm. He was giddy about the scoop and the traffic it would bring. But then Carlson's tone turned somber. When the *Caller* launched just six months earlier, he'd boasted, "I don't really have any enemies." But now he said that the JournoList story was going to make the *Caller* enemies. "People are going to hate you," he warned his staff. "Be prepared." "I think Tucker was sensitive to the fact that he had a whole stable of young reporters with big dreams in his office who might struggle in the future if they were associated with this," Moody said. "He wanted to make sure we knew what was coming."

Strong followed up his Weigel story with nine additional articles about JournoList. The series featured fairly thin gruel. It quoted opinion writers and reporters for avowedly liberal publications, like *The Nation* and *The New Republic*, rejoicing over Obama's election and bellyaching about what they considered unfair coverage of him or obscure liberal bloggers saying something intemperate about conservatives or NASCAR fans. Occasionally one of the JournoList members would issue some sort of urgent call to action, which, with one exception—a public letter complaining about questions asked by ABC News during a Democratic presidential primary debate that was signed by forty-one of the listserv's members—were never acted upon. The series made no mention of the fact that a *Caller* staffer belonged to JournoList or that Klein had tried to grant Carlson membership. But the *Caller* articles nonetheless painted JournoList as the hub of a media conspiracy to get Obama elected with headlines like "Documents show media plotting to kill stories about Rev. Jeremiah Wright" and "When McCain picked Palin, liberal journalists coordinated the best line of attack." As Carlson, who not so long ago had blasted conservatives for their "contempt for journalists," put it during an appearance on a conservative talk radio show to plug the series: "We've discovered that all of the worst preconceptions you ever had about the liberal media, all the kind of foaming, conservative conspiracy theories about how they were in league against Republicans, they're all true."

That sort of talk naturally didn't sit well with liberals. And Carlson's warning to his staff proved true: The JournoList series did make the *Caller* an object of hatred on the left. "I've never dealt with someone who was quite so opportunistically mendacious as Carlson was here," Klein complained to the *Columbia Journalism Review*. *Caller* staffers certainly felt the chill. "When he did the CPAC speech, I think people were pretty open to the *Daily Caller* and the idea of the *Daily Caller* had some potential liberal acceptance," Strong said. "And then the JournoList stories very much cemented the idea that the *Daily Caller* is the enemy."

What's more, it wasn't just liberals who now held the *Caller* in low regard because of its JournoList series. Many objective journalists did, too—recognizing a puffed-up story when they saw one. The coin of the realm in political journalism in 2010 was *Politico*'s *Playbook* newsletter, an early-morning email tip sheet that was authored by Mike Allen, a veteran political reporter whom *The New York Times Magazine*, in a profile, dubbed "the man the White House wakes up to." Carlson had long been chummy with Allen. Before the *Caller*'s launch, Allen and *Politico*'s other top brass "couldn't have been nicer, offering all sorts of advice, no trade secrets or anything, but just welcoming," Carlson said. Once the *Caller* got going, *Playbook* gave *Caller* stories copious mentions, which didn't deliver the same amount of traffic as a Drudge link, but carried far more prestige. But after the JournoList series, the Playbook mentions dried up. When Strong published a subsequent scoop about Minnesota congresswoman and Tea Party darling Michele Bachmann suffering debilitating migraines, throwing into question her presidential candidacy, *Politico* reassigned the story to a couple of its reporters to "confirm" it and described the *Caller* as "a conservative online publication."

Carlson was both livid about and hurt by the snubs. He ordered that the *Caller*'s house style be changed so that *Politico* was described as "a liberal publication based in suburban Virginia," before eventually abandoning the idea, and assigned a reporter to document the many times *Politico* reporters appeared on MSNBC as proof of its "left-of-center bias." When Allen stopped by to say hello to Carlson, Carlson's son, Buckley, and some *Caller* reporters at a New Hampshire restaurant on the eve of that state's presidential primary, Carlson told Allen that the next day was Buckley's fifteenth birthday and how nice it would be if Allen mentioned it in *Playbook*. Allen assured him he would. Once Allen, who also picked up the *Caller* table's dinner tab, was out of earshot, Carlson told his staffers that Buckley's birthday was in fact two weeks away. "Tucker was just fucking with *Politico*," one of them said. "All of us were laughing." They laughed some more the next morning when they saw Buckley's name in *Playbook*. And Carlson, at least, had an annual residual laugh for the next eight years before *Politico* finally caught the error.

But being the enemy of liberals and the mainstream media certainly had its advantages. In July, when the *Caller* published the bulk of its JournoList series, it enjoyed its best traffic month to date with 1.35 million unique visitors—almost three times as many unique visitors as it had in its first month. Carlson was exquisitely attuned to these sorts of metrics. The *Caller* was an early client of the "content intelligence" company Chartbeat, which offered real-time web analytics about the site. Chartbeat tracked, among other things, which articles were being read the most at any given moment, where those readers came from, and how long those readers stayed. Chartbeat's constantly updating statistics were displayed on a giant television in the *Caller*'s newsroom that was strategically placed so that Carlson had a direct view of it from his office. If his view was ever blocked, or if he wasn't in the office, he'd look at Chartbeat's dashboard on his laptop.

Carlson soon detected a common thread that ran through the *Caller*'s most popular articles. They obviously weren't the sober, straightforward stories that were adding to the sum total of known facts about politics and government. But they weren't necessarily the more partisan stories—ones that reflected or advocated a conservative worldview—either. Rather, the most popular *Caller* stories fell into a third category. They were stories that, in addition to appealing to conservatives, actively antagonized liberals. Those were the articles that earned Drudge links, went viral, and drew millions of readers. And those were the stories that Carlson now craved from his staff. "The thing that Tucker valued most of all," Riggs said, "was a person's willingness to write something that would make liberals mad."

Matt Boyle was more than willing. A graduate student at American University in Washington, DC, he'd applied—and been rejected—for internships at *Politico*, CNN, even the

Washington City Paper. When he interviewed with Carlson and Patel at the *Caller* in the fall of 2010, Patel asked him what his politics were. "Whatever you want them to be," Boyle replied. He got the internship. It wasn't hard to see why the other media outlets had turned up their noses at Boyle. Doughy and baby faced, he was socially awkward in the extreme—as a child he'd been diagnosed with a nonverbal learning disability, which made it difficult for him to read body language or tone of voice—and seemed to subsist on a diet of Mountain Dew and Marlboro Lights.

But what Boyle lacked in polish he more than made up for in aggressiveness. He proved to be a relentless reporter. When a whistleblower accused Eric Holder, Obama's attorney general, of trying to cover up a federal gun-trafficking investigation called Operation Fast and Furious that had allowed guns to fall into the hands of criminals, Boyle began going to members of Congress, one by one, to ask them if Holder should resign; he would threaten congressional spokespeople for Democrats that if they didn't respond to his query about Holder by his deadline, he would report that their boss no longer supported the attorney general. This resulted in a lengthy series of articles with headlines like "35 congressmen now calling for Holder's resignation," "At least 36 members of Congress want Holder's immediate resignation," and "Two more Congressmen demand Eric Holder's immediate resignation, 46 now calling for it." Democratic flacks accused Boyle of blackmail, and Holder complained that Boyle was manufacturing a scandal. "It's not an organic thing that's just happening," Holder lectured another *Caller* reporter. "You guys are behind it." But Carlson loved Boyle's stories—and the traffic they brought. He told colleagues that Tea Party media stars like Dana Loesch spoke to him about Boyle in "hushed tones." Before long Carlson promoted Boyle to a full-time reporter and the erstwhile intern dropped out of grad school.

Boyle's aggressiveness often crossed over into recklessness. He wrote one article claiming that the Environmental Protection Agency was "asking for taxpayers to shoulder the burden" of hiring "up to 230,000 new bureaucrats," at a cost of $21 billion, to regulate greenhouse gas emissions as part of the Clean Air Act. The seemingly blockbuster scoop—the EPA at the time had 17,000 employees and an $8.7 billion budget—went viral, earning a Drudge link and segments on Fox News. But the article was inaccurate. Boyle had misinterpreted an EPA court filing that cited those numbers as a worst-case outcome that the agency explicitly sought to avoid. When an EPA spokesman called out Boyle for his "comically wrong" article, the *Caller* refused to concede the error, with its executive editor arguing that "the EPA is well-known for expanding its reach."

Boyle's investigation into Democratic senator Bob Menendez of New Jersey was an even bigger journalistic disaster. In the run-up to the 2012 elections, the *Caller* was one of several media outlets, including *The Washington Post* and ABC News, chasing a story being shopped by Republican operatives that the scandal-plagued Menendez had hired prostitutes during visits to the Dominican Republic. Reporters at those other outlets eventually concluded that the story was false—or, at the very least, that they couldn't confirm it—and abandoned their pursuit. But Boyle persevered. A week before the election, he informed Carlson that he had nailed Menendez; Carlson in turn excitedly alerted Drudge, with whom he'd achieved a détente, that the *Caller* would imminently be sending him a blockbuster story that could upend the New Jersey senate race.

But when Carlson began to edit Boyle's article, he was dismayed to discover how thin it was. Boyle had interviewed over Skype two anonymous Dominican women who, through a translator provided by the women's attorney, alleged that a man that they said they later recognized as Menendez had paid them for sex. Boyle had no corroboration for their claims. It was awfully meager reporting on which to hang such a fantastic charge; indeed, ABC had interviewed the same two women before ultimately dropping the story "because of doubts about the women's veracity and identity." But Carlson felt that, at that point, he had no choice but to run Boyle's article. "Drudge was the business, basically," a former *Caller* staffer said. "Better to just publish than risk pissing off Drudge."

Boyle's story did great traffic, but it had no impact on the New Jersey Senate race, which Menendez won five days later in a cakewalk. And while Menendez would later be convicted in 2024 on federal bribery and corruption charges for acting as an agent for the Egyptian government, the FBI investigated the Dominican Republic prostitution allegations and found no evidence for them. One of the Dominican women interviewed by Boyle later claimed in an affidavit that she and the other woman were paid by a local lawyer to make up the allegations in an effort to frame Menendez, whom she'd never met. And *The Washington Post* later reported that the CIA had obtained "credible evidence" that, while the prostitution story was shopped to media outlets by GOP operatives, it actually originated with agents working for the Cuban government, who hoped to damage Menendez, a staunch supporter of the US embargo against Fidel Castro's regime.

These and other misfires by Boyle were a source of great consternation among many *Caller* staffers, who frequently complained to Carlson about their problematic colleague. Carlson didn't disagree with—and would sometimes join—them when they lampooned Boyle's appearance and mannerisms. A former *Caller* staffer told *Washingtonian* that, behind Boyle's back, Carlson "would make fun of him and say that he had Asperger's." Still, Carlson liked to say that he viewed staffing the *Caller* as akin to casting a sitcom or a reality show—and that there was always a slot for a "crazy person." "The *Daily Caller* was Tucker's menagerie," a former *Caller* staffer said. "That was the guiding principle for hiring: These are such weird people. What would happen if we put them all in one room together?" With his desk covered in Mountain Dew dead soldiers and his penchant to type so violently that he sometimes damaged his keyboard, even Boyle's harshest critics at the *Caller* had to admit that he added to the newsroom's madcap entertainment value.

But Carlson refused to countenance their criticism of Boyle's journalism. In the summer of 2011, he invited Jonathan Strong to his vacation home in Maine. Like many of the *Caller*'s early employees, Strong had gone to work there in large part because of Carlson's CPAC speech. "I felt like conservatives needed people who did real, straight news," he said. He believed—justifiably—that he was doing just that at the *Caller*. Even his JournoList series was, in his mind, perhaps a little exaggerated but ultimately newsworthy. He did not feel the same way about Boyle's work. As he and Carlson sat in a canoe fishing for smallmouth bass, he took the opportunity to tell Carlson that he believed Boyle was taking the *Caller* away from Carlson's original vision for it. "I really laid into him," Strong recalled. Carlson did not appreciate it. "He got pretty pissed at me," Strong said. "I can still see his face. He was unhappy." When another *Caller* staffer lamented to Carlson that Boyle was hurting the *Caller*'s credibility, Carlson shot back, "The story he filed yesterday got a million views. When was the last time you wrote a story that a million people read?" On another occasion, Mike Riggs told Carlson that he thought one of Boyle's error-plagued stories "crossed the line." "There is no line. The line is fake," Carlson replied. "They impose the line to put you in place. The sooner you stop believing in the line, the better off you'll be."

Perhaps no *Caller* reporter was more concerned about the site's diminishing credibility than Jon Ward. Even before Boyle's arrival, Ward feared that his publication was heading in the wrong direction. The JournoList stories were "a demarcation for the *Caller*," he said. "It was like a signal that read, 'Hey, this is not what I signed up for.'" And it wasn't just the work of other *Caller* reporters that troubled him; increasingly it was his own.

A couple of months after the JournoList series earned the *Caller* a traffic windfall, Ward scored what appeared to be his own major scoop—one that he hoped would please Carlson, who'd begun teasing him that he had a "nose for the boring." Ward wrote a story accusing *National Review* of colluding with John Boehner, the House minority leader, to drum up support for House Republicans' legislative blueprint; in it, he quoted two anonymous "high-level Republican sources" who alleged that the venerable conservative publication wrote an editorial, which one of them described as "a political blowjob," endorsing the agenda in exchange for receiving an advance copy of it. The article was very inside baseball reporting, but in the Tea Party–infused tenor of the times, when right-wing Republicans were livid that the House GOP's blueprint didn't include a ban on earmarks or a promise to pass a balanced-budget amendment, it was red meat for dissatisfied conservatives.

It was also a source of irritation for *National Review*. The magazine's editor, Rich Lowry, cried foul, denying that there was any sort of quid pro quo. He called Ward and vehemently protested. Ward told Carlson about Lowry's protest, and Carlson called Lowry. The two editors had a heated conversation—so heated that almost everyone in the *Caller*'s office overheard Carlson's end of it. At one point, Carlson shouted at Lowry, "Fuck you!" (Carlson later regaled the *Caller*'s staff by informing them that Lowry's retort was "Did you just say, 'Eff you?!'") Carlson told Lowry that the *Caller* stood by the story and that there would be no corrections.

Initially, Ward was gratified that Carlson had his back. What reporter doesn't want an editor who tells someone complaining about a story to eff himself? But as Ward thought more about Lowry's objections to his article, he began to fear that they had merit. Neither of the two "high-level Republican sources" who alleged the quid pro quo was actually in a position to know. What's more, both had obvious ideological axes to grind against House GOP leadership and *National Review*. "It was that time in journalism where you could kind of play fast and loose with sourcing," Ward recalled. "And a journalist like me, who was young and able to kind of get around the Hill and talk to people, could make hay." His story, he ultimately concluded, "was pretty much bullshit."

Ward found himself ruminating on the direction he wanted his career, and his life, to take. "I think anybody who was doing daily journalism at that time was actually getting a crash course in the incentive structure that every single human being on Earth now has to deal with," he said. "Which is: Do you put stuff online that's hyped up and provocative so that you can get attention? Or do you actually take a sense of responsibility?" He concluded that he wanted to do the latter, which he believed would be impossible at the *Caller*. In February 2011, a little more than a year after the *Caller*'s launch, Ward resigned and soon took a job at *The Huffington Post* covering the 2012 Republican presidential primaries.

WARD'S DEPARTURE KICKED OFF A mini exodus from the *Caller*, as many of the site's original crew soon followed him out the door. Riggs quit to work at *Reason*. Mulligan took a job training journalists in Tunisia. Moody went to *Yahoo! News*. And Strong defected to *Roll Call*. Carlson was not unhappy about any of this. Publicly, he could portray the *Caller* as a talent incubator and launching pad—and take credit for his former staffers' future successes. Privately, he was excited for the opportunity to hire a new group of reporters and editors who were more aligned with his evolving vision for the *Caller*—a website that would be less about facts and more about feelings, less about analysis and more about provocations. A website that wouldn't just be more financially successful but would be more in keeping with the increasingly brutish nature of American politics.

To replace Ward as White House correspondent, Carlson tapped Neil Munro, an almost comically belligerent former science journalist who quickly endeared himself (and the *Caller*) to conservative readers when he interrupted an Obama speech about immigration in the Rose Garden by shouting at the president, "Why do you favor foreign workers over Americans?" Caroline May, an intern who became a full-time reporter, covered immigration, developing a close journalist-source relationship with Stephen Miller, a young aide to Alabama Republican senator Jeff Sessions, who fed her a steady stream of stories about the perfidy of immigrants and their deleterious effects on the United States. (A representative headline from a May article: "Illegal immigrants leave tons of trash in Arizona desert, devastating environment.") And Patrick Howley, a volatile young college dropout who came from *The American Spectator*, assumed the role of gender-wars correspondent, proudly waving the flag for male chauvinism. "Women are like Indians now," Howley wrote in one dispatch. "Pretty soon, looking at a woman's chest will legally be a 'hate' crime instead of a love crime."

At the same time, the *Caller* developed an intense focus on—and stoked fears about—Black-on-white crime. Trayvon Martin, the unarmed Black teenager who was fatally shot by a neighborhood watch volunteer in Florida in 2012, was a recurring character on the site. In one story, the *Caller* reported that a white man in Alabama was beaten by a mob of nearly two dozen Black teenagers seeking revenge for Martin's killing. (Law enforcement officials later said that only one person was involved in the assault and that it started after the victim used a racial slur.) In another article, the *Caller* published the occasionally obscene and juvenile contents of Martin's closed Twitter account, seemingly in order to muddy the dead teen's image. "I was struck by the immediate, uncloaked assumption by the media that Trayvon Martin was innocent," Carlson explained. "Of course we got attacked and people said we were racist, but I didn't care."

All the while, the *Caller*'s traffic continued to grow. After a year and a half, the site was getting more than three million unique visitors a month. Foster Friess decided to re-up his investment. While some conservative sites, including *FrumForum*, were folding, Patel was projecting that his site would be profitable in 2012. The *Caller* was extraordinarily mindful of what conservatives wanted to read, and it was committed to delivering it. "Subscription publications are very distant from the consumer because the reporters and editors sit at headquarters and write articles that they each think the readers will be interested in," Munro, who'd worked at the print *National Journal* before going to the *Caller*, explained two months after he heckled Obama. "In the online world, we know precisely what they're interested in. We feel the hits. Which means we're in much closer contact with our readers."

The *Caller*'s formula was proving such a success that other conservative websites began copying it—none more than *Breitbart News*. *Breitbart News* was founded in 2007 by Andrew Breitbart, an Internet savant who worked for Matt Drudge on the Drudge Report and then helped Arianna Huffington launch *The Huffington Post* before starting his own network of sites. Breitbart called himself a "reluctant culture warrior," but there was nothing shy and retiring about him. After a dissolute and relatively liberal youth, he was radicalized in his early twenties by Clarence Thomas's Supreme Court confirmation hearings, and he became a brash and outspoken conservative. "I realized

I liked being hated more than I liked being liked—that's when the game began," he said. He believed that "politics is downstream from culture," and his websites that operated under the *Breitbart* banner—*Big Government*, *Big Hollywood*, and *Big Journalism*—waged a ferocious, oftentimes underhanded battle against the citadels of liberal power.

Breitbart News brought down New York Democratic congressman Anthony Weiner by exposing the sexually explicit messages Weiner sent to young women over Twitter. The site also posted a video of Shirley Sherrod, an obscure Black US Department of Agriculture official, that was misleadingly edited to make it appear that Sherrod had discriminated against white farmers, when in fact she'd worked to help them. (Sherrod, who was forced to resign from her USDA job before the dishonest edits were exposed, subsequently sued *Breitbart News* for libel. The lawsuit was settled on confidential terms.) Breitbart put himself at the center of the sites, generating many of their articles by either writing them or featuring prominently in them; most of their other content came from unpaid bloggers and aggregated wire copy. He was a Barnumesque figure whose journalism was a form of performance art. At the press conference Weiner called to address *Breitbart News*'s reporting on his lewd pictures, Breitbart showed up and, before Weiner arrived, commandeered the podium to hold his own press event. "I've seen a lot of Congressman Weiner's body," he taunted. "He's in very good shape."

Although *Breitbart News* and *The Daily Caller* theoretically competed for the same conservative audience, Breitbart and Carlson were more friends than rivals. Before the *Caller*'s launch, Breitbart gave Carlson and Patel advice on the ins and outs of running an online publication. Later, Carlson and Breitbart would go pheasant hunting together in the Dakotas, and the *Caller* would cohost (with Grover Norquist's Americans for Tax Reform) a Washington, DC, book party for Breitbart.

When Carlson, as a Breitbartesque publicity stunt for the *Caller*, paid twenty-five hundred dollars in a charity auction to have a home-cooked dinner with Bill Ayers—the Vietnam-era left-wing radical and Weather Underground cofounder who'd been friendly with Obama and was the focus of several conservative conspiracy theories about the president—he was afforded the opportunity to bring five guests with him. He chose a *Caller* reporter; a *Caller* contest winner; his brother, Buckley; Labash; and Breitbart. Carlson and Breitbart had concluded that the conservative online space was big enough for both of their publications, and they'd agreed to a division of labor of sorts: *Breitbart News* would be dedicated to whatever spectacle Breitbart himself was making. The *Caller*, whose newsroom had grown to thirty, would continue to produce reported articles that hit the conservative base's sweet spot.

But then in March 2012, just a few weeks after Ayers's dinner party, Breitbart collapsed outside his home in Los Angeles and died of heart failure. He was forty-three. Breitbart, Carlson wrote in a eulogy, was "decent as hell, a loyal friend in a business with too few of them." He would not feel the same way about the man who soon took over *Breitbart News*: Steve Bannon.

Bannon was a former Goldman Sachs banker who'd become a right-wing filmmaker, directing propagandistic documentaries about Ronald Reagan, Sarah Palin, the global financial crisis, and illegal immigration. Breitbart, who met Bannon in the exceedingly small world of conservative Hollywood, described Bannon as "the Leni Riefenstahl of the Tea Party movement." (He meant it as a compliment.) Breitbart enlisted Bannon, who had an MBA from Harvard, to help with *Breitbart News*'s business side. Shortly before Breitbart's death, Bannon secured a ten-million-dollar investment from the right-wing financier Robert Mercer and his daughter Rebekah to fund *Breitbart News*'s relaunch and expand its staff. When Breitbart died,

Bannon became *Breitbart News*'s executive chairman, and the relaunch became his baby.

Like Carlson had two years earlier when he launched the *Caller*, Bannon declared that he wanted *Breitbart News* to become "the *Huffington Post* of the right." But Bannon had learned from Carlson's mistakes. He had no interest in spending the Mercers' money on sober, serious-minded reporters. Instead, he wanted bomb throwers. More specifically, he wanted the bomb throwers Carlson had hired for the *Caller* 2.0. At the top of his list was Matt Boyle, whom Bannon dubbed "our No. 1 draft pick." In late 2012, he poached Boyle from the *Caller*; then, over the next few years, *Breitbart News* also hired Caroline May, Patrick Howley, and two other *Caller* reporters, as well as the *Caller*'s publicist. When Neil Munro, the last of the *Caller*'s major traffic drivers from its second wave still at the site, finally quit in early 2015, Carlson wrote in a staff memo: "Where is Neil going? Honestly, I have no idea. . . . I got not a single detail from him other than, 1) he's leaving with great affection for *The Daily Caller*, and 2) he's not going to Breitbart." Shortly thereafter, Munro went to *Breitbart News*.

Carlson tried to find a way for the *Caller* to compete with *Breitbart News*—and, just as acutely, the Mercers' millions. In 2013, he believed his site was close to landing a significant investment from Fox News CEO Roger Ailes, but the deal ultimately fell through. Carlson suspected that Bannon—who was helping Ailes run a smear campaign against the journalist Gabriel Sherman in anticipation of Sherman's forthcoming critical biography of Ailes, *The Loudest Voice in the Room*—had talked Ailes out of it.

Those weren't Carlson's only suspicions about the man who replaced his dearly departed friend atop *Breitbart News*. "Bannon is full of shit about everything," Carlson told Charles Johnson, a right-wing blogger who'd done some freelance stories for the

Caller. "The guy's a total fraud." Johnson was a controversial media figure, a "troll on steroids," in the assessment of *The New York Times* media critic David Carr; he was later banned from Twitter for soliciting funds to help him "take out" a Black Lives Matter protest leader. But he was a resourceful reporter who specialized in digging up dirt on people. One of his *Caller* stories had busted Elizabeth O'Bagy, a prominent foreign policy analyst and leading advocate for Syrian rebels, for inflated academic credentials and undisclosed financial ties to the rebels. Carlson asked Johnson to conduct a similar investigation into Bannon. Had he really gone to Harvard Business School? Was *Breitbart News*'s money actually from the Mercers? Everything was on the table. Johnson, who'd also written for *Breitbart News* and harbored his own dislike of Bannon, did a deep dive. He came up with very little. "Tucker wanted me to prove him correct," Johnson said. "I always felt like I had sort of disappointed him."

In the end, Carlson could only watch as Bannon treated the *Caller* as *Breitbart News*'s farm team and torqued up its populist-nationalist journalism to the extreme. Not content to only have Caroline May write up anti-immigration stories that revolved around Washington-based tips and leaks from Stephen Miller, Bannon opened up a *Breitbart News* bureau in Lubbock, Texas, to provide on-the-ground reporting from the southern border that illustrated the issue more vividly. Where the *Caller* had taken a scattershot approach to its racist articles about Trayvon Martin, *Breitbart News*, under Bannon, created an entire "black crime" vertical. Bannon's version of *Breitbart News* was like the *Caller* on steroids.

The business benefits of *Breitbart News*'s new approach quickly became apparent: The site doubled its number of unique visitors in the first six months after its relaunch. But Bannon—and the Mercers—were less interested in traffic than influence, which was a longer game. Bannon recognized that, while right-wing populism had long flourished on talk radio, the Internet was an even more effective medium for it. (For all of Limbaugh's and talk radio's supposed political power, they were unable to prevent John McCain and Mitt Romney from winning the Republican presidential nominations in 2008 and 2012.) Bannon viewed *Breitbart News* less as a political website dedicated to covering the news than a political weapon designed to advance his—and the Mercers'—ideological agenda.

In 2013, that agenda's top item was torpedoing bipartisan immigration-reform legislation. The bill had the support of the GOP's rising star Marco Rubio and Fox News, but with an unrelenting avalanche of alarmist anti-immigration stories that often peddled false information—including the bogus claim that the legislation would give undocumented immigrants free mobile phones—*Breitbart News* sparked a revolt among the conservative base, and the bill failed. Following that success, Bannon and the Mercers turned their attention toward finding a populist-nationalist candidate that *Breitbart News* could throw its weight behind in the 2016 Republican presidential primaries. After Bannon tried and failed to recruit Jeff Sessions to run for the White House, he and the Mercers initially favored Texas senator Ted Cruz, and *Breitbart News* assiduously promoted Cruz's candidacy. But Bannon and the Mercers soon pivoted to Donald Trump, and fawning coverage of the New York real estate developer overtook the site, providing him a crucial boost that ultimately helped him win the Republican nomination.

Trump himself recognized the role *Breitbart News* played in his success. During the primaries, he declared Matt Boyle "the best reporter in the country." Then, as he headed toward the general election, he appointed Bannon the chief executive of his campaign.

Carlson didn't just resent *Breitbart News*'s—and Bannon's—good fortune; he was baffled by it. At the *Caller*, he had heavily edited writers like Boyle, sometimes even sitting down next to him and commandeering his keyboard in order to rewrite his stories top to bottom. At *Breitbart News*, though, Boyle's and others' articles often read as if they'd been published without so much as even a cursory copy edit to check for subject-verb agreement. "Tucker was very frustrated that he had thought he was making something better than *Breitbart*—but the market didn't recognize it as better than *Breitbart*," Mike Riggs said.

What Carlson failed to appreciate about *Breitbart News*'s rise was the programmatic discipline that Bannon brought to the website. *Breitbart News* articles may have lacked writerly polish, not to mention proper grammar and accuracy, but they were hardly careless. There was a purpose and an intentionality to everything Bannon published. "*Breitbart*'s home page was designed for killing a bill or boosting a candidate," a former *Caller* staffer, who did grasp what Bannon was up to, said. "If they were against a piece of legislation, they'd flood the zone on it with all of their best writers and put everything on the home page." By contrast, the former *Caller* staffer explained, "The *Daily Caller*'s home page was designed for getting clicks. Whatever was drawing traffic would be on the home page." As Carlson himself put it at the time, "Links are what I'm after."

This heedless pursuit of clicks soon took the *Caller* in a new and even more extreme direction. To the extent that Carlson thought he understood *Breitbart News*'s success, he attributed it to the fact that Bannon, after raiding the *Caller*'s staff and then amping up their inflammatory takes on immigration, race, and gender, had positioned *Breitbart News* to the *Caller*'s right. The

Caller's response, therefore, would be to try to outflank *Breitbart News*—which, considering how far to the right *Breitbart News* had tacked, wouldn't be an easy feat. But the new crop of reporters and editors that Carlson began hiring to replace those whom Bannon lured away was more than up to the task.

One new hire was Scott Greer, who became a *Caller* writer and editor shortly after he graduated from the University of Tennessee at Chattanooga in 2013. While in college, Greer attended gatherings of the Wolves of Vinland, a neo-pagan white supremacist group that met in the woods of central Virginia. With their worship of the Norse god Odin and their fixation on feats of strength, the Wolves might have appeared to be a ridiculous, harmless group, but they were deadly serious: One of their members was convicted of trying to burn down a Black church. After Greer was hired by the *Caller*, he began writing under a pseudonym for the *Radix Journal*, a website founded by the white nationalist leader Richard Spencer. As the journalist Rosie Gray later revealed in 2018, Greer's *Radix* contributions were rife with hatred. In one *Radix* article about a new California sexual-consent law, he complained that "while sex laws become more draconian for White men and they are further assaulted for trying to be men, the more virile Arabs, Blacks, and Hispanics that are swarming into our countries will continue to victimize our people." In another article about European Jews, he attributed the anti-Semitism they face to "the Jewish role in promoting the root causes of this problem through their support of mass immigration, multiculturalism, and hate speech laws that only go after Whites." Greer responded to Gray's reporting with a statement that read, in part, "As the political situation has evolved in recent years, so have my views. That said, I do not apologize for honestly stating what I believed to be correct at the time."

Another new hire was Jonah Bennett, a young Canadian who joined the *Caller* as a reporter not long after Greer's arrival—and who participated in a secret email listserv called Morning Hate. Morning Hate was a bit like JournoList—if instead of liberals engaging in wonky policy debates, it was white nationalists expressing their visceral hatred of Blacks, Jews, and immigrants. According to journalist Hannah Gais, who later exposed the Morning Hate listserv in 2019, its members wrote in code: "Hawaiians" meant "Hebes," "Alaskans" stood for the N-word, and "our good friend" or "AH" was a reference to Hitler. Upon joining Morning Hate, Bennett was introduced by one of its participants as "a good boy who knows the issues." Bennett replied that "although my first name may insinuate otherwise, I am not, in fact, a Hawaiian." In a subsequent email to Morning Hate, Bennett mocked a CNN article about an Austrian Holocaust survivor: "I VAS THREE YEEES OLD WHEN THE NAHZEES CUT OFF MY SCHMECKLE OYY," he wrote. In another email to the listserv, he lamented that Gavin McInnes, the founder of the Proud Boys, had substituted the word "Western" for "white" when on his podcast he recited the neo-Nazi "14 words" slogan that reads "we must secure the existence of our people and a future for white children." Bennett responded to Gais's reporting with a statement that read, in part: "I was on a lot of gossip mailing lists years ago—as journalists are. This mailing list in particular was a good place to get info and scoops, which led to several good stories. I hammed it up in sometimes regrettable and cynical ways to go along with the temperament of the list. . . . I've never been a white nationalist."

There was Chuck Ross, who was hired by the *Caller* as a reporter in 2013 and who prior to joining the *Caller* maintained a personal blog called *Gucci Little Pig*. On *Gucci Little Pig*, Erik Wemple later reported for *The Washington Post*, Ross discoursed about the genetic inferiority of women ("When given equal opportunity women don't have the tools to perform as well in business as men") and Blacks ("Blacks' higher testosterone levels lead to increased aggression which in today's confined society inevitably leads to increased violence and crime"). Ross later apologized for his blog, telling Wemple in 2017, "I've matured immeasurably since then, and I regret that I put these ill-formed thoughts out in the public domain."

And then there was Katie McHugh, a self-described white nationalist who joined the *Caller* as a reporter shortly before Ross and who, not long after her arrival at the website, began dating Kevin DeAnna, the founder of the white nationalist campus group Youth for Western Civilization. Through McHugh, DeAnna and several of his white nationalist friends became fixtures at the *Caller*'s office happy hours and holiday parties. McHugh, meanwhile, brought her *Caller* affiliation with her to a private dinner in Washington, DC, with the British Holocaust denier David Irving, where his admirers peppered him with questions about Hitler. McHugh later recanted her white nationalist beliefs. "I take responsibility for all my actions," she told Gray. "Everything I said that was terrible was my fault."

Carlson has maintained that he was completely unaware of the white nationalist beliefs, writings, and associations of these *Caller* staffers. "I think it kind of goes without saying that I didn't know anything about that," Carlson told Wemple after Ross's racist and misogynistic blog posts were revealed. "Maybe it doesn't go without saying. Let me just say: I had no idea that Chuck Ross had written anything like that." He offered similar denials about Greer, Bennett, and McHugh.

But these staffers didn't seem overly concerned about hiding their odious views from their *Caller* colleagues. Greer, according to a former *Caller* staffer, called his newsroom desk the Eagle's Nest, which was the name of Hitler's mountain lair. McHugh, who interned at the *Caller* two years before she joined the site as a full-time staffer, told Matt Lewis, a *Caller* opinion columnist, at the end of her internship that she believed "Jews control the media." When Ross was considering going to work at the *Caller*, he emailed McHugh about a picture she'd posted online of herself at a *Caller* party with DeAnna and two other men whom Ross recognized as prominent white nationalists. "Do any of the [*Caller*] people know who they are?" he asked. McHugh replied, "Our enemies and their sympathizers are lazy and are weaklings for the most part," before going on to boast that "no one was going to say anything even though" DeAnna and one of the men in the picture were featured on the websites of prominent anti-hate groups like the Southern Poverty Law Center and One People's Project, while the other man in the picture "commandeered my laptop to update AmRen"—the white supremacist magazine *American Renaissance*—"in the office." She added, "It's good not to tiptoe around everything. Posting photos like that implies a certain boldness, like we're not going to have a heart attack and immediately start apologizing at the first hint of a thoughtcrime accusation. The best first response is reframing the scenario with a 'What?' or 'So what?'"

Moreover, their work for the *Caller* often hinted at—and occasionally outright betrayed—their extremism. Greer was fixated on race. He pooh-poohed "how supposedly bad the American justice system is for blacks" and repeatedly defended white police officers accused of (and often caught on video) using excessive force against Blacks. He dismissed Ta-Nehisi Coates's writing as "white guilt porn" and attacked the NFL for allowing Beyoncé to perform during the Super Bowl halftime and "signal a black power message to the entire country." He celebrated the Confederate flag. And he wrote up a horrific local news story from Wisconsin in which a pregnant woman was gang-raped during a home invasion—seemingly just so he could note that the "six suspects charged are African-American."

Bennett, meanwhile, worked to prop up—and soft pedal the awfulness of—white nationalists who, in the course of the 2016 presidential campaign, were coming to national prominence as the "alt-right." In one *Caller* article, Bennett attempted to preempt a controversy over Donald Trump Jr. retweeting an attack on Hillary Clinton by the notorious anti-Semitic evolutionary psychologist Kevin MacDonald—who argues that Jews are genetically predisposed to try to destroy Western countries—by describing MacDonald "as a leading intellectual for his innovative work on group evolutionary theory and advocacy of Western culture" who "has written more than 100 scholarly articles and seven books" and "has been translated into Danish, Dutch, Finnish, German, Russian and many other languages." (Only at the end of the article did he offer a grudging mention that the Southern Poverty Law Center had accused MacDonald of anti-Semitism.) In another piece, he hailed and revealed the identity of an anonymous "alt-right personality" who had hoaxed *Politico* about voter-suppression efforts on the eve of the 2016 elections—falsely telling a *Politico* reporter that he and his ideological allies planned to go "in to the ghettos in Philly with 40s and weed to give out to the local residents, which we think will lead to more of them staying home." The merry prankster, Bennett reported, was a man named Mike Enoch, whom Bennett described as "owner of The Right Stuff (TRS) [website], a main node of the alt-right"; Bennett did not mention that Enoch, whom he approvingly quoted complaining about the mainstream media's unfair coverage of the alt-right, hosted a neo-Nazi podcast called *The Daily Shoah* and was the creator of "the echo," the online tactic of placing three sets of parentheses around the names of Jewish individuals in order to call attention to their Jewishness.

And while Ross eventually became a solid investigative reporter for the *Caller* covering national security and foreign policy, his initial work for the site was just a slightly more refined version of the noxious musings about race from *Gucci Little Pig*. He frequently rewrote local news stories from across the United States about instances of Black-on-white crime ("Teens Rob, Punch Elderly Woman In The Face" and "Group Attacked For Being White In Cincinnati"). Covering the Trayvon Martin trial for the *Caller*, Ross seemed less an objective reporter than a PR person for George Zimmerman, the man charged with murdering Martin, writing a series of stories that portrayed Martin as a dangerous thug with "a burgeoning penchant for violence" who forced Zimmerman to shoot him in self-defense. After Zimmerman was acquitted, Ross kept up the PR work, reporting that Zimmerman had helped rescue a family from an overturned SUV. The first line of the story quoted Zimmerman's actual spokesman asking, "What if George hadn't gotten out of his truck?"—a taunting reminder that prosecutors had argued that Zimmerman would have never physically encountered Martin if he hadn't gotten out of his vehicle to follow the teenager.

McHugh was the only one whose racist and anti-Semitic views weren't obviously reflected in her *Caller* stories. It wasn't until *Breitbart News* hired her away in 2014 that she began giving those sentiments full voice in public, mostly on her Twitter feed, where she wrote things like "British settlers built the USA. 'Slaves' built the country as much as cows 'built' McDonald's. Amateur . . ." and "Indian tribes never bothered to build any kind of civilization. They killed each other and chased bison. Yawn~."

The *Caller*'s efforts to outflank *Breitbart News* did not achieve the results that Carlson was hoping for. While his site's web traffic did continue to climb, rising to 10.2 million unique visitors by October 2016, it still trailed *Breitbart News*'s, which boasted 19.2 million unique visitors that same month. What's more, the *Caller* never began to approach its rival's influence. That was partly because it was difficult for the *Caller*, even with its white nationalist staffers, to get to the right of *Breitbart News*, which was doubling down on its own extremism. An analysis of Twitter during the 2016 campaign by the Investigative Fund found that 31 percent of key influencers who used the white supremacist hashtag #whitegenocide followed *Breitbart News*. (By comparison, 10 percent followed the *Caller*, and 5 percent followed *National Review*.) When a *Daily Beast* reporter confronted *Breitbart News* editor Alex Marlow with McHugh's racist tweets in 2016, Marlow replied: "Neither Steve [Bannon] nor I are big fans of Twitter, but after reviewing these tweets, we're considering giving Katie a weekly column."

The bigger impediment was that Carlson did not instill in the *Caller* the same fanatical message discipline exhibited by *Breitbart News*. Under Bannon, *Breitbart News* relentlessly hammered away at the populist-nationalist issues of trade, crime, and above all, immigration. According to a study by Harvard's Berkman Klein Center for Internet & Society, nearly one out of every twenty-five sentences in *Breitbart News*'s 2016 election coverage mentioned immigration, more than three times as many as Fox News devoted to the issue. After Trump embraced *Breitbart News*'s set of issues and *Breitbart News*, in turn, threw its support behind his campaign, Bannon purged anyone from the site who refused to get on board the Trump train. Ben Shapiro, one of the departing staffers, complained that *Breitbart News* had become "Trump's personal Pravda."

The *Caller*'s message was comparably muddled. While its white nationalist writers and reporters produced the toxic sludge that was expected of them, Carlson also continued to employ and publish more conventional conservative voices, ones who openly blanched at Trumpian populism. Matt Lewis—the *Caller*'s perhaps most prominent opinion columnist who came to the site from AOL in 2011 after it merged with *The Huffington Post* and he concluded he couldn't work for "a far-left liberal" like Huffington—routinely inveighed against Trump's candidacy, even begging his boyhood hero Rush Limbaugh to "sack up" and oppose Trump during the GOP primaries. After Trump became the nominee, Lewis decided to sit out the 2016 election altogether. "I have criticized both candidates for their sins," Lewis wrote of Clinton and Trump. "But I can't, in good conscience, vote for either of them." Jamie Weinstein, a *Caller* staffer who primarily wrote about foreign policy from a neoconservative perspective, did Lewis one better, actually backing Clinton. "In a White House race between Hillary Clinton and Donald Trump, I'd prefer Clinton, just as I'd prefer Malaria to Ebola," Weinstein wrote. "In most cases, Malaria is curable. Ebola is more often deadly."

The result was that the *Caller* existed in a sort of political-journalism no-man's-land during the 2016 elections. On one side of conservative media, there were the resolutely anti-Trump publications: most notably, *National Review*, which ran an entire "Against Trump" issue featuring twenty-two essays by conservative luminaries opposing Trump's candidacy and a scathing editorial that declared Trump "a menace to American conservatism who would take the work of generations and trample it under foot in behalf of a populism as heedless and crude as the Donald himself"; and *The Weekly Standard*, which launched a fusillade of articles attacking Trump, including a memorable cover story by Matt Labash cataloging nine instances of "Trump at his Trumpiest," from his incorrigible cheating at golf to his multiple business failures. Newer, online-only outfits, like *RedState* and *The Federalist*, also weighed in against Trump. These anti-Trump fulminations even spilled off the page: After Trump clinched the GOP nomination, *The Weekly Standard* editor Bill Kristol tried and failed to recruit *National Review* writer David French to launch an independent presidential bid. On the other side of conservative media, the *Claremont Review of Books*, *The*

American Conservative, and of course, *Breitbart News* were solidly in Trump's corner, providing intellectual (and, at times, anti-intellectual) arguments for his candidacy. It was a brutal internecine struggle. When Trump appointed Bannon his campaign chairman, *The Weekly Standard*'s Stephen Hayes wrote that Trump was

> choosing to end his campaign living in the alternate reality that *Breitbart* creates for him on a daily basis—where everything he does is the best, where everyone who questions him is an idiot or a traitor, where big rallies portend electoral victories, where House speaker Paul Ryan is the problem with modern conservatism, where polls that find him down are fixed, where elections he loses are rigged, where immigration and trade are the nation's most pressing issues, and where, truly, Trump alone can fix it all.

Breitbart News, for its part, branded Kristol not just a "Republican spoiler" but a "renegade Jew."

The Daily Caller managed to stay out of the crossfire. But in this particular instance, that was actually a bad place to be: In the 2016 election, the most important story of its existence, the *Caller* was relegated to the role of bystander. Still, that didn't trouble Carlson as much as it once would have. As Trump emerged and began to completely upend the American political system—and conservative media—Carlson was turning his focus away from the world of online journalism and toward another route to prominence and power. It looked a lot like a route he'd taken once before.

SIX

IN THE WINTER OF 2009, not long after his ignominious departure from MSNBC but before the launch of *The Daily Caller*, Carlson received an unexpected phone call. It was from Roger Ailes. The Fox News chief had never much cared for Carlson's preppy, fraternity-rush-chair shtick; his taste in cable-news hosts (male ones, that is) ran toward confrontational populists like Chris Matthews, who got his first television show when Ailes hired him at the NBC-owned America's Talking, and Bill O'Reilly, Fox's biggest star. Ailes also wasn't one to forget a slight. "I don't ignore anything," he once boasted. "Somebody gets in my face, I get in their face." He no doubt remembered all the nasty things Carlson had said over the years about Fox ("a mean, sick group of people"), O'Reilly ("a humorless phony"), and Ailes himself ("sucking up to power").

Now Ailes was calling Carlson. According to one version of the call that Carlson later recounted to Neil Patel, Ailes began their conversation with a gratuitous insult. "You're a loser, and you screwed up your whole life," he taunted. It seemed as if he just wanted to get in Carlson's face. But then, before Carlson could hang up, Ailes got to the heart of the matter. "The only thing you have going for you is that I like hiring talented people who have screwed things up," he told Carlson, "because once I do, you're going to work your ass off for me." Ailes offered Carlson a contributor contract at Fox. It was the same type of deal Carlson received from CNN a decade earlier, when he was still a magazine writer and was just breaking into the cable-news business—five figures a year to appear on the network's various programs when they needed to fill airtime with a talking head. It was quite a comedown, in both compensation and prestige, from having his own prime-time show. But, for Carlson, it was a lifeline. He was grateful for the extra money, even if it was a pittance compared to the salary he'd earned as an anchor. And he was grateful to still have a toehold, even if it was a tenuous one, in television. "I'm doing whatever they want me to do," he told *The New York Times* when his Fox deal was announced.

Granted, Ailes didn't offer this lifeline out of the goodness of his heart. Even in the cutthroat world of television, he stood out for his ruthlessness. He started in the business in 1961, fresh out of Ohio University, as a production assistant on *The Mike Douglas Show*, a local talk show in Cleveland; three years later *The Mike Douglas Show* was nationally syndicated, and Ailes was its executive producer. When Richard Nixon was a guest on the show in the run-up to his 1968 presidential bid, he came away impressed by Ailes's television know-how; Nixon's ignorance of the then-new medium, of course, had been his undoing in the 1960 presidential contest against John F. Kennedy. Nixon subsequently hired Ailes to run the television strategy for his victorious 1968 campaign. It was the start of a two-decade detour into Republican politics for Ailes, who went on to mastermind the media strategies for Ronald Reagan's and George H. W. Bush's winning presidential campaigns—and, in the process, develop a unified theory of how to use television to move people politically.

Ailes returned to the television business in the early 1990s, helming CNBC, NBC's once-struggling business cable-news channel whose fortunes he reversed, and running America's Talking (which eventually became MSNBC). In 1996, Rupert Murdoch approached him with a straightforward but daunting mission. "Can you build me a network that can beat CNN?" Murdoch asked. Ailes said he could. A mere five years later, Fox News sat atop the cable-news ratings. Much of Fox's success was attributable to its ideological positioning. The promotional slogans that Ailes devised for Fox—"Fair and Balanced" and "We Report, You Decide"—appealed to an underserved news audience, "the audience of the disaffected," as one Ailes lieutenant called it. This audience believed the mainstream media was hopelessly biased in favor of liberals; Fox's conservative tilt was, in their view, simply leveling the playing field.

It wasn't just Fox's politics that accounted for its strong ratings, however. There was the news channel's showmanship as well. Ailes introduced bold graphics and whooshy sound effects to signal breaking news; he had his female anchors deliver that news wearing short skirts while sitting on couches or behind Lucite desks so that viewers could ogle their legs. Ailes had an intuitive grasp of what did—and did not—work on television, frequently watching shows with the sound off. "If there was nothing happening on the screen in the way the host looked or moved that made me interested enough to stand up and turn the sound up," he explained, "then I knew that the host was not a great television performer." Even Ailes's competitors—and ideological opponents—recognized his genius. "There's a sort of, like, respecting the game, in terms of people who are doing well and people who are good at it," Rachel Maddow said of Ailes. Her opinion of the Fox News chief was so high that she sought his advice. "I wanted tips from him about how to be better on TV," Maddow recalled. "And he was willing to talk to me about what I was doing well, and doing poorly, to help me get better."

Ailes especially relished hiring broadcasters who'd flamed out at other networks. (O'Reilly, who'd been a correspondent at ABC and CBS and anchored the syndicated tabloid show *Inside Edition*, had left television entirely and was studying for a master's degree in public administration at Harvard when Ailes brought him to Fox.) "I look for people who haven't reached their potential," he said. "I think I'm pretty good at developing talent." By resurrecting careers, Ailes was able to prove his own genius—that the network he built was so strong, that the audience he convened was so large and so loyal, that Fox was capable of making almost anyone a star. "I could have put a dead raccoon on the air this year," he once boasted, "and got a better rating than last year."

But Ailes had other, baser motives for hiring has-beens and never-weres. "Roger liked to bring people on who would be completely beholden to him," a former Fox executive said. Most notoriously, Ailes liked to bring on women whom he then expected would repay him with sexual favors. In the summer of 2016, Gretchen Carlson (no relation to Tucker)—whom Ailes had hired at Fox ten years earlier and who once anchored the channel's weekday morning show, *Fox & Friends*—filed a sexual harassment lawsuit against Ailes, alleging that Ailes asked her for a sexual relationship and that when she rebuffed him he reduced her pay and airtime and declined to renew her contract. (21st Century Fox, Fox News's parent company, ultimately paid Gretchen Carlson twenty million dollars and offered her a public apology to settle her lawsuit.) After lawyers hired by 21st Century Fox to investigate Gretchen Carlson's claims found more than two dozen other women at Fox, including the star prime-time anchor Megyn Kelly, who alleged that Ailes had harassed them, Murdoch forced Ailes to resign. He soon disappeared to a mansion in Florida and, less than a year later, died in exile from the media world he once commanded.

While Ailes's horrendous mistreatment of women would eventually be his downfall, he tormented certain male employees, as well. He grew up in the blue-collar town of Warren, Ohio, where his father worked in the Packard Electric factory. His boyhood memory of seeing "college boys give my dad orders in the shop in an inappropriate manner," he later said, was seared into his brain. No matter how much wealth and power Ailes accrued, he never lost the chip on his shoulder. "They think I'm this rube from Ohio," he complained of his fellow inhabitants of New York's elite media circles. "They all look down their noses at me." He never stopped looking for ways to even the score. Counterintuitively, hiring Tucker Carlson at his absolute nadir presented just such an opportunity. "Roger liked the idea of Tucker coming to him on his hands and knees," a former Fox executive said. "Roger took no small amount of pleasure in being able to tell Tucker Swanson McNear Carlson, 'You're a loser.'"

Carlson knew that he was low in the pecking order at Fox. Still, he had ambitions. His biggest, and a seemingly attainable one, was to become a regular on *Special Report*, Fox's 6:00 p.m. political-news show. Created by Ailes in haste in 1998 to cover the breaking news of Bill Clinton's affair with Monica Lewinsky—hence the name *Special Report*—the show quickly became a must-watch for political junkies and, over time, established itself as Fox's highest-brow, most cerebral program. The original anchor of *Special Report* was Brit Hume, who shared Ailes's conservative ideology but was also a serious newsman; prior to Fox, he'd been ABC News's chief White House correspondent. Hume was joined each night in Fox's Capitol Hill studio by the show's All-Star Panel, a rotating trio comprised of some of Washington's most prominent and respected political journalists, including Carlson's old *Weekly Standard* colleagues Bill Kristol, Fred Barnes, and Charles Krauthammer, as well as reporters and writers from National Public Radio, *The Wall*

Street Journal, and *The Washington Post*. The All-Star Panel was almost invariably stacked in favor of the right: Two openly conservative columnists or writers, like Barnes and Krauthammer, were typically paired with one objective reporter from a mainstream-media outlet, like NPR's Mara Liasson. If you were looking for an avowedly liberal point of view on the Lewinsky scandal or the Florida recount or the invasion of Iraq, you wouldn't find it on the All-Star Panel. But you would get a level of discourse that was significantly more intelligent, more informed, and more civil than the lowest-common-denominator, right-wing dreck that made up most of Fox's programming. For Fox, *Special Report*, which typically had about two-thirds as many viewers as *The O'Reilly Factor*, qualified as Prestige TV.

In January 2009, a few weeks before Barack Obama's inauguration (and four months before Carlson joined Fox), Hume relinquished his anchor chair. Taking his place was Bret Baier. A lantern-jawed, Ken-doll reporter who'd initially impressed Ailes on 9/11 by driving the six hundred miles from Atlanta, where he was Fox's bureau chief, to Virginia to cover the attack on the Pentagon, Baier was eventually made the news channel's White House correspondent for the final years of the Bush administration. He was known for truly fair and balanced coverage—asking Bush during the 2008 financial crisis, "Are you worried about being the Herbert Hoover of the 21st century?"—and, unlike Hume, he claimed that he was nonideological. Just thirty-eight at the time he took over *Special Report*, he vowed to maintain Hume's "high standards" but also to freshen things up a bit by adding younger, newer pundits to the All-Star Panel. One was Jonah Goldberg, who'd parlayed his mother Lucianne's starring role in the Lewinsky scandal into a blogging job at *National Review*'s nascent website before going on to become a syndicated columnist and the best-selling author of an anti–Hillary Clinton jeremiad called *Liberal Fascism*. Another was Stephen Hayes, the

Weekly Standard writer and Dick Cheney cat's-paw who'd been Baier's fraternity brother at DePauw University.

Carlson, who made his Fox debut on the day he turned forty, believed he should be part of this *Special Report* youth movement. Although he was friends with both Goldberg and Hayes, he couldn't help but still view them as upstarts and his journalistic inferiors; if they were deemed All-Star caliber, then surely he was too. In his cockier moments, he even fantasized about supplanting Baier in the anchor chair, convinced he was a more natural heir to Hume, whom he revered. "Bret's a nice guy," Carlson told one friend, "but he's not really a thinker." Whenever a *Special Report* producer asked Carlson if he would appear on that night's panel, he jumped at the opportunity; then, before the show, he'd often hole up in *The Daily Caller* office of Jamie Weinstein—who by dint of his Cornell and London School of Economics degrees, not to mention neoconservative views, was arguably the site's brainiest staffer and closest approximation to Krauthammer—to prepare and rehearse his arguments. When he went on air, he seemed to acquit himself well. He was appropriately deferential to Krauthammer, the panel's most esteemed member: The term "climate change," Carlson ingratiatingly noted in one appearance, was "a handily elastic phrase that covers, as Charles suggested, virtually everything." At the same time, he reliably pushed the then-standard conservative talking points, even when they ran counter to the tenets of paleoconservatism: "Free trade actually might help the American economy in ways that are tangible," he said in another *Special Report* hit, slagging Obama for being insufficiently committed to globalization.

Nonetheless, Carlson did not earn a spot in the *Special Report* rotation. His appearances became fewer and farther between, and he grew increasingly dismayed that his friends who were regulars on the show weren't going to bat for him. He was especially upset with Bill Kristol—"the best boss" he'd ever had—who was generous with advice about how to run *The Daily Caller* but chary about sticking his neck out to try to help Carlson revive his television career. "He felt like Kristol betrayed him," a person who was friendly with both men said. "He was the enfant terrible of the establishment Republican Party, all these people loving his untied bowtie, and then when he fell on hard times, they ditched him."

Even if Kristol and other All-Stars had lobbied for Carlson, it wouldn't have mattered. Much like the fictional Hollywood studio head Jack Woltz insists that "Johnny Fontane never gets that movie," in *The Godfather*, the very real Fox News chief Ailes was determined that Carlson never get a regular seat on the All-Star Panel. (And, unlike Fontane, Carlson didn't have a godfather who was unconcerned about humane equine treatment.) "Roger loved kicking Tucker down the stairs and beating him up," a former Fox executive said. That meant not just denying Carlson the opportunities he craved, but saddling him with obligations he hoped to avoid—like coanchoring the weekend version of *Fox & Friends*, which was less political and even more aggressively stupid than its weekday counterpart. "Roger's idea was to throw Tucker onto the worst thing—the weekend morning show," the former Fox executive said. "It's early. He has to go to New York. He has to drive go-karts. It was inconvenient and humiliating."

Outwardly, Carlson appeared to embrace the assignment, eventually rising from fill-in weekend coanchor to full-time one. He not only careened around the set in a go-kart; he participated in cooking segments with guests like Billy Ray Cyrus, played the cowbell with Blue Öyster Cult, and competed against (and lost to) his female coanchor in a Spartan Race, thereby subjecting himself to a dunk tank. Just as Ailes had predicted, he worked his ass off—and he did it all with a smile. "He brought the same energy to *Fox & Friends Weekend* that he brought to *Dancing with the Stars*," the former Fox executive said. "He never acted too good for it. A lesser person would have said, 'I had two prime-time shows!'"

But, while Carlson might not have said it, he certainly thought it. According to friends, he did in fact consider the morning-show hijinks to be beneath someone who once had two prime-time shows, not to mention a highbrow talk show on PBS. He struggled with the *Fox & Friends* predawn call time, at one point even dozing off while on air. ("Is this honestly live?" he asked upon waking.) And he hated being away from his family and his social circle in DC on the weekends. When Susie sent an email inviting some of Carlson's Washington friends up to New York to celebrate his forty-fifth birthday on a Saturday night, she enticed guests with the prospect that, if they woke up early enough on Sunday morning, "We can throw eggs at the Fox studio window!" When his wife and friends weren't visiting him, Carlson tended to spend his New York weekends alone, hunkered down in his hotel room tying flies and then walking a dozen blocks to Central Park to fish in one of its ponds.

One afternoon while fly casting in Central Park, Carlson noticed a man with a video camera standing in some nearby bushes. Assuming he was a paparazzo or a liberal stalker, Carlson angrily confronted him. "Are you videotaping me?" he demanded. The man confessed that he was—because he'd never seen anyone fishing in Central Park before. He explained that he videotaped things that he found "interesting and unique about the city of New York" and then uploaded them to his YouTube channel, which, he said, had about fifteen thousand subscribers. "Really?!" Carlson exclaimed. "That's so neat."

As the man peppered Carlson with questions—"Where did you grow up?" "Do you live in New York now?"—it became clear to Carlson that the man wasn't a paparazzo or a stalker. Indeed, the man had no idea who Carlson was. Disarmed and charmed,

Carlson proceeded to show the man his flies and rhapsodize about fly-fishing. "It's a great pleasure and a great sport," he said.

They continued to talk, and the man told Carlson about his other pastime—pranking journalists. "I'm kind of a media terrorist," he boasted.

Now Carlson was no longer so happy about his anonymity.

"What's your favorite cable channel?" he asked.

CNN, the man told him, still not realizing whom he was talking to.

"Do you watch Fox?" Carlson pressed, perhaps hoping to cause a spark of recognition.

"I watch Fox," the man replied. But no, still not so much as a glimmer. Even to a self-professed cable-news junkie, Carlson was now just some random weirdo fishing in Central Park.

MAKING CARLSON MISERABLE WAS NO doubt enjoyable for Ailes, but the Fox News chairman was faced with far more pressing matters. First among them was figuring out how to position the cable-news channel in the Obama era.

For the briefest of moments, it seemed possible that Fox might actually give Obama a fair shake, or at least not be flagrantly biased against him. Fox had clearly favored Hillary Clinton in its coverage of the 2008 Democratic primaries. "Are you surprised that Fox News has been fairer to you than NBC News and a lot of other liberal news networks?" O'Reilly asked Clinton when she appeared on his show in May of that year. "I wouldn't expect anything less than a fair and balanced coverage of my campaign," she replied with an ingratiating grin. All the while, Fox took a sledgehammer to Obama, oftentimes in racist ways—referring to his wife, Michelle, as his "baby mama" and dubbing a loving fist bump between the couple at a rally as "a terrorist fist jab." But after Obama clinched the Democratic nomination and appeared to be on his way to becoming the country's first Black president, Murdoch, worried about being judged harshly by history, began to take a liking to the Illinois senator. He praised Obama as a "highly intelligent man with a great record at Harvard" and "a rock star." That summer, Murdoch and Obama held a secret meeting at the Waldorf Astoria hotel in New York City. Murdoch came away even more impressed. Obama left the meeting happy too. His campaign had largely avoided Fox News, but now he agreed to end the freezeout. In September, on the night that John McCain accepted the Republican Party's nomination, Obama appeared on *The O'Reilly Factor* for an interview.

But Ailes, who accompanied Murdoch to the Waldorf Astoria sit-down, was not as placated. He thought that staking out an anti-Obama position was good for Fox's ratings and, therefore, Murdoch's bottom line—which, more than history's judgment, is what his boss truly cared about. "Our relationship isn't about love—it's about arithmetic," Ailes once said of working for Murdoch. "Survival means hitting your numbers. I've met or exceeded mine in fifty-six straight quarters. The reason is: I treat Rupert's money like it is mine." Moreover, Ailes despised Obama and considered him a threat to the Republic. "People need to be reminded this guy never had a job. He's a community organizer," he vented to Fox executives. On one occasion, Ailes told David Axelrod, Obama's messaging guru with whom he'd maintained a cordial relationship ever since they'd helmed rival campaigns in an Illinois Senate race in the 1980s, he was worried Obama would install a national police force. Axelrod was incredulous, so Ailes played him a YouTube clip from an Obama campaign speech, in which Obama proposed creating a new civilian corps to help the US military on foreign aid missions. As Axelrod later told *New York Magazine*, that was when he realized that Ailes believed everything Fox was broadcasting.

In the end, Murdoch chose to defer to Ailes on what was best for Fox News. In November, a couple of weeks after Obama's election, he signed Ailes to a new five-year contract that guaranteed him editorial independence. The "tentative truce" Murdoch had negotiated with Obama a few months earlier was just that—tentative. He left it up to Ailes to decide if—or, more realistically, when—to break it.

That moment arrived on a February morning in 2009. It was right around the time Rush Limbaugh was stiffening Republican spines with his CPAC speech, and Rick Santelli, a CNBC financial reporter who covered the bond markets, was doing one of his regular hits from the floor of the Chicago Board of Trade. That's when Santelli launched into a rant about Obama's housing bailout plan. "The government is promoting bad behavior!" he shouted. With traders in the background cheering him on, Santelli continued, "We're thinking of having a Chicago Tea Party in July." The clip of Santelli went viral; Ailes took notice. It's a historical oddity that the Tea Party movement began with a speech on CNBC—because no one was more responsible for fanning its flames, and turning it into the most potent force of the conservative backlash against Obama, than Fox News and Ailes. As Sal Russo, the leader of the Tea Party Express, one of the movement's largest groups, later said, "There would not have been a Tea Party without Fox."

The tip of the spear of Fox News's campaign against Obama was Glenn Beck, whom Ailes had hired away from CNN's Headline News to anchor Fox's 5:00 p.m. show—and who made his Fox debut the day before Obama's inauguration. A self-described "rodeo clown," he was a departure from the hypermasculine, hyperpatriotic hosts, like Hannity and O'Reilly, who ruled the Fox roost during the war on terror and the Bush years. Beck, who often wept on air, spent his hour-long show lamenting the current state of America and offering apocalyptic visions of its future. According to Beck, Obama possessed "a deep-seated hatred for white people or the white culture"; indeed, Beck claimed that Obama's entire legislative agenda—from health care reform to combating climate change to the stimulus plan—was driven by his desire for "reparations" and his goal of "creating a new America, a new model, a model that will settle old racial scores through new social justice." When he wasn't calling Obama a "racist," Beck was declaring that "progressivism is the cancer in America and it is eating our constitution"; drawing from Goldberg's *Liberal Fascism*, he likened liberals to Nazis and Stalinists, since they all supported universal health care. In a dog whistle heard around the fever swamps, he introduced many Fox viewers to the Jewish billionaire financier and philanthropist George Soros, whom Beck portrayed as a "puppet master" at the center of a liberal conspiracy "to bring America to her knees, financially" and "to reap obscene profits off us as well."

Beck's brand of populism seemed to match—and exacerbate—conservatives' anxiety about the country's first Black president. His program sometimes drew more than three million viewers, an unheard-of number in what had been a cursed time slot at the news channel. (The previous year, Laura Ingraham held down the 5:00 p.m. hour at Fox for just three weeks before her show was canceled; a video compilation of Ingraham's off-the-air meltdowns later emerged in which she deemed her own program a "train wreck.") More than any politician, much less any other media figure, Beck became the face of the Tea Party movement, with one opinion poll finding him "the most highly regarded individual among Tea Party supporters." (Another poll found him to be the country's second-favorite TV personality, behind Oprah Winfrey.) In late August 2010, Beck drew three hundred thousand people to the National Mall in Washington, DC, for his Restoring Honor rally. A little more than two months later, Republicans, fueled by the Tea Party, romped in the midterm elections, gaining sixty-three seats in the US House of Representatives and taking the majority back from the Democrats.

Beck's success naturally made him the target of criticism. "I've got one television station entirely devoted to attacking my administration," Obama complained about Fox, singling out Beck as "troublesome." Nearly three hundred companies asked Fox that their advertising not run during Beck's show. Even some conservatives blanched at his racist rhetoric and conspiracy theories. David Frum diagnosed Beck's ascent as "a product of the collapse of conservatism as an organized political force, and the rise of conservatism as an alienated cultural sensibility." Matthew Continetti, the latest hotshot young *Weekly Standard* writer (who'd go on to marry Bill Kristol's daughter, Anne), likened Beck to John Birch Society founder Robert Welch, whom William F. Buckley famously banished from the conservative movement in the 1960s. "Not even the stupidest American liberal," Continetti argued, "shares the morality of the totalitarian monsters whom Beck analogizes to American politics so flippantly." Just as it had fifteen years earlier with Pat Buchanan, *The Standard* was trying to write Beck out of the right.

Beck wore the scorn like a badge of honor; he was early to recognize that the new coin of the realm in American politics was having the right enemies. "People like Bill Kristol, I don't think they stand for anything anymore," he fired back. "I don't even know if you understand what conservatives are anymore, Billy." But there was one person Beck could not afford to displease: Ailes. The Fox News chairman had long insisted that no one at the cable network was bigger than Fox News itself, and he bristled at Beck's extracurricular activities. Like Hannity and O'Reilly, Beck hosted a syndicated radio show and wrote best-selling books; unlike his fellow Fox stars, he had his own production company, which published a magazine, operated a subscription website, and sold enough merchandise that it boasted thirty million dollars in annual revenue. Ailes considered Beck insufficiently appreciative of the enormous boost his Fox show gave to his other ventures; he liked to tell people that if Beck were still at Headline News, only thirty people would have shown up to his rally on the Mall.

Worse, Ailes started to view Beck as a political liability. The star host, and the Tea Party movement more broadly, was too extreme—even for the Fox News chief. While Beck and the Tea Party helped the GOP take back the House in 2010, Ailes did not believe they could propel Republicans to the White House in 2012; Beck's doom mongering was not a successful, or sustainable, political message. "The problem with predicting the end of the world," Ailes complained, "was that sooner or later you have to deliver." He tried to rein in Beck, summoning him with increasing frequency to his office for meetings about how he could tone things down, but he was unsuccessful. When Beck told Ailes during one such meeting that he had spoken to God and he was simply doing God's will, Ailes replied, "Jesus, Glenn, I think God's a little too busy to be dealing with producing your show." In April 2011, Beck and Ailes jointly announced that Beck would be ending his Fox News show.

Ailes surmised correctly that, without his Fox News megaphone, Beck would fade away. (Compared to the three million viewers he drew at Fox, Beck's new streaming channel had just three hundred thousand subscribers.) But, while Ailes was able to make Beck disappear, he could not conjure a strong Republican presidential candidate. The 2012 Republican primaries were often called the "Fox News primary" because of the outsize influence Ailes and his news channel were expected to have on selecting the GOP nominee. But Ailes was unimpressed with the candidates who seemed eager to throw their hats in the ring, even though a number of them—including Newt Gingrich,

Mike Huckabee, Rick Santorum, and Sarah Palin—were paid Fox contributors. He blamed Beck and the Tea Party, in part, for making them want to run in the first place. He tried to recruit New Jersey governor Chris Christie and US Army general David Petraeus, but both rejected his entreaties.

When Mitt Romney wound up as the Republican nominee, Ailes did what he could to drag him across the finish line; Fox News devoted hundreds of hours of airtime to various Obama outrages that, while far less loony than the ones Beck once trafficked in, were still sufficiently juicy, Ailes hoped, to deny Obama a second term. But the Operation Fast and Furious, Benghazi, and New Black Panther Party scandals were not enough. In November, Obama defeated Romney by nearly four percentage points. As Ailes left the Fox News election-night party, before the official results were announced but after it was becoming clear that Republicans were going to come up short, he told one attendee, "If Romney wins, it's good for the taxpayers. If Obama wins, it's great for the ratings."

Obama's reelection occasioned a round of soul-searching among Republican leaders. The most tangible result was a Republican National Committee report issued four months after Romney's defeat. Officially titled the *Growth & Opportunity Project*, the report was known as "the autopsy." The autopsy concluded that the GOP was "marginalizing itself" with its harsh treatment of minorities and its reactionary social policies. Its most dramatic recommendation was for Republicans to abandon their anti-immigration stance and "embrace and champion comprehensive immigration reform."

Even before the autopsy was published, some Republican politicians were already trying to seize the moment on immigration reform—with the hope of riding it to the White House in

2016. The most aggressive was Marco Rubio, a young US senator from Florida whose parents were Cuban immigrants and who'd soon appear on the cover of *Time* under the headline "The Republican Savior." Working with seven other senators—three Republicans and four Democrats who, with Rubio, were known as the Gang of Eight—he authored immigration reform legislation that, among other things, introduced a path to citizenship for most of the country's eleven million undocumented immigrants. Of course, Rubio knew that the last time Republicans attempted to pass immigration reform that created such a path, when George W. Bush joined with Senate Democrats to try to overhaul the country's immigration system in 2007, the effort had been scuttled by a conservative grassroots revolt led, in large part, by cable-news hosts like Hannity and O'Reilly who blasted it as "amnesty." He was determined to avoid that fate this time around.

In January, Rubio traveled to Manhattan to have dinner with Murdoch and Ailes. Eating in News Corporation's executive dining room, he and Chuck Schumer, a Democratic senator from New York and a fellow Gang of Eight member, lobbied the two most powerful men in conservative media to get Fox's hosts to support this new attempt at immigration reform—or, at the very least, refrain from savaging it. It was an easier ask than Rubio had anticipated. Murdoch, an immigrant himself, agreed with the business arguments in favor of immigration reform. During Obama's first term, he had once buttonholed Axelrod at a dinner party and pushed him to move forward on the issue. Axelrod said that immigration reform would be more doable if Fox were less nativist. "You'll have to talk to Roger about that," Murdoch replied. But now Ailes, too, could see the logic of immigration reform. Whatever his personal views, he'd come to agree with the political argument, soon to be spelled out in the autopsy, that Republicans should embrace the issue. The two media men told the senators that Fox News would help.

Hannity and O'Reilly, Fox's biggest stars and among the biggest critics of the 2007 immigration-reform effort, would be the crucial players. Ailes was confident they'd cooperate. While both hosts were prima donnas, with their constant demands for more money and various power plays, they were, in the end, good and loyal soldiers. When Ailes was trying to defuse some of Beck's and the Tea Party's madness that he believed was damaging the news channel, O'Reilly pitched in by aggressively attempting to debunk an emerging conservative conspiracy theory that Obama had been born in Kenya, not Hawaii, and was ineligible to be president. And Hannity didn't squawk when Ailes made him embarrassingly cancel an appearance at a Tea Party event that he'd been promoting on his show. Now, they delivered again. Both invited Rubio on their shows to tout the legislation, before giving it their own seals of approval. "I like your program. I think it's fair," O'Reilly told Rubio, while Hannity proclaimed, "I think it's probably the most thoughtful bill that I have heard heretofore."

Ultimately, Fox News's support for immigration reform wasn't enough. After the legislation passed the Senate, it died in the House—the victim, again, of a conservative grassroots rebellion, only this time a rebellion largely led by new-media outlets, such as *Breitbart News*, that didn't even exist in 2007. But Murdoch and Ailes did not waver from their shared conviction that the GOP needed the sort of course correction recommended by the autopsy. And as their attention turned to the 2016 Republican (and another Fox News) primary, they were in search of a candidate who could deliver that message. They weren't certain who could—at some points the news channel favored Rubio, at others it was Jeb Bush, for a time it was Ben Carson. But there was one candidate who they knew for certain could not: Donald Trump.

In 2014, Ivanka Trump arranged a lunch with her father and Murdoch, according to Joshua Green's *Devil's Bargain*. "My father has something big to tell you," she announced. "What's that?" Murdoch asked. "He's going to run for president," she replied. "He's not running for president," Murdoch said, not even bothering to look up from his soup, before changing the subject. Murdoch and Trump had been friendly enough with one another for decades, as they traveled in some of the same New York social circles, but Murdoch did not take Trump seriously—not as a person, not as a businessman, and certainly not as a presidential candidate.

Once Trump came down his golden escalator in June 2015 and told the world that he was running, Murdoch made his doubts public. Responding to Trump's contention that Mexican immigrants were "rapists" and bringing drugs into the United States, Murdoch wrote on Twitter: "Mexican immigrants, as with all immigrants, have much lower crime rates than native born. . . . Trump wrong." After Trump mocked John McCain for having been shot down as a Navy pilot during the Vietnam War, Murdoch took to Twitter again to ask, "When is Donald Trump going to stop embarrassing his friends, let alone the whole country?"

For his part, Ailes had long recognized that Trump was good for Fox News's ratings. Back in 2011, he'd given the businessman a regular weekly segment on *Fox & Friends*, where, among other ramblings, Trump promoted the birther conspiracy theory about Obama with no pushback from the show's hosts. (Ailes left it to O'Reilly to invite Trump on his prime-time show and then demolish the theory to Trump's face.) In 2015, as Trump teased a presidential bid and then eventually made it official, Ailes made sure that Fox lavished plenty of attention on him. But in that respect, Fox was no different from CNN or MSNBC, which gave the topic of Trump's presidential run—and Trump himself—just as much airtime as Fox. At MSNBC, Joe Scarborough and Mika Brzezinski had Trump on *Morning Joe* so often—even letting him call in for his interviews, rather than making him appear on set—that Trump at one point referred to the pair as "supporters" and gushed to them, "You have me almost as a legendary figure." Meanwhile, CNN—whose president, Jeff Zucker, helped Trump create *The Apprentice* when he ran NBC—was in the habit of airing live shots of the empty podium before Trump's rallies with the chyron: "DONALD TRUMP EXPECTED TO SPEAK ANY MINUTE." Indeed, some at Fox believed that Trump was such an obvious disaster as a presidential candidate that CNN's and MSNBC's decision to pay so much attention to him could only be explained by nefarious motives. "I can assure you one thing," Krauthammer grumbled on *Special Report* the day of Trump's announcement. "The mainstream media who wished the Republicans no good will lavish upon him enormous coverage."

In August, Fox News hosted the first Republican presidential debate. Murdoch and Ailes hoped to use it to deal Trump's candidacy a serious, perhaps even fatal, blow. The debate's first question, from Bret Baier, asked: "Is there anyone on stage, and can I see hands, who is unwilling tonight to pledge your support to the eventual nominee of the Republican party and pledge to not run an independent campaign against that person?" Trump had already made clear that he refused to take such a pledge, and so after he was, predictably, the only one of the ten candidates on the stage to raise his hand, Baier singled him out with a follow-up. "Experts say an independent run would almost certainly hand the race over to Democrats and likely another Clinton," Baier told Trump. "You can't say tonight that you can make that pledge?" Then it was Megyn Kelly's turn. Confronting Trump with a litany of sexist insults he's flung at women over the years—"fat pigs, dogs, slobs, and disgusting animals"—she asked, "Does that sound to you like the temperament of a man we should elect as president, and how will you answer the charge from Hillary Clinton, who is likely to be the Democratic nominee, that you are part of the war on women?" Finally, Chris Wallace, the third debate moderator, cited Trump's claim that he had evidence the Mexican government was intentionally sending criminals to the United States and asked, "Why not use this first Republican presidential debate to share your proof with the American people?" After the debate, Fox News broadcast a focus group, conducted by the Republican pollster Frank Luntz, that featured a couple dozen Republican voters; most of them had gone into the evening saying they had a positive view of Trump, but now they ripped him to shreds. "He just crashed and burned," said one middle-aged man. "He was mean, he was angry, he had no specifics."

Trump did not respond well to the onslaught. The day after the debate, appearing on CNN, he crudely attacked Kelly. "You could see there was blood coming out of her eyes," he said. "Blood coming out of her wherever." A few weeks later, he announced on Twitter that he was boycotting Fox News altogether; the news channel, he wrote, "has been treating me very unfairly & I have therefore decided that I won't be doing any more Fox shows for the foreseeable future."

For most of his time at Fox News, Carlson was far, far removed from the decisions that were made—and the dramas that played out—on the second floor of the news channel's Manhattan headquarters, where Ailes and his top lieutenants had their offices. On his trips to New York, he'd sometimes stop by the second floor to schmooze with Fox executives and remind them of his existence. "He seemed a little lost," a person who encountered Carlson on one such visit remembers. And he was always on the lookout for opportunities to demonstrate that he was aligned with the news channel's biggest and most important projects. When Mickey Kaus, a columnist for *The Daily Caller*, wrote a 2015 story attacking Fox News for not rallying opposition to immigration reform, Carlson ordered the column taken down, telling Kaus, "We can't trash Fox on the site." Kaus quit in protest. As Carlson half-jokingly told a shock jock radio host, "I'm 100 percent [Rupert Murdoch's] bitch. Whatever Mr. Murdoch says, I do." But these demonstrations of loyalty didn't seem to boost his standing inside the news channel. Relegated to the frivolous afterthought of *Fox & Friends Weekend*, Carlson was on the outside looking in at Fox.

Until, that is, Trump's presidential campaign. Carlson was, by no means, a Trump fan. In 1999, when he was still a magazine writer, he branded the New York real estate developer "the single most repulsive person on the planet." A few years later, after Carlson had become a cable-news host, he made a throwaway joke about Trump's hair on CNN—and Trump responded with a short voicemail. "It's true you have better hair than I do," he told Carlson's answering machine. "But I get more pussy than you do." Carlson thought the episode was funny; it maybe even made him like Trump the same way he liked Jim Traficant. It didn't, however, make Carlson think that Trump had what it takes to be president.

But by 2015, Carlson's thinking had begun to change. Part of the shift was a result of his usual contrarianism. "On my street in Northwest Washington, D.C., there's never been anyone as unpopular as Trump," he wrote later in the campaign. "Idi Amin would get a warmer reception in our dog park." Carlson viewed it as his long-held role, even his duty as the skunk invited to the political and media elite's garden party, to defy that consensus.

There was a deeper, more substantive reason for the change, as well. Ever since he'd launched *The Daily Caller* five years earlier, he'd been immersing himself in its web-traffic metrics; they served as an early-warning system for Carlson about where the conservative base was headed—and how a populist candidate who explicitly ran on nativism, white grievance, and sexism might have a lane in a Republican primary.

This insight made Carlson unusual at Fox. Much like Murdoch had initially dismissed the notion of Trump running for president when Ivanka first told him, so did the pundits at his cable-news channel. "Even among conservatives in Fox, there was the view that Trump's an idiot, he's not a serious person, that there wasn't a chance of him winning," Ken LaCorte, a former Fox News executive, recalled. This posed a problem for Fox, especially since Ailes knew covering Trump was good for ratings; to make for compelling television, the news channel needed to put people on air who wouldn't simply dismiss Trump out of hand. "The project at Fox of trying to find normal-seeming, television-camera-ready human beings who would make a sensible case for Donald Trump was no small lift," a former Fox producer said.

Enter Carlson. Fox producers had taken notice of the heterodox views on Trump that he was offering on *Fox & Friends*. Soon he began appearing with increasing regularity on other Fox shows, particularly *Special Report*, whose All-Star Panel had become something of a Never Trump redoubt. A few days after Trump's official announcement, while Krauthammer was hailing Jeb Bush's own official announcement as "unexpectedly good, energetic" and "the biggest news" of the campaign, Carlson countered that Trump's entry was more significant. Trump was "filling the role" of the candidate who "has his opinions," Carlson said. "Some of them are kind of interesting. Some of them are right, by the way. He can say exactly what he wants. I think it could potentially be a problem." As the campaign went on, he urged his fellow panelists to, essentially, get over themselves.

"Avert your gaze from Trump, look at what he is saying or what he stands for in the eyes of voters," Carlson said. "I think it's a pretty compelling message, obviously." As Carlson explained during another episode of *Special Report*, "The economy and our culture and the population have totally changed in the last 25 years, and the people in charge didn't notice. And so everything is changing, not just our politics." Two decades earlier, Bill Kristol, David Frum, and other intellectual gatekeepers had managed to excommunicate Pat Buchanan from the conservative movement. But now publications like *The Weekly Standard* and *National Review* stood powerless in the face of Trump.

So, in a way, did Fox. Going into 2016, Murdoch and Ailes believed that Fox had the power to make the GOP's nominee, but as the campaign went on, and Trump's hold on the Republican primary electorate became increasingly clear, Murdoch and Ailes recognized that Trump had the power to unmake Fox. Before long, Hannity, O'Reilly, and eventually even Megyn Kelly were boosting him on their shows, and Trump, abandoning his boycott of the news channel, returned to its airwaves. In September, two months before the election, Hannity filmed a testimonial for Trump that was featured in a campaign video. Carlson never went that far, but Murdoch didn't forget his prescience. After Ailes's departure from Fox in August 2016, the octogenarian media tycoon took direct control of the news channel, appointing himself its interim CEO. Murdoch sought to stabilize Fox but also plot a course for its future—a future that, no matter what happened on Election Day, would have to take into account a viewing audience that had been deeply affected by, and was now extremely loyal to, Donald Trump. In November, five days before the election, Murdoch made his first big move, when Fox News announced its new 7:00 p.m. show: *Tucker Carlson Tonight*.

SEVEN

Tucker Carlson Tonight premiered on November 14, 2016. Approximately 3.7 million viewers tuned in—either out of curiosity about the Fox News Channel's newest evening host or, perhaps more likely, out of habit. The presidential campaign, culminating in Donald Trump's election six days earlier, was an unprecedented ratings boon to Fox. Not only did the news channel maintain its lead over its rivals CNN and MSNBC (which also enjoyed huge campaign-fueled ratings bumps), but for the first time in its twenty-year history, Fox became the most-watched network on all of basic cable, topping the traditional leaders ESPN and USA.

But Trump's victory offered Fox something even more compelling than eyeballs: power. Still more of a media creature than a political one, Trump was not entering the White House with the usual retinue of—not to mention reverence for—seasoned policy advisers. He promised to be an unusually accessible—and malleable—president for the television executives and on-air personalities whose opinions he respected and solicited.

In the two and a half months between the election and Trump's inauguration, Rupert Murdoch became a frequent visitor to Trump Tower, where he congratulated the president-elect on his stunning victory, advised him on how to fill his cabinet, and maybe ventured a thought or two about his own parochial priorities—like stopping AT&T from acquiring Time Warner, which owns CNN. (In November 2017, Trump's Justice Department filed a lawsuit to block the $85 billion deal on antitrust grounds, but the lawsuit was unsuccessful, and the merger was ultimately completed in 2018.) Fox News personalities like Eric Bolling, Pete Hegseth, and Jeanine Pirro stopped by Trump Tower, too, as did Fox News president Bill Shine. Sean Hannity, meanwhile, was lobbying Trump and those around him to become White House chief of staff. Where Fox News had long been the Republican Party's media arm, it now seemed as if the Trump White House was going to become the political arm of Fox News.

As the host of one of Fox's evening shows, a job he landed because he was one of the first people at the network to recognize Trump's political appeal, Carlson was well positioned to wield influence in the new administration. Yet he wanted no part of that political project. It was, in some respects, simply a failure of his imagination. While his more established Fox News colleagues were suddenly alive to the new political possibilities a Trump presidency offered them, Carlson was focused on the television nuts and bolts of his role—which, superficially, would differ little from the rest of the Fox lineup. He insisted that he do the new show from his "natural habitat" behind an anchor's desk—"a safety barrier," as he called it—so that, unlike on *Fox & Friends* or, even worse, *Dancing with the Stars*, the viewing audience would not have to "see my lower half." He submitted to a more grown-up haircut—trading in his self-described "reefer-smoking, revolutionary" shag for a shorter, conservative style that, combined with a weight gain, made him a dead ringer for his father during his banker days. "Wouldn't you invest money with me?" he joked.

Most critically, Carlson concentrated his energies on putting together a team to back him up—a group that would later be known inside Fox as the "Tuckertroop." Many initial members of the Tuckertroop were inherited from Greta Van Susteren's canceled show that previously occupied the 7:00 p.m. slot, including the executive producer, Justin Wells. But Carlson made sure to have some familiar faces, as well. One was Blake Neff, an education reporter for *The Daily Caller* who was a former *Dartmouth Review* editor and, according to one *Caller* colleague, "the most brilliant guy" at the website; Carlson made Neff his show's head writer. Later, he hired Alex Pfeiffer, his son Buckley's former prep school friend whom Carlson had given a reporting job at the *Caller* after Pfeiffer dropped out of Sewanee; Carlson made Pfeiffer an investigative producer on his show. After eight years in the cable-news wilderness and the long, arduous climb back to prime time, Carlson had no illusions about whether he'd get another shot at helming another eponymous show. He was putting together a staff that wasn't for his amusement but for his success. "Tucker knew that Fox was his last chance," a former Fox producer said. He was determined not to blow it.

But, at the dawn of Trump's presidency, it wasn't just short-sightedness that stopped Carlson from angling for the political power that captivated so many of his Fox colleagues. It was also prudence. Despite his clairvoyance about candidate Trump's political appeal, he nursed serious, even grave doubts about president-elect Trump's fitness for office. This was partly a matter of sensibility. A pure product of La Jolla and St. George's School, Carlson's aesthetic preference remained those of an old-money WASP—preppy, shabby chic, expensive but understated. Like everyone, he'd seen the pictures of Trump's gold-and-marble rococo apartment in Trump Tower—and he was repulsed. Trump had an "innkeeper's mentality," Carlson complained to friends: Trump was desperate, too desperate to impress with glitz and glam. Carlson thought such a mentality was unbecoming in a president.

More important, Carlson questioned Trump's political judgment. While he believed many of Trump's critics were hysterical in their condemnations, he certainly had his own reservations. In March 2016, as it was becoming more and more apparent that Trump would be the Republican nominee, Carlson bumped into John McCormack, a young *Weekly Standard* writer (whom Carlson had once tried to hire at the *Caller*) in the greenroom of Fox News's Washington studio. Carlson's old magazine had recently run a piece attacking the "Vichy Republicans" who were falling in line behind Trump and Carlson had a minor bone to pick. "Come on, Trump's not evil," he told McCormack. "He's just mentally ill." Now that Trump had won, Carlson concluded that he simply had too much riding on his new show to completely throw in with the new president. He knew that, as a Fox host, it wasn't tenable for him to oppose Trump, or even so much as criticize him—Carlson's qualms were for the greenroom, not the studio. But that didn't mean he was going to join Hannity and his other Fox colleagues who were gleefully gluing themselves to Trump either. The last time Carlson had swallowed his doubts in the name of partisan allegiance, he'd supported the Iraq War. What if a Trump presidency was a similar disaster? He did not want the success of his new show to hinge on Trump's.

Carlson previewed his solution to the bind in which he found himself on the first episode of *Tucker Carlson Tonight*, when he offered his viewers a mission statement. "What's the show going to be about? You can judge for yourself, but here's the basic theme of it," he announced.

> People in power tend to lie. Not that they want to but because they can't help themselves. That's human nature.

> The more power people have, the bigger the temptation to misuse it. The press is supposed to be the watchdog against all of this, and it worked fine for a couple of centuries, but then the press decided they had more in common with certain politicians than with readers or viewers, and that's when it fell apart. We're going to get back to basics here. We're going to hold the powerful accountable, pierce pomposity, translate doublespeak, mock smugness, and barbecue nonsense every night.

With the GOP having hit the so-called government trifecta in the 2016 elections—winning control of the White House, the House of Representatives, and the Senate—it stood to reason that Trump and his fellow Republicans now had the most power in Washington and therefore, according to human nature, the greatest temptation to misuse it. That was certainly the conclusion of most mainstream media outlets, which were reinvigorated as they made watchdogging Trump their new identities—and enjoyed a spike in readers and viewers as a result. *The Washington Post*, which saw its digital subscriptions triple over the course of the first Trump administration, went so far as to adopt the slogan "Democracy Dies in Darkness" and portentously slap it on its front page.

But on *Tucker Carlson Tonight*, the people in power, the ones who needed to be held to account, were not the president and cabinet secretaries and members of Congress. Rather, they were academics and actors and activists—the people who (occasionally) took to the streets and (with greater regularity) social media to oppose Trump and his new administration, the people who fashioned themselves as the anti-Trump #Resistance. For Carlson, in the early days of his show, the #Resistance was the ultimate foil, providing a seemingly inexhaustible supply of pomposity to pierce, smugness to mock, and nonsense to barbecue. There was no need for Carlson to become a Trump cheerleader or even a Trump defender when, instead, he could devote his airtime to opposing Trump's opponents—helping to invent the ideological escape hatch now known as anti-anti-Trumpism.

In real life, and in his past cable-news simulacra of real life, Carlson was the consummate schmoozer; he relished the conversations he had over multicourse lunches and, when on the job, in greenrooms and during commercial breaks. "After food, water, and sex," he once wrote, "the strongest human desire may be for someone interesting to talk to." But on *Tucker Carlson Tonight*, there was scant opportunity for those sorts of interactions. Instead of having the show's guests come on set, Carlson did most of his interviews remotely, with his guest beaming in from a different studio (even if, as was sometimes the case, that studio was in Fox's Capitol Hill offices where Carlson was broadcasting from). The setup may have deprived Carlson of his strongest human desire, but it offered him control. If a guest was winning an argument or threatening to upstage him—by, say, calling him a "dick" and accusing him of "hurting America"—the guest's feed could be cut and the interview brought to a hasty end; Carlson was guaranteed to always have the last word.

What's more, the remote interviews afforded Carlson the ability to score points even when he wasn't talking. His producers would "box" Carlson's face alongside his guest's, allowing viewers to watch his facial expressions react in real time—with incredulity, outrage, disdain, or any other negative emotion—to whatever his guest happened to be saying. Unlike his previous cable-news interactions with sparring partners like James Carville and Rachel Maddow, which always seemed to end on a cordial, let's-agree-to-disagree note, the setup on his Fox show was engineered to elicit and then highlight Carlson's contempt for his guests.

And Carlson was certainly blessed with a surfeit of Trump opponents and critics for him to invite on his show to attack. Some were more worthy, and consequential, foes than others.

Like Ben Smith, then the editor of *BuzzFeed News*, who, shortly before Trump's inauguration, published a thirty-five-page dossier of unverified allegations about ties between Trump and Russia—including, most infamously, the allegation that Russian intelligence services possessed an incriminating videotape of Trump enjoying a golden shower from prostitutes at Moscow's Ritz-Carlton hotel. The dossier, which was written by a former British intelligence officer named Christopher Steele at the behest of Hillary Clinton's campaign, drove and dominated news coverage of Trump's alleged collusion with Russia; for almost two years, rarely a night went by that Maddow didn't cite it on MSNBC. But the Steele dossier, and its publication, turned out to be a blessing in disguise for Trump. It was so rife with explosive but ultimately disproven (by the Justice Department's inspector general and others) allegations—including the one about the so-called "pee tape"—that by the time special counsel Robert Mueller issued his *Report on the Investigation into Russian Interference in the 2016 Presidential Election* in March 2019, which exhaustively documented how Russia sought to help elect Trump and how Trump and his advisers welcomed that assistance, Mueller's report seemed like small beer. Indeed, Trump and his supporters claimed Mueller's report as exoneration.

Still, when *BuzzFeed* published the Steele dossier in January 2017, it was initially considered quite damaging to Trump—and Carlson invited Smith on his show later that month. "Let's say I had an unverified document given to me by one of your enemies, claiming that you had committed a sex crime," Carlson proposed to Smith. "Let's say I had no evidence at all that it was true, but I did know that releasing it would gravely damage your reputation. Should I release it? Or let me phrase it another way. Of course I would never publish that because it would be unfair." Smith parried that *BuzzFeed* published the dossier because it was already in wide circulation among elected officials and journalists, who were "making dark intimations" about it in press releases and reports. "Show them the document and let people see the thing that is being referred to," Smith argued. "We're living in this world where there's tons of unverified information, and where we have to figure out ways to help our audience navigate and reckon with that." Carlson wasn't having it. "I'm for openness. I'm for transparency," he told Smith. "But by setting yourself up as a champion of press freedom, you're being slightly disingenuous because there is a political component here."

Then there was Max Boot. He and Carlson had once been colleagues at *The Weekly Standard*. There, Boot wrote a series of influential articles cheerleading for George W. Bush's war on terror and the invasions of Afghanistan and Iraq—predicting that the latter would "mark the moment when the powerful antibiotic known as democracy was introduced into the diseased environment of the Middle East, and began to transform the region for the better"; he later became a foreign policy adviser to Republican presidential candidates John McCain and Mitt Romney and advocated for American military intervention in Libya and Syria. In 2016, Boot, for the first time in his life, voted against a Republican presidential nominee, explaining, "I would sooner vote for Josef Stalin than I would vote for Donald Trump." Like many neoconservatives, Boot became part of the Never Trump movement. Trump's subsequent election only strengthened Boot's Never Trump convictions, which he gave ample voice to on Twitter and eventually a weekly column in *The Washington Post*.

In the summer of 2017, Boot was attacking Trump for cozying up to Vladimir Putin when Carlson invited him on his show. Carlson told Boot he didn't see Russia as a serious threat. Boot told Carlson that he was being a "cheerleader" for Moscow and, by extension, its allies in Tehran and Damascus. Carlson called Boot's accusation "grotesque." Then Carlson went in for the kill. "To dismiss people who disagree with you as immoral, which is your habit, isn't a useful form of debate; it's a kind of moral preening," he lectured Boot. "And it's a little odd coming from you, who really has been consistently wrong in the most flagrant and flamboyant way for over a decade."

Carlson's debates with Smith and Boot—accomplished individuals who wielded considerable influence in American politics and media—made for good, useful television; the segments produced plenty of heat but also a lot of light. More often than not, though, Carlson's sparring partners weren't heavyweights like Smith and Boot. They were the cut outs and straw men of the "Big Brother" format Carlson once derided—guests he brought in from the fringes or elevated from irrelevancy just so he could slap them around.

Like Alex Mohajer, a self-described "political commentator" who, in an article for *The Huffington Post*'s contributor section—i.e., the section of the website that was devoted to stories by unpaid citizen journalists—argued that "Hillary Clinton is the rightful President-elect of the United States" and that a federal judge should enjoin Trump and install her in the White House. "How does this work exactly?" Carlson asked Mohajer, who gave a predictably stumbling and unconvincing answer. "This is so stupid," a cackling Carlson said, before dismissing Mohajer as "a crackpot" and declaring the interview over.

Or like Matthew Hughey, a University of Connecticut sociology professor who planned to argue in an upcoming lecture titled "Make America White Again: The Racial Reasoning of American Nationalism"—of which Carlson's crack researchers got wind—that Trump's victory was attributable to white supremacy. As Hughey repeated his argument for Fox viewers—"It's not just white supremacy, but it's gender dynamics, it's heteronormativity, it's capitalism"—Carlson made a spectacle of trying to follow along, a baffled look spreading across his face. "Do you have tenure, by the way?" Carlson asked Hughey, who replied that he did. "So nothing you say, no matter how silly, can ever get you fired," Carlson said. "Is that true?!"

Or, most memorably, like Shane Saunders, a Los Angeles man who participated in one of the Not My President's Day anti-Trump protests across the country on Presidents' Day. Saunders had no connection to the protest organizers (who'd refused Carlson's booker's invitations to appear on the show). He was an actor but not a well-known one (his credits were mostly as an extras casting assistant). And, although he did take part in the nationwide protests, so did thousands of other people—any of whom, it seemed, would have been better equipped to debate Carlson on the merits of the demonstrations.

"What's the point of it?" Carlson asked Saunders, who, for more than five minutes, tried and repeatedly failed to answer that simple question—to Carlson's increasing bemusement. "I'm making the mistake of taking you seriously," a laughing Carlson told Saunders, "which I will never do again, I can promise you that. Shane, thanks a lot for joining us."

Carlson's fans clipped and posted his best smackdowns to YouTube, Twitter, and Reddit. Stills from the videos—Carlson framed in one window wearing a look of incredulity or bewilderment; his hapless guest caught mid-yammer in the other window—became a sort of digital diptych of the early Trump era. It turned out that millions of Americans loved watching someone who could reliably, and serially, humiliate people they despised. As one Carlson superfan, who wound up compiling nearly twenty hours of Carlson's most contentious and withering interviews on his YouTube channel, put it: "You Can't Cuck The Tuck." Indeed, the challenge for Carlson became finding people who disagreed with him and were dumb or shameless enough to go on his show; he began to focus less on his guests and more on his opening monologue, which would soon become the centerpiece of *Tucker Carlson Tonight*. "The reason the debate era of the show ended isn't because Tucker couldn't handle the debate," said a former Fox producer. "It's because good people wouldn't come on anymore."

Tucker Carlson Tonight WAS SUCH a ratings success at 7:00 p.m. that when, at the start of 2017, Megyn Kelly decamped to NBC News—where she would make twenty-three million dollars a year and, she hoped, find an audience that did not resent her for having once aggressively questioned Trump—Rupert Murdoch immediately slid Carlson into Kelly's now-vacant 9:00 p.m. slot. His ratings, averaging 3.7 million viewers a night, soon surpassed hers. Three months later, *The New York Times* revealed that Fox News and Bill O'Reilly, the highest-rated host in all of cable news who'd anchored the crucial 8:00 p.m. block at Fox for more than two decades, had paid about thirteen million dollars to five women who'd accused him of sexual harassment or other inappropriate behavior. In the wake of the Roger Ailes scandal, and the more than fifty advertisers who abandoned O'Reilly's show following the *New York Times* report, Murdoch forced O'Reilly out. It was a difficult but necessary decision—made easier by the fact that Murdoch knew he could move Carlson to 8:00 p.m. A mere five months after being stuck in the netherworld of weekend mornings, Carlson now occupied the most prestigious and powerful hour in cable news—a remarkable reversal of fortune that, as he confided to friends, sometimes even he didn't believe.

And Fox News, in many respects, now occupied the White House. Hannity, who eventually helmed the 9:00 p.m. hour in Fox's revamped, post-O'Reilly prime-time lineup, didn't get the chief of staff job, but his phone calls and visits with Trump were so frequent and influential that some White House aides now referred to him as "the unofficial chief of staff," with one telling *The Washington Post* that "he basically has a desk in the place." Laura Ingraham, whom Murdoch plucked from talk radio to fill Fox's 10:00 p.m. slot, was also in regular contact with Trump; before she got the prime-time gig, Trump had even contemplated making her White House press secretary or communications director. (When Ingraham joined Carlson as a guest on the first episode of *Tucker Carlson Tonight*, Carlson told her, "I wanted to get you on before you get drafted by the Trump people.") Trump's entwinement with Fox was so profound that one morning *Fox & Friends* featured a live shot of the White House with a light blinking in a second-floor window after its cohost Steve Doocy, addressing the president, asked him to flick the lights if he was watching the show; after the clip went viral on Twitter, Fox had to clarify that the lights were a "video effect" and that the bit had been a joke.

Despite his anti-anti-Trump, rather than explicitly pro-Trump, stance, Carlson still enjoyed warm relations with some Trump administration officials. He was old friends with White House press secretary Sean Spicer, a veteran Republican flack whom Carlson first met when they were both teenagers and Spicer attended the Portsmouth Abbey School in Newport, St. George's rival, and they wrestled against each other. Stephen Miller was a newer acquaintance of Carlson's, but an important one. Miller had gone from the Senate to the Trump campaign and was now a White House policy adviser in charge of crafting the administration's restrictionist immigration policy. He and Carlson immediately hit it off, with Carlson coming back from a White House meeting with Miller early in the administration gushing that the sepulchral adviser was "perhaps the smartest person" he'd ever met in politics. And Carlson held Jeff Sessions, Trump's attorney general (and Miller's old boss in the Senate), in especially high regard—not just because of Sessions's hard-line anti-immigration views but also Sessions's genuine economic populism, which Carlson believed made Sessions unique, even in Trump's administration. The two developed such a strong relationship that, in July, Sessions allowed Carlson to accompany him on an official trip to El Salvador so that Carlson could produce a special report on the country's MS-13 gang problem. Over ominous footage of heavily tattooed young men in steel cages inside one of the Central American country's notorious prisons, Carlson warned Fox viewers, "Before long, some of these guys may wind up in LA or Long Island. It's happening now."

Yet, even while he parroted similar Trumpian talking points, Carlson remained one of the few Fox hosts who kept a wary personal and professional distance from the president himself. Still, there was nothing he could do to prevent Trump from watching his show—nor could he stop Trump from calling him when the show was over. "Tucker didn't seek it," says a former White House official. "Tucker wasn't calling Trump. Trump was calling him." The first time Trump reached out to Carlson to talk shop, Carlson was flabbergasted. The TV host mused to friends and colleagues that the president had to have more important matters to tend to than watching a cable news show and offering notes on it to its host. (Trump seemed to share these concerns, at least when it came to public perception, writing on Twitter early in his presidency: "The W.H. is functioning perfectly, focused on HealthCare, Tax Cuts/Reform & many other things. I have very little time for watching T.V.") But as Trump continued calling him, Carlson's attitude went from bemusement to paranoia. He confided to multiple people that he suspected the phone calls were being recorded by intelligence agencies or Trump himself; as a result, he tried to keep his side of the conversation to a polite minimum to prevent Trump or anyone else from being able to use any of his words against him some day. "If you heard a tape of their early conversations," said one person who worked with Carlson at Fox, "you'd mostly just hear Tucker laughing a lot and saying, 'Okay' and 'Interesting.'"

On a Friday in February, when Carlson had the night off from hosting duties, *Tucker Carlson Tonight* ran a prerecorded interview Carlson did with Ami Horowitz, a conservative documentary filmmaker/provocateur who'd recently made a ten-minute digital short for Fox News about Sweden's influx of Muslim refugees. According to Horowitz, the Swedish government was covering up a crime surge of rape and gun violence committed by these Muslim immigrants. "Sweden had its first terrorist, Islamic attack not that long ago, so they're now getting a taste of what we've been seeing across Europe already," Horowitz reported. "The masochism of the West really knows no bounds, at all," Carlson intoned.

It was a throwaway segment—the sort of evergreen, in-house promotional interview Fox hosts were in the habit of banking so that they could fulfill their company man responsibilities and enjoy the occasional three-day weekend. And that's all it would have been if the president of the United States hadn't been watching. Less than twenty-four hours after Carlson's interview with Horowitz aired, Trump addressed a campaign rally in Florida—never mind that the next election was still almost four years away—and made the case, as he often did, for stronger borders. He cited a host of European cities that had suffered terrorist attacks—Brussels, Nice, Paris—as examples of the dangers posed by Muslim refugees. "You look at what's happening in Germany," Trump went on. "You look at what's happening last night in Sweden. Sweden! Who would believe this? Sweden."

White House reporters—and everyone else—were baffled. There hadn't been a terrorist attack in Sweden the night before. (In fact, there hadn't been a terrorist attack in Sweden since

2010, when a suicide bomber in Stockholm injured two people.) On Twitter, the former Swedish prime minister Carl Bildt wrote, "Sweden? Terror attack? What has he been smoking? Questions abound." The next day, Trump took to Twitter to offer an answer. "My statement as to what's happening in Sweden was in reference to a story that was broadcast on @FoxNews concerning immigrants & Sweden," he wrote.

It was one of countless through-the-looking-glass moments of Trump's first presidency. ("From an Anchor's Lips to Trump's Ears to Sweden's Disbelief," read the headline on *The New York Times* article about the episode.) But for Carlson, it was a revelation. While he was obviously, at times painfully, aware that Trump watched his show, that the president was in fact addicted to cable news and to Fox News in particular, Carlson had been operating under the assumption that if a cable host wanted to wield real influence over Trump, he needed to do it off air, with special pleadings during late-night phone calls or Oval Office visits. But the Sweden episode showed Carlson that one-on-one lobbying and cajoling—the sort of behavior that, unlike Hannity and so many of his other Fox colleagues, he was unwilling to engage in—was unnecessary. Carlson realized that the words—and, ultimately, the deeds—of the president could be manipulated through the television itself.

Carlson began to conceive of *Tucker Carlson Tonight* as a show for an "audience of one." Although he never lost sight of the wants and needs of the broader universe of Fox News viewers—indeed, within the network, Carlson was known to be keenly attuned to the "minute-by-minutes," the expensive ratings data Fox paid for that offered a far more granular view of viewer behavior than Nielsen's tracking of fifteen-minute blocks—he started to write his monologues, plan his segments, and book his guests with an eye toward influencing the president. He wanted to, as Fred Barnes used to put it, affect the game.

Carlson was particularly interested in swaying Trump on foreign policy. Although Trump had broken sharply with Republican dogma during the campaign by condemning military adventurism and even blaming George W. Bush for 9/11, Carlson worried that his cabinet and White House staff picks (including secretary of state Rex Tillerson, secretary of defense Jim Mattis, and national-security adviser H. R. McMaster) were neocons, not realists, and were wedded to the GOP's old way of foreign policy thinking. He sought to counter their, in his view, malign influence.

When Tillerson was on the verge of appointing Elliott Abrams, a neoconservative grandee who'd served on George W. Bush's National Security Council and was one of the architects of the Iraq War (and the son-in-law of Norman Podhoretz to boot), to be his deputy at the State Department, Carlson had Kentucky senator Rand Paul on his show to disparage Abrams as a Never Trumper. Paul noted that during the campaign Abrams had written an article for *The Weekly Standard* titled "When You Can't Stand Your Candidate." Trump, who had met with Abrams and come away favorably disposed to his nomination, saw the segment and abruptly changed his mind, telling Tillerson that Abrams couldn't work for him after all. Later, when Trump was considering tapping Dina Powell, a Goldman Sachs executive who'd previously served as his deputy national-security adviser, to be US ambassador to the United Nations, Carlson devoted a short monologue to pouring water on the idea. "Powell seems like a nice person and lots of people like her," he said, before noting that she'd once worked with the Clinton Foundation, was friends with Valerie Jarrett and Arianna Huffington, and as an official in the Bush administration had once boasted about the number of and speed with which student visas were being granted, concluding that "she's worked on behalf of virtually every idea that President Trump ran against in his 2016 campaign." The next morning Powell withdrew from consideration.

Carlson's foreign policy influence wasn't limited to stopping Trump from making certain hires. More than once he helped stop Trump from launching an imminent military attack. In the summer of 2019, after Iran shot down an American surveillance drone, Trump's top national-security advisers—including his secretary of defense, secretary of state, national-security adviser, and the chairman of the Joint Chiefs of Staff—were unanimous in their recommendation that he retaliate with air strikes against Iranian radar and missile batteries. On Fox, Hannity was also in favor of military action. "The president will have no choice: He will bomb the hell out of them," he said on his show. "We have the most advanced weapons systems, and a strong message needs to be sent that a huge price will be paid if you take on the United States of America." Trump appeared as if he was going to heed their advice. On the afternoon of June 20, he gave the green light to launch the attack. But three hours later, just ten minutes before the missiles were to be launched, he changed his mind and called off the strikes.

One contributor to the president's change of mind was Carlson, who'd been offering a lonely albeit impassioned voice of dissent. On his show—and, in this instance, in off-air conversations with Trump—he argued that attacking Iran would be a mistake, not least because, he said, it would cost Trump reelection. Indeed, Carlson claimed that the people pushing Trump to attack Iran actually favored that outcome. "The neocons still wield enormous power in Washington," he said on his show. "They don't care what the cost of a war with Iran is. They certainly don't care what the effect on Trump's political fortunes might be. They despise Donald Trump." After Trump aborted the strikes, Carlson was giddy. "Policy makers in Washington crave a war with Iran," he told Fox viewers. "Last night was supposed to be the first domino. At the last minute the president thwarted their plans."

Carlson found himself in a similar spot six months later in the aftermath of a targeted US air strike that killed Iranian military commander Qasem Soleimani. He was critical of the attack. Announcing the breaking news on Fox, he warned his viewers that "America appears to be lumbering toward a new Middle East war." By contrast, Hannity, who was on vacation that evening, called in to his show to hail the strike as "a huge victory and total leadership by the president." After Iran responded to Soleimani's assassination with retaliatory strikes against military bases housing US troops in Iraq, it seemed likely that Trump would launch another round of attacks. "Their hostility will now be met with the full force of the greatest, most advanced, most sophisticated military the world has ever seen," Hannity predicted/counseled on his Fox show. Most other Fox hosts offered similarly bellicose sentiments, with Pete Hegseth going so far as to encourage Trump to commit war crimes by targeting Iranian cultural sites. "If Iran could," Hegseth argued, "they would destroy every single one of our cultural sites and build a mosque on top of it."

But Carlson, again, urged caution—and did so with an argument that was tailor-made to appeal to Trump. "The people demanding action against Iran tonight, the ones telling you the Persian menace is the greatest threat we face," he said, "are the very same ones demanding that you ignore the invasion of America now in progress from the south, the millions, the tens of millions of foreign nationals living among us illegally." And, once again, Trump listened to Carlson and opted to forgo additional attacks. "The United States is ready to embrace peace with all who seek it," Trump said.

Tucker Carlson Tonight helped make Trump's domestic policy, as well. In the summer of 2020, Carlson interviewed Christopher Rufo, a conservative researcher in Washington state who'd recently written a series of articles for the Manhattan Institute's website about anti-racism trainings being conducted by diversity consultants at federal agencies. On Fox, Rufo said the trainings were based on "critical race theory," which he described as a "cult indoctrination" that held that American society was irredeemably and systematically racist. "It's absolutely astonishing how critical race theory has pervaded every aspect of the federal government," Rufo told Carlson. Then, addressing his own audience of one, Rufo said, "The President and the White House—it's within their authority to immediately issue an executive order to abolish critical-race-theory training from the federal government. And I call on the President to immediately issue this executive order—to stamp out this destructive, divisive, pseudoscientific ideology."

The next morning, Rufo received a phone call from a 202 number that he didn't recognize. It was Mark Meadows, the White House chief of staff, telling Rufo that the president had seen his appearance on Fox and was inviting him to Washington, DC. A few days later, Rufo helped draft an executive order that put new restrictions on how contractors talk about race when conducting diversity seminars in federal agencies—kicking off the conservative war against critical race theory that is still going on today. "Tucker frames the narrative for conservative politics," Rufo later said. "Tucker doesn't react to the news; he creates the news."

Indeed, Carlson's influence was actually enhanced by his insistence on talking to Trump through his show rather than off air—not only largely refraining from calling Trump himself but, on more than one occasion, refusing to answer the phone when Trump called him. "Tucker was the hot girl that didn't want to fuck him," said one former Trump White House official. "Trump was like, 'What do you mean you don't want to?' He was intrigued." At one of the first White House senior staff meetings that Alyssa Farah Griffin attended upon becoming White House communications director in the spring of 2020, some of Trump's other advisers were discussing a segment that had aired on *Tucker Carlson Tonight* the previous evening when Griffin admitted that she hadn't watched. Jared Kushner, Trump's son-in-law and a senior adviser to the president, snapped at her, "You can't work in this White House and not watch Tucker Carlson."

Taking a page from Steve Bannon's old *Breitbart News* playbook, Carlson had turned *Tucker Carlson Tonight* into a political weapon. "The show itself was effectively a senior adviser to the president," a former Fox producer boasted, "and could change government policy." For all practical purposes, during Trump's first presidency the interagency process was replaced by the *Tucker Carlson Tonight* A block.

AT THE SAME TIME THAT Carlson was seeking to influence the Trump administration, he was also, in some ways, attempting to supplant it. In the aftermath of the 2016 election, a small group of conservative intellectuals began trying to reconcile their ideological movement to the man who now, improbably, sat atop it. They identified themselves as national conservatives, or NatCons. At think tanks like the Claremont Institute and in journals and on websites such as *American Greatness* and *The Federalist*, the NatCons tacked hard to the right on culture-war issues, denouncing critical race theory and drag queen story hours, while voicing a set of economic concerns more typically associated with the left, supporting child subsidies and industrial policy. Depending on your point of view, NatCons were either attempting to add intellectual heft to Trumpism or trying to reverse engineer an intellectual doctrine to match Trump's lizard-brain populism.

Either way, it was a difficult, frequently futile task. Trump proved to be a vexing ideological lodestar—aggressively anti-intellectual in his attitudes and consistently inconsistent in his views. Trying to construct a coherent ideology out of his administration's official positions, much less his off-the-cuff speeches and interviews, was not only frustrating; for anyone with a modicum of self-seriousness, to say nothing of self-respect, it was often humiliating.

Which is where Carlson came in. Each night on Fox, he was articulating a populist-nationalist ideology that was far more coherent than anything being offered by Trump himself. Eventually described as Trumpism without Trump, Carlson's worldview mixed anti-immigrant and, oftentimes, outright racist tropes with a clinical dissection of consumer capitalism and the deleterious effects it's had on American families, the working class, and civic society in general. It was a highbrow version of white grievance that painted the country as imperiled by a callous ruling elite and the desperate and violent migrant hordes infiltrating its borders. Pairing his staple rep ties and Rolex with this new populist streak, he assumed the role of class traitor.

The entire package was irresistible to NatCons, who began to view Carlson, as much as Trump, as their standard-bearer. At the inaugural National Conservatism Conference in 2019, Carlson was invited to give the keynote address. Meanwhile, Carlson began to borrow from new-right intellectuals themselves, including the neo-reactionary blogger Curtis Yarvin and Claremont Institute fellow Michael Anton, smuggling their fringe ideas—about how the United States would work better as a monarchy, for instance—into the conservative mainstream.

In one prolonged monologue in January 2019, Carlson railed against the "finance-based economy" and "internationalist foreign policy," favored by mainstream Republicans and Democrats alike, that had immiserated working-class Americans. "We are ruled by mercenaries who feel no long-term obligation to the people they rule," he told his viewers. "They're day traders. Substitute teachers. They're just passing through. They have no skin in this game, and it shows. They can't solve our problems. They don't even bother to understand our problems." He went on, "At some point, Donald Trump will be gone. . . . What kind of country will it be then? How do we want our grandchildren to live? These are the only questions that matter."

Later that year, Carlson devoted an eleven-minute segment—an eternity in cable news, longer even than his old nemesis Keith Olbermann's old Special Comments—to the plight of Sidney, Nebraska. The small town had once thrived as the headquarters of the sporting goods store Cabela's, but it was decimated after Cabela's merged with Bass Pro Shops and the headquarters closed, costing the town of six thousand more than two thousand jobs. The merger, Carlson explained, was done at the behest of a hedge fund run by the billionaire Paul Singer, which had taken an ownership stake in Cabela's and netted nearly a billion dollars after the merger drove up Cabela's short-term share prices. This sort of "vulture capitalism," Carlson told his viewers,

> bears no resemblances whatsoever to the capitalism we were promised in school. It creates nothing. It destroys entire cities. It couldn't be uglier or more destructive. So why is it still allowed in the United States? The short answer: because people like Paul Singer have tremendous influence over our political process. Singer himself was the second-largest donor to the Republican Party in 2016. He's given millions to a super PAC that supports Republican senators. You may never have heard of Paul Singer, which

> tells you a lot in itself. But in Washington he is rock star famous. And that may be why he's almost certainly paying a lower effective tax rate than your average fireman, just in case you're still wondering if our system is rigged.

That same month, Carlson took aim at the American Enterprise Institute, one of Washington's most venerable conservative think tanks (whose office building Carlson worked in when he was at *The Weekly Standard*). Citing reporting by *ProPublica*, Carlson told his viewers that AEI had played a hidden role in fueling the opioid epidemic by producing articles and op-eds that described OxyContin as "a godsend" and attacked law enforcement for overzealous prosecution of doctors for prescribing OxyContin—all without ever disclosing that Purdue Pharma, the maker of OxyContin, was a major donor to AEI. Noting that the opioid epidemic was particularly bad in red states, Carlson said, "A conservative think tank ran interference for a company whose products were disproportionately killing conservatives. Yeah, just another day in Washington. If you're starting to suspect that the conservative establishment doesn't really represent your interests, there's a reason for that. They're every bit as corrupt as you think they are."

Just as Carlson's show specialized in finding relatively unknown liberals for Carlson to slap down, it also excelled at taking stories from obscure corners of the conservative Internet and putting them in prime time. One evening on *Tucker Carlson Tonight*, its host would run a segment about the Romanian immigrants (except he didn't refer to them quite as kindly) who had settled in a Pennsylvania town and who—in a presumably unintentional echo of the type of anti-immigrant rhetoric he'd condemned on *The Wall Street Journal* editorial page some two decades earlier—"defecate in public, chop the heads off chickens, leave trash everywhere, and more." On another he'd complain in his monologue that America's leaders insist that "we've got a moral obligation to admit the world's poor . . . even if it makes our own country poorer, dirtier and more divided." And on another, just days after a racist white gunman killed twenty-three people in an attack on Hispanic shoppers at a Texas Walmart, Carlson would insist that "white supremacy" was "actually not a real problem in America" and that it was, in fact, "a hoax." In the summer of 2018, Carlson devoted multiple segments to South African land reform policy, falsely claiming that the country's Black-led government was seizing the farms of white South Africans because, according to Carlson, "they are the wrong skin color." He went on: "That is literally the definition of racism. Racism is what our elites say they dislike most."

Blake Neff, *Tucker Carlson Tonight*'s head writer, was responsible for many of these words that came out of Carlson's mouth. As he once boasted to Dartmouth's alumni magazine, "Anything he's reading off the teleprompter, the first draft was written by me." The anti-immigrant and racist sentiments that dominated the show came naturally to him. At the same time Neff was writing for Carlson—first as a reporter at *The Daily Caller* and then as a staffer on *Tucker Carlson Tonight*—he was also writing posts at a racist and sexist message board called AutoAdmit.

Posting under the username CharlesXII—the eighteenth-century Swedish warrior king who later became an icon for Swedish neo-Nazis—Neff joked about "foodie faggots" and proposed an "Urban business idea: He Didn't Do Muffin!" that would sell "Sandra Bland's Sugar-free Shortbreads!"—a reference to the twenty-eight-year-old Black woman who, in 2015, was taken into custody by a Texas state trooper after a traffic stop and was later found dead in her jail cell, becoming an early symbol of the Black Lives Matter movement. Neff agreed with other AutoAdmit commenters who argued that Michael Brown deserved to be killed by a Ferguson, Missouri, police officer, complaining that "the violent criminals are even MORE heroic to Black people." He claimed that the four liberal congresswomen known as "The Squad"—Alexandria Ocasio-Cortez, Ilhan Omar, Ayanna Pressley, and Rashida Tlaib—want to "MAKE YOUR COUNTRY A DUMPING GROUND FOR PEOPLE FROM THIRD WORLD SHITHOLES." In another post, Neff warned that "once Democrats have the majorities to go full F**K WHITEY, things are going to get really wacky really quickly" and lamented that there is a "large minority of whites who are fully supportive of a F**k Whitey agenda" and that "there's a suicidal impulse to Western peoples that honestly feels almost biological in origin."

After a CNN reporter discovered Neff's AutoAdmit posts in July 2020, Neff resigned from Fox News. (Years later, Neff, who eventually went to work as a producer on Charlie Kirk's podcast, would maintain that he was "the least racist person on AutoAdmit," noting that, unlike many of the site's users, "I never posted the n-word.") Carlson, for his part, claimed that he was unaware of the posts. "We don't endorse those words," he said. "They have no connection to this show." But Neff's AutoAdmit habit was not a secret to everyone he worked with. At *The Daily Caller*, Neff used to brag about his posts on the site to at least one colleague. "He was really proud of his AutoAdmit persona," the former *Caller* staffer recalled. And Neff's connection to Carlson was not a secret on AutoAdmit, either. When Scott Greer, Carlson and Neff's old *Daily Caller* colleague, appeared on *Tucker Carlson Tonight* to promote his book *No Campus for White Men* in 2017 (before Greer's own pseudonymous racist ratings for *Radix Journal* were uncovered), Neff dropped a favorite AutoAdmit catchphrase, "the sweet treats of scholarship," into Carlson's script introducing Greer. Neff's fellow board members didn't miss the Easter egg. "We maed [*sic*] it," one wrote.

Given all this, it's little wonder that among the nearly four million people who regularly tuned in to *Tucker Carlson Tonight*, some of them were white supremacists. One Carlson viewer was apparently Dylann Roof, who killed nine Black parishioners at the Emanuel African Methodist Episcopal Church in Charleston, South Carolina, in 2015. In a letter to Carlson that was purportedly written by Roof in 2019 from death row at a federal prison in Indiana—and that J. J. MacNab, a fellow at George Washington University's Program on Extremism, discovered on a white supremacist website and believes is authentic—Roof told the Fox host, "I watch your show almost every night, and most of the time I enjoy it." While Roof faulted Carlson for inviting "plenty of jews and blacks on your show," he praised him as "a relatively free thinker." Roof told Carlson he was writing him for a simple reason: "You are uniquely positioned because [of] your high profile to help the White race."

Mike Enoch, another prominent white supremacist, shouted out Carlson's segment about Paul Singer on his *Daily Shoah* podcast, noting that Carlson began the segment by mentioning that the notoriously anti-Semitic Henry Ford once raised the wages of his workers. "If you didn't catch the German shepherd whistles where he praised Henry Ford and then went into a diatribe of a Jewish financier," Enoch said approvingly, "I don't know what universe you're existing in."

One analysis of the neo-Nazi website *The Daily Stormer* found that between November 2016 and November 2018, Carlson had been mentioned in 265 articles on the site, most of them featuring clips of his show, with titles like "Tucker FILLS Liberal Kike with LEAD for Demanding Gun Control" and "Tucker Carlson FORCES Fat Beaner Whore to CHOKE to DEATH on GREASY TACOS." (Hannity, by comparison, was the subject of twenty-seven *Daily Stormer* articles during that time period; Ingraham was the subject of four.) As one blog post on the site celebrated: "Tucker Carlson is basically 'Daily Stormer: The Show.' Other than the language used, he is covering all our talking points."

Carlson maintained that he couldn't control who watched—and liked—his show. He insisted that he himself was not a white supremacist and, moreover, that white supremacists didn't even exist. "I've lived here for fifty years and I've never met anybody, not one person who ascribes to white supremacy," he said, adding, "I don't know a single person who think that's a good idea." But he didn't seem to want to know. In 2019, after Carlson hosted an anti-immigration North Carolina Congressional candidate named Pete D'Abrosca on his show, Carlson's old friend Jonah Goldberg sent him a text message alerting him to the fact that D'Abrosca was being strongly supported by Nick Fuentes, a prominent white-nationalist activist. Carlson sent Goldberg a text in response threatening to destroy him.

IN JULY 2020, *TUCKER CARLSON Tonight* became the highest-rated program in US cable-news history with an average nightly audience of 4.33 million viewers. But even before that feat, Carlson had, in many ways, become bigger than Fox News.

That was something that was never supposed to happen. When Ailes ran Fox News, the pecking order was clear. If a host or reporter stepped out of line, Ailes would simply yank that person off the air, instructing producers to "show 'em the red light." When Beck or O'Reilly or Hannity or any of the channel's other big names threatened to quit—which they seemed to do every six months, arguing that they no longer needed Fox since they had popular talk radio shows or best-selling books—Ailes would call their bluffs. "Go ahead," he told them. "You'll last two days." He practically dared them to decamp to Newsmax or One America News Network, a couple of Fox News imitators that launched in the 2010s. Under Ailes, the talent wasn't the star; Fox News was the star. "I create monsters and they bring in monster ratings," Ailes once said. "But then I have to control them." If Ailes couldn't control them, as was the case with Beck, he got rid of them.

The executive team that ultimately replaced Ailes did not enforce as much discipline. Fox News chief executive Suzanne Scott and Rupert Murdoch's son Lachlan, who was the chief executive of the Fox Corporation, were managers, not monster tamers, and the network's stars treated them as such—no one more than Carlson.

From the moment Murdoch moved Carlson into Fox's evening lineup, and Carlson moved into a corner office inside Fox's Washington headquarters, he started pissing off his colleagues. Chris Wallace, who hosted *Fox News Sunday*, the channel's most prestigious politics show after Baier's *Special Report*, took a particular dislike to him. Part of the bad blood stemmed from a decades-old incident involving the two men's fathers. In the early 1980s, when Dick Carlson was a vice president for a California savings and loan and Mike Wallace was in his prime at *60 Minutes*, the CBS news magazine ran an investigative story about the bank's home foreclosures of Black and Hispanic customers. Before being interviewed by Wallace for the story, Carlson requested and received permission to hire his own camera crew to tape the interview. After the *60 Minutes* story aired, Carlson leaked his recording to the *Los Angeles Times*, which revealed that, during a break when Wallace assumed the cameras were off, Wallace had joked that the people whose homes were foreclosed didn't read their mortgage contracts because they were "probably too busy eating their watermelon and tacos." Wallace maintained that he made the quip to try to elicit any possible "latent racist" sentiment from Carlson, but he was humiliated, and the moment dogged him. Six years later, when

Wallace gave the commencement address at the University of Michigan, his alma mater, students protested. That sort of family history might have made Tucker Carlson tread lightly around Chris Wallace, but he didn't. The hallway outside of Wallace's office in Fox's Washington headquarters was festooned with positive press clippings about the veteran anchorman. Carlson decided to decorate the hallway outside of his own office with negative press clippings about himself. Wallace was not amused.

Carlson's relationship with Hannity was even worse. Hannity resented Carlson's ratings success. After O'Reilly's departure, he'd thought he'd be Fox's biggest star, and Carlson had usurped him. Carlson, meanwhile, thought Hannity was an idiot—and he wasn't shy about sharing that view with others, especially his fellow journalists. Word of Carlson's barbs inevitably got back to Hannity. The tension between the two men made their nightly handoffs, when Carlson's show ended and Hannity's began, oddly compelling television. In one instance, after Carlson had just done a segment excoriating Amazon founder Jeff Bezos for making thirteen billion dollars in one day during the coronavirus pandemic, essentially profiting from so much suffering, Hannity felt compelled to put in a plug for the free market system. As Carlson looked on with the pinched, pained look he typically saved for liberal professors, Hannity said, "People can make money. They provide goods and services people want, need, and desire. That's America. It's called freedom, capitalism. And as long as it's honest, right? People decide. All right, Tucker, great show."

Carlson's biggest enemy at Fox, however, wasn't an on-air talent. It was Irena Briganti, the head of the network's vaunted and feared media relations department. Ostensibly Fox's chief publicist, Briganti, who started working for Ailes in the run-up to Fox's launch, was in fact its chief enforcer. For years, she was suspected of helping Ailes tame Fox's monsters, leaking damaging stories about them to friendly media outlets whenever they stepped out of line or made what Ailes deemed to be excessive demands in their contract renegotiations; she also, most infamously, was accused of using the same leaking strategy to help Ailes silence some of the women who thought about going public with their accusations of sexual harassment against him. After Ailes's departure, Briganti's power actually seemed to increase. When *Fox & Friends* coanchor Brian Kilmeade was up for a new contract in 2017 and tried to drive a hard bargain, a series of damaging gossip items appeared about him in the *New York Post*. Carlson, who was friends with Kilmeade, suspected the stories were Briganti's handiwork and, feeling flush with his newfound success, went to Lachlan Murdoch and demanded that he rein Briganti in. Murdoch didn't, and the move earned Carlson Briganti's endless enmity, making Carlson paranoid in the process. He became so convinced that Briganti was leaking damaging stories about him that he eventually refused to work with her; instead, Carlson insisted that Raj Shah, a former Trump White House deputy press secretary who was a Fox senior vice president, handle his and his show's PR duties and ultimately made Fox give a consulting contract to Arthur Schwartz, a New York political operative and Trump dirty trickster, to run a pro-Carlson PR campaign.

And Carlson desperately needed a good public relations team. His ratings success and inflammatory remarks had made him a fat target for liberal groups trying to force Fox to pay a financial penalty for its programming. In 2018, Carlson became the target of multiple overlapping advertiser boycotts. Where commercial breaks during the early days of *Tucker Carlson Tonight* featured spots from blue-chip brands like Lexus, T-Mobile, and Disney, by 2020 more than a third of the ad spending on the show was coming from just one company—MyPillow, owned by the Trump-supporting, conspiracy-loving Mike Lindell.

But the advertising boycotts and the enmity of many of his

colleagues ultimately didn't matter because Carlson had something that trumped all of that: the staunch and enthusiastic support of both Rupert and Lachlan Murdoch. Carlson had diligently tended to both relationships. Publicly, he never let an opportunity pass to heap praise on the pair, often thanking them by name on his show and raving about them to reporters. "You couldn't ask for a better relationship," he told *The Washington Post*. "They are completely supportive. They are nice. They are fun to eat with. They've never asked me to go easy on this person or tough on that person. They always stood by the show when people were clamoring for my firing."

Privately, he kept in regular contact with both men, particularly Lachlan, whom Rupert had tapped to oversee Fox after a bitter power struggle with his younger brother, James. Lachlan had come into the job with scant experience or understanding of the news channel; he'd spent the previous decade in his father's native Australia. So Carlson offered himself up to his new boss as a kind of cable-news Sherpa. The fact that Carlson and Lachlan were roughly the same age with similar hobbies—hunting and fishing—and, more important, similar politics—right-wing—cemented their bond. While Suzanne Scott was Carlson's nominal boss, he dismissed her as "a mediocrity"—perhaps his most damning insult. ("I'm an elitist by temperament," he once explained. "I want to take instructions from people who are more impressive than I am.") Whenever he needed something or had a problem, he bypassed Scott and went directly to Lachlan. He wasn't shy about letting others at Fox know about their relationship. Walking into Fox's annual Christmas party at a Capitol Hill steak house in 2018, Carlson was conspicuously talking on his cell phone. When the call was over, he let the partygoers know who had been on the other end. It was Lachlan, Carlson told them, who'd just wanted to let him know that, in the midst of an advertiser boycott, Carlson had his and his father's full support.

BUT FOR ALL THE GOOD the Murdochs' support did Carlson in his professional home, his personal home, Washington, DC, was becoming increasingly inhospitable.

Carlson had lived in Washington under Democratic and Republican administrations. It didn't matter who was in the White House. Permanent Washington, of which Carlson had been a fixture for more than two decades, never really changed. The fact that he was conservative, while most of his DC friends were liberals, wasn't a problem. They helped him, and he helped them.

When Carlson's son, Buckley, was a senior at St. George's and applying to college, Georgetown University was his first choice, so Tucker and Susie reached out to one of their Washington friends who was a well-connected Georgetown alum—Hunter Biden, the son of the then vice president; Hunter's then-wife Kathleen and Susie were especially close. "Tucker and I would be so grateful if you could write a letter or speak to someone in the Georgetown Admission's [*sic*] Office about Buckley," Susie wrote Hunter in a 2014 email. "I realize you don't really know Buckley. Maybe you could meet or speak to him and he could send you a very brief resume with his interests and grades attached." In another email, Tucker, who once claimed that he tried to convince his children not to go to college because it's "totally counterproductive and stupid and probably pretty bad for you," filled in Hunter on Buckley's grades—all A's save for a B+ in physics—and his talents as a squash player and fly fisherman, adding, "He loves Washington, for all the right reasons I think, and really wants to go to school here." Buckley ultimately didn't attend Georgetown—he had to make do going to the University of Virginia, after which he landed a job as the press secretary for the young, ambitious, and media-savvy Indiana congressman Jim Banks—but Carlson was grateful to Biden for the help.

And so when, a year later, the London tabloid the *Daily Mail* was working on a story about how Hunter Biden's name was discovered in a leaked user list for Ashley Madison, a website for people seeking to have extramarital affairs, Biden sought the help of Carlson, who was friends with the *Daily Mail*'s Washington editor. "Just lost my shit on the editor over there," Carlson wrote in an email to Biden reporting back on his efforts. "He claims the London office forced him to do it. He's a pig either way, and I told him so." When Biden apologized to Carlson for troubling him, Carlson wouldn't have it. "Are you kidding? I'm glad you called," he wrote in another email. "What they did was repulsive and immoral and I hope I wrecked their day. I certainly tried to. Fuck them. Let me know if there's any way we can help."

But ever since Trump entered the White House, the mutual aid society of permanent Washington—you try to help my kid get into an elite college, I try to help you defuse an embarrassing sex scandal—was unraveling. The Washington friends who used to roll their eyes at or laugh about Carlson's contrarian statements now recoiled. The haunts he had frequented for decades were suddenly unwelcoming. A waiter at the Metropolitan Club cursed him out. So did a fellow diner at the Palm. Carlson eventually began taking all his meals at the Prime Rib, a stodgy and often empty supper club on K Street that he deemed a safe space. "I can't really go to a lot of restaurants anymore because I get yelled at," he lamented to his old *Daily Caller* colleague Jamie Weinstein. "And it's just, I don't feel threatened, but, like, having someone scream, 'Fuck you!' at a restaurant, it just wrecks your meal." He added, "I'm not a restaurant guy anymore. It's sad. I can't wait for this revolution to end."

Then the revolution came to his doorstep. On a Wednesday evening in November 2018, twenty members of a local anti-fascist group called Smash Racism DC showed up outside Carlson's house in Northwest Washington. Standing in the dark and speaking through a bullhorn, one of them accused Carlson of "promoting hate" and "an ideology that has led to thousands of people dying." Then the group broke into a chant: "Tucker Carlson, we will fight! We know where you sleep at night!" As it turned out, Carlson was at Fox getting ready for his show, but Susie, who was home alone, locked herself in the pantry and called 911. Police arrived, dispersed the protesters, and stationed officers outside Carlson's home.

For a moment, the protest seemed to rekindle the spirit of solidarity that once permeated permanent Washington, drawing condemnations from Carlson's friends and foes alike. "I think Tucker is a terrible influence on modern America but that doesn't justify harassing him at home," Max Boot wrote on Twitter. "Go high, not low." Nonetheless, the episode left Carlson deeply unsettled. "It wasn't a protest. It was a threat," he fumed. "They were threatening me and my family and telling me to leave my own neighborhood in the city that I grew up in." He decided to accede to their demand and began looking at homes in Florida.

In December, a month after the protests at his home, Carlson went to a party—one of the last parties he'd attend in Washington for a good while—at the home of his old colleague Andy Ferguson. It was a wake for *The Weekly Standard*.

Unlike *National Review* and *RedState* and *The Federalist* and almost every other conservative publication that fulminated against Trump during the 2016 campaign, only to fall in line behind him (or at least adopt an anti-anti-Trump posture) once he won the election, *The Standard* had stubbornly stuck to its Never Trump convictions. Stephen Hayes, to whom Kristol had handed the magazine's editorship a few weeks before Trump's inauguration (Kristol kept a column and an office), positioned *The Standard* as loyal not to Trump but to the truth. "We're an unapologetically conservative magazine," Hayes said. "But I don't want people coming to *The Weekly Standard* seeking *affirmation*, I want people coming to *The Weekly Standard* seeking *information*."

That position ultimately did not sit well with *The Standard*'s owner, Philip Anschutz, a Colorado billionaire businessman who bought the magazine from Murdoch in 2009 (two years after Murdoch bought *The Wall Street Journal*). Anschutz and his media executives pressed Hayes to hire pro-Trump writers and adopt a pro-Trump editorial line. When he refused, they slashed *The Standard*'s budget. Hayes and Kristol worked to find a buyer for the magazine. At one point James Murdoch, who, after losing the succession battle to Lachlan, had become critical of the Trumpy tilt of Fox News, was interested; several other potential buyers emerged, as well. But, in the end, Anschutz decided not to sell. He preferred to kill the magazine. On December 17, *The Weekly Standard* published its 1,124th and final issue. "The pathetic and dishonest *Weekly Standard*, run by failed prognosticator Bill Kristol (who, like many others, never had a clue), is flat broke and out of business," Trump celebrated on Twitter. "Too bad. May it rest in peace!"

Carlson had the good manners to be more circumspect, but privately he was also happy about *The Standard*'s demise. As was the case with so many of his old friends in Washington, he and Kristol had fallen out since Trump's election—with Kristol taking swipes at Carlson on social media (after Carlson did a Fox segment criticizing the removal of Confederate monuments, Kristol wrote on Twitter, "They started by rationalizing Trump. They ended by rationalizing slavery") and Carlson firing back on his show ("Washington is littered with formerly impressive people who now just shout and preen on social media, but I hate to see it with him"). Indeed, it wasn't long before Carlson had retconned their entire relationship. He began telling the story—seemingly as much for himself as for his audience—of how, as a young journalist, he'd been used as a cat's-paw by Kristol and the neocons to promote disastrous foreign wars and unfair trade deals and to attack the truth tellers who opposed them. "Kristol was always encouraging me to write hit pieces on Pat Buchanan," Carlson now recalled. With his prime perch on Fox and the political sorties he was launching from it, Carlson claimed that he was making amends for all the harm he—and, more to the point, Kristol and the neocons—had done to white, working-class Americans. *Tucker Carlson Tonight* was his penance. When Carlson published a quickie book in the fall of 2018 to cash in on his renewed TV fame—his deal with Simon & Schuster was reported to be eight figures—he titled it *Ship of Fools: How a Selfish Ruling Class Is Bringing America to the Brink of Revolution*. The cover illustration featured caricatures of familiar villains including Jeff Bezos, Hillary Clinton, Nancy Pelosi, and Mark Zuckerberg—as well as a caricature of a much less recognizable figure whom Carlson had specifically requested: Bill Kristol.

But on that December evening, Carlson tried to forget about all of that. *The Standard*'s staff and alums—Steve Hayes and Bill Kristol, John McCormack and John Podhoretz—were gathering at Ferguson's house to celebrate its life and mourn its demise. Matt Labash, Carlson's first—and now quite possibly last—friend at the magazine, had impressed upon him that he should be there too. When Carlson arrived at the party, Labash greeted him and brought Carlson over to Kristol. The two men shook hands for everyone to see. But as soon as the handshake was over, Carlson and Kristol went their separate ways. And then, before the toasts and speeches had even begun, Carlson slipped out. He had a TV show—the second-highest-rated news show in all of prime time—to do that night, after all.

EIGHT

When Tucker Carlson left his new home on Florida's Gasparilla Island in March 2020 and set off on the 180-mile drive across the state to Palm Beach, where he would meet with Donald Trump at Mar-a-Lago to try to convince the president to take the emerging COVID pandemic seriously, he did not have high hopes.

Carlson understood that he owed both his professional and political success to Trump. He now enjoyed an outsize voice in American politics not just because his show had the most viewers of any on cable news, but because one of those viewers was Trump himself, who often seemed to take Carlson's advice over that of his actual aides. Still, Carlson was careful to try to maintain some plausible deniability. Unlike Sean Hannity, he did not want to be the "unofficial chief of staff"; he often insisted to friends and colleagues that he wasn't an adviser, even an informal one, to the White House. But he knew that wasn't true. Speaking of Trump's presidency to one person, he admitted, "I'm implicated in this too."

And yet Carlson had begun to sour on Trump. The doubts he held about him at the outset of his presidency—doubts he once managed to push aside—were returning.

He was angry about the way Trump had treated Jeff Sessions, his first attorney general whom he fired after the 2018 midterms. Sessions—one of the few politicians Carlson professed to personally like—had been advocating anti-immigration, anti-free-trade, and anti-interventionist views for years, often alone, before Trump adopted them as his own. It was why Sessions was the first Republican US senator to endorse Trump in 2016. As Carlson saw it, Trump owed Sessions. But a little more than a month into his tenure as attorney general, Sessions recused himself from overseeing the FBI's investigation into Russian election interference in the 2016 election on the grounds that he had worked on Trump's campaign—and Trump never forgave him. Carlson complained to one person that Trump, in his inability to let go of his grudge against Session, was "a fucking baby." When Sessions decided to try to reclaim his old Alabama Senate seat in 2020, Carlson let him announce his campaign on *Tucker Carlson Tonight*. Then Trump endorsed Tommy Tuberville in the Alabama Republican primary, torpedoing Sessions.

Carlson was similarly miffed about the way Trump had treated their mutual friend Roger Stone. Carlson became friends with Stone in 1996, when Stone was working for Bob Dole's presidential campaign and Carlson was covering it. Stone and Trump went back even further. They first met when Stone was raising money for Ronald Reagan's 1980 presidential campaign and Roy Cohn suggested he hit up Trump. In 2000, Stone masterminded Trump's short-lived, ill-fated attempt to run for president on the Reform Party ticket. Sixteen years later Stone helped Trump's more successful GOP presidential campaign. In 2017, that work landed Stone in front of the House committee investigating potential collusion between the Trump campaign and Russia; the committee wanted to know if Stone had served as an intermediary between the Trump campaign and WikiLeaks, which published a trove of emails that Russian hackers had stolen from Democratic computers in an effort to damage Hillary Clinton. Stone was not forthcoming, and in 2019 federal prosecutors charged him with seven felony counts of obstructing the congressional inquiry, lying to investigators, and witness intimidation. Later that year he was convicted on all seven counts. Prosecutors initially recommended that Stone, who was sixty-seven, serve nine years in prison, before attorney general William Barr prevailed upon them to knock down the sentence request, and they asked for three years.

Carlson nonetheless expected that Trump would pardon Stone. After all, the president had been on something of a pardoning and commutation spree, granting get-out-of-jail-free cards to everyone from Governor Rod Blagojevich, the former Illinois Democratic governor who'd tried to sell a Senate seat, to Crystal Munoz, a Texas woman who'd been sentenced to twenty years in prison for dealing marijuana. Surely Stone, a loyal friend and adviser who'd obstructed the congressional investigation seemingly at Trump's behest, was worthy of similar treatment. When Trump didn't offer Stone clemency, Carlson visited Jared Kushner, who was serving as Trump's de facto pardon czar. In a tense White House meeting in February 2020, Carlson addressed Kushner as "son" (one of his favorite put-downs) and threatened that if Trump didn't grant Stone a pardon, Carlson would begin pushing for one on his show—and raising questions about the people Trump, on Kushner's advice, had been pardoning. Kushner wouldn't commit, so shortly thereafter, Carlson took to the airwaves. "The typical rapist in this country spends four years in prison. Armed robbers, three years. Thugs who commit violent assault, less than a year and a half," he told his viewers. "But Roger Stone must do nine years, until he's 76 years old, for lying." He added, "The president must pardon Roger Stone or commute his sentence before he goes to jail."

And so Carlson was disappointed but hardly surprised when, at Mar-a-Lago in March, he failed to scare Trump straight about COVID. Nothing he said—not even his dire warning that the pandemic could destroy Trump's reelection chances—managed to penetrate the president's bubble of denial. That evening at Trump's club, Carlson was dragooned into attending the lavish fifty-first birthday party of Kimberly Guilfoyle, his former Fox colleague and Donald Trump Jr.'s girlfriend at the time. As he sat in the gilded ballroom surrounded by about a hundred other revelers—including the entire Trump family (save for Melania Trump) and a coterie of Republican senators, congressmen, and administration officials—he could only shake his head at their obliviousness about what was about to befall the country. Across the United States, people who recognized the threat posed by COVID were beginning to adjust their lives (including Rupert Murdoch, who would turn eighty-nine a few days later and opted to cancel his own birthday party at his California vineyard out of concern for his and his guests' health). But at Mar-a-Lago, it was as if nothing was amiss. Turning to the Florida congressman Matt Gaetz, who was seated next to him at the head table, Carlson said, "This is the end of something."

For a time, it certainly seemed to be the end of Carlson's relationship with Trump. As the COVID pandemic spread and worsened, Carlson could not hide his frustration with the Trump administration's lack of a response. While his fellow Fox hosts dismissed COVID as a liberal plot to damage Trump—"They're scaring the living hell out of people and I see it again as like, 'Oh, let's bludgeon Trump with this new hoax,'" Hannity told his viewers—Carlson continued to sound the alarm on his show. "Nobody wants to be manipulated by a corrupt media establishment—and it is corrupt. And there's an election coming up. Best not to say anything that might help the other side. We get it," he conceded in one monologue. "But they're wrong. The Chinese coronavirus is a major event. It will affect your life. And by the way, it's definitely not just the flu." Trump might not have listened to Carlson, but Carlson's viewers apparently did. A University of Chicago study later found that "greater viewership of *Hannity* relative to *Tucker Carlson Tonight*" was associated with COVID-19 cases and deaths in the early stages of the pandemic.

But as the pandemic continued, Carlson's own views on its severity and the existential danger it posed began to change. By late April, he was telling his viewers, "The virus just isn't nearly as deadly as we thought it was, all of us, including on this show." He lambasted Anthony Fauci, Zeke Emanuel, and other public health authorities for calling for lockdowns and stay-at-home orders—and he criticized Trump for listening to them. Indeed, Carlson's beef with Trump was no longer that he was underestimating COVID but that he was overreacting to it. "In many places in this country, Americans cannot go to the park with their children," Carlson complained during one monologue in April. "They can't go to church. They can't have family dinners with their relatives. They can't go to the dentist. They can't get a knee replacement. They can't get married. Tens of millions of them can't afford to do much of anything right now because they're unemployed."

Then came the murder of George Floyd. Unsurprisingly, Carlson took a dim view of the Black Lives Matter protests that sprung up in cities across the country in response to Floyd's murder in late May by the Minneapolis police officer Derek Chauvin. "This may be a lot of things, this moment we're living through, but it is definitely not about black lives," Carlson said near the end of a twenty-five-minute monologue in June.

"Remember that when they come for you, and at this rate, they will." Fox News subsequently claimed that the "they" to whom Carlson was referring was Democratic politicians, not BLM protesters. But his comments triggered a number of companies, including Disney and Papa John's, to stop advertising on Carlson's show.

Still, Carlson reserved his greatest anger for Trump. After a group of BLM protesters swarmed a Fox News reporter near the White House, Carlson addressed the president on his show. "If you can't keep a Fox News correspondent from getting attacked directly across from your house, how can you protect my family?" he asked. "How are you going to protect the country? How hard are you trying?" Noting that Trump had posted on Twitter that, despite the protests outside the White House, he and his family were fine, Carlson said: "Their federally funded bodyguards had kept them safe. He did not mention protecting the rest of the nation, much of which was on fire. He seemed aware only of himself." When White House communications director Alyssa Farah Griffin called Carlson to assure him that Trump would be cracking down on violent protesters, he wasn't placated. "It's too bad our streets are on fire!" Carlson yelled at Farah Griffin. "These fucking animals looted the Hermès in Buckhead!"

Trump appeared to take Carlon's criticisms to heart. Throughout the summer of 2020, as the pandemic and protests roiled the country and he fought for a second term in the White House against Joe Biden, the president often seemed most concerned about being on the television host's bad side. "He'd say, 'Tucker's crushing us. Our base is going to leave us,'" Farah Griffin recalled. Trump tried to get back in Carlson's good graces. In July, he commuted Roger Stone's prison sentence. (Appearing on *Hannity* shortly after the commutation, Stone thanked Carlson rather than Trump. "He's a man of incredible loyalty and he's a great friend," Stone said of Carlson. "He may be the best friend a man can have.") After Carlson began doing nightly segments on the summerlong protests in Portland, Oregon—"another beautiful city destroyed by the mob," he lamented—Trump ignored the objections of the White House counsel and White House chief of staff, not to mention Oregon's governor, and ordered federal law enforcement officials, many of them members of the US Customs and Border Protection's SWAT-team equivalent, to the city to aggressively crack down on the protesters.

Carlson was somewhat mollified by Trump's actions. On Fox, he muted his criticisms of the president and, as Election Day drew closer, amped up his attacks on Biden. Back in his CNN days, Carlson had hailed Biden as "by far the most articulate senator I've ever spoken to about foreign policy. . . . He knows an awful lot about an awful lot." But now Carlson tried to link Biden to Antifa, which he called "the armed wing of the Democratic Party." In one monologue, Carlson told his viewers, "The leaders of today's Democratic Party . . . despise this country. They have said so. They continue to. That is shocking but it is also disqualifying. We cannot let them run this nation because they hate it. Imagine what they would do to it." His show returned to its anti-anti-Trump roots. While Hannity and Ingraham and other Fox hosts continued to fawn over Trump, Carlson seemed to almost be trying to ignore him, focusing instead on Biden—or, after the attacks on Biden didn't seem to find much purchase, on Biden's running mate, the "radical" Kamala Harris, who he told his viewers would actually be running the country if Trump was defeated. "America is still a great country, the best in the world. But our ruling class is disgusting," he declaimed the night before the election. "A vote for Trump is a vote against them."

Carlson's approach to the election was, not surprisingly at this point, the mirror image of Bill Kristol's. After *The Weekly*

Standard folded in 2018, Kristol had regrouped and, with the help of investors including James Murdoch, founded an online publication called *The Bulwark* as a new Never Trump redoubt. Just as he tried and failed to recruit an independent candidate to run in the general election in 2016, he tried and failed to recruit a Republican to challenge Trump in the 2020 GOP primaries. Finally, he availed himself of the only option left—and endorsed Joe Biden in the Democratic primaries, assuming an anti-anti-Biden stance. "You are a normal American. You don't like demagogues of the right or the left," he wrote in *The Bulwark*. "And so you don't want to face a choice—you don't want the country to face a choice—between Donald Trump and Bernie Sanders in November." As November drew closer, Kristol's efforts on Biden's behalf revolved all around Trump. With a couple of *Bulwark* colleagues, he created a new group, Republican Voters Against Trump, that solicited testimonials from regular Republicans who'd voted for Trump in 2016 but couldn't bring themselves to do so again. These testimonials, which were broadcast as part of a ten-million-dollar digital and TV ad campaign, were hardly ringing endorsements of Biden. "I suppose I'll be voting for Biden," one man said in a resigned tone, while another man rationalized, "This guy has one term written all over him. Let him win. We'll have four years to rebuild the base, re-educate the party, bleach out the Trump cult stain and then come back." The people in the ad shared Kristol's hatred of Trump—and that was motivation enough.

Carlson, by contrast, didn't seem to have his heart in it. After Trump's disastrous performance in his first debate with Biden in late September—in which he failed to denounce the Proud Boys—Trump accused Chris Wallace, the debate's moderator, of asking unfair questions and siding with Biden. As much as Carlson disliked Wallace, he couldn't bring himself to agree; Trump's debate face-plant, Carlson privately told people, had been Trump's fault. While Carlson instructed his viewers to ignore the polls that showed Trump trailing in the race and focus on things like isolated, impromptu parades of Trump supporters driving pickup trucks—"Certainly if enthusiasm is any measure," Carlson said, "Donald Trump has a real shot at reelection"—off the air he confided to friends and coworkers that he was all but certain Trump was going to lose. "They're fucked," he frequently said. He later confided to multiple people that on Election Day, he voted for Kanye West. When Trump did lose, he and his supporters shot the messenger and lashed out at Fox, which had been the first network to project that Biden would win Arizona, making Trump's chances of victory remote, but Carlson was clear-eyed about who deserved the blame for Trump's defeat. "If Trump had run on law and order and re-opening the schools," Carlson wrote in a text message to Laura Ingraham shortly after the election, "he would have won in a landslide."

CARLSON'S RUEFUL ACCEPTANCE OF TRUMP'S defeat is why, in the initial days after the election, he resorted to metacoverage of Trump's claims that the election had been stolen. To be sure, he rotely faulted "the media" for refusing to entertain Trump's and his supporters' conspiracy theories about the race, claiming that the ever-present "they" were "demanding that you shut up and accept Joe Biden." But Carlson—unlike Fox News and Fox Business colleagues Hannity, Ingraham, Maria Bartiromo, and Lou Dobbs—was reluctant to entertain those conspiracy theories on his own show. As he wrote in a text message one week after the election to his producer Alex Pfeiffer, who'd told him that viewers were mad he wasn't covering Trump's election fraud claims, "I just hate that shit."

His reluctance turned into outright defiance in the case of Sidney Powell, a lawyer on Trump's election legal team who—in interviews with Bartiromo, Dobbs, and other conservative media figures—claimed that the voting software made by Dominion Voting Systems, which was used in several key states, had switched millions of votes from Trump to Biden. Carlson—who acknowledged in a text to Pfeiffer that it had been a "mistake" not to cover Trump's election-fraud claims, considering his viewers' feelings—reached out to Powell to ask for evidence for her Dominion theory, with the hope of having her on his show. When the evidence she sent Carlson proved insufficient, he pressed her. "You keep telling our viewers that millions of votes were changed by the software," he wrote Powell. "I hope you will prove that very soon. You've convinced them that Trump will win. If you don't have conclusive evidence of fraud at that scale, it's a cruel and reckless thing to keep saying." Powell told Carlson to stop contacting her, so he did. Then he went on his show and nuked her—telling his audience that she had failed to provide him, or the Trump campaign, any evidence for the claims she was making about Dominion. "She never demonstrated that a single actual vote was moved illegitimately by software from one candidate to another," he told his viewers. "Not one."

If Carlson thought his viewers were mad that he wasn't covering Trump's claims of election fraud, he quickly discovered they were livid that he was now debunking those claims. Powell herself fueled their anger, appearing on Newsmax to attack Carlson as "abrasive" and "disrespectful." Raj Shah, the former Trump aide and Fox Corporation senior vice president, whose job it was to fight back against liberals calling for advertiser boycotts of Carlson, was now tasked with shoring up the host's support among conservatives. He and Carlson pushed the Trump campaign to disavow Powell—which the campaign soon did, issuing a statement that she was "not a member" of Trump's legal team and that she was "practicing law on her own." But that did little to assuage the anger of many conservatives. The "irrational reaction" to his Powell segment was "totally disgusting and crazy and dispiriting," Carlson wrote in a series of text messages to Pfeiffer, who was starting to function more like a shrink than a producer for the embattled cable news star. "Can't have a country like this." In a separate text exchange with Shah, Pfeiffer complained that the fallout from the Powell segment, and the delicate sensibilities of Fox viewers, was "surreal." "Like negotiating with terrorists," he added, "but especially dumb ones. Cousin fucking types, not Saudi royalty."

Indeed, even before Carlson's debunking of Powell, Fox News executives and hosts were panicking about the election outcome—and how to report it, truthfully, without alienating their audience. Chris Wallace's handling of the first debate and then the Fox News Decision Desk's Arizona projection on election night had already angered Trump and his supporters. In the days after the election, Fox News executives watched in horror as their ratings sank and those of Newsmax skyrocketed. In a text message to Fox News chief executive Suzanne Scott, Jay Wallace, the network's president, wrote: "The Newsmax surge is a bit troubling—truly is an alternative universe when you watch, but it can't be ignored. Trying to get everyone to comprehend we are on war footing." Scott, Wallace, and other Fox executives aggressively policed—and smacked down—the channel's reporters who applied appropriate scrutiny to Trump's bogus claims. In a text conversation in mid-November, on the day Trump supporters were rallying in Washington to protest the election results, Lachlan Murdoch wrote Scott, "News guys have to be careful how they cover this rally. So far some of the side comments have been slightly anti, and they shouldn't be. The narrative should be this huge celebration of the president." As Scott had tried to reassure Murdoch in an earlier text message, "[W]e will highlight our stars and plant flags letting the viewers know we hear them and respect them."

If anything, those stars were even more alarmed—and, for a moment, they put aside their enmity and rivalries. In a group text in the days and weeks after the election, Hannity, Ingraham, and Carlson commiserated.

"We are screwed," Ingraham wrote.

"The network is being rejected," Hannity agreed.

"I've heard from angry viewers every hour of the day all weekend, including at dinner tonight," Carlson reported.

They scapegoated.

Complaining about the reporters and executives on the news, rather than the opinion, side of Fox, Hannity wrote, "In one week and one debate they destroyed a brand that took 25 years to build and the damage is incalculable."

"It's vandalism," Carlson replied. "It needs to stop immediately, like tonight. It's measurably hurting the company. The stock price is down. Not a joke."

And they engaged in gallows humor.

"Laura let's all move to Florida and move in With [*sic*] Tucker!" Hannity wrote.

"Film a reality show[.] Huge hit," Ingraham replied.

But, while Carlson wasn't above joining his fellow millionaire anchors to kvetch about Fox's news side, he still placed the blame for Fox's—and the country's—predicament squarely on the billionaire president. "I hate him passionately," Carlson wrote of Trump in a text message to Pfeiffer on January 4. And it wasn't just Trump's postelection behavior that made Carlson feel this way. Although Trump's presidency had afforded Carlson the sort of professional success and political influence that, even in his most ambitious and heady moments, he'd never dreamed was possible, he now looked back on the last four years as a waste. "We're all pretending we've got a lot to show for it," he wrote in another text message, "because admitting what a disaster it's been is too tough to digest. But come on. There isn't really an upside to Trump."

On January 6, 2021, the downside of Trump became glaringly obvious. As his supporters stormed the Capitol, Trump's biggest cheerleaders at Fox sent desperate text messages to Mark Meadows, the White House chief of staff, begging him to get the president to intervene. "Can he make a statement," Hannity wrote. "Ask people to peacefully leave the capital." Ingraham pleaded: "Mark, the president needs to tell people in the Capitol to go home. This is hurting all of us. He is destroying his legacy." But Carlson did not reach out to Meadows. He spent part of the day on the phone with his son, Buckley, who was in the Capitol working for Jim Banks, to make sure he was safe. And he began to plan for a post-Trump future.

"Trump has two weeks left," he wrote in a text message to Pfeiffer. "Once he's out, he becomes incalculably less powerful, even in the minds of his supporters. My view is that the most important thing we can do maybe the only thing we can do is try to save the things that make America worth living in."

Pfeiffer told Carlson he was worried that Trump would do even more damage in those remaining two weeks.

"There's no question he will," Carlson replied. "He's a demonic force, a destroyer. But he's not going to destroy us. I've been thinking about this every day for four years."

It wasn't just Carlson who was ready to move on from Trump. In the immediate aftermath of January 6, so were Rupert and Lachlan Murdoch—and, by extension, the rest of Fox News. In the days and weeks after the election, the father and son, and the Fox executives who worked for them, were clearly terrified of crossing Trump and losing his supporters as viewers.

But the storming of the Capitol was such a shocking event that it changed their thinking. Paul Ryan, the former Speaker of the House who was on the Fox Corporation board of directors, told a fellow board member that, after January 6, he communicated to Rupert and Lachlan that Fox was now at "a huge inflection point to keep Trump down and move on for the future of the conservative movement." Ryan added: "Both Rupert and Lachlan fully agree. The key is to execute our collective will." On January 8, Rupert emailed a former Fox executive: "Fox News [is] very busy pivoting . . . We want to make Trump a non person." Rupert knew this would be a difficult mission. As he acknowledged in a subsequent email to Lachlan, "We have to lead our viewers which is not as easy as it might seem."

For a time, the Murdochs and Fox were hoping to lead those viewers to Florida governor Ron DeSantis. DeSantis owed his governorship to Fox—and to Trump. It was his numerous appearances on the news channel as a Florida congressman, in which he fulsomely praised Trump, that first brought him to the president's attention and led Trump to offer him his endorsement in the 2018 Republican gubernatorial primary. (DeSantis capitalized on the endorsement by running ads that showed him reading *The Art of the Deal* to his toddler son.) After Trump's defeat in 2020, DeSantis, who'd raised his national profile among conservatives by reopening Florida months before the rest of the country during the COVID pandemic, began plotting his own White House run. Fox tried to give him a boost. In the four months after the election, DeSantis appeared on Fox 113 times, almost once a day. As one Fox producer told DeSantis's deputy director of communications in a 2021 email obtained by the *Tampa Bay Times*, "We see him as the future of the party."

Carlson, ever the good soldier for the Murdochs, was happy to pitch in on the effort, hosting the Florida governor on his show six times in the first six months of 2021. But in many ways, Carlson offered not DeSantis but himself as Trump's replacement. Now liberated from having to defend or triangulate around Trump—to say nothing of trying to influence his policies—Carlson was free to devote all his efforts to prosecuting the culture wars and positioning himself as the new leader of the conservative movement. He cast doubt on the new COVID vaccines, telling his viewers that the Biden administration was using them as a form of "social control" and hosting Robert F. Kennedy Jr., who claimed that that the COVID vaccine had already killed more people "than all vaccines, the billions and billions of vaccines combined over the past thirty years." He picked up the cause of QAnon adherents, defending them as "gentle people waving American flags." He attacked Biden for "feminizing" the US military by allowing pregnant women to serve and hosted Tulsi Gabbard, who accused the Biden administration of trying to "turn our country into a police state with KGB-style surveillance." After Mark Milley, the chairman of the Joint Chiefs of Staff, defended a West Point course that taught critical race theory, Carlson blasted him on his show. "He's not just a pig," Carlson said of the decorated US Army general. "He's stupid."

Most significantly, Carlson introduced his more than four million viewers—who were, by then, the largest audience in the history of cable news—to replacement theory. A tenet of the far-right, white nationalist, racist fringe, replacement theory holds that liberal elites, typically at the behest of Jews, seek to increase the number of non-white immigrants to the United States so that they can "replace" and disempower white Americans at the ballot box. Carlson gave it a full airing on his show. "I know that the left and all the little gatekeepers on Twitter become literally hysterical if you use the term 'replacement,' if you suggest that the Democratic Party is trying to replace the current electorate, the voters now casting ballots, with new people, more obedient voters from the Third World," he said in April. "But they become hysterical because that's what's happening, actually. Let's just say it: That's true." He went on,

> If you change the population, you dilute the political power of the people who live there. So every time they import a new voter, I'd become disenfranchised as a current voter. . . . Everyone wants to make a racial issue out of it. "Oh, the White replacement?" No, no, no. This is a voting rights question. I have less political power because they're importing a brand new electorate. Why should I sit back and take that?

He began to refer to "legacy Americans"—a term typically found on white nationalist websites like *The Daily Stormer*—as the people who were being replaced.

But Carlson didn't just take aim at the left. He policed the right, too, in an effort to make sure that things didn't go back to the way they were in the GOP before Trump rode down the golden escalator—to make sure that the future of the conservative movement didn't look, as Paul Ryan clearly hoped, like its past. In a text exchange with Ingraham in January, Carlson complained about Wyoming Republican congresswoman Liz Cheney, who'd just announced that she was going to vote to impeach Trump over his actions on January 6. "The Establishment bites back," Ingraham wrote. "Nothing speaks change like open borders and endless wars." Carlson replied: "As soon as Trump is gone, I'm going to devote part of every single day to attacking them."

And he regularly delivered on that pledge. He revealed that Republican leader Kevin McCarthy shared a luxury DC apartment with the veteran GOP messaging guru Frank Luntz who, Carlson claimed, advised Congressional Republicans to stake out pro-immigration positions; Luntz was "a conventional liberal," according to Carlson, whose "main clients are left-wing corporations like Google." On the occasion of the US military's disastrous withdrawal from Kabul, when most of Fox was bashing Biden, Carlson instead highlighted South Carolina senator Lindsey Graham's long track record of being wrong about the prospects of success in Afghanistan. When Republicans joined with Democrats to condemn Vladimir Putin on the eve of Russia's invasion of Ukraine, Carlson struck a discordant note, complaining that "hating Putin has become the central purpose of America's foreign policy." He added,

> It might be worth asking yourself, since it is getting pretty serious: What is this really about? Why do I hate Putin so much? Has Putin ever called me a racist? Has he threatened to get me fired for disagreeing with him? Has he shipped every middle-class job in my town to Russia? Did he manufacture a worldwide pandemic that wrecked my business and kept me indoors for two years? Is he teaching my children to embrace racial discrimination? Is he making fentanyl? Is he trying to snuff out Christianity? Does he eat dogs? These are fair questions, and the answer to all of them is no.

For Carlson, the old Reaganite shibboleths of free trade, immigration, and hawkish foreign policy were as big a problem as anything being peddled by liberals.

With Trump seemingly well on his way to nonpersonhood—banned from Twitter and Facebook and almost entirely absent from Fox—Carlson was now presenting himself as the vessel for the grievances and resentments of the seventy-four million Americans who'd just voted for the former president. He quickly established himself as the right's standard-bearer, occupying the same mental real estate, among both conservatives and liberals, that Trump once did. Just as Rush Limbaugh had stood for conservative opposition to Barack Obama in the early days of Obama's presidency a dozen years earlier, when CNN and Fox News carried his CPAC speech live, Carlson was now playing the same role with Biden. When Biden gave his first prime-time address as president in March (about a month after Limbaugh died), Fox News, like all the major networks and cable-news channels, carried it live. But Fox added a twist: a "Live Tucker Reaction" box in the bottom corner of the screen, which showed Carlson making his trademark facial expressions as he watched the speech. "BIDEN SPEECH NEARLY FINISHED," a Fox chyron read toward the end of the president's address. "TUCKER WILL RESPOND."

CARLSON WAS NO LONGER JUST a cable host. He was a movement leader. And he worked to bring the GOP in line with his views. For guidance and inspiration, he looked overseas. Ever since becoming the prime minister of Hungary in 2010, Viktor Orbán had methodically consolidated his power—neutering the judiciary, clamping down on journalists, and curtailing academic freedom. All the while Orbán kept up a steady drumbeat of invective against immigrants, asylum seekers, Romani, gays, lesbians, transgender people, George Soros, the European Union, and basically anyone, or anything, that he deemed a threat to what he called Hungary's "Christian democracy." He boasted that, in Hungary, he was building an "illiberal state."

This was catnip for national conservatives, or NatCons, who began flocking to Budapest for audiences with Orbán and paid fellowships at the Danube Institute, a conservative think tank with close ties to the Hungarian government. In the NatCon imagination, a Central European country with a population a bit larger than New Jersey's and a gross domestic product one-twentieth the size of California's became a model and beacon for the United States. As Orbán's boosters wandered Budapest's cobbled streets and admired its baroque and art nouveau architecture, the city came to resemble, in the estimation of the liberal American writer John Ganz, a NatCon Epcot.

Carlson wanted to go to Disney World too. In 2019, he invited Hungary's US ambassador to his office at Fox, where they talked about their mutual love of fly-fishing and Carlson lobbied to interview Orbán. On his show, he hosted a minister from Orbán's party to discuss the Hungarian government's efforts to encourage its citizens to have more children. "I've rarely thought we could learn something important from another country," Carlson said, "but I think in this case, we really can." And yet for all of Carlson's special pleading and sucking up, he could not persuade the Hungarian government to let him visit with Orbán.

Finally, Rod Dreher intervened. Dreher, a writer for *The American Conservative*, a leading NatCon thinker, and one of Carlson's texting pals, was doing a fellowship at the Danube Institute in the spring of 2021 when he learned of Carlson's difficulties. Dreher had developed a deep admiration for Orbán and his ideological project. "Trump fights like a drunk falling off a barstool," he said. "Orbán fights like people say Trump fights." (The next year, Dreher would leave the United States and move permanently to Budapest, a city he deemed "synonymous with intellectual conservatism.") But he had some misgivings about the Orbán team's understanding of the American media landscape. He explained to them that, back in the United States, Carlson was kind of a big deal—that he was, in fact, America's most important conservative media figure. More importantly, he assured Orbán's team that Carlson was on their side in the great struggle in which they were engaged—that he was someone who could be trusted. Before long, Carlson's interview with Orbán was given the green light.

On the first Monday in August, *Tucker Carlson Tonight* broadcast from Budapest. "It's a place we're going to be telling you a lot about in the coming days," Carlson said from the rooftop bar of a luxury hotel, the city's Hapsburg skyline in the background. "If you care about western civilization and democracy and families and the ferocious assault on all three of those things by the leaders of our global institutions, you should know what is happening here right now." Then, for the rest of that week he treated his American viewers to an infomercial about the wonders of Hungary under Orbán—or, as Carlson called it, "the small country with a lot of lessons for the rest of us."

What lessons could Americans possibly glean from Hungary?

For Carlson, there was a lesson about public safety. "Notice as you watch what you don't see here," he said as the camera broadcast footage of Budapest. "There are not tent cities of drug addicts living in the parks here. There isn't garbage and human waste littering the sidewalks. People don't get beheaded at intersections. BLM is not allowed to torch entire neighborhoods in Budapest."

Or lessons about immigration. Carlson helicoptered to Hungary's southern border with Serbia, where Orbán had erected a barbed wire fence to repel refugees from the civil wars in Libya and Syria. There, Carlson was warmly received by a pair of imposing Hungarian border guards. They gave him a tour of Hungary's side of the border, which Carlson marveled was "perfectly clean and orderly" and devoid of the "trash," "chaos," and "human suffering" found on the US border with Mexico. Carlson watched as the border guards dealt with two Syrian men who'd been caught trying to sneak into Hungary from Serbia. Instead of bringing the Syrians "to meet their attorneys or some Soros-funded NGO, and then moved into some other part of Hungary to stay there forever," Carlson reported, the guards sent the men right back to Serbia, whose side of the border, he "couldn't help but notice," had "trash and filth everywhere." Stopping illegal immigration, Carlson concluded, "doesn't require a GDP the size of the United States' GDP. It doesn't require high-tech walls or guns or surveillance equipment. All it requires is the will to do it."

He then pivoted to leadership. What gave Orbán the courage and wisdom to have Hungary turn away the wave of Muslim immigrants that were wrecking other European countries like Germany? Was it "bewildering" to him that Biden had unfairly called him "a totalitarian thug"? Will Christians and conservatives in Europe seek sanctuary in Hungary? Even with the softball questions, Orbán did not give a polished, American-style performance. He was difficult to understand with his thick accent, and his answers tended to meander. But it didn't really matter since, when the interview was over, Carlson told his viewers exactly what they should take away from it. "You don't have to watch your country collapse," he said. "You don't have to have leaders who hate the population or divide their own people against each other, who make the country worse, who open the borders, who increase crime, who encourage people to live on the sidewalk, and do drugs. If there's any lesson in talking to Viktor Orbán, maybe that's it."

On one of his last nights in Budapest, Carlson had dinner with Orbán and some of his advisers at the prime minister's office. Under a colonnade that overlooked the Danube River, he rose to offer his hosts a toast. They loved their country, and they were willing to fight for it, Carlson told them, and in that love, and in that willingness to fight, they had earned the opprobrium of the very forces with whom they were engaged in a fierce, civilizational struggle. It was that opprobrium, as much as anything else, that proved that their struggle was just and that they were on the path to victory. Looking at Orbán and his advisers, but also perhaps thinking of himself, Carlson said reassuringly, "You're truly hated by all the right people."

In the months after Carlson's trip to Hungary, a host of other American conservative leaders made their own pilgrimages there. Mike Pence went and celebrated Hungary's declining abortion rate. Jeff Sessions showed up and declared that Hungary did a better job with border security and immigration than the United States. The next summer, the American Conservative Union, which sponsors CPAC, hosted its first ever CPAC in Europe—in Budapest, because, as American Conservative Union head Matt Schlapp explained, Hungary "represents Christian conservative values." CPAC Hungary is now an annual event featuring leading Republicans. And it hasn't all been a one-way transaction. American conservatives began hosting Hungarians on their home turf too. Three months after the first CPAC Hungary, another CPAC was held in Dallas, where the opening speech was delivered by Orbán. In 2024, Trump hosted Orbán at Mar-a-Lago on three separate occasions.

Carlson had somehow made the entire American conservative movement fall in love with a country that most Americans could probably not identify on a map. The cable news host's Hungary idyll, Dreher said, was "the week that changed American conservatism."

CLOSER TO HOME, CARLSON SET out to make the entire American conservative movement fall in love with—or at least no longer feel ashamed of—what happened on January 6.

In the immediate aftermath of the storming of the Capitol, Carlson, like everyone else at Fox, was privately livid; also like everyone else at Fox, he made certain not to give full voice to that anger on-air. He minimized what took place, describing it as "a political protest [that] got out of hand after a president recklessly encouraged it." And he engaged in his usual hand-waving, criticizing Democrats and CNN for labeling January 6 as "domestic terrorism" and comparing it to Pearl Harbor. He even spent airtime taking it to a New England boarding school for, in a letter to parents, condemning the rioters for their "racism." "Whatever you thought about what happened yesterday, what was racist about it?" he asked, wearing his trademark befuddled look. "The Berkshire School is lying! So is everyone else on the left."

Still, in those early days, Carlson did not try to deny to his viewers what had occurred at the Capitol that Wednesday afternoon in January. Indeed, in some moments, he was unable to hide his anger and despair. On the day of the attack, discussing the death of Ashli Babbitt, the protester who was shot and killed by a US Capitol police officer after she tried to vault through a window near the House chamber, he seemed near tears. Describing the video of Babbitt's death—which he refused to broadcast on his show, because it was "too upsetting," but could be found many places online—he said, "The camera closes in on the woman's face. She looks stunned. She stares ahead unblinking. In her eyes you can see that she knows she's about to die, which in the end she did."

"So what can we learn from this?" he plaintively asked.

> It's not enough to call it a tragedy. Imagine getting the call and learning that was your daughter. The last time you spoke to her she was heading to Washington for a political rally. Now she's dead. You'll never talk to her again.

Seriously, imagine that. If you have children it will put you in the right frame of mind. That's what we're watching.

But as time went on, and the memories of January 6 became less fresh, the pain less raw, Carlson began to change his on-air tune. In April, on the three-month anniversary of the storming of the Capitol, he described the rioters as "a mob of older people from unfashionable zip codes" who "wandered freely through the Capitol, like it was their building or something." These people "didn't have guns," he continued, "but a lot of them had extremely dangerous ideas. They talked about the Constitution, and something called 'their rights.' Some of them made openly seditious claims. They insisted, for example, that the last election was not entirely fair." In September, he complained that the Justice Department was refusing to release thousands of hours of surveillance footage of the Capitol from January 6 because, he claimed, it would show that "the vast majority of people inside the Capitol on January 6 were peaceful. They were not insurrectionists. . . . They weren't trying to overthrow the government."

Carlson was laying the groundwork for an even bigger lie. During the 2020 election interregnum, when Fox News executives were scrambling to hold on to their viewers, he and Justin Wells, his executive producer, decided to do a little empire building. They pitched the creation of an investigative-reporting unit that would produce long-form documentaries for Carlson to anchor. They would call them Tucker Carlson Originals. "Given everything that's happening right now," Carlson wrote in a November email to Suzanne Scott, "I believe it would be wise, and reassuring to our viewers, to announce an initiative like this sooner rather than later." Scott soon gave Carlson and Wells the green light, and in April, Tucker Carlson Originals began airing on Fox's subscription-only digital streaming service, Fox Nation. TCO's early efforts featured Carlson's familiar hobbyhorses—green-energy scams, MS-13, vigilantism—and barely caused a ripple. Then TCO decided to tackle January 6.

The result was *Patriot Purge*, a three-part series that debuted on Fox Nation in November. Directed by Scooter Downey, a filmmaker who previously worked with the far-right conspiracy theorist Mike Cernovich, and featuring as a talking head Darren Beattie, the proprietor of the right-wing website *Revolver News*, *Patriot Purge* was an attempt to not just minimize but completely rewrite the history of January 6. In Carlson's retelling, the violence that occurred that day at the Capitol was a false flag operation, instigated by undercover FBI operatives in the crowd, so that the Biden administration could then persecute—and prosecute and imprison—Americans for the crime of being conservative. "The helicopters have left Afghanistan, and now they've landed here at home," Carlson said, comparing the government's response to January 6 to its response to 9/11. "They've begun to fight a new enemy in a new War on Terror . . . hunting down American citizens, purging them from society, throwing some of them into solitary confinement." He ended the series with an ominous warning to his viewers. "They're pushing you toward violence and they're doing it on purpose," Carlson told them. "But don't fall for it. Build the country. Love your family and each other. Be the light. That's how it gets better."

It was an outlandish, completely unhinged conspiracy theory, but it wasn't an entirely new one. Beattie had extensively workshopped and promulgated it on *Revolver News*. What was so striking was that the conspiracy theory was now being offered by Carlson. For most of his media career, he had recoiled from this sort of paranoid thinking. In 2008, Carlson, who'd recently lost his MSNBC show, had agreed to serve as the emcee for Ron Paul's Rally for the Republic event during that year's Republican National Convention; he'd developed a genuine appreciation for Paul—"the only politician with zero interest in controlling other people"—after he'd written about his long shot presidential bid for *The New Republic*. (The uproarious, insightful article, in which Carlson brought a Nevada brothel owner and two prostitutes to a Paul press conference, was the last good magazine story he ever wrote.) At the rally, former Minnesota governor Jesse Ventura gave a speech questioning whether Osama bin Laden had carried out the 9/11 attacks. Carlson didn't hear Ventura's remarks, but when Matt Labash, who was covering the event for *The Weekly Standard*, told Carlson about Ventura's 9/11 trutherism, Carlson was aghast. "This is crazy," he said to Labash. "I've got to get out of here. Let's go get dinner." Carlson abandoned his emcee job mid-rally, before Paul even spoke.

Four years later, Carlson appeared on the online radio show of Scott Ledger, a prominent 9/11 truther, for the sole purpose of humiliating him in a combative hour-long interview. After Ledger alleged that the Project for the New American Century, Bill Kristol's old foreign policy think tank that shared office space with *The Standard*, had ginned up the Iraq War—in part by staging the 9/11 attacks as a false flag operation—so that it could increase its arm sales, Carlson lit into him. "You got the wrong guy on your show today," he lectured Ledger. "I know a lot about PNAC, because I worked next door, and they were not selling weapons, and you're saying they are, which reveals that you are a moron. You do not deserve to talk about this."

Now Carlson was promoting a conspiracy theory about January 6 that was just as moronic as Ledger's about 9/11—and he wasn't doing it in the fever swamps of online radio but on a glitzy platform owned and operated by the most powerful company in conservative media. Even worse, unlike Alex Jones and other prominent promulgators of conspiracy theories and unhinged rhetoric, who began their careers on, and still present themselves as, the fringe, Carlson possessed a certain trustworthiness, even gravitas, making him much more persuasive—and dangerous. It was too much even for some people inside Fox. Privately, Chris Wallace and Bret Baier both protested to Scott that *Patriot Purge* was damaging Fox's credibility. Publicly, Wallace had Liz Cheney, the vice chair of the House committee investigating the January 6 riots, on *Fox News Sunday* to essentially rebut Carlson's claims. Was there "any truth," Wallace asked, to the "talk that January 6th was a false flag operation?" "None at all," Cheney replied. "It's the same kind of thing that you hear from people who say that 9/11 was an inside job. . . . It's un-American to be spreading those kinds of lies. And they are lies." Baier, meanwhile, ran a segment on *Special Report* by Fox News's veteran national security correspondent Jennifer Griffin debunking false flag theories about January 6. Neither Wallace nor Baier ever mentioned Carlson or *Patriot Purge* on their shows, but it wasn't hard to figure out why they suddenly felt the need to address false flag theories about January 6.

Others inside Fox were less passive-aggressive in their opposition. Stephen Hayes and Jonah Goldberg, who'd enjoyed lucrative contributor contracts and had been mainstays on *Special Report* for a dozen years, resigned from the news channel in protest. Two years earlier, after their longtime professional homes had been rendered uninhabitable—Hayes's at *The Weekly Standard* because it went out of business, Goldberg's at *National Review* because it had become irredeemably Trumpy—they had founded *The Dispatch*, an online publication that billed itself as "a place where thoughtful readers can come for conservative, fact-based news and commentary." *The Dispatch* was undoubtedly anti-Trump, but unlike Kristol's *Bulwark*, that wasn't its entire identity; it envisioned a future for conservatism—and conservative media—that didn't involve Trump at all, when there was no longer a need for there to be a resistance. Now, in a letter posted on *The Dispatch*'s site, they explained that "the tension between doing that work well and remaining loyal to Fox has tested us many times over the past few years. But with the release of *Patriot Purge*, we felt we could no longer 'do right as we see it' and remain at Fox News. So we resigned." Carlson hailed Goldberg's and Hayes's resignations as "great news" in an interview with *The New York Times*. "Our viewers will be grateful," he taunted his erstwhile friends.

Goldberg and Hayes got off easy compared to Jon Ward. Ward, who'd been Carlson's first hire at *The Daily Caller*, was now a politics reporter for *Yahoo! News*. He set out to do a "detailed examination" of *Patriot Purge*'s claims. It was the sort of fact-heavy, diligent, responsible work that Ward and his nose for the boring had tried to do at the *Caller* before he quit after concluding that Carlson was taking the website in a direction that made that sort of work impossible. Still, Ward and Carlson had remained on friendly terms. Carlson had even hosted Ward and his wife and three children at his summer home in Maine. Before Ward's story ran on *Yahoo! News*, he texted Carlson to basically fact-check his fact-check. They went back and forth over the course of a couple of days. At one point, Ward texted Carlson his words, as Ward had transcribed them, from the end of the series: "They're pushing you toward violence and they're doing it on purpose . . . Tell the truth. Build the country. Love your family and each other. Be the light. That's how it gets better." Carlson pointed out to Ward that he'd removed his admonition "But don't fall for it" in his transcription. Ward admitted that he'd missed that and thanked Carlson for the correction. "I'm glad I checked," he wrote his old boss. "It's important to get it right before we publish."

But before *Yahoo! News* could publish, Carlson beat him to the punch. On his show, alongside an unflattering photo of Ward, Carlson recounted their text exchange. "You'll notice in that transcription, there's a series of dots between two of those sentences. Those are called ellipses. They signify that something has been removed from the original quote," he told his viewers. "The phrase 'Don't fall for it' was removed." Of course, Ward had told Carlson he would—and in fact did—publish the correct transcript in his story. But Carlson didn't tell his viewers that. Instead, he claimed that this was an "example of media dishonesty." And he offered up Ward as a cautionary tale. "He's a very nice person. He's a sincere family man. He's also weak," Carlson said. "And in a moment like this, weak people get crushed by the forces above them. Weak people conform. They do what it takes." Carlson, who was being paid twenty million dollars a year by a corporation whose annual revenues were more than ten billion dollars, continued his attack on *Yahoo!*, which was in the midst of a seemingly endless cycle of layoffs and retrenchments, and Ward. "If you want to draw a salary from a big media company right now, you do what you're told," he said. "You toe the line. If it comes down to it, you lie. The whole thing is heartbreaking to watch. What an awful moment this is."

Two years later, Ward left *Yahoo! News*, and journalism entirely, to become a strategic consultant. "I was quite an idealist," he explained, "and the last several years have been chastening."

THE 2022 MIDTERMS PROVIDED CARLSON with an opportunity to flex his political muscle like never before—to demonstrate that he could turn his viewers into voters, that he could use his show to send Republicans in his own populist-nationalist image to Washington. Thinking as much like a political strategist as a television host, he converted *Tucker Carlson Tonight*'s booking operation into a quasi congressional-campaign committee. But instead of showering millions of dollars on his preferred candidates, Carlson offered them airtime. For some candidates, winning the "Tucker Primary" was tantamount to winning the Republican primary.

Joe Kent was running in a Washington state congressional district, trying to unseat Jaime Herrera Beutler, a six-term incumbent who was one of just ten Republicans to vote for Trump's impeachment in 2021. Kent was a former Green Beret who flirted with white nationalists, argued that the January 6 riots were a deep state conspiracy, and railed against "pointless or unwinnable wars"; he became a frequent guest on *Tucker Carlson Tonight*. "I was up against a Republican who was backed by the full weight of the Republican establishment," Kent said after he defeated Herrera Beutler in the primary. "Being able to get on Tucker for free and have him say, 'I hope you win, I agree with what you're saying,' was really important."

Blake Masters, who was running for the US Senate in Arizona, was another *Tucker Carlson Tonight* regular. It was the thirty-five-year-old Masters's first campaign. Before entering politics, he spent eight years working for the billionaire tech investor Peter Thiel. His political beliefs largely mirrored those of Thiel, the avatar of techno-libertarianism who once infamously mused that he "no longer believe[d] that freedom and democracy are compatible." But Masters's political style and rhetoric owed everything to Carlson. His campaign ads were, essentially, repurposed Carlson monologues, borrowing Carlson's favorite topics—the piggishness of "woke" US military generals and the ignorance of American teachers—and, occasionally, stealing

Carlson's exact phraseology. "Does anyone still believe that cheaper iPhones or more Amazon deliveries of plastic garbage from China are going to make us happy?" Carlson once asked his viewers. Masters told voters, "Amazon will send you some useless Chinese junk at the press of a button. But the things people actually need—housing, health care, education—this stuff just keeps getting more and more expensive every year."

The results were odd, bordering on off-putting. While Carlson, of course, delivered his dire pronouncements from the familiar setting of a cable-news studio, Masters's stark positions had not yet been reduced to the simple shorthand images political ads normally rely on. He couldn't declare that schools are making kids dumber over footage of himself talking to kindergartners. His living room would be an incongruously cozy place from which to convey the message that the country is run by psychopaths. So, instead, Masters's ads showed him prophesizing doom from a desert or a hayfield, radiating a weird, dark energy. But Arizona Republicans didn't seem to mind: Masters won the GOP primary in a rout.

No 2022 midterm candidate enjoyed as much airtime on *Tucker Carlson Tonight*, and enjoyed as close a personal relationship with its host, as JD Vance, who was running for the US Senate in Ohio. Carlson and Vance met for the first time, not too long after Trump's election, at a bankers' conference at a California resort. Carlson was new in his prime-time role at Fox News, his populist persona in its embryonic stages, but he was a veteran of the buckraking circuit, where he'd been engaging in chummy, bloodless political debates with Paul Begala or James Carville or some other liberal talking head since his CNN days. Wall Street types still viewed him as a fellow traveler, not the dangerous class traitor he'd soon become.

Vance was the coastal elite's shiny new toy. Having moved on from *FrumForum*, he was now a best-selling author. *Hillbilly*

Elegy, his memoir about his rise from a dysfunctional childhood in a working-class family in Ohio to Yale Law School, was published in the summer of 2016, in the heat of the presidential campaign. It was immediately hailed by the commentariat as a key to understanding the peculiar political moment—"a compassionate, discerning sociological analysis of the white underclass that has helped drive the politics of rebellion, particularly the ascent of Donald J. Trump," as *The New York Times* put it in its review. Vance, who was in his early thirties and working at a Silicon Valley venture capital firm (owned by Thiel), suddenly found himself gracing the stages of the Aspen Institute, the 92nd Street Y, and other highbrow forums, explaining to anxious, upper-crust audiences why so many downtrodden white people loved Trump. He always reassured his elite interlocutors that he himself had no use for Trump—calling him, in an essay for *The Atlantic*, "cultural heroin" and, in private, a "moral disaster" and "America's Hitler." But he told them that the problems of the white working class that Trump identified—deindustrialization, the opioid epidemic, immigration—were very real, and that white working-class support for Trump, while regrettable, was understandable. He'd found fame—and, increasingly, fortune—as polite society's Trump translator.

But at the bankers' conference in California, something inside Vance seemed to break. As he later recounted to a friend, standing on stage he began to feel contempt for his audience. Where he once thought America's ruling class was incompetent, now he viewed them as evil, caring less about American citizens than global ones. And so he deviated from his script; rather than explain the plight of the working class to the elites, he attacked the elites for not doing enough to alleviate—and, in some respects, for actually causing—the working class's plight. When his talk was over, he recalled, there was little applause, and the bankers avoided him for the rest of the conference. In Vance's retelling, the only person who came up to him afterward was Carlson, who praised him for delivering an excellent speech. Carlson and Vance hit it off, their mutual self-loathing about being at the bankers' conference marrying with their shared self-seeking recognition that the future of conservative politics resided outside of—and, in fact, in opposition to—that confab. As Vance later explained his populist pivot to the journalist Simon van Zuylen-Wood: "Dominant elite society is boring, it is completely unreflective, and it is increasingly wrong. I kind of had to make a choice."

Carlson and Vance stayed in touch. After Vance moved back to Ohio and began laying the groundwork for a political career there, Carlson turned into an informal adviser. When Mitch McConnell tried to recruit Vance to run for the US Senate against the Democratic incumbent Sherrod Brown in 2018, Carlson counseled him against it: Brown was a tough candidate with his own working-class appeal, and running as the hand-picked choice of McConnell and other establishment Republicans would not wear well. Better to wait for another race. Four years later, after the other Ohio Senate seat opened up with the retirement of Republican Rob Portman, Carlson encouraged Vance to take the plunge; when he did, Carlson gave him ample airtime. In the ten months between Vance's campaign launch and the Republican primary, he appeared fifteen times on *Tucker Carlson Tonight*, which, as one Fox producer noted, was "the most-watched news program of any news program in Ohio" among the state's GOP primary voters. "I probably shouldn't say this: I'm really glad you're doing it," Carlson told the newly minted Senate candidate when he went on Carlson's show hours after entering the race. "JD Vance, I admire you and I wish you luck, very much."

It certainly helped that Vance sounded so much like his host. He promoted replacement theory, warning of an immigrant "invasion" while claiming that Democrats "have decided that they can't win reelection in 2022 unless they bring a large number of new voters to replace the voters that are already here." He sloughed off Vladimir Putin's imperial ambitions, declaring, "I don't really care what happens to Ukraine one way or another." And he dismissed "Silicon Valley technology companies as the enemies of western civilization." Like Carlson, he embraced—and gave voice to—the NatCons, delivering the closing speech at their second annual conference. Like Carlson, he attempted to co-opt the harshest criticisms that were leveled against him, releasing a TV ad that began "Are you a racist? Do you hate Mexicans? The media calls us racist for wanting to build Trump's wall." "I think Tucker looks at JD as a reflection of Tucker's own worldview," a Vance adviser said.

Just as important as offering Vance airtime and a worldview, Carlson worked to get him into Trump's good graces. Although Carlson was still angry at the former president—his own conspiracy theorizing about January 6 did not mean he'd forgotten Trump's behavior in the postelection period—he had started talking to Trump again. And most of those conversations, in early 2022, revolved around Vance's Senate race. Trump was initially skeptical of Vance; the other Republicans running in the primary, and vying for Trump's endorsement, made sure that Trump was aware of all the negative things Vance had said about him during the 2016 campaign. But Carlson, along with Donald Trump Jr., slowly brought Trump around on the elegiac hillbilly. At one point Carlson spent nearly two hours on FaceTime with Trump, while Trump golfed in Florida, making the case that Vance believed what Trump believed and that, were Trump to run for president again, he needed someone like Vance in the Senate. At the end of the call, Trump told Carlson, "You'll be happy." A few weeks later, Trump endorsed Vance, propelling him to the Republican nomination. In his victory speech on the night of the primary, Vance made sure to thank both Trump and Carlson for their support.

As the midterms drew closer, Republicans were giddy with anticipation. Polls, many of them conducted by right-leaning pollsters, showed the GOP reclaiming the House, picking up as many as thirty-five seats, and taking back the Senate, as well. Republican politicians and Fox hosts gleefully predicted a "red wave." Some even talked about a "red tsunami." Carlson was one of them. "The conventional view among people who follow politics is that the Democratic Party is about to suffer a humiliating repudiation in next week's midterm elections," Carlson told his viewers six days before the midterms. But that didn't come to pass. While Republicans did take back the House, their nine-seat majority was the fifth-smallest margin of control in modern history; what's more, Democrats not only held on to the Senate but gained a seat.

For Carlson, though, the results were mixed. Almost all the candidates he invited and promoted on his show—a group he once hailed as "surging outsiders" that included Kent, Masters, Vance, Kari Lake, and Mehmet Oz—went down to defeat. "I've never gotten anything wronger in my life," he told the audience at a Turning Point USA conference shortly after the midterms. But the one Carlson-stamped candidate who did win was Vance—and Carlson took tremendous satisfaction from that. As he told one friend during the campaign, Vance was the candidate in whom he was most invested because Vance was the candidate who, he believed, had the greatest potential. "Occasionally, you run into somebody who could actually change things," Carlson said in an interview before the Ohio primary. "That would be JD Vance."

NINE

SIX MONTHS AFTER THE MIDTERMS, on a Friday evening in April 2023, Tucker Carlson delivered the keynote speech to more than two thousand people at the Heritage Foundation's fiftieth-anniversary gala. He appeared to be at the pinnacle of American conservatism.

Admittedly, the previous few months had been a little rocky. After the disappointment of the midterms (save for the silver lining of Vance) Carlson had to contend with one particularly nasty bit of fallout from the 2020 election interregnum—a lawsuit. Dominion Voting Systems, the software company that was at the center of Sidney Powell's conspiracy theory about a stolen election, had sued Fox for $1.6 billion for defaming it by repeatedly broadcasting Powell's bogus claims. Carlson—along with Hannity and Ingraham and both Murdochs and dozens of other Fox hosts and executives and staffers—had to sit for an unpleasant deposition. Even more unpleasant, as part of the lawsuit, Dominion obtained thousands of emails and text messages from Carlson and other Fox employees that were eventually made public—revealing the yawning gap between what Carlson said publicly and privately about Trump and voter fraud. But in April, right before the case went to trial—where Carlson would have been forced to take the stand—Fox agreed to settle the case for $787 million. It was a shocking sum, but Fox could afford it, and disposing of the case seemed to be in the interests of everyone at the network. They could all move on.

And so three days after the settlement was reached, as Carlson stood in a hotel ballroom outside of Washington to celebrate America's most powerful conservative think tank—and to be celebrated in return—he was not just in a jovial mood, but a reflective one. He noted his long-ago internship at Heritage and how, the week he started there in 1991, the Soviet Union collapsed—a development that completely unmoored American politics. "Our entire political orientation was based on this war between the United States and the Soviet Union, this Cold War," he explained. When the Cold War ended, things went off the rails, and now "the country's really going at high speed in the wrong direction . . . in ways that are just unfathomable," he said. He lamented the "cowards" and "quislings" who are "saying things they don't believe"—about "George Floyd and COVID and the Ukraine war"—because "they want to keep their jobs." But he hailed the truth tellers—the people who "stand up in the middle of a DEI meeting at Citibank and say, 'This is nonsense'"—and said that their example "gives me hope." Thanks to them, he went on, "we can also see rising in the distance, new things, new institutions led by new people who are every bit as brave as the people who came before us." He left little doubt that he believed himself to be one of them.

The following Monday morning, Carlson was back home in Florida. He'd just sent his producers the first draft of his monologue for that evening's show—a lengthy attack on Alexandria Ocasio-Cortez, or as Carlson called her, invoking her high school nickname, Sandy Cortez—when he got a phone call from Suzanne Scott. That was something of a rarity. But Carlson didn't have time to wonder why Scott was calling him. She got right to the point. "We're taking you off the air," Scott told him. He was being fired. Scott offered him the opportunity to include his own statement in the press release Fox would send out in fifteen minutes announcing his departure—a face-saving gesture that would make it seem like a mutual parting of the ways. But Carlson refused. If Fox was firing him, he wanted the world to know. When the phone call was over, he sent an email to the Tuckertroop telling them the shocking news. A minute later Fox sent out the press release telling the world.

In the days after Carlson's firing, there was much speculation, both inside and outside of Fox, about the reasons behind his defenestration. Some thought it had to do with offensive comments he made about Fox executives, including calling Irena Briganti a "cunt," in text messages uncovered in the Dominion suit. Others wondered if it could have been because of another lawsuit, from Abby Grossberg, a former head of booking on his show, accusing him and the network of creating a hostile work environment. And others speculated that it had something to do with a potential lawsuit from Ray Epps, a January 6 protester from Arizona who was at the center of Carlson's and *Patriot Purge*'s false conspiracy theory about the day that alleged that Epps was a government provocateur. In fact, a sympathetic profile of Epps had appeared on *60 Minutes* the evening before Carlson's firing. Perhaps Rupert Murdoch, who at the tender age of ninety-two fit squarely in the CBS television news magazine's viewer demographic, had seen it and gotten spooked.

Among Fox hosts and executives, stories circulated about a recent dinner Carlson had at Murdoch's California vineyard with Murdoch and his then fiancée, Ann Lesley Smith, during which Smith, who believed Carlson was "a messenger from God," treated him as such. The evening left Murdoch extremely weirded out, and a few days later, he canceled the engagement. Now, the theory went, he was canceling Carlson. For his part,

Carlson came to believe—as eventually relayed by his longtime Boswell, Michael Wolff, in his 2023 book about Fox, *The Fall*—that his firing was part of Fox's settlement with Dominion: Murdoch refused Dominion's demand to fork over $1 billion, so he got the plaintiffs to yes by offering $787 million and Carlson's scalp instead. None of the explanations were especially satisfying.

But, while it was human nature for Carlson to dwell on what just befell him, he did not have the luxury of everyone else to perseverate on it. He needed to find a new platform, a new way for him to keep his voice out there, and he needed to do it fast. The presidential election, just eighteen months away, was already in full swing, He'd assumed, with good reason, that *Tucker Carlson Tonight* would be a major player in that race. But now that he'd lost his Fox megaphone, he'd have to come up with a new vehicle. Carlson was determined not to go the way of Beck and Kelly and O'Reilly and all the other stars who'd left the cable channel and, while defying Ailes's taunting prediction that they wouldn't last two days, had not come anywhere close to matching the success they enjoyed at Fox. Complicating matters, Fox was keeping him under his contract, which ran through 2024, with the express intent of keeping him off the air. That meant he'd be making the nearly twenty million dollars a year Fox owed him, but he wouldn't be able to take his show to Newsmax or OAN. Carlson knew that, in the attention economy, twenty million dollars was worthless if it didn't come attached to a deal that put him on people's screens multiple times a week.

Fortunately for Carlson, he had no shortage of other offers that didn't run afoul of Fox's noncompete clause. Just hours after his firing, Elon Musk—who, six months earlier, had bought Twitter and was in the process of reshaping the social media platform into a right-wing media hub, eventually rebranding it as

X—called him to talk about doing a deal. So did Omeed Malik, who together with Rebekah Mercer ran 1789 Capital, a venture capital firm that invests in conservative companies. "The world is his oyster," said one person who was talking to Carlson as the offers came in. "Many billionaires and others with deep pockets would be eager to fund a new venture." Enlisting the help of Neil Patel and Justin Wells, Carlson immediately began laying the groundwork for a new digital-media company, the Tucker Carlson Network, securing Musk's help to boost Carlson's content on X and fifteen million dollars in seed money from Malik and others. He became a frequent visitor to Doha, Dubai, and Riyadh—cities he once derided as "chintzy" and "prefab"—in pursuit of Gulf investors. In the rapidly fracturing conservative-media space, he was establishing a very firm toehold. (So firm that in 2025, Carlson and Patel would buy out their investors and gain complete independence and total control of their media company.)

But no one would be more important to Carlson's efforts to preserve his standing, his power, his relevance, than one very crucial ally: Donald J. Trump.

EVEN BEFORE CARLSON WAS FIRED from Fox, he had achieved something of a rapprochement with the former president. For a long time after January 6, it was Trump who was courting Carlson—calling him, inviting him to Mar-a-Lago and Bedminster, his golf resort in New Jersey, letting it be known that he was still watching Carlson's show, making it clear that he still wanted to have a relationship. But Carlson had gone back to playing hard to get. While he would get on the phone, and occasionally even FaceTime with Trump, when he wanted something from him—like an endorsement for JD Vance—he refused Trump's offers of a sit-down. Finally, in July 2022, Donald Trump Jr. traveled to Maine to visit Carlson at his home there. As he and Carlson hunted and fished together, Trump Jr. pressed Carlson to meet with his father. A few weeks later, Carlson showed up at Bedminster on the same weekend it was hosting the Saudi-backed LIV Golf tour. The result was widely circulated pictures of Carlson yukking it up with Trump and Marjorie Taylor Greene in the tournament's VIP section. Although Carlson hates golf—when people ask him if he plays, he typically answers, "No, I'm sorry, I still have sex"—he appeared to be having a great time.

As Trump laid the groundwork for another run for the White House in 2024, Carlson weighed whether to back the former president. On the one hand, he was dead set opposed to Nikki Haley, for whom he developed an intense personal dislike during an ill-fated hunting weekend a decade earlier. After Haley announced her 2024 presidential candidacy, Carlson told his viewers, "Nikki Haley believes in collective racial guilt," going on to say, "She believes identity politics is our future. 'Vote for me because I'm a woman,' she says. That's her pitch." On the other hand, Carlson, along with everyone else at Fox News, had been trying to boost DeSantis. But the more he saw of the Florida governor, the less he liked—especially after DeSantis and his wife visited Carlson and Susie at their home on Gasparilla Island for lunch and Susie gave him the thumbs-down. When the text messages of Carlson trashing Trump were released as part of the Dominion suit, Carlson called Trump and offered a fulsome apology; it was water under the bridge, Trump told him. A few weeks later, Carlson visited Mar-a-Lago and *Tucker Carlson Tonight* devoted an entire hour to a one-on-one softball interview of Trump, who'd recently been arraigned in New York City on thirty-four counts of falsifying business records; at the time, it stood as one of Trump's longest appearances on the cable network since he'd left the White House. "For a man who is caricatured as an extremist," Carlson told his viewers, "we think you'll find what he has to say moderate, sensible, and wise."

If Carlson was already leaning toward Trump in the 2024 presidential race, his firing from Fox practically forced him onto Trump's lap. Indeed, cozying up to Trump became a central pillar of Carlson's post-Fox plans. When Carlson had his Fox show, it was relatively easy for him to hold on to America's attention, but now he was going to need some help. Fortunately for Carlson, Trump needed him too. Their interests aligned most immediately in their mutual desire to stick it to Fox. Despite his once-again warm relations with Hannity and Ingraham and others at the network, Trump had not forgiven Murdoch for trying to disappear him—and for so flagrantly trying to boost DeSantis. He accused Fox of having gone to the "dark side." And so when Scott, Hannity, Baier, and other Fox figures began lobbying Trump to appear in the first GOP presidential-primary debate in August, which was going to air on Fox—knowing that, without Trump, the debate's ratings would suffer—Trump strung them along for months. All the while, Trump was talking to Carlson about some sort of counterprogramming. Eventually, Carlson and Trump settled on a pretaped interview between the two that would be posted on X at the same time Fox was hosting the debate. The Trump-less debate was a relative dud, drawing eleven million viewers—fewer than half as many as the first Republican debate of the contested 2016 primaries, further confirming for Fox that the GOP was still Trump's party.

Even Trump and Carlson haters had to concede their counterprogramming made for oddly compelling viewing—certainly more compelling than the debate—as Carlson steered the interview and Trump to some unusual and dark places. "They started with protests against you . . . then it moved to impeachment twice. And now indictment. I mean, the next stage is violence,"

Carlson said. "Are you worried they're going to try and kill you? Why wouldn't they try and kill you? Honestly?"

"They're savage animals," Trump replied. "They are people that are sick, really sick."

For his final question, Carlson asked, "Do you think we're moving towards civil war?"

Trump's answer was hardly reassuring. "I can say this, there's a level of passion that I've never seen," he said. "There's a level of hatred that I've never seen, and that's probably a bad combination."

Later in the campaign, Trump granted unprecedented access to Wells for a behind-the-scenes documentary miniseries, *Art of the Surge*, that ran on the Tucker Carlson Network. It was a predictably schlocky product—with lots of slow-motion footage of Trump walking onto stages and American flags rippling in the wind—but the access did produce at least one riveting and stomach-turning moment: Wells's cameras were about fifteen feet away from Trump at the July campaign rally in Butler, Pennsylvania, when Trump was shot by a would-be assassin.

But Carlson couldn't rely solely on Trump to maintain the public's attention. Without Fox's built-in audience—not to mention the guardrails of a publicly traded media company or even nominal corporate supervision—he descended further into the fever swamps in the pursuit of eyeballs for his new show. On one episode, he hosted the notorious conspiracy theorist Alex Jones, telling his viewers that Jones "is not a crazy person." On another, he interviewed Larry Sinclair, an ex-con who during the 2008 presidential campaign made a long-since-debunked claim that he smoked crack and had sex with Barack Obama when Obama was a little-known state senator. (Ironically, Carlson had cited his own refusal to cover Sinclair's claims in 2008—"I just thought it was unfair to report that"—when he debated Ben

Smith in 2017 about *BuzzFeed*'s decision to publish the Steele dossier.) For another episode, Carlson traveled to Romania to conduct a friendly two-and-a-half-hour interview with the misogynistic online influencer Andrew Tate, who was under house arrest there while being investigated for human trafficking and rape allegations. Carlson later argued that Tate's arrest was "obviously a setup" and the "definition of a human-rights violation" while repeatedly hailing Tate as a role model for young men. (Tate was eventually charged with human trafficking and rape by Romanian authorities; additionally, the Crown Prosecution Service in Britain charged Tate with human trafficking, rape, and assault charges.)

There was a through-line in many of Carlson's most unhinged and conspiratorial musings: a deep antipathy toward Jews and a visceral loathing of Israel. Attacking Ukraine's Jewish president Volodymyr Zelensky, Carlson employed classic anti-Semitic tropes in describing Zelensky as "ratlike" and a "persecutor of Christians." In the midst of the Israel-Hamas War, he accused Israel of "blowing up churches and killing Christians" and criticized the conservative commentator Ben Shapiro, an Orthodox Jew, and other pro-Israel Americans for being "focused on a conflict in a foreign country as their own country becomes dangerously unstable"; contrasting Shapiro's and his compatriots' supposed disdain for America with his own abiding love of it, Carlson said, "I'm from here, my family's been here hundreds of years. I plan to stay here. I'm shocked by how little they care about the country." On one show, Carlson hosted Darryl Cooper, a Nazi apologist historian who has argued that concentration camps were a "humane" solution to widespread hunger during World War II—and whom Carlson introduced to his viewers as "the best and most honest popular historian in the United States." He'd come a long way from the days when he described himself as a pro-Israel, Episcopalian neocon.

In February 2024, Carlson made his biggest splash, and drew his greatest number of eyeballs, when he traveled to Moscow to interview Vladimir Putin. It was the Russian strongman's first interview with a Western journalist in the nearly two years since his country invaded Ukraine—and Carlson was preemptively pilloried by his critics for doing it at all. "He's what's called a useful idiot," Hillary Clinton told MSNBC. "He says things that are not true. He parrots Vladimir Putin's pack of lies about Ukraine, so I don't see why Putin wouldn't give him an interview." After the interview was broadcast, Clinton seemed to have had a point. While it was hard to fault Carlson for doing the interview—Putin was perhaps the most newsworthy subject in the world, and any journalist would want to talk to him—Carlson seemed very much out of his depth. For more than two hours, sitting in a gilded hall in the Kremlin, Putin filibustered with lengthy and tendentious history lessons about Russia's supposed claims to Ukraine and other Eastern European lands—history lessons that Carlson was unable to interrupt, much less correct.

Carlson had gone to Moscow with the goal of freeing Evan Gershkovich, a thirty-two-year-old *Wall Street Journal* reporter who was imprisoned by Russian authorities eleven months earlier on trumped-up espionage charges. Carlson had told Putin's aides that he planned to ask Putin to release Gershkovich to him during the interview and, presuming Putin said yes, that he'd take Gershkovich with him on his flight back to the United States. Putin's aides seemed receptive to the idea. It would be the ultimate public relations coup for Carlson—returning to the United States with a "corporate-media" reporter (for a Murdoch publication, no less) who'd been taken hostage by Putin, the man Carlson's critics alleged he was in cahoots with, and that the Biden administration had been unable to free. But when Carlson did raise the subject of Gershkovich's imprisonment toward the end of his interview with Putin—"The guy is obviously not a spy. He's a kid," Carlson told the Russian president—Putin demurred. He said that he'd only release Gershkovich in exchange for "a person serving a sentence in an allied country of the U.S. . . . [who], due to patriotic sentiments, eliminated the bandit in one of the European capitals during the events in the Caucasus." Experienced Russia hands—and maybe even Carlson—knew that Putin was referring to Vadim Krasikov, a Russian hitman who was convicted by German authorities of killing a Georgian citizen, who'd fought Russian troops in Chechnya, in Berlin. Carlson obviously had no truck with the German government. Regardless, after the interview, as Putin gave him a late-night tour of the Kremlin, Carlson raised Gershkovich once again. "Why are you doing this?" he asked Putin. "It's hurting you." Once again Putin rebuffed him. Carlson returned home without the reporter. (Six months later, as part of a prisoner swap negotiated by the US and Russian governments, Krasikov was freed from a German prison and returned to Russia in exchange for Gershkovich's release and return to the United States.)

But if Carlson didn't have the influence over Putin that he hoped for, he still had Trump. And, as the presidential campaign continued, Carlson's relationship with the former president took on new dimensions. Where Carlson once tried to reach Trump through his Fox show, he now recognized that Trump did not have the wherewithal to watch (or listen, after Carlson began releasing his online show as a podcast) to a two-hour-plus program. He began to communicate with Trump more directly—by text message, on the phone, and in person. And he was pleasantly surprised that Trump was even more receptive to his advice than he had been when he was in the White House and Carlson was on Fox. The people around Trump who'd once pushed him to ignore Carlson's counsel were long gone. Instead, Trump was surrounded almost entirely by people who shared Carlson's worldview—most importantly Stephen Miller and Donald Trump Jr.

As Trump began to think about a running mate, Carlson was a constant voice in his ear. Trump told reporters he was entertaining the idea of tapping Carlson as his veep. "I like Tucker a lot; I guess I would," Trump said in response to a radio interviewer who asked if he was considering Carlson as a running mate. "I think I'd say I would, because he's got great common sense." Publicly, Carlson said he was at least open to the idea. "God would have to yell at me very loud." But, privately, he insisted he wasn't interested in joining the ticket. The person he did want Trump to pick was JD Vance. Since his election to the Senate, Vance had, if anything, become even closer to Carlson—both personally and ideologically. And Carlson, along with Trump Jr., became Vance's most crucial advocate with Trump. In June, after receiving word that Trump was leaning away from Vance and toward Senator Marco Rubio of Florida or Governor Doug Burgum of North Dakota, Carlson called Trump from Australia, where he was on a speaking tour. He warned Trump that Rubio and Burgum were neocons who supported military adventurism overseas. If Trump chose one of them for his running mate, Carlson said, US intelligence agencies would try to assassinate him. Trump picked Vance.

And it was Carlson who connected Robert F. Kennedy Jr., who was running as an independent presidential candidate and threatening to siphon votes from Trump, with Trump on a three-way text chain in July after Trump survived the assassination attempt; six weeks later, Kennedy dropped out of the presidential race and endorsed Trump.

Carlson's influence even filtered down to the staff level. In August, Trump's campaign hired Alex Pfeiffer, Carlson's former Fox producer, as a campaign aide. A month later, Pfeiffer dug up Kamala Harris's 2019 candidate interview with the American Civil Liberties Union, in which she said she supported providing gender transition surgery to detained migrants; the next day, in their one debate, Trump attacked Harris on the issue, and the Trump campaign launched tens of millions of dollars in attack ads against Harris mentioning her stance and ending with the line "Kamala is for they/them. President Trump is for you."

Trump returned these favors, embracing Carlson and giving him a prominent public role in his campaign. At the Republican National Convention in Milwaukee in July, he invited Carlson to sit in his private box on the first night and gave him a prime-time speaking slot on its final, most watched night. In October, Carlson spoke at Trump's massive Madison Square Garden rally. When Carlson launched his own sixteen-city speaking tour that fall, Trump and Vance both lent a hand, appearing as the evening's "special guest" in Arizona and Pennsylvania respectively. Far from fading away, Carlson was firmly at the center of the MAGA movement.

He wasn't above flaunting his position. At the Republican convention, he paid a surprise visit to Fox News's studio inside the venue, accompanying Donald Trump Jr. when he went to do an interview with Sean Hannity. As Carlson was mobbed by old colleagues like Brit Hume and Jeanine Pirro, Fox executives could only look on in awkward silence. Carlson just grinned, relishing their discomfort.

On January 20, 2025, Carlson strolled through downtown Washington, DC. It was Inauguration Day, and he had come to the nation's capital like de Gaulle returning to Paris. Dressed for the bitter cold in a field coat and with a red, white, and blue scarf slung around his neck, Carlson was swarmed by people on the street, who shook his hand and snapped his picture. "Hey, Tucker!" one man shouted. "Our country's back, sir!" Carlson smiled and pointed and put his hand over his heart. "Happy inaugural!" he exclaimed as he threw his arm around another man's shoulders. "You're a hero!" the man told him. Carlson was overwhelmed by his reception in a city that, just a few years earlier, he had essentially fled. "Not one person was rude to me. Not one person was anything but nice to me," he later marveled. "And that's all because of Trump. It had nothing to do with me. And so Trump's total control of the city was shocking."

Just as shocking was the amount of power Carlson himself now wielded in Trump's Washington. Unlike the last time Trump was elected, when Carlson had pointedly passed up the opportunity to influence the transition, he'd been deeply involved in this one. Carlson subscribed to the old Washington dictum that "personnel is policy." In multiple postelection visits to Mar-a-Lago and countless phone calls and texts, he vigorously weighed in on how he believed Trump should fill out his cabinet and staff. "Trump wanted Tucker's opinion," a Trump adviser said, "and Tucker didn't ever hesitate to offer it."

In some instances, Carlson exercised a veto. When Trump was on the verge of appointing Mike Pompeo, who served as CIA director and secretary of state in his first administration (and, perhaps just as importantly in Trump's eyes, had lost a tremendous amount of weight and was now, according to Trump, "so handsome"), as secretary of defense in his second administration, Carlson, together with Donald Trump Jr., launched a furious lobbying campaign to scuttle the move. Carlson nursed both ideological and personal grudges against Pompeo. Like Trump Jr., he considered Pompeo a neocon—a "warmonger" and "a criminal," as Carlson told more than one person—and believed that, as CIA director, Pompeo had plotted to have WikiLeaks founder Julian Assange killed. He also had not forgotten the time that a lawyer for Pompeo, who was then secretary of state, had called and threatened him with criminal prosecution after he mentioned on his Fox show that a source had told him that the CIA had been involved in the assassination of John F. Kennedy. Talking to Trump, though, Carlson mostly focused on Pompeo's loyalty, or lack thereof. He reminded Trump that Pompeo had distanced himself from Trump's claims that the 2020 election had been stolen and that Pompeo had criticized the actions of Trump supporters on January 6 as "unacceptable." Carlson was so persuasive that not only did Trump pass over Pompeo for secretary of defense, instead choosing Carlson's old Fox News colleague Pete Hegseth; shortly after being sworn in, Trump revoked the security detail that Biden's State Department had provided Pompeo, whom the Iranian government had targeted for assassination after the United States, during Trump's first presidency, killed Iranian general Qasem Soleimani in a drone strike.

In other instances, Carlson made more affirmative arguments. Howard Lutnick, Trump's transition-team cochair, had promised before the election that Robert F. Kennedy Jr. would not be Health and Human Services secretary—a promise that was much appreciated by pharmaceutical-industry executives, who blanched at Kennedy's anti-vaccine conspiracy theories. But Carlson was a Kennedy fan. He believed that Kennedy's Make America Healthy Again agenda, which Carlson had assiduously promoted on his own show, was good politics. (Carlson's August 2024 podcast interview with Calley and Casey Means, a brother-and-sister duo of wellness influencers and Kennedy acolytes, was Apple's most-shared episode of that year.) Carlson prevailed upon Trump to ignore what his transition chair had promised and to put Kennedy in charge of HHS. Similarly, Carlson was a key backer of Tulsi Gabbard in her bid to become Trump's director of national intelligence. He pushed for her privately with Trump; then, after Trump nominated Gabbard for the role and some Republican senators expressed hesitation about voting to confirm her, owing to her past statements in support of Vladimir Putin and Syrian leader Bashar al-Assad, Carlson declared that any Republican senator who voted against Gabbard was "an enemy of the United States." She was confirmed, with Mitch McConnell being the only Republican to vote against her.

Carlson didn't confine himself to just the cabinet. His influence extended to Trump's subcabinet and even deeper into the new administration. Elbridge Colby was a low-level Pentagon official in Trump's first administration who, as a frequent guest on Carlson's Fox show during the interregnum, became a leading "realist" voice on foreign policy, particularly on Iran; a few days after the 2024 election, Carlson hosted Colby on his podcast, billing him as "one of the very few experienced national security officials who actually agrees with Donald Trump" and predicting that Colby would "play a large and meaningful role in this administration." A month later, over the objections of conservative pro-Israel activists, Trump tapped Colby as undersecretary of defense for policy, a job in which he serves as the Pentagon's in-house intellectual. Darren Beattie, the far-right conspiracy theorist who was given ample airtime in Carlson's documentary about January 6, *Patriot Purge*—and who, on social media, had previously written that "Competent white men must be in charge if you want things to work" and "130+ IQ white males under the age of 20 is pretty much the only demographic that matters," among other racist and sexist sentiments—was appointed the State Department's acting undersecretary for public diplomacy and public affairs. Alex Pfeiffer, Carlson's former tyro producer, landed a job in the White House press office; Carlson's son, Buckley, got a job on JD Vance's staff. "Tucker has people everywhere," the Trump adviser said.

Even more than personnel, Carlson's influence could be detected in Washington's new vibe. In the months that followed the inauguration, as the Trump administration conducted a shock-and-awe campaign to bring the federal government to heel and to bend the country—and, indeed, the world—to its will, so many of its actions and initiatives, its provocations and outrages, seemed as if they originated in the dark and dangerous corners where Carlson tread and toiled the previous decade.

The Trump administration's use of a centuries-old wartime act to deport, without due process, more than two hundred Venezuelan immigrants accused of being gang members to a maximum-security prison in El Salvador, where they may spend the rest of their lives? It was Carlson who, in a Tucker Carlson Original documentary in 2021, hailed El Salvador's then new president Nayib Bukele for his brutal crackdown on Salvadoran gangs, highlighting Bukele's construction of special prisons to house gang leaders. Indeed, the video US Homeland Security secretary Kristi Noem later released of her visit to the Salvadoran prison where the Venezuelan immigrants were sent—which featured Noem standing in front of a teeming jail cell of shirtless, tattooed men—was almost identical to a video of Carlson visiting a similar prison that was featured in his documentary.

JD Vance's remarkable dressing-down of Ukrainian president Volodymyr Zelensky, in front of assembled media during Zelensky's visit with Trump in the Oval Office, for being insufficiently grateful to the United States? It was a direct echo of the criticisms Carlson had been leveling against Zelensky on his shows for the previous three years.

The Trump administration's decision to grant refugee status to white South Africans, who claim to be victims of racial discrimination, at the same time the administration was making it impossible for refugees from war-torn and famine-stricken countries to seek asylum in the United States? It was Carlson who injected the issue of supposed racial discrimination and violence against white South African landowners whose ancestors invented apartheid—portraying it as a cautionary tale for the United States about racial-equality efforts run amok—into the MAGA bloodstream back in 2018, when he hosted Ernst Roets, a South African lobbyist for white rights, on his Fox show.

Donald Trump's landmark speech in Riyadh, in which he effectively denounced decades of American policy in the Middle East by declaring that "the interventionists were intervening in complex societies they did not even understand" and that "the so-called 'nation-builders' wrecked far more nations than they built"? It was a distilled version of the anti-neoconservative jeremiad Carlson had given countless times in the years since he realized the error of his ways about the Iraq War.

The Trump administration's simultaneous assault on the judiciary, universities, journalists, and any part of civil society that refused to bend its knee in abject submission—an assault that had democracy experts worrying that the United States was descending into the form of government known as competitive authoritarianism? It appeared to be cribbed directly from the playbook Viktor Orbán used to such great effect in turning Hungary into an illiberal state—a playbook that Carlson introduced to Trump and the rest of American conservativism back in 2021, in that week that changed everything.

To be sure, Carlson's influence had its limits. In the summer of 2025, as Trump contemplated assisting Israel in its war against Iran, Carlson pleaded with him to keep the US out of the conflict. A war with Iran, he predicted in a lengthy X post, would lead to thousands of American deaths, thirty-dollar-a-gallon gasoline, and the collapse of the US economy; it would also be, he said, a "profound betrayal of [Trump's] supporters" who voted for him, believing he was "a peace candidate." Speaking with Steve Bannon, who also opposed a US strike on Iran, Carlson accused his hawkish former employer Fox News and hawkish former colleague Sean Hannity of "turning up the propaganda hose to full blast" trying to rally support for a war "and knock elderly Fox viewers off their feet and make them submit to where you want them to." In the end, Carlson's protests were for naught. Trump, the world's most powerful elderly Fox viewer, went ahead and authorized US airstrikes on three Iranian nuclear facilities; he dismissed Carlson as "kooky" and taunted, "I don't know what Tucker Carlson is saying. Let him go get a television network and say it so that people listen."

Similarly, Carlson's criticisms of the Trump administration for failing to release the FBI's files on the convicted sex offender Jeffrey Epstein fell on deaf ears in the White House. But, unlike other MAGA media figures, who dropped their Epstein conspiracy theories once it became clear that the Trump administration was abandoning them, Carlson continued to press Trump on the issue. "Donald Trump ran for president on the promise that he would tell us, and that he'd end corruption in Washington," he said. "Can one man fix that? No. But you have to make a good faith effort."

Still, these were seemingly minor ruptures. And if they broadened into bigger ones, some observers surmised that they could redound to Carlson's benefit, since he could then portray himself to a disillusioned MAGA base as the true leader of their movement—and run for president himself in 2028.

DESPITE CONTINUING TO SPLIT HIS time between the Maine backwoods and a Florida island, Carlson was seemingly omnipresent in Trump's Washington. His old friends and colleagues, by contrast, carved out narrower niches in the new political and media landscapes.

Sam Feist, Carlson's producer and "corner man" on *Crossfire*, left CNN after thirty-five years to run C-SPAN, the unglamorous, nonprofit public affairs network. There, he announced plans for C-SPAN's first new weekly program in two decades: *Ceasefire*, which would feature two politicians, a Democrat and a Republican, trying to find things they agreed on, assuming C-SPAN could find enough Democrats and Republicans to participate; Feist insisted that his new show was not penance for his old one.

David Frum settled into a perch at *The Atlantic*, the venerable, century-and-a-half-old monthly magazine that, during Trump's second presidency, refashioned itself into a hub of daily "accountability journalism." (It accomplished this, in part, by raiding *The Washington Post*'s newsroom; although *The Post* had proclaimed that "democracy dies in darkness" during Trump's first stint in the White House, its owner, Amazon billionaire Jeff Bezos, ditched the slogan and adopted a much more conciliatory posture toward Trump the second time around.) While his *Atlantic* colleagues churned out damaging scoop after damaging scoop about the Trump administration, Frum penned lugubrious essays bemoaning the state of American democracy and launched a weekly podcast.

Stephen Hayes and Jonah Goldberg stubbornly stuck to their plan to make *The Dispatch* a media company for news consumers who opposed Trump *and* the Democrats—offering, as Hayes put it, "an alternative to the persistent progressivism of the mainstream media and the increasingly conspiratorial infotainment world on the right." They faced stiff headwinds, to say the least. But more than fifty thousand people valued *The Dispatch* enough to pay at least one hundred dollars a year to subscribe (in addition to seven hundred thousand people who subscribed to its free offerings); its staff, which numbered eight when it launched in 2019, now stood at more than twenty, many of them refugees, like *The Dispatch*'s founders, from *National Review* and *The Weekly Standard*.

Other members of *The Weekly Standard* diaspora now worked at *The Bulwark*, which Bill Kristol had grown from a Never Trump sanctuary into a thriving anti-Trump YouTube, podcast, and newsletter operation, with one hundred thousand paid subscribers and one million unpaid ones; *The Bulwark*'s staff of twenty came not just from conservative media but also from mainstream outlets, including *The Washington Post* and *Politico*, and even liberal ones, like *The Huffington Post*. Along the way, Kristol reinvented himself from neoconservative bogeyman to "former conservative" elder statesman; unlike in the 2020 presidential campaign, when he staked out an anti-anti-Biden position, he now embraced—and, increasingly, was embraced by—Democrats.

Kristol and the others had long since given up trying to figure out what had happened to the Carlson they once knew. Indeed, many of Carlson's old friends and colleagues now simply reviled him. After Carlson hosted on his show a Palestinian Christian pastor and Hamas supporter, who accused the Israeli government of harming Christians, John Podhoretz attacked Carlson as "Anti Semite filth." (Later, after Trump's description of some bankers as "Shylocks" drew criticism from Jewish leaders, Podhoretz declared, "Trump bombed Iran. He can say Shylock 100 times a day forever as far as I'm concerned.") Even Matt Labash had given up on Carlson. Their once-daily talk, text, or email—a staple in each of their lives for more than two decades—had, not long after Trump's first election, been reduced to an every-couple-of-days occurrence. Then it became weekly. Then monthly. Labash still harbored the hope that he could bring his old friend around. Andy Ferguson encouraged him "to keep the lines of communication open" with Carlson, telling him that he could be Carlson's "last contact with reality." But then some time not long before Trump's second election—when their disagreements became too pronounced, their exchanges too hostile—Labash and Carlson ceased contact altogether.

At times, it seemed as if these and other losses gnawed at Carlson. Although he could now walk unmolested through the streets of Washington, DC, at least when it was flooded with the MAGA faithful on Inauguration Day, he feared for his personal safety—so much so that he began trying to make peace with the fact that he was increasingly of the belief that he'd meet a violent end. "I think he'd love to get assassinated," a friend of Carlson said. "He's put away enough money for Susie and the kids that he doesn't have to worry about that anymore, and he thinks there'd be honor to die in a blaze of glory." He was convinced that, on one occasion, he was the victim of a supernatural attack: A "demon" or "something unseen," he told the Christian influencer John Heers, had mauled him in his bed while he was sleeping, leaving him with "four claw marks on either side, underneath my arms and on my left shoulder."

But whatever regrets or dark thoughts Carlson might have had quickly evaporated when he reflected on his current situation. As he saw it, he'd exchanged one set of comrades for another—and his new set of friends offered him so much more than his old ones. Instead of invitations to Washington, DC, dinner parties, he now hobnobbed with the richest man in the world. Yes, he no longer had the respect of editors and columnists, but he enjoyed direct lines—which he no longer had qualms about using—to both the vice president and the president of the United States. He had traded up.

Thirty years ago, as a young man, Carlson liked to make sport of Joseph Sobran, the once great conservative writer who'd been banished from the kingdom of respectability on account of his descent into anti-Semitism and racism; Carlson had joked that he'd run into a rambling, disheveled Sobran at a suburban Denny's, where he sat by himself in a booth, holding court to an audience of no one. It is tempting to think that Carlson has followed in Sobran's ignominious footsteps, that he has suffered the same fate as the man he once ridiculed. Except Carlson is not sitting in an empty restaurant booth. He has the ears of heads of state and billionaires. He is selling out basketball arenas and constantly streaming onto our phones. He has descended into madness, but he is speaking to millions.

ACKNOWLEDGMENTS

The idea for this book originated in a phone call not long after January 6, 2021. Chris Parris-Lamb, my agent, and I were discussing another book idea—one that would be about the civil war inside the Republican Party between MAGA and establishment forces that we were certain was about to take place now that Donald Trump's political career had obviously come to such an ignominious end. (Oops.) I was explaining to Chris that I didn't relish the prospect of writing that book, primarily because I didn't think any of the Republican presidential aspirants angling to inherit Trump's supporters—Ted Cruz, Josh Hawley, Ron DeSantis—would be successful; no matter how much they aped Trump's nationalist-populist policies, they lacked his charisma and his showmanship. Trumpism without Trump, I said, was a nonstarter. "The only person who could pull that off," I added offhandedly, "is Tucker Carlson." As I remember it, Chris and I were silent for a few seconds. Then, simultaneously, we both said, "That's the book!" It's been a long and winding road since that conversation, but Chris has been by my side for every step—not just as an agent but as a sounding board, a cheerleader, and a friend. This book wouldn't have happened without him.

I'm similarly grateful to the team at Zando and Crooked Media. Sarah Ried, my editor, has been a close and invaluable collaborator, offering big-picture thoughts and razor-sharp line edits. Jordan Koluch's copyediting and fact-checking saved me from countless (and embarrassing) grammatical and factual errors. Sarah Goldstein demonstrated infinite patience fielding my dumb technological questions. David Eber was exactly the kind of lawyer you want in these times when powerful people are trying to intimidate and prevent journalists from subjecting them to scrutiny. And Molly Stern, Lucinda Treat, Tommy Vietor, Reid Cherlin, Katie Long, Sam Mitchell, Julia McGarry, and Julia Talley were all great champions of this project. Before the book came to Zando and Crooked, Vanessa Mobley and Pronoy Sarkar provided important editorial guidance on its early chapters. And thank you to Henry Rosenbloom at Scribe for his steadfastness.

Zane Irwin, Oviya Kumaran, Rachel Papalski, and Candice Reed were dogged and resourceful researchers, digging through various physical and electronic archives on my behalf.

New America awarded me a fellowship and, more importantly, welcomed me into a community of writers and thinkers that offered crucial intellectual and emotional support. Awista Ayub and Sarah Baline made the fellowship particularly valuable.

The New York Times Magazine and *The New York Times* Opinion section allowed me to develop small portions of this book in their pages. Nitsuh Abebe and Laura Reston were excellent editors, and Gita Daneshjoo, Jamie Fisher, and Eileen Lepping were fantastic fact-checkers of those stories.

I owe an enormous debt of gratitude to the people who shared with me their memories, opinions, and theories about Tucker Carlson. Those who are named, and those who asked to remain anonymous, all entrusted me to faithfully and accurately retell their parts of this story, and I hope that the final product is worthy of their trust. I'm also in debt to the other journalists and academics whose work on Carlson and conservative media and conservative politics has informed my own. I've tried to cite all of them in the text or in the notes, but a few deserve special recognition: Gabriel Sherman, whose *Loudest Voice in the Room* remains, more than a decade after it was published, the definitive book about Roger Ailes and Fox News; Nicole Hemmer for her two books on conservative media, *Messengers of the Right* and *Partisans*; Joshua Green for *Devil's Bargain* and its account of Steve Bannon's tenure at *Breitbart* and the role both played in the 2016 campaign; and Matthew Continetti for his history of American conservatism, *The Right*.

Writing a book can be a lonely endeavor, and I want to thank the friends and colleagues who helped me along the way—doing everything from reading chapters to sharing sources to talking through ideas to just checking in. So, to Philip Bennett, Jonathan Chait, Doug Bock Clark, Jonathan Cohn, Nicholas Confessore, Zeke Faux, Franklin Foer, David Graham, David Grann, Charles Homans, John Judis, Andrew Keller, Charles Lane, Peter Leone, Jessica Lustig, Katherine Marsh, Jonathan Martin, Jennifer Medina, Todd Pruzan, Jim Sailer, Michael Schaffer, Ben Seigel, Willy Staley, Brian Stelter, and Ed Wilson: Thank you!

Words cannot adequately express my gratitude to my parents, Joe and Lynda Zengerle. They remain my most devoted readers and have encouraged and supported my writing long before I began working on this book—indeed, long before I even became a journalist. I cannot imagine having better parents and role models. Special thanks also to my brother Tucker Zengerle (whose iPhone contact I was always careful to double- and triple-check before calling or texting him these last few years) and my sister-in-law Daniela Zengerle. My in-laws Paul and Anita Farel, sister-in-law Lily Farel, and brother-in-law Spence Hanemann have also been remarkably supportive of this effort.

But my biggest thanks go to my wife, Claire Farel, to whom this book is dedicated. For twenty-seven years, she has made my life immeasurably richer with her beauty, wit, intelligence, and kindness. The life cycle of this book corresponded with an extremely challenging time in her own professional life—and her ability to be both a loving spouse and a caring physician never ceased to amaze me. I am forever grateful to her and our two children, Asa and Georgia. They serve as a constant reminder that while it may no longer hold true in politics, in life there's nothing more important than to be loved by the right people.

NOTES

PROLOGUE

x **Carlson—who spends his winters in Florida:** Joe Hagan, "'Dishonesty . . . Is Always an Indicator of Weakness': Tucker Carlson on How He Brought His Coronavirus Message to Mar-a-Lago," *Vanity Fair*, March 17, 2020, www.vanityfair.com/news/2020/03/tucker-carlson-on-how-he-brought-coronavirus-message-to-mar-a-lago.

xi **A who's who of the MAGA universe:** Emily Goodin, "Kimberly Guilfoyle celebrates her 51th at lavish Mar-a-Lago birthday bash as Trump loudly sings happy birthday before the former Fox News presenter shows off her dance moves with beau Don Jr," *Daily Mail*, last updated March 17, 2020, 5:15 p.m. EDT, www.dailymail.co.uk/news/article-8088531/Kimberly-Guilfoyle-celebrates-50th-lavish-Mar-Lago-birthday-bash.html.

xiii **In the days to come:** Andrew Howard, "'Morning Joe' hosts visited Mar-a-Lago for Trump meeting," *Politico*, last updated November 18, 2024, 10:17 a.m. EST, www.politico.com/live-updates/2024/11/18/congress/morning-joe-trump-meeting-joe-scarborough-mika-brzezinski-00190100; Adriana Gomez Licon, "Zuckerberg dines with Trump in Mar-a-Lago," *AP News*, last updated November 27, 2024, 11:08 p.m. EST, apnews.com/article/facebook-trump-zuckerberg-meta-03b409b31deb17ecf3c6d8913e999550; Mike Wendling, "Musk joins Bezos and Trump dinner at Mar-a-Lago," *BBC News*, December 19, 2024, www.bbc.com/news/articles/c5ygvjpxn17o.

xiii **But on this evening:** Theodore Schleifer and Maggie Haberman, "Musk to Spend Election Night with Trump," *The New York Times*, November 5, 2024, www.nytimes.com/2024/11/05/us/politics/elon-musk-trump-election-night.html.

xiii **The party's guest list:** Meridith McGraw, "Trump at Mar-a-Lago with Elon Musk, RFK Jr., others," *Politico*, last updated November 5, 2024, 10:00 p.m. EST, www.politico.com/live-updates/2024/11/05/2024-election-results-live-coverage-updates-analysis/trump-elon-musk-rfk-jr-00187624.

xiii **where they ate beef Wellington:** "Tucker Carlson Election Night LIVE From Mar-a-Lago With Special Guests," streamed live on November 5, 2024, by Tucker Carlson, YouTube, 3 hr., 6 min., 35 sec., www.youtube.com/watch?v=284VFHrO8Nc.

xiii **Carlson was a crucial voice in Trump's ear:** Jonathan Swan and Maggie Haberman, "How Tucker Carlson Helped Sell JD Vance as Trump's Running

Mate," *The New York Times*, July 16, 2024, www.nytimes.com/2024/07/16/us/politics/tucker-carlson-jd-vance-trump.html.

xiv **at the Republican National Convention in July:** "Watch: Tucker Carlson speaks at 2024 Republican National Convention," *PBS News*, July 18, 2024, www.pbs.org/newshour/politics/watch-tucker-carlson-speaks-at-2024-republican-national-convention.

xiv **During Carlson's own sixteen-city speaking tour:** Jason Zengerle, "The Strange Afterlife of Tucker Carlson," *The New York Times*, September 20, 2024, www.nytimes.com/2024/09/20/opinion/vance-tucker-carlson-interview.html.

xiv **he had Vance and Trump join him:** "Former President Trump Campaigns with Tucker Carlson in Glendale, Arizona," C-SPAN, October 31, 2024, www.c-span.org/program/campaign-2024/former-president-trump-campaigns-with-tucker-carlson-in-glendale-arizona/651374.

xiv **Speaking at a Trump rally in Georgia:** Maggie Astor, "Tucker Carlson Tells Crowd Trump Will Give Country a 'Spanking,'" *The New York Times*, October 24, 2024, www.nytimes.com/2024/10/24/us/politics/tucker-carlson-trump-spanking.html.

xiv **At Madison Square Garden:** "Full Speech: Tucker Carlson Delivers Remarks at Madison Square Garden," uploaded on October 27, 2024, by Right Side Broadcasting Network, YouTube, 8 min., 49 sec., www.youtube.com/watch?v=BDMjEu9IaVk.

xiv **"You're truly hated by all the right people":** Rod Dreher (@roddreher), "Says the lesson of Hungary is that people here genuinely love their country and its traditions, and are willing to fight for them. Final good thing about Hungary says @TuckerCarlson : 'That you're truly hated by all the right people.' He's absolutely right," Twitter (now X), August 4, 2021, x.com/roddreher/status/1423000728776286210.

xv **"I don't think anyone has spoken":** "Tucker Carlson Election Night LIVE."

xv **over the next three hours:** "Tucker Carlson Election Night LIVE."

xv **"an absolute beast":** "Tucker Carlson Election Night LIVE."

xv **"I appreciate what you've done, Tucker":** "Tucker Carlson Election Night LIVE."

xv **"You just went more all in":** "Tucker Carlson Election Night LIVE."

xv **"I've never seen anything like this in my life":** "Tucker Carlson Election Night LIVE."

CHAPTER ONE

2 **These memos, which were soon dubbed Kristolgrams:** Daniel J. Balz and Ronald Brownstein, *Storming the Gates: Protest Politics and the Republican Revival* (Little, Brown, 1996), 250.

2 **"Mr. Kristol—you've probably never heard of him":** Michael Crowley, "Last Man Standing," *Politico Magazine*, July/August 2016, www.politico.com/magazine/story/2016/07/2016-bill-kristol-republicans-conservative-movement-donald-trump-politics-214025.

3 **At Harvard in the early '70s:** Nina J. Easton, *Gang of Five: Leaders at the Center of the Conservative Ascendancy* (Simon & Schuster, 2002), 27.

3 **Their parents, and their parents' cohort of conservative intellectuals:** Godfrey Hodgson, "How the Rebels Seized the Palace," *The New York Times*, October 5, 1986, www.nytimes.com/1986/10/05/books/how-the-rebels-seized-the-palace.html.

3 **"He takes things for granted":** Hanna Rosin, "Oedipus & Podhoretz," *New York Magazine*, January 5, 1998, nymag.com/nymetro/news/media/features/1968.

4 **knew "his DNA pretty well":** Balz and Brownstein, *Storming the Gates*, 249.

4 **John P. Normanson:** Rosin, "Oedipus & Podhoretz."

4 **"mini-cons":** James Atlas, "The Counter Counterculture," *The New York Times Magazine*, February 12, 1995, www.nytimes.com/1995/02/12/magazine/the-counter-counterculture.html.

5 **A few months later, Rupert Murdoch:** Daniel Jeffreys, "US right hoists its Standard," *Independent*, September 12, 1995, www.independent.co.uk/news/media/us-right-hoists-its-standard-1600728.html.

5 **Over dinner, Kristol pitched Murdoch:** Jeffreys, "US right hoists its Standard"; Fred Barnes, "In the Beginning . . ." *Washington Examiner*, September 19, 2005, www.washingtonexaminer.com/weekly-standard/in-the-beginning-7223.

6 **"Let's try to make sure we don't lose too much money on this":** John Podhoretz, "Autopsy of *The Weekly Standard*," *The Commentary Magazine Podcast*, December 17, 2018, www.commentary.org/john-podhoretz/commentary-podcast-on-the-weekly-standard.

6 **who'd briefly been the paper's film critic:** David Brooks, interview with *Life Stories*, April 11, 2025, www.lifestories.org/interviewees/david-brooks.

7 **In 1992, the Corporation for Public Broadcasting (CPB):** John Carmody, "The TV Column," *The Washington Post*, March 26, 1992, www.washingtonpost.com/archive/lifestyle/1992/03/27/the-tv-column/97de21b9-123c-4464-b88b-86ace4914d3b.

7 **"zero fund":** "Necessity of funding CPB challenged in congressional hearing," Reporters Committee for Freedom of the Press, January 23, 1995, www.rcfp.org/necessity-funding-cpb-challenged-congressional-hearing.

8 **the Dale wasn't just a dud but a scam:** John Pashdag, "The Incredible Dale Hoax," *TV Guide*, January 10, 1976.

8 **He also revealed that Carmichael:** *The Lady and the Dale*, episode 3, "The Guilty Fleeth," directed by Nick Cammilleri and Zackary Drucker, aired February 7, 2021, on HBO, www.hbo.com/the-lady-and-the-dale/season-1/3-the-guilty-fleeth.

8 **There, he made national news:** Renée Richards with John Ames, *No Way Renée: The Second Half of My Notorious Life* (Simon & Schuster, 2007).

8 **Dick carried himself with a macho swagger:** *The Lady and the Dale*, episode 2, "Caveat Emptor: Buyer Beware," directed by Nick Cammilleri and

Zackary Drucker, aired January 31, 2021, on HBO, www.hbo.com/the-lady-and-the-dale/season-1/2-caveat-emptor-buyer-beware.

9 **"a black eye":** Barry M. Horstman, "Hedgecock Resigns as Mayor, Gets Year Term: San Diego Official 'Violated the Public Trust in Onerous Way,' Judge Says of Election Funds Case," *Los Angeles Times*, December 11, 1985, www.latimes.com/archives/la-xpm-1985-12-11-mn-851-story.html.

9 **he lent his campaign nearly five hundred thousand dollars:** Lanie Jones, "Final Tallies Show Record Costs in Race to Be Mayor," *Los Angeles Times*, February 2, 1985, www.latimes.com/archives/la-xpm-1985-02-02-me-9036-story.html.

9 **Hedgecock trounced him:** Associated Press, "San Diego Mayor Wins Despite an Indictment," *The New York Times*, November 8, 1984, www.nytimes.com/1984/11/08/us/san-diego-mayor-wins-despite-an-indictment.html.

9 **Eleven months later, Hedgecock was convicted:** Barry M. Horstman, "Hedgecock to Resign as San Diego Mayor Friday," *Los Angeles Times*, October 12, 1985, www.latimes.com/archives/la-xpm-1985-10-12-mn-14434-story.html.

10 **"I thought once that I would own the whole State of California":** Frank Parker Stockbridge, "Greatest Land Estate; Henry Miller, Cattle King, Had Vast Tracts, Which Are About to Be Sold Piecemeal," *The New York Times*, May 2, 1921, www.nytimes.com/1921/05/01/archives/greatest-land-estate-henry-miller-cattle-king-had-vast-tracts-which.html.

10 **Kappa Kappa Gamma:** Molly Barnes, interview with the author; "Pi Deuteron," Kappapedia, last updated December 15, 2021, wiki.kkg.org/index.php?title=Pi_Deuteron.

10 **"Killings, Guts & Orgies":** Richard Carlson, "Signs of the Zodiac," *Washington Examiner*, September 9, 2013, www.washingtonexaminer.com/magazine/1665912/signs-of-the-zodiac.

11 **an autodidact who'd eventually assemble a personal library of more than ten thousand books:** Michael J. Kerrigan, *Politics with Principle: Ten Characters with Character* (Wheatmark, 2010), 46.

11 **criticizing her for her lack of self-discipline:** "Tucker Carlson on the Media's Deception, the ADL's Attacks, and Armor Against Criticism," uploaded on September 24, 2021, by Megyn Kelly, YouTube, 1 hr., 35 min., 38 sec., www.youtube.com/watch?v=OOx0ap1CSkA.

11 **"would in fact be raised by hired help":** Exhibit A in April 29, 1976, filing from Lisa Carlson.

12 **"had repeated difficulties with abuse of alcohol, marijuana, cocaine and amphetamines":** Declaration of Richard Carlson in Support of Order to Show Cause RE: Modification (Custody and Visitation) filed on January 14, 1977.

12 **So concerned was Dick about Lisa:** person familiar with, interview with the author.

12 **According to court records, she had left the country:** Order Re Probation Report, Visitation, and Attorneys Fees, entered May 23, 1977.

12 **After McDermott drank himself to death in 1988:** "Hockney: The Biography, Volume 2, 1975–2012, A Pilgrim's Progress,' by Christopher Simon Sykes," *Financial Times*, September 5, 2014

12 **the couple eventually moved to France:** "Lisa McNear (Lombardi) Vaughan (1945–2011)," WikiTree, April 11, 2025, www.wikitree.com/wiki/Lombardi-59.

12 **"I got this call, like":** "Tucker Carlson on the Media's Deception."

13 **In her will, Lisa left Tucker and Buckley one dollar each:** Bickel v. Carlson, Cal. Ct. App. (2019).

13 **He traded in his classic Mercedes-Benz:** "SETTLEMENT AGREEMENT," November 2, 1976.

13 **Ford Country Squire station wagon:** Tucker Carlson, "In Praise of Adventure: How to Fill a Child's Life with Excitement and Danger (Without Getting Them Killed)," in *The Dadly Virtues: Adventures from the Worst Job You'll Ever Love*, ed. Jonathan V. Last (Templeton Press, 2015), 67.

13 **He packed Tucker and Buckley brown-bag lunches every morning before school:** Kerrigan, *Politics with Principle*, 55.

13 **lecturing them on the importance of good manners:** Kerrigan, *Politics with Principle*, 48.

13 **"The fact that a few bugs bother you is just pathetic":** Kerrigan, *Politics with Principle*, 55.

13 **The nannies he hired were men:** person familiar with, interview with the author.

13 **a former Korean intelligence officer whom Tucker and Buckley addressed as Colonel Kwon:** person familiar with, interview with the author.

14 **"the cigarette pack is your friend":** "The dadly virtues: Adventures from the worst job you'll ever love," streamed live on May 11, 2015, by American Enterprise Institute, YouTube, 1 hr., 12 min., 36 sec., www.youtube.com/watch?v=I8SMOk2T5DI&t=3235s.

14 **"Liberals were everywhere":** Tucker Carlson, *Ship of Fools: How a Selfish Ruling Class Is Bringing America to the Brink of Revolution* (Free Press, 2018), 22.

14 **"full of tired old men and tired old money":** *La Jolla Light*, February, 21, 2018, www.lajollalight.com/sd-cm-ljl-raymond-chandler-20180221-htmlstory.html.

14 **There was scant discussion of the Hopi and the humpbacks:** Howard Kurtz, "The Opinionated Journalist," *The Washington Post*, August 16, 1999, www.washingtonpost.com/archive/lifestyle/1999/08/17/the-opinionated-journalist/4340b332-e33d-442b-b681-fbb97cffee71.

14 **The scent of patchouli was well-nigh indetectable:** person familiar with, interview with the author.

15 **after consulting a copy of *The Anarchist Cookbook*, pilfered from Dick's library:** Carlson, "In Praise of Adventure."

16 **"kicked out":** Urs Gehriger, "Tucker Carlson: 'Trump is not capable,'" *Die Weltwoche*, 2018, web.archive.org/web/20200813024543/https:/www

.weltwoche.ch/ausgaben/2018-49/weltwoche-international/trump-is-not-capable-die-weltwoche-ausgabe-49-2018.html.

16 **sporting natty Brooks Brothers blazers and an impressive collection of bow ties:** Aaron Short, "The Tucker Carlson origin story," *Business Insider*, May 5, 2022, www.businessinsider.com/the-tucker-carlson-origin-story-2022-5.

17 **he hung an elephant poster:** Kelefa Sanneh, "Tucker Carlson's Fighting Words," *The New Yorker*, April 3, 2017, www.newyorker.com/magazine/2017/04/10/tucker-carlsons-fighting-words.

17 **That fall, one of St. George's few Black students:** Short, "The Tucker Carlson origin story."

17 **"She was the cutest 10th grader in America":** Steve Dougherty, "Meet Mister Right," *People*, November 6, 2000, people.com/archive/meet-mister-right-vol-54-no-19.

17 **Carlson became something of a campus legend:** Short, "The Tucker Carlson origin story."

18 **Although Carlson found religion:** Tucker Carlson, "When the Fun Stopped," *Washington Examiner*, March 7, 2005, www.washingtonexaminer.com/magazine/1042709/when-the-fun-stopped.

19 **"What do you mean you told Susie?":** Short, "The Tucker Carlson origin story."

19 **"If you want to get into a top American college":** "Tucker: How did Chris Cuomo get into Yale?" *Tucker Carlson Tonight*, Fox News, July 8, 2019, www.foxnews.com/video/6056751869001.

20 **But in the spring of Carlson and Patel's freshman year:** person familiar with, author interview.

21 **"I think you're all a bunch of greasy chicken fuckers":** Stephen Rodrick, "Tucker Carlson Is Sorry for Being Mean," GQ, September 19, 2017, www.gq.com/story/tucker-carlson-profile-2017.

21 **Founded in 1980 with an initial ten-thousand-dollar grant from IEA:** Dudley Clendinen, "Conservative Paper Stirs Dartmouth," *The New York Times*, October 13, 1981, www.nytimes.com/1981/10/13/us/conservative-paper-stirs-dartmouth.html.

21 **"Dem white mo-fo":** Keeney Jones, "Dis sho' ain't no jive, bro," *The Dartmouth Review*, March 15, 1982, journeys.dartmouth.edu/lesttheoldtraditionsfail/dis-sho-aint-no-jive-bro.

21 **a *Review* reporter surreptitiously recorded:** Associated Press, "Dartmouth Group in Privacy Battle," *The New York Times*, July 16, 1984, www.nytimes.com/1984/07/16/us/dartmouth-group-privacy-battle-concord-nh-july-15-ap-student-reporter-s-taping.html.

22 **a libel lawsuit from a Dartmouth professor:** Fer M. Jebsen, "Dartmouth Prof. Sues Review for $2.4 Million," *The Harvard Crimson*, May 4, 1983, www.thecrimson.com/article/1983/5/4/dartmouth-prof-sues-review-for-24/

22 **they drew up plans for their own conservative publication:** person familiar with, author interview.

22 **"The truth is that due to angry and confused activists":** T.S.M. Carlson, "Ms. Levin Is Paranoid," *Trinity Tripod*, November 24, 1987.

23 **"Professor Greenberg does not, or will not":** T.S.M. Carlson, "Force-feeding of Opinions Is Not Intellectual Freedom," *Trinity Tripod*, November 22, 1988.

23 **"I am offended by the idea":** T.S.M. Carlson, "TGLBA Homophobic Labelling Questioned," *Trinity Tripod*, May 9, 1989.

23 **Carlson and Susie were wed in August 1991:** "Andrews-Carlson," *Detroit Free Press*, August 28, 1991, www.newspapers.com/article/17438093/detroit-free-presswed-28-aug-1991.

24 **"That's the terrible secret of college":** Tucker Carlson, "College's Hidden Secret," *Slate*, November 2, 2000, slate.com/human-interest/2000/11/college-s-hidden-secret.html.

24 **With Carlson's help, Bill forged a letter to the professor:** Tucker Carlson, *Politicians, Partisans, and Parasites: My Adventures in Cable News* (Warner Books, 2003), 176–179.

24 **"He said, 'Please don't take this personally'":** Janice Farnham, author interview.

25 **His 1.9 GPA was deemed too low:** Short, "The Tucker Carlson origin story."

25 **In 1985, journalists of color:** Ruth Shalit, "Race in the Newsroom," *The New Republic*, October 2, 1995, newrepublic.com/article/120886/ruth-shalit-race-newsroom.

26 ***The Spectator*'s hotshot young investigative reporter, David Brock:** David Brock, "His Cheatin' Heart," *The American Spectator*, January 1994, spectator.org/his-cheatin-heart/.

26 **"be written off as a wing nut":** Kurtz, "The Opinionated Journalist."

27 **"I called everyone I ever met":** Kurtz, "The Opinionated Journalist."

27 **When it was over, Kristol and Barnes:** Bill Kristol, author interview.

CHAPTER TWO

28 **Mark Gerson was working on a book about neoconservative intellectuals:** Mark Gerson, *The Neoconservative Vision: From the Cold War to the Culture Wars* (Madison Books, 1996).

28 **where he edited the conservative newspaper:** Gabriel Sherman, "Power Punk: Mark Gerson," *Observer*, December 15, 2003, observer.com/2003/12/power-punk-mark-gerson.

29 **"I remember thinking":** Gerson, author interview.

29 **"He was terrible":** Gerson, author interview.

29 **Susie had been a religious-school teacher:** a person familiar with, author interview.

29 **A dozen years later, Barnes and a majority of the Falls Church congregation:** Julie Zauzmer Weil, "Seven years after losing its fight with the

Episcopal denomination, The Falls Church Anglican opens its new home," *The Washington Post*, October 13, 2019, www.washingtonpost.com/religion/seven-years-after-losing-its-fight-with-the-episcopal-denomination-the-falls-church-anglican-opens-its-new-home/2019/10/13/b351168c-eded-11e9-b648-76bcf86eb67e_story.html; Fred Barnes, "When the Pastor Says It's 'A Time to Sow,'" *The Wall Street Journal*, March 20, 2009, www.wsj.com/articles/SB123751393100191463.

30 **"How many people of Bill's stature":** Gerson, author interview.

30 **"It's pretty cost free":** Kristol, author interview.

30 **he had considered giving it a geographic marker:** "*The Weekly Standard: A Reader, 1995–2005*," C-SPAN, September 20, 2005, www.c-span.org/video/?189151-1/the-weekly-standard-reader-1995-2005.

30 **The cover featured:** *The Weekly Standard*, September 18, 1995, archive.org/details/the-weekly-standard-1995-09-18.

30 **Inside, Barnes wrote a typically credulous story:** Fred Barnes, "GOP on Offense," *The Weekly Standard*, September 18, 1995, archive.org/details/the-weekly-standard-1995-09-18/page/n5/mode/2up.

30 **an access-driven, laudatory account:** David McClintick, "Scenes from a Speakership," *The Weekly Standard*, September 18, 1995, archive.org/details/the-weekly-standard-1995-09-18/page/n15/mode/2up.

31 **"it is not the business of conservatives to offer utopias":** Charles Krauthammer, "A Critique of Pure Newt," *The Weekly Standard*, September 18, 1995, archive.org/details/the-weekly-standard-1995-09-18/page/n33/mode/2up.

31 **Carlson's contribution to the inaugural issue:** Tucker Carlson, "Mumia Dearest," *The Weekly Standard*, September 18, 1995.

32 **"This kid was born":** Andrew Ferguson, author interview.

33 **"*Mad Men* without the sexual harassment":** Matt Labash, author interview.

33 **Carlson's office at the magazine:** people familiar with, author interviews.

33 **"looked like some WASP":** Labash, author interview.

33 **For the next two decades:** Tucker Carlson, interview with the author; person familiar with, interview with the author.

34 **"guided populism":** Easton, *Gang of Five*, 46.

34 **Barnes emulated the punchy, ideologically slanted reportage:** Matthew Continetti, "What I Learned from the Beadle," *The Washington Free Beacon*, June 18, 2021,https://freebeacon.com/columns/what-i-learned-from-the-beadle/.

34 **"sociological journalism":** Sasha Issenberg, "David Brooks: Boo-Boos in Paradise," *Philadelphia*, April 1, 2004, www.phillymag.com/news/2004/04/01/david-brooks-booboos-in-paradise.

34 **"affect the game":** Tad Friend, "It's, You Know, About Opinions and Stuff," *The New York Times Magazine*, June 15, 1997, www.nytimes.com/1997/06/15/magazine/it-s-you-know-about-opinions-and-stuff.html.

34 **a high-low mix of *Foreign Affairs* and *Mad* magazine:** Podhoretz, "Autopsy of *The Weekly Standard*."

34 **"merry pranksters":** David Brooks, author interview.

34 **"difficulty balancing economy-class rhetoric":** Tucker Carlson, "James Carville, Populist Plutocrat," *The Weekly Standard*, March 18, 1996, archive .org/details/the-weekly-standard-1996-03-18/page/n17/mode/2up.

35 **"One of the major tenets of the Perot faith":** Tucker Carlson, "Temperamental Tycoon," *The Weekly Standard*, April 8, 1996.

35 **"giving a soul handshake to a man in the crowd":** Tucker Carlson, "Jack Kemp, Apostle to the Unconvertible," *The Weekly Standard*, September 16, 1996.

35 **"Luntz is legendary for flattering his clients":** Tucker Carlson, "Billy Tauzin, Earl Long of the GOP," *The Weekly Standard*, January 19, 1998.

35 **"Gore cultivates this image":** Tucker Carlson, "The Real Al Gore," *The Weekly Standard*, May 19, 1997.

36 **who as a twentysomething took a LARPing expedition to Angola:** Thomas B. Edsall, "Right in the Middle of the Revolution," *The Washington Post*, September 3, 1995, www.washingtonpost.com/archive/politics/1995 /09/04/right-in-the-middle-of-the-revolution/52c49f99-6b61-4166-bc88 -ba42eebe9dbc.

36 **The reason Podhoretz gave Carlson:** Jacob Weisberg, "The Conintern," *Slate*, June 29, 1997, slate.com/news-and-politics/1997/06/the-conintern .html.

37 **"Newt Melts":** David Plotz, "Other Magazines," *Slate*, March 30, 1997, www.slate.com/articles/news_and_politics/other_magazines/1997/03/_2.html.

37 **"roadkill on the highway of American politics":** Peter King, "Why I Oppose Newt," *The Weekly Standard*, March 31, 1997, archive.org/details/the -weekly-standard-1997-03-31/page/n17/mode/2up.

37 **"cash-addled, morally malleable lobbyist":** Tucker Carlson, "What I Sold at the Revolution," *The New Republic*, June 9, 1997, newrepublic.com /article/171072/sold-revolution-grover-norquist-profile.

37 **"to get it down to the size where we can drown it in the bathtub":** Grover Norquist (@GroverNorquist), "'My goal is to cut the government in half in twenty-five years, to get it down to the size where we can drown it in the bathtub,'" Twitter (now X), January 26, 2016, twitter.com/grovernorquist /status/691989279774527489.

38 **ATR was an Islamist front group:** Molly Ball, "Grover Norquist, the Happiest Man in Washington," *The Atlantic*, April 18, 2017, www.theatlantic .com/politics/archive/2017/04/grover-norquist-the-happiest-man-in-washington /523206.

38 **"His father and I were on opposite sides of the fight for democracy in the Seychelles":** Howard Kurtz, "Carlson-Norquist: Feud for Thought," *The Washington Post*, July 21, 1997, www.washingtonpost.com/archive/lifestyle /1997/07/22/carlson-norquist-feud-for-thought/fa95dd63-69d8-44f5-a121 -6d015a450445.

39 **"it would be easier than ever for the White House to tar":** Laura Ingraham, "The Wrong Man for a Sensitive Job," *The New York Times*, November 20, 1996, www.nytimes.com/1996/11/20/opinion/the-wrong-man-for-a-sensitive-job.html.

39 **He was caught doctoring transcripts:** George Lardner Jr., "Democrats Hit Burton over Tapes of Hubbell," *The Washington Post*, May 3, 1998, www.washingtonpost.com/archive/politics/1998/05/04/democrats-hit-burton-over-tapes-of-hubbell/cf6267d2-83d8-4775-baae-c548b144602a.

39 **"If Bill Clinton didn't have Rep. Dan Burton (R-Ind.) in the House":** Robert G. Beckel, "You Want a Non-Partisan Investigation? Don't Get Burton," *Los Angeles Times*, May 10, 1998, www.latimes.com/archives/la-xpm-1998-may-10-op-48171-story.html.

40 **"a supposedly conservative activist":** Robert Novak, "The Odd Couple," *The Washington Post*, December 15, 1996, www.washingtonpost.com/archive/opinions/1996/12/16/the-odd-couple/43bbf629-29d4-4328-a3cc-0298671ceae0/.

40 **"whether to be with us or against us":** Weisberg, "The Conintern."

40 **"No one who believes what we believe should be attacking Grover":** Weisberg, "The Conintern."

41 **"a mean-spirited, humorless, dishonest little creep":** Tucker Carlson, "Right-Wing Journalism," *Slate*, July 17, 1997, slate.com/news-and-politics/1997/07/right-wing-journalism-4.html.

41 **"I took a notebook and I wrote down":** Ben Domenech, author interview.

41 **"The celery stuck behind Grover's ear":** Tim Mak, "Tucker and Grover End Bitter Feud," *FrumForum*, January 4, 2011, frumforum.com/entry/tucker-and-grover-end-longtime-feud.

42 **"difficult, maybe impossible, to defend as a species of logic":** Tucker Carlson, "What Pro-Choice Republicans Believe," *The Weekly Standard*, June 24, 1996.

42 **"the eugenic utility of abortion":** Tucker Carlson, "Eugenics, American Style," *The Weekly Standard*, December 1, 1996.

42 **"tighter national borders":** Tucker Carlson, "The Intellectual Roots of Nativism," *The Wall Street Journal*, October 2, 1997, www.wsj.com/articles/SB875739465952259500.

43 **"a combative journalist":** Otis L. Graham, Jr., *Immigration Reform and America's Unchosen Future* (pub. by author, 2008), 302–304.

43 **"I had this crisis":** Kurtz, "The Opinionated Journalist."

44 **"He sent me a handwritten letter":** Mitch Horowitz, author interview.

44 **"national greatness conservatism":** David Brooks, "A Return to National Greatness," *Washington Examiner*, March 3, 1997, www.washingtonexaminer.com/weekly-standard/a-return-to-national-greatness.

44 **"Wishing to be left alone isn't a governing doctrine":** William Kristol and David Brooks, "What Ails Conservatism," *The Wall Street Journal*, September 15, 1997, www.wsj.com/articles/SB874276753849168000.

44 **"Saddam Must Go":** [by Kristol & Kagan], "Saddam Must Go," *Washington Examiner*, November 17, 1997, www.washingtonexaminer.com/weekly-standard/saddam-must-go.

44 **"Tucker was always less ideologically defined":** Brooks, author interview.

45 **"Every time Bill Clinton appears in public":** David Tell, "Clinton Must Go," *Washington Examiner*, August 31, 1998, www.washingtonexaminer.com/weekly-standard/clinton-must-go.

45 **"He was very schmoozy and friendly about it":** Jonah Goldberg, author interview.

45 **The friend gave Carlson the phone number:** "Tucker Carlson from the *Daily Caller*," Hugh Hewitt and Duane Patterson, August 5, 2010, hughhewitt.com/tucker-carlson-from-the-daily-caller.

46 **"She would have to be very sick to fantasize to that degree":** Tucker Carlson, "Monica's Therapist Speaks," *Washington Examiner*, March 23, 1998, www.washingtonexaminer.com/weekly-standard/monicas-therapist-speaks.

47 **"You're not trying to get a job":** Ferguson, author interview.

47 **"create a new form for a magazine":** Alex Kuczynski, "Editor Who Thrives on Celebrity Is Pleased with Latest Sensation," *The New York Times*, July 26, 1999, www.nytimes.com/1999/07/26/business/editor-who-thrives-on-celebrity-is-pleased-with-latest-sensation.html.

47 **"hot" or, even better, "v. hot":** Alessandra Stanley, "Talk Ends and Spin Begins: Tina Brown Has No Regrets," *The New York Times*, January 20, 2002, www.nytimes.com/2002/01/20/us/talk-ends-and-spin-begins-tina-brown-has-no-regrets.html.

47 **"gadfly scamp":** Alex Shephard, "How Tucker Carlson Lost It," *The New Republic*, September 16, 2021, newrepublic.com/article/163567/tucker-carlson-profile-lost-mind.

48 **It was a source-greasing tactic:** William F. Buckley Jr., "The Way They Are," *Vanity Fair*, June 1985, www.vanityfair.com/magazine/1985/06/reagans198506.

48 **The story that resulted:** Tucker Carlson, "Devil May Care," *Talk*, September 1999.

50 **"You fucked us!":** Carlson, *Politicians, Partisans, and Parasites*, 153.

50 **"Mr. Carlson misread, mischaracterized me":** Associated Press, "Bush Meets Rush," *CBS News*, August 12, 1999, www.cbsnews.com/news/bush-meets-rush; Timothy Noah, "Bush's Tookie," *Slate*, December 2, 2005, slate.com/news-and-politics/2005/12/bush-s-tookie.html.

50 **"I don't remember those words being used":** George F. Will, "Bush Lite," *The Washington Post*, August 11, 1999, www.washingtonpost.com/archive/opinions/1999/08/11/bush-lite/77308fa1-0f07-4f18-b365-e83983cd8211.

50 **"to demand that she stop slandering me":** Carlson, *Politicians, Partisans, and Parasites*, 154.

50 **"Tucker Carlson was a journalist for a magazine":** David Frum, author interview.

51 **"dopey middle-aged Canadian Twitter celebrity":** Peter Weber, "Tucker Carlson casually maligns David Frum, who responds by deconstructing his former friend's 'cowardly' act," *Yahoo!* May 5, 2021, www.yahoo.com/video/tucker-carlson-casually-maligns-david-044237748.html.

51 **"He's great at digging up stuff":** Kurtz, "The Opinionated Journalist."

52 **"In an increasingly conservative America":** David Frum, "Patrick J. Buchanan, Left-Winger," *Washington Examiner*, November 27, 1995, www.washingtonexaminer.com/weekly-standard/patrick-j-buchanan-left-winger-8164.

53 **"Don't worry. I'll protect you guys when the pitchforks come":** Bret Stephens and David Brooks, "The Party's Over for Us. Where Do We Go Now?" *The New York Times*, January 11, 2023, www.nytimes.com/2023/01/11/opinion/republican-party-future.html.

53 **"Blame-America-Firster":** William Kristol, "A Party of Appeasement?" *Washington Examiner*, October 11, 1999, www.washingtonexaminer.com/weekly-standard/a-party-of-appeasement.

54 **"Let me tell you about Mr. Kristol":** Howard Kurtz, "Right Face, Right Time," *The Washington Post*, February 1, 2000, www.washingtonpost.com/archive/lifestyle/2000/02/01/right-face-right-time/d1de7dfc-6f00-436f-9a15-890e5772fa29/.

54 **Carlson's contributions to the anti-Buchanan effort:** Tucker Carlson, "Buchanan and His Friends," *The Weekly Standard*, September 27, 1999, archive.org/details/the-weekly-standard-1999-09-27/page/n7/mode/2up; Tucker Carlson, "Pat Buchanan Loses a Press Secretary," *The Weekly Standard*, June 26, 2000; Tucker Carlson, "Pat Buchanan Heads into the Fire," *Talk*, December 1999/January 2000.

54 **"You work for Bill Kristol, correct?":** "News Review," *Washington Journal*, C-SPAN, September 24, 1999, www.c-span.org/video/?152331-1/news-review.

55 **Carlson had a running joke:** people familiar with, author interviews.

55 **"The Anointed One":** Fred Barnes, "The Anointed One," *Washington Examiner*, June 14, 1999, www.washingtonexaminer.com/weekly-standard/the-anointed-one.

56 **"Either by accident or by design":** William Kristol and David Brooks, "The Politics of Creative Destruction," *Washington Examiner*, March 13, 2000, www.washingtonexaminer.com/weekly-standard/the-politics-of-creative-destruction.

56 **"about the coolest guy who ever ran for president":** Tucker Carlson, "On the Road," *The Weekly Standard*, March 27, 2000.

56 **"Each of them had a sense of humor":** Mark Salter, author interview.

56 **Six years later, Carlson would give a toast:** a person familiar with, author interview.

57 **"a bidding war":** William Kristol and David Brooks, "The High Road to High Office," *The Weekly Standard*, September 25, 2000, www.washingtonexaminer.com/magazine/984439/the-high-road-to-high-office/.

57 **"profound national humiliation":** "A National Humiliation," editorial, *The Weekly Standard*, April 15, 2001.

57 **"the impending evisceration of the American military":** "No Defense," editorial, *The Weekly Standard*, July 23, 2001, ia600900.us.archive.org/5/items/the-weekly-standard-2001-07-23/the-weekly-standard-2001-07-23.pdf.

58 **who gave him an approval rating of 90 percent:** "Presidential Approval Ratings—George W. Bush," Gallup, accessed April 11, 2025, news.gallup.com/poll/116500/presidential-approval-ratings-george-bush.aspx.

58 **"simple and direct, with an unhackneyed vigor of language":** David Remnick, "The Trap," *The New Yorker*, September 23, 2001, www.newyorker.com/magazine/2001/10/01/the-trap.

58 **"War and Destiny: The White House in Wartime":** Christopher Buckley, "War and Destiny: The White House in Wartime," *Vanity Fair*, February 2002, archive.vanityfair.com/article/2002/2/war-and-destiny-the-white-house-in-wartime.

58 **"In fact this analysis is exactly backward":** Max Boot, "The Case for American Empire," *Washington Examiner*, October 15, 2001, www.washingtonexaminer.com/weekly-standard/the-case-for-american-empire.

58 **"The wider conflict ahead":** William Kristol and Robert Kagan, "The Gathering Storm," *The Weekly Standard*, October 29, 2001, www.washingtonexaminer.com/magazine/1616614/the-gathering-storm-2/.

59 **It was not a coincidence:** David Carr, "White House Listens When Weekly Speaks," *The New York Times*, March 11, 2003, www.nytimes.com/2003/03/11/arts/white-house-listens-when-weekly-speaks.html.

59 **"It's probably fair to say":** "Old Standard," *On the Media*, WNYC, December 2, 2005, www.wnycstudios.org/podcasts/otm/segments/128930-old-standard.

59 **We charge that a cabal of polemicists and public officials:** Patrick J. Buchanan, "Whose War?" *The American Conservative*, March 24, 2003, www.theamericanconservative.com/whose-war.

60 **"began by hating the neoconservatives":** David Frum, "Unpatriotic Conservatives," *National Review*, April 7, 2003, davidfrum.com/article/unpatriotic-conservatives.

60 **"constructed one of the most":** John Podhoretz, *Bush Country: How Dubya Became a Great President While Driving Liberals Insane*, St. Martin's Press, 2004.

60 **"Oh, I think we've played a big role":** "*The Weekly Standard: A Reader*," C-SPAN.

CHAPTER THREE

61 **Gathered at the base of the Statue of Liberty:** Alex Kuczynski, "For *Talk* Magazine, Electric Party and a 'Hip' List," *The New York Times*, August 3, 1999, www.nytimes.com/1999/08/03/nyregion/for-talk-magazine-eclectic-party-and-a-hip-list.html; Tina Brown, "Farewell to the King of Parties," *The*

Daily Beast, July 12, 2009, www.thedailybeast.com/farewell-to-the-king-of-parties; David Carr, "10 Years Ago, an Omen No One Saw," *The New York Times*, August 3, 2009, www.nytimes.com/2009/08/03/business/media/03carr.html?hp.

61 **"This one is for you, Salman":** Brown, "Farewell to the King of Parties."

61 **"It was the end of something extraordinary":** Carr, "10 Years Ago, an Omen No One Saw."

61 **Ever since he was twelve:** Carlson, "When the Fun Stopped."

62 **"Magazine buyers are people who've chosen reading":** Tucker Carlson, "Brill's Follies," *Slate*, November 30, 1999, slate.com/human-interest/1999/11/brill-s-follies.html.

63 **"His highest journalism ideal":** Labash, author interview.

63 **"He wanted to know":** Ferguson, author interview.

63 **By 1992, more than 60 percent of US households had cable:** Nicole Hemmer, *Partisans: The Conservative Revolutionaries Who Remade American Politics in the 1990s* (Basic Books, 2022), 188.

64 **"the news is the star":** Jason Zengerle, "Fiddling with the Reception," *The New York Times Magazine*, August 17, 2003, www.nytimes.com/2003/08/17/magazine/fiddling-with-the-reception.html.

64 **"news talk-radio with video":** Gabriel Sherman, *The Loudest Voice in the Room: How the Brilliant, Bombastic Roger Ailes Built Fox News—and Divided a Country* (Random House, 2014), 178.

64 **At MSNBC, the network went so far as to use a health care staffing model:** Marjorie Williams, "Laura, Get Your Gun," *Vanity Fair*, January 1997, archive.vanityfair.com/article/1997/1/laura-get-your-gun.

65 **"Suddenly we were hot, and they wanted us":** Chris Stirewalt, host, *The Hangover*, podcast, "Chapter 6: Chris Stirewalt and John Podhoretz," June 24, 2021, podcasts.apple.com/us/podcast/the-hangover-chapter-6-chris-stirewalt-and-john-podhoretz/id1291144720?i=1000526703402.

65 **"The Friends":** Friend, "It's, You Know, About Opinions and Stuff."

65 **"transforming our culture into one vast arena for show business":** Neil Postman, *Amusing Ourselves to Death: Public Discourse in the Age of Show Business* (Penguin Books, 2006), 80, 155–156.

65 **"people like you [who] caused us to lose that war":** Howard Kurtz, "The Blonde Flinging Bombshells at Bill Clinton," *The Washington Post*, October 16, 1998, www.washingtonpost.com/wp-srv/politics/special/clinton/stories/coulter101698.htm.

66 **"When Laura Ingraham was still a lawyer":** Friend, "It's, You Know, About Opinions and Stuff."

66 **"The world of talk show guests is like a closed union":** Carlson, *Politicians, Partisans, and Parasites*, 133.

67 **Indeed, the next day:** Sanneh, "Tucker Carlson's Fighting Words."

67 **its only contributor under the age of thirty-five for its first few years was Monica Crowley:** Friend, "It's, You Know, About Opinions and Stuff."

67 **CNN's and MSNBC's ratings grew:** Sherman, *The Loudest Voice in the Room*, 225.

67 **"Monica was a news channel's dream come true":** Jane Mayer, "Roger Ailes, the Clintons, and the Scandals of the Scandalmongers," *The New Yorker*, August 24, 2016, www.newyorker.com/news/daily-comment/roger-ailes-the-clintons-and-the-scandals-of-the-scandalmongers.

67 **"I wouldn't be surprised if six months from now":** Bruce Gottlieb, "The Comeback Kid," *Slate*, September 27, 1998, slate.com/news-and-politics/1998/09/the-comeback-kid.html.

68 **Carlson ranked just behind David Gergen:** Edgar Ortega Barrales, Alistair Christopher, and Ian Judson, "Pundits' Jamboree," CNN, August 10, 1998, www.cnn.com/ALLPOLITICS/1998/08/10/time/pundits.html.

68 **Barnes preferred *The McLaughlin Group*:** David Daley, "'Beltway' Takes Buddy Approach to Punditry," *Los Angeles Times*, December 1, 1999, www.latimes.com/archives/la-xpm-1999-dec-01-ca-39160-story.html; Howard Kurtz, "Bill Kristol Dumped in 'This Week' Makeover," *The Washington Post*, December 23, 1999, www.washingtonpost.com/wp-srv/WPcap/1999-12/23/042r-122399-idx.html.

68 **In the spring of 2000:** Mark Landler, "McCain, in Vietnam, Finds the Past Isn't Really Past," *The New York Times*, April 27, 2000, www.nytimes.com/2000/04/27/world/mccain-in-vietnam-finds-the-past-isn-t-really-past.html.

68 **"McCain in Vietnam turned out to be":** Carlson, *Politicians, Partisans, and Parasites*, 123.

69 **Carlson was able to spend the night:** Gabriel Snyder, "Red Tape: Tucker Carlson Gets Held Up in Ho Chi Minh City," *Observer*, May 8, 2000, observer.com/2000/05/red-tape-tucker-carlson-gets-held-up-in-ho-chi-minh-city.

69 **"Vietnam Detains Journalist on McCain Trip":** Howard Kurtz, "Vietnam Detains Journalist on McCain Trip," *The Washington Post*, April 29, 2000, www.washingtonpost.com/archive/lifestyle/2000/04/29/vietnam-detains-journalist-on-mccain-trip/a358d25d-d752-4986-bddc-741d21516f41.

70 **"That sobered me up":** Brooks, author interview.

70 **"He was amused":** Ferguson, author interview.

70 **"When you're on TV":** Brooks, author interview.

70 **"knock out colorful":** Labash, author interview.

70 **Carlson was a terrible procrastinator:** Tucker Carlson, "Diary: Tucker Carlson," *Slate*, September 18, 1998, slate.com/human-interest/1998/09/tucker-carlson-3.html.

71 **"I have a lot of trouble writing":** Kurtz, "The Opinionated Journalist."

71 **"he accidentally boarded a flight to Cleveland":** Betsy Rothstein, "Redefining Tucker," *The Hill*, May 5, 2008, thehill.com/capital-living/20836-redefining-tucker/.

71 **And yet he was starting more and more of his days:** Chadwick Moore, *Tucker* (Skyhorse Publishing, 2026), 122.

71 **"acting like what I said is important":** Kurtz, "The Opinionated Journalist."

71 **"Wordloaf doesn't work":** Carlson, author interview.

72 **"The trick is to care, but not too much":** Carlson, *Politicians, Partisans, and Parasites*, 28.

72 **"The disappointment to CNN":** Kurtz, "The Opinionated Journalist."

72 **"Keep your day job":** Kristol, author interview.

73 **"I'm always struck that if you're in Gambia"**: Kerry Lauerman, "You burn out fast when you demagogue," *Salon*, September 14, 2003, www.salon.com/2003/09/14/carlson_4.

73 **"It was CNN or us":** former *Weekly Standard* editor, author interview.

74 **"I'm not a magazine writer anymore":** Tucker Carlson, "The Write Stuff," *The Weekly Standard*, March 5, 2001, archive.org/details/the-weekly-standard-2001-03-05/page/n3/mode/2up.

74 **"Tucker isn't tainted by Republican rage":** Michael Wolff, "Pundit's Progress," *New York Magazine*, January 15, 2001, nymag.com/nymetro/news/media/columns/medialife/4272.

75 **"Ronald Reagan is like Lassie":** Bobby Garon, author interview.

75 **"There were some issues":** Bill Press, author interview.

75 **"She has an illegal alien live in her house for a while":** *The Spin Room*, "Did the Bush Team Abandon Linda Chavez?" CNN, January 10, 2001, www.cnn.com/TRANSCRIPTS/0101/09/tsr.00.html.

76 **"probably the dumbest idea in TV to date":** *The Spin Room*, "Did the Bush Team Abandon Linda Chavez?"

76 **On one of his visits to *The Spin Room* set:** Carlson, *Politicians, Partisans, and Parasites*, 76.

77 **Jim Traficant Legal Defense Fund:** Carlson, *Politicians, Partisans, and Parasites*, 19.

77 **the House voted 420 to 1:** Juliet Eilperin, "House Votes 420 to 1 To Expel Traficant," *The Washington Post*, July 25, 2002, www.washingtonpost.com/archive/politics/2002/07/25/house-votes-420-to-1-to-expel-traficant/1429ba03-a9f8-4019-8b83-2904833ded27/.

77 **As Carlson slugged a martini:** Carlson, *Politicians, Partisans, and Parasites*, 25.

78 **"not a real Republican":** Carlson, *Politicians, Partisans, and Parasites*, 28.

78 **"an unreconstructed McCainiac who did not like Bush":** Robert D. Novak, *The Prince of Darkness: 50 Years Reporting in Washington* (Three Rivers Press, 2007), 580–581.

78 **"Underneath the asshole is a nice guy":** David Margolick, "What About Novak?" *Vanity Fair*, January 1, 2007, www.vanityfair.com/news/2005/04/novak200504.

79 **But after the sugar high of the Lewinsky scandal wore off**: Joe Flint, "CNN's Ratings Decline as Rivals CNBC, Fox Lure Away Viewers," *The*

Wall Street Journal, March 31, 2000, www.wsj.com/articles/SB954460577842383089.

79 **"The genius of Rupert Murdoch and Roger Ailes":** Charles Krauthammer, "How Fox News Opened America," *The New York Post*, June 10, 2009, nypost.com/2009/06/10/how-fox-news-opened-america.

79 **"the human straw man":** "No Liberal Limbaughs," *On the Media*, WNYC, January 10, 2003, www.wnyc.org/story/130997-no-liberal-limbaughs.

79 **"We grew up watching Crossfire":** Ken LaCorte, author interview.

79 **"Sean basically served as executive producer of the show":** Sherman, *The Loudest Voice in the Room*, 240.

80 **"He is Everyman on a barstool":** Evan Thomas, "Life of O'Reilly," *Newsweek*, February 11, 2001, www.newsweek.com/life-oreilly-155263.

80 **"a thin-skinned blowhard":** Lauerman, "You burn out fast when you demagogue."

80 **"a mean, sick group of people":** Associated Press, "CNN's Tucker Carlson angry over phone flap," *USA Today*, September 29, 2003, usatoday30.usatoday.com/life/television/news/2003-09-29-carlson_x.htm.

80 **"I don't like partisanship because it abets lying":** Lauerman, "You burn out fast when you demagogue."

80 **"The only thing America won't forgive you for is under-reaching":** Bill Carter and Jim Rutenberg, "Fox News Head Sent a Policy Note to Bush," *The New York Times*, November 19, 2002, www.nytimes.com/2002/11/19/us/fox-news-head-sent-a-policy-note-to-bush.html.

80 **"Roger Ailes is the editorial chief of Fox News":** *Crossfire*, "Weapons Inspectors Return to Iraq," CNN, November 18, 2002, transcripts.cnn.com/show/cf/date/2002-11-18/segment/00.

80 **"Being called a secret liberal was a serious charge":** Carlson, *Politicians, Partisans, and Parasites*, 28.

81 **"One benefit of hosting a talk show":** Carlson, *Politicians, Partisans, and Parasites*, 35.

81 **"the corner man in a boxing match":** Carlson, *Politicians, Partisans, and Parasites*, 36.

81 **"For one thing, the Confederates were traitors":** Carlson, *Politicians, Partisans, and Parasites*, 34.

82 **"terrifying and depressing statistics":** *Crossfire*, "Celebrities Attracting Attention Regarding Anti-war Movement," CNN, January 21, 2003, transcripts.cnn.com/show/cf/date/2003-01-21/segment/00.

82 **"a genius politically":** *Crossfire*, "How Will Conflict with North Korea Affect a War with Iraq?; FBI Seek Five Men Who Illegally Entered U.S. from Canada," CNN, December 30, 2002, transcripts.cnn.com/show/cf/date/2002-12-30/segment/00.

82 **"the perfect man":** *Crossfire*, "Democratic, Republican Economic Plans Unveiled; Anti-SUV Campaign Heats Up," CNN, January 8, 2003, transcripts.cnn.com/show/cf/date/2003-01-08/segment/00.

82 **"I just want to remind us how lucky we are":** *Crossfire*, "America's New War: Grading the Players," CNN, November 2, 2001, transcripts.cnn.com/show/cf/date/2001-11-02/segment/00.

83 **"Senator McCain, it's not as if":** *Crossfire*, "Interview with John McCain; Elections Are Closing In," CNN, April 24, 2002, transcripts.cnn.com/show/cf/date/2002-04-24/segment/00.

83 **"I think people will like Tom DeLay":** *CNN Live Today*, December 12, 2001.

84 **Dick created and hosted a weekly radio show:** "Richard W. Carlson (1968–1991)," VOA Public Relations, July 25, 2018, www.insidevoa.com/a/4499736.html.

84 **"putting pressure on the Soviet Union in an indirect way":** Ambassador Richard W. Carlson, interview by Charles Stuart Kennedy, Association for Diplomatic Studies and Training Foreign Affairs Oral History Project, March 2, 1993, www.adst.org/OH%20TOCs/CARLSON,%20Richard%20W.toc.pdf.

84 **"The continuing conflict between the United States and the Soviet Union":** "Voice of America," C-SPAN, July 1, 1988, www.c-span.org/video/?3298-1/voice-america.

84 **Dick's résumé has led some of his son's current critics:** John Ganz, "The Preppie in Decline," *Unpopular Front*, April 25, 2023, www.unpopularfront.news/p/the-preppie-in-decline.

84 **"CIA fanboy":** a former VOA official, author interview.

85 **A favorite parlor game:** a former VOA official, author interview.

85 **"We are both extremely political":** Jason Savage, "Students Trek to Nicaragua to Witness Elections," *The Trinity Tripod*, March 13, 1990.

86 **"wing-tipistas":** P. J. O'Rourke, *Give War a Chance: Eyewitness Accounts of Mankind's Struggle Against Tyranny, Injustice, and Alcohol-Free Beer* (Grove Press, 1992), 65.

87 **"an Episcopalian neo-con":** Bill Steigerwald, "Q&A: Tucker Carlson, before he became King of Cable—and GOP presidential timber," BillSteigerwald.com, July 1, 2020, billsteigerwald.com/qa-tucker-carlson-the-early-years.

87 **"Call this self-serving, if you will":** *Crossfire*, "Target Terrorism: Anti-American Sentiment Justified?" CNN, October 19, 2001, transcripts.cnn.com/show/cf/date/2001-10-19/segment/00.

87 **"All three are evil":** *Crossfire*, "Is It Time to Take War on Terror to the Axis of Evil?; Should Inmates Receive Organ Transplants?" CNN, January 31, 2002, transcripts.cnn.com/show/cf/date/2002-01-31/segment/00.

87 **who'd once selected a *Weekly Standard* story by Carlson:** Christopher Hitchens and Christopher Caldwell, eds., *Left Hooks, Right Crosses: A Decade of Political Writing* (Bold Type Books, 2002).

87 **he occasionally attended salons:** *Slow Burn*, podcast, season 5, episode 4, "Fighting Words," Slate Podcasts, May 12, 2021, slate.com/transcripts/RHI5NGkrdkJoZS9pUzB6anBZQVRiekhIcXBhQ2xxT0NTSG1FRWZLd3dEdz0=.

88 **"not a clear they-bombed-Pearl-Harbor kind of argument":** *Crossfire*, "Senators Respond to State of the Union," CNN, January 29, 2003, transcripts.cnn.com/show/cf/date/2003-01-29/segment/00.

88 **"Cheney's Dick Cheney":** Eric Schmitt, "Indicted aide had been 'Cheney's Dick Cheney,'" *The New York Times*, October 30, 2005, www.nytimes.com/2005/10/30/world/americas/indicted-aide-had-been-cheneys-dick-cheney.html.

89 **"Freedom matters":** Benjamin Wallace-Wells, "Who Killed *The Weekly Standard*?" *The New Yorker*, January 3, 2019, www.newyorker.com/news/the-political-scene/who-killed-the-weekly-standard.

89 **"When you try and kill an American president":** *Crossfire*, "National Terrorism Alert Goes Up; Interview with Saddam's Bomb Maker," CNN, February 7, 2003, transcripts.cnn.com/show/cf/date/2003-02-07/segment/00.

89 **"Those claims are uncontested":** *Crossfire*, "Democratic Hopefuls for 2004; Interviews with Janeane Garofalo, Randy Larsen," CNN, February 19, 2003, transcripts.cnn.com/show/cf/date/2003-02-19/segment/00.

89 **"Wouldn't the president be irresponsible":** *Crossfire*, March 19, 2003.

89 **"elderly, increasingly irrelevant nations":** *Crossfire*, "Are France and Germany Sabotaging America's Policy in Iraq?" CNN, February 10, 2003, transcripts.cnn.com/show/cf/date/2003-02-10/segment/00.

89 **"Joe, at the end of World War II":** *Crossfire*, "Will Hussein Destroy Al Samoud Missiles?; What Is Karl Rove's Role in the Bush Administration?; Interview with Jesse Jackson," CNN, February 28, 2003, transcripts.cnn.com/show/cf/date/2003-02-28/segment/00.

90 **"I like your answers in this forum":** Tucker Carlson, "Politics," *The Washington Post*, March 11, 2003, www.washingtonpost.com/wp-srv/liveonline/03/special/politics/sp_politics_carlson031103.htm.

90 **"No day will come":** David Brooks, "The Collapse of the Dream Palaces," *Washington Examiner*, April 28, 2003, www.washingtonexaminer.com/weekly-standard/the-collapse-of-the-dream-palaces.

91 **"You said a moment ago":** *Crossfire*, CNN, April 16, 2003.

91 **"Transitions are difficult":** *Crossfire*, CNN, April 11, 2003.

91 **"If the goal is to control the country":** Tucker Carlson, "Inside the (Not So) Secret Armies of Operation Iraqi Freedom," *Esquire*, September 9, 2016, www.esquire.com/news-politics/a48032/private-armies-operation-iraqi-freedom.

92 **"We have no second thoughts":** Howard Kurtz, "*New Republic* Editors 'Regret' Their Support of Iraq War," *The Washington Post*, June 18, 2004, www.washingtonpost.com/archive/lifestyle/2004/06/19/new-republic-editors-regret-their-support-of-iraq-war/d2a85a98-29ed-467f-a36f-3297e5cda1fe.

92 **"sullen and suspicious and conspiracy-minded":** Fred Barnes, "The Bumpy Road to Democracy in Iraq," *Washington Examiner*, April 5, 2004, www.washingtonexaminer.com/weekly-standard/the-bumpy-road-to-democracy-in-iraq.

92 **"an operational relationship":** Stephen F. Hayes, "Case Closed," *Washington Examiner*, November 24, 2003, www.washingtonexaminer.com/weekly-standard/case-closed-4618.

92 **"best source of information":** Faiz Shakir and Aaron Rupar, "Cheney Chooses Chief Propagator of False Iraq-9/11 Link to Be Official Biographer," *ThinkProgress*, August 28, 2006.

92 **"to politicize the war in Iraq":** *Crossfire*, "Iraq Out of Control?" CNN, April 7, 2004, www.cnn.com/TRANSCRIPTS/0404/07/cf.00.html.

92 **"a completely open question":** *Crossfire*, "New Hampshire Gets Set for Primary," CNN, January 26, 2004, transcripts.cnn.com/show/cf/date/2004-01-26/segment/00.

93 **"I am embarrassed that I supported the war in Iraq":** Kurtz, "*New Republic* Editors 'Regret' Their Support of Iraq War."

93 **"I think it's a total nightmare and disaster":** Joe Hagan, "Newly Dovish, Tucker Carlson Goes Public . . . Kimmel Writer Ribs *Times*," *Observer*, May 12, 2004, observer.com/2004/05/newly-dovish-tucker-carlson-goes-publickimmel-writer-ribs-times.

93 **"You're the asshole":** person familiar with, author interview.

93 **who now served as the vice chairman:** "Richard Carlson Joins Anti-Terrorism Think Tank," Foundation for Defense of Democracies, April 3, 2003, www.fdd.org/analysis/2003/04/01/richard-carlson-joins-fdd; Eli Clifton, "AIPAC, FDD websites erase all evidence of their Iraq War cheerleading," *Responsible Statecraft*, March 20, 2023, responsiblestatecraft.org/2023/03/20/aipac-fdd-websites-erase-all-evidence-of-their-iraq-war-cheerleading.

CHAPTER FOUR

95 **David Brooks ascended:** "*The New York Times* Appoints a Columnist," *The New York Times*, July 25, 2003, www.nytimes.com/2003/07/25/us/the-new-york-times-appoints-a-columnist.html.

95 **Jeffrey Goldberg, who wrote an influential article for *The New Yorker*:** Jeffrey Goldberg, "The Great Terror," *The New Yorker*, March 17, 2002, www.newyorker.com/magazine/2002/03/25/the-great-terror.

95 **sent ponies to his house:** Howard Kurtz, "*The Atlantic*'s Owner Ponies Up," *The Washington Post*, August 6, 2007, www.washingtonpost.com/wp-dyn/content/article/2007/08/05/AR2007080501576.html.

96 **accommodated a live audience of two hundred people:** Sam Feist, "CNN's *Crossfire*," *The Washington Post*, May 15, 2002, www.washingtonpost.com/wp-srv/liveonline/02/politics/feist051502.htm.

96 **The show's new opening credits:** Caryn James, "Critic's Notebook; The Hard News Smackdown," *The New York Times*, April 4, 2002, www.nytimes.com/2002/04/04/arts/critic-s-notebook-the-hard-news-smackdown.html.

96 **"the Ragin' Cajun":** Eric Boehlert, "In the crossfire: 'Crossfire,'" *Salon*, April 10, 2002, www.salon.com/2002/04/10/crossfire.

96 **"Look me right in the eyes and tell me truthfully":** *Crossfire*, "Did the FBI Drop the Ball?; Who Should Be Blamed for the Intelligence Snafu?" CNN, May 20, 2002, transcripts.cnn.com/show/cf/date/2002-05-20/segment/00.

97 **"The new *Crossfire*":** Novak, *The Prince of Darkness*, 581.

97 **After shows, he'd go with Carville:** Feist, "CNN's *Crossfire*."

97 **"one of my favorite people":** Carlson, *Politicians, Partisans, and Parasites*, 33.

97 **where the pair could pocket checks in the mid five figures:** Andrew Perez, David Sirota, Walker Bragman, and Julia Rock, "Tucker Carlson Calls Himself a Populist. He Has No Problem Taking Private Equity Money," *Jacobin*, November 19, 2020, jacobin.com/2020/11/tucker-carlson-speaking-fees-private-equity.

97 **"I'm afraid the deer was not long for this world":** Richard Leiby, "The Reliable Source," *The Washington Post*, October 27, 2004, www.washingtonpost.com/archive/lifestyle/2004/10/28/the-reliable-source/5e9da18f-ab14-4554-a0c3-57a90dcfa9ce.

97 **"Members of Congress don't make enough money":** *Inside Politics*, "Interview with Al Sharpton; Bush Compares Iraq Standoff to Bad Rerun," CNN, January 21, 2003, transcripts.cnn.com/show/ip/date/2003-01-21/segment/00.

97 **"Congressman Pete King of New York":** *Crossfire*, "109th Congress in Session," CNN, January 4, 2005, transcripts.cnn.com/show/cf/date/2005-01-04/segment/01.

97 **"First envisioned as an explanation of how she could have put up with a husband like that":** *Crossfire*, "Where Is Saddam Hussein?; Will Hillary Clinton Tell All in New Book?" CNN, April 28, 2003, transcripts.cnn.com/show/cf/date/2003-04-28/segment/00.

98 **"I really want you to notice, Tucker":** *Crossfire*, "Interview with Senator Hillary Rodham Clinton," CNN, July 9, 2003, transcripts.cnn.com/show/cf/date/2003-07-09/segment/00.

98 **he'd stopped drinking in August 2002:** Moore, *Tucker*, 121.

98 **he unsuccessfully tried to convince Matt Labash:** person familiar with, author interview.

99 **The *Crossfire* bookers had desperately pursued him as a guest:** Josh Cowen, "My Profane, Revealing Year Working for Tucker Carlson," *Slate*, April 25, 2003, slate.com/business/2023/04/tucker-carlson-fired-crossfire-cnn-fox-news-offensive-jokes.html.

99 **"a good-natured tweaker of Republicans and Democrats":** Novak, *The Prince of Darkness*, 628.

99 **Carlson, meanwhile, felt warmly toward Stewart:** Chris Smith, *The Daily Show (The Book): An Oral History as Told by Jon Stewart, the Correspondents, Staff and Guests* (Grand Central Publishing, 2016), 143.

99 ***The Daily Show* averaged about 1 million viewers per episode:** Pamela McClintock, "Stewart Adds Years to 'Daily Show,'" *Variety*, March 18, 2004, variety.com/2004/tv/news/stewart-adds-years-to-daily-show-1117901903/.

100 **"Both of us were excited":** Ben Karlin, author interview.

100 **"He's either the funniest smart guy on TV":** *Crossfire*, "Jon Stewart's America," CNN, October 15, 2004, transcripts.cnn.com/show/cf/date/2004-10-15/segment/01.

101 **"energy and excitement":** Laura Ewald, "Lights, Camera, *Crossfire*," *GW Magazine*, Fall 2003, www2.gwu.edu/~magazine/archive/2003_fall/docs/feat_crossfire.html.

101 **For another ninety minutes:** Paul Begala, "Begala: The day Jon Stewart blew up my show," CNN, last updated February 12, 2015, 4:26 p.m. EST, www.cnn.com/2015/02/12/opinion/begala-stewart-blew-up-crossfire/index.html.

102 **The episode drew 867,000 viewers:** Matt Hines, "Jon Stewart 'Crossfire' feud ignites Net frenzy," *CNET*, October 19, 2004, www.cnet.com/culture/jon-stewart-crossfire-feud-ignites-net-frenzy.

102 **Those download stats:** Loen Kelley, "Frenemies: Network News and YouTube," Joan Shorenstein Center on the Press, Politics and Public Policy Discussion Paper Series, February 2010, shorensteincenter.org/wp-content/uploads/2012/03/d57_kelley.pdf.

102 **which boasted some of New York's most acclaimed (and expensive) restaurants:** Florence Fabricant, "Famous Chefs! Sumptuous Food! Luxuriant Settings!" *The New York Times*, January 21, 2004, www.nytimes.com/2004/01/21/dining/famous-chefs-sumptuous-food-luxuriant-settings.html.

102 **Carlson told Klein that he had a job offer:** Jon Klein, author interview.

103 **like Albert Brooks's character in *Broadcast News*:** "Albert Brooks Sweating (*Broadcast News*)," uploaded on May 26, 2013, by Peter Murphy, Vimeo, 6 min., 26 sec., vimeo.com/67010349.

103 **But Carlson actually did fine:** *CNN NewsNight*, "Devastating Tsunami Kills Tells of Thousands in South Asia," CNN, December 27, 2004, transcripts.cnn.com/show/asb/date/2004-12-27/segment/01.

103 **"He clearly wasn't going to be":** Klein, author interview.

103 **"I don't know what CNN is saying":** Bill Carter, "CNN Will Cancel 'Crossfire' and Cut Ties to Commentator," *The New York Times*, January 6, 2005, www.nytimes.com/2005/01/06/business/media/cnn-will-cancel-crossfire-and-cut-ties-to-commentator.html.

104 **"Radio is where I feel most like myself":** "Q&A: Laura Ingraham," C-SPAN, December 5, 2005, www.c-span.org/video/?190221-1/qa-laura-ingraham.

104 **For a time after 9/11:** Gabriel Sherman, "Chasing Fox," *New York Magazine*, October 1, 2010, nymag.com/news/media/68717; Kelefa Sanneh, "Twenty-Four-Hour Party People," *The New Yorker*, August 26, 2013, www.newyorker.com/magazine/2013/09/02/twenty-four-hour-party-people.

104 **"difficult public face for NBC in a time of war":** Paul Waldman, *Fraud: The Strategy Behind the Bush Lies and Why the Media Didn't Tell You* (Sourcebooks, Inc., 2004), 155.

104 **The only constant was:** "News Audiences Increasingly Politicized," Pew Research Center, June 8, 2004, www.pewresearch.org/politics/2004/06/08/i-where-americans-go-for-news.

104 **"There's less pressure on our show to perform":** Phil Rosenthal, "Carlson 'sorry' to be walking away from PBS," *Chicago Tribune*, last updated August 22, 2021, 10:26 p.m. CDT, www.chicagotribune.com/news/ct-xpm-2005-06-12-0506120147-story.html.

105 **"an angry, weird guy":** Tucker Carlson, interview with the author.

105 **"banal":** Howard Kurtz, "The Campaign of a Comedian," *The Washington Post*, October 23, 2004, www.washingtonpost.com/archive/politics/2004/10/23/the-campaign-of-a-comedian/fde6e8bd-e32e-4950-937f-8c0effcfe127.

105 **"because he's more famous":** Carlson, interview with the author.

105 **"Big Brother format":** Carlson, interview with the author.

105 **"I'm not interested in institutional positions":** Rosenthal, "Carlson 'sorry' to be walking away from PBS."

106 **"cut outs":** Carlson, interview with the author.

106 **"dinner party":** a person familiar, interview with the author.

106 **"When a man gets dissed on his own show":** Alynda Wheat, "Tonight's Best TV," *Entertainment Weekly*, June 13, 2005, www.cnn.com/2005/SHOWBIZ/TV/06/13/ew.best.mon/.

107 **"the first openly gay Rhodes scholar":** Ken Tucker, "Rooting for Lefty," *New York Magazine*, July 7, 2005, nymag.com/nymetro/arts/tv/reviews/12171.

107 **"I'll be honest with you":** *The Situation with Tucker Carlson*, MSNBC, June 13, 2005, www.nbcnews.com/id/wbna8216294.

107 **debating him on everything from polygamy to foreign aid:** *The Situation with Tucker Carlson*, MSNBC, June 14, 2005, www.nbcnews.com/id/wbna8229402; *The Situation with Tucker Carlson*, MSNBC, June 15, 2005, www.nbcnews.com/id/wbna8242510.

107 **"You're smarter than what you're saying right now":** Frances Martel, "Part 1—Before She Was *the* Rachel Maddow: The Best of the Maddow–Tucker Carlson Debates," *Mediaite*, January 9, 2017, www.mediaite.com/online/part-1-before-she-was-the-rachel-maddow-the-best-of-the-maddow-tucker-carlson-debates.

107 **"She was unbelievably prepared":** Jessica Pressler, "The Dr. Maddow Show," *New York Magazine*, October 31, 2008, nymag.com/news/media/51822.

107 **"What's the first thing":** "Tucker Carlson and Rachel Maddow on Democratic Control & Changing Perspectives in America," uploaded on November 20, 2012, by PoliticalVideosArchive, YouTube, 4 min., 41 sec., www.youtube.com/watch?v=jfxnMChoMNY&t=51s.

108 **"From the first dinner I had with him":** Rob LeDonne, "Breakout Star Willie Geist Might Just Be the Next Matt Lauer," *Observer*, May 30, 2014, observer.com/2014/05/breakout-star-willie-geist-might-just-be-the-next-matt-lauer/amp.

108 **like the security camera video of a Nebraska man:** *Tucker*, MSNBC, January 16, 2007, www.nbcnews.com/id/wbna22708292.

108 **"The loathsome versus the loathsome":** *Tucker*, MSNBC, December 22, 2006.

108 **to move his show from nine o'clock to eleven o'clock:** Brian Stelter, "Carlson's Situation Moves to Late-Night," *Adweek*, July 29, 2005, www.adweek.com/tvnewser/carlsons-situation-moves-to-late-night/?ver=1704492350956; brianlname, "Late-Night Situation: Tucker Carlson Calls It a 'Bold' Move by MSNBC's President," *Adweek*, July 29, 2005, www.adweek.com/tvnewser/late-night-situation-tucker-carlson-calls-it-a-bold-move-by-msnbcs-president.

109 **One episode Carlson might interview Harvard professor Graham Allison:** *The Situation with Tucker Carlson*, MSNBC, June 22, 2005, www.nbcnews.com/id/wbna8331191; *Tucker*, MSNBC, September 19, 2006, www.nbcnews.com/id/wbna14921944.

109 **Carlson liked to book as guests his old colleagues from *The Standard*:** Andrew Walzer, "In Tucker discussion, *Weekly Standard*'s Ferguson on Clinton and liberal Protestants: '[T]hey believe in everything but God,'" *Media Matters for America*, June 17, 2007, www.mediamatters.org/tucker-carlson/tucker-discussion-weekly-standards-ferguson-clinton-and-liberal-protestants-they; *The Situation with Tucker Carlson*, MSNBC, October 27, 2005, www.nbcnews.com/id/wbna9849852.

109 **"to create or maintain a serf class":** *Tucker*, MSNBC, January 4, 2007, www.nbcnews.com/id/wbna16485187.

110 **"breathtaking demagogic, xenophobic ads":** *Tucker*, MSNBC, January 5, 2007.

110 **"security fence":** *The Situation with Tucker Carlson*, MSNBC, November 28, 2005, www.nbcnews.com/id/wbna10254944.

110 **"I honestly don't think":** former worker on Carlson's MSNBC show, interview with the author.

110 **"no-man's-land":** MSNBC on-air personality, interview with the author.

111 **"I really do owe him a percentage of my salary":** Peter J. Boyer, "One Angry Man," *The New Yorker*, June 15, 2008, www.newyorker.com/magazine/2008/06/23/one-angry-man.

111 **"Keith Olbermann is our brand":** "Counting Down on MSNBC's Keith Olbermann," NPR, November 23, 2007, www.npr.org/transcripts/16517458.

112 **"nappy-headed hos":** Robert Smith, "CBS Radio Fires Don Imus in Fallout over Remarks," NPR, April 12, 2007, www.npr.org/2007/04/12/9556159/cbs-radio-fires-don-imus-in-fallout-over-remarks.

112 **Presenting them with a laminated page of bullet points:** Jacques Steinberg, "TV Host Is in His Prime with a Morning Audience," *The New York Times*, June 5, 2008, www.nytimes.com/2008/06/05/arts/television/05joe.html.

112 **"How can such a fanatic be so likable?":** Sam Tanenhaus, "When Pat Buchanan Tried to Make America Great Again," *Esquire*, April 5, 2017, www.esquire.com/news-politics/a54275/charge-of-the-right-brigade.

113 **Robert Novak, a septuagenarian pundit no less:** Novak, *The Prince of Darkness*, 586.

113 **"I want to have an interesting life":** Carlson, interview with the author.

113 ***Wheel of Fortune* host Pat Sajak:** Prem Thakker, "Don't Pour One Out for Pat Sajak, *Wheel of Fortune*'s Die-Hard Right-Wing Host," *The New Republic*, June 13, 2023, newrepublic.com/post/173587/pat-sajak-wheel-of-fortune-right-wing-host.

114 **"He thought that would just":** Carlson friend, interview with the author.

114 **"a chance for a big audience to see":** Willie Geist, "Dancing with Springer," *NBC News*, March 22, 2006, www.nbcnews.com/id/wbna11961531.

114 **"What an awful mess":** "Tucker Carlson & Elena Grinenko—Cha-Cha-Cha on *Dancing with the Stars*," uploaded on January 19, 2011, by Elena Grinenko (Elena Grinenko Dance), YouTube, 6 min., 24 sec., www.youtube.com/watch?v=FRTYvygTArs.

114 ***Do You Trust Me?* was the brainchild of Phil Gurin:** Josef Adalian, "Carlson to host CBS gameshow pilot," *Variety*, April 12, 2007, variety.com/2007/scene/markets-festivals/carlson-to-host-cbs-gameshow-pilot-1117963015.

115 **"He was very poised":** Ray Giuliani, interview with the author.

115 **The only Gurin game show pilot:** Felicia R. Lee, "Forget Naming That Tune, Try Naming Those Lyrics," *The New York Times*, August 14, 2007, www.nytimes.com/2007/08/14/arts/television/14bee.html.

115 **"Phil thinks he's my boss":** Boyer, "One Angry Man."

115 **Back in 2005, when McCain appeared:** *The Situation with Tucker Carlson*, MSNBC, June 20, 2005, www.nbcnews.com/id/wbna8301716.

115 **"You look at John McCain":** *Hardball with Chris Matthews*, MSNBC, January 3, 2008, 5:00 p.m. ET, www.nbcnews.com/id/wbna22505260.

116 **"I come on this show":** *Tucker*, MSNBC, March 14, 2008.

116 **Six months later:** Chris Ariens, "Maddow's Show to Be Called . . . *The Rachel Maddow Show*," *Adweek*, August 20, 2008, www.adweek.com/tvnewser/maddows-show-to-be-called-the-rachel-maddow-show/21619.

CHAPTER FIVE

117 **eyeing the young and dynamic new president's sky-high approval ratings:** "Presidential Approval Ratings—Barack Obama," Gallup, April 11, 2025, news.gallup.com/poll/116479/barack-obama-presidential-job-approval.aspx.

117 **he'd turned Keene down:** David Keene, interview with the author.

118 **Speaking to the eighty-five hundred CPAC attendees:** Edward Hudgins, "CPAC 2009: A Focus on Freedom," Atlas Society, June 9, 2011, www.atlassociety.org/post/cpac-2009-a-focus-on-freedom.

118 **as well as the hundreds of thousands of people watching on Fox News and CNN:** CNN Live Event/Special, "Rush Limbaugh's Address to the CPAC Winter Meeting," CNN, February 28, 2009, transcripts.cnn.com/show/se/date/2009-02-28/segment/01.

118 **"Where is the compromise between good and evil?":** "Rush Limbaugh's Speech at CPAC 2009," *RealClearPolitics*, February 28, 2009, www.realclearpolitics.com/articles/2009/02/rush_limbaughs_speech_at_cpac.html.

118 **Limbaugh had recently come under fire:** "Limbaugh: I Hope Obama Fails," Rush Limbaugh Show, January 16, 2009, www.rushlimbaugh.com/daily/2009/01/16/limbaugh_i_hope_obama_fails.

118 **as Florida governor Charlie Crist discovered:** Charlie Crist, "The Hug That Killed My Republican Career," *Time*, February 4, 2014, time.com/4608/the-hug-that-killed-my-republican-career.

118 **"the biggest speech":** Keene, interview with the author.

118 **"pale pastels":** Carl P. Leubsdorf, "Leubsdorf: Reagan, Trump: CPAC heroes," *The Columbian*, March 12, 2023, www.columbian.com/news/2023/mar/12/leubsdorf-regan-trump-cpac-heroes.

119 **He bought a nine-thousand-square-foot mansion:** "25 Midwood Ter," NJ Parcels, April 11, 2025, njparcels.com/property/1417/4402/4; "25 Midwood Ter, Madison, NJ 07940," Zillow, April 11, 2025, www.zillow.com/homedetails/25-Midwood-Ter-Madison-NJ-07940/39440209_zpid.

119 **"I looked around and I was like":** "Tucker Carlson on the Media's Deception."

119 **he dramatically upped his Nicorette consumption:** Tom Bartlett, "The Bearable Lightness of Being Tucker Carlson," *Washingtonian*, November 26, 2012, www.washingtonian.com/2012/11/26/the-bearable-lightness-of-being-tucker-carlson.

119 **Chatsworth Osborne Jr.:** Elmer Lightman, *Everything You Need to Know About Rush Limbaugh* (pub. by author, 2014), 127.

119 **"Most speakers hate to be interrupted":** Joel Meares, "The Great Right Hype," *Columbia Journalism Review*, July 13, 2011, www.cjr.org/feature/the_great_right_hype.php.

120 **"refused to put accuracy first":** "CPAC: Tucker Carlson Tries to Defend *The New York Times*, Gets Booed [RightWingWatch.org]," uploaded on February 26, 2009, by RightWingWatchdotorg, YouTube, 2 min., 15 sec., www.youtube.com/watch?v=6tD2H6AX1fE.

121 **"Tucker Carlson calls for the professionalization of conservative media":** Ta-Nehisi Coates, "Notes from CPAC," *The Atlantic*, February 27, 2009, www.theatlantic.com/entertainment/archive/2009/02/notes-from-cpac/6789.

121 **Shortly after the 2008 election:** a person familiar, interview with the author.

121 **Although Patel's mentor, Scooter Libby, had resigned:** "Timeline: The CIA Leak Case," NPR, July 2, 2007, www.npr.org/templates/story/story.php?storyId=4764919.

122 **"Do we really want":** James Hamel, "Defending the Best and the Brightest," FrumForum, July 27, 2010, http://frumforum.com/entry/defending-the-best-and-the-brightest.

122 **"Internet newspaper":** Brian Stelter, "Citizen Huff," *The New York Times*, March 31, 2008, www.nytimes.com/2008/03/31/business/media/31huffington.html.

123 ***The Tucker Report*:** a person familiar, interview with the author.

123 ***News Queue*:** Chris Moody, interview with the author.

123 **Carlson liked *Punji Stick*:** Meares, "The Great Right Hype."

123 **"suggestive of kind of a traditional":** Carlson, interview with the author.

123 **"virtually impossible to find":** Matt K. Lewis, "How the *Daily Caller* got its name (a true story)," *Daily Caller*, October 18, 2012, dailycaller.com/2012/10/18/how-the-daily-caller-got-its-name-a-true-story/.

123 **Patel came up with the controversial press strategy:** John C. Moritz, "'Vice' the movie: How the *Caller-Times* broke the story on the Dick Cheney shooting accident," *Corpus Christie Caller-Times*, December 13, 2018, www.caller.com/story/news/local/texas/state-bureau/2018/12/13/vice-movie-dick-cheney-shooting-accident-caller-times-broke-story/2291298002; Lewis, "How the *Daily Caller* got its name (a true story)"; Sanneh, "Tucker Carlson's Fighting Words."

123 **One of the first people:** a person familiar, interview with the author.

124 **all of Scaife's money was tied up:** Michael Joseph Gross, "A Vast Right-Wing Hypocrisy," *Vanity Fair*, January 2, 2008, www.vanityfair.com/news/2008/02/scaife200802.

124 **Carlson and Patel hired:** a person familiar, interview with the author.

124 **His investment firm famously held its rare staff meetings:** Peter J. Tanous, *Investment Gurus: A Road Map to Wealth from the World's Best Money Managers* (Prentice Hall, 1997), 217.

125 **"I don't want to run your lives":** a person familiar, interview with the author.

125 **"Tucker and Neil present a huge opportunity":** Howard Kurtz, "Media Notes: A look at Tucker Carlson's political Web site, the *Daily Caller*," *The Washington Post*, January 11, 2010, www.washingtonpost.com/wp-dyn/content/article/2010/01/10/AR2010011002388_pf.html.

125 **save for attending the annual antiabortion March for Life:** Jon Ward, *Testimony: Inside the Evangelical Movement That Failed a Generation* (Brazos Press, 2023), 22, 49.

125 **traveling the country and the world:** Ward, *Testimony*, 110.

125 **"the instrument in spreading the truth about God to the world":** Harrison Smith, "Wesley Pruden, *Washington Times* editor and pugnacious conservative columnist, dies at 83," *The Washington Post*, July 18, 2019, www.washingtonpost.com/local/obituaries/wesley-pruden-washington-times-editor-and-pugnacious-conservative-columnist-dies-at-83/2019/07/18/cd73c342-a96a-11e9-9214-246e594de5d5_story.html.

126 **"It was going to be":** Jon Ward, interview with the author.

126 **Megan Mulligan, a well-regarded:** Mike Allen, "Tucker Carlson launching Jan. 11," *Politico*, December 5, 2009, www.politico.com/story/2009/12/tucker-carlson-launching-jan-11-030234.

126 **Labash agreed to write the *Caller*'s advice column:** dailycaller.com /author/mlabash/.

126 **Roger Stone signed up:** Roger Stone, "The beauty of the indispensable black knitted tie," *The Daily Caller*, February 8, 2010, dailycaller.com /2010/02/08/the-beauty-of-the-indispensable-black-knitted-tie/.

127 **Ginni Thomas, the wife of:** Kenneth P. Vogel and Jennifer Epstein, "Ginni Thomas Joins *The Daily Caller*," *Politico*, March 22, 2011.

127 **"That was then":** Carlson, interview with the author.

127 **"I want to be like Bill Kristol":** Carlson, interview with the author.

127 **"We think that with the crisis in the news business":** "News Review," C-SPAN, November 22, 2009, www.c-span.org/video/?290181-3/news -review.

127 **"lots of original and, I hope, hard-nosed reporting":** Mike Allen, "Tucker Carlson launching Jan. 11," *Politico*, December 5, 2009, www.politico.com /story/2009/12/tucker-carlson-launching-jan-11-030234.

127 **"try to increase the amount of useful information in the world":** Sanneh, "Twenty-Four-Hour Party People."

127 **"stories that add to the sum total of known facts":** Jason Zengerle, "The Scribbler," *The New Republic*, February 18, 2010, newrepublic.com /article/72794/the-scribbler.

128 **"You haven't made it in D.C.":** Patrick Gavin, "*Daily Caller* Party: Glover opens her Kalorama home," *Politico*, January 13, 2010, www.politico.com /click/stories/1001/glover_opens_her_kalorama_home.html.

128 **The tab was being picked up:** David Weigel, "Take a Ride on Tucker Carlson's Spaceship," *The Washington Independent*, January 5, 2010, web .archive.org/web/20100108090457/https://washingtonindependent.com /73240/take-a-ride-on-tucker-carlsons-spaceship.

128 **And the guest list included:** Jim Treacher, "You haven't lived until you've done Jell-O shots with Paul Begala," *Daily Caller*, January 13, 2010, dailycaller.com/2010/01/13/you-havent-lived-until-youve-done-jell-o-shots -with-paul-begala.

128 **As women in French-maid outfits passed hors d'oeuvres:** Tara Palmeri, "Carlson's *Daily Caller* kicks off with flair," *Washington Examiner*, January 14, 2010, www.washingtonexaminer.com/?p=1350564.

128 **"It hasn't been a big month for sleeping":** "Tucker Carlson Lands His 'Most Permanent' Gig Yet," *NBC Washington*, last updated January 20, 2010, 4:02 p.m., www.nbcwashington.com/local/call-tucka/147477.

128 **Then Carlson and Glover's dog:** Patrick G. Ryan, "*Daily Caller* Launch Party," *SnarkInfested*, January 13, 2010, snarkinfested.com/2010/01/13/daily -caller-launch-party.

129 **"a frat house vibe":** former *Daily Caller* staffer, interview with the author.

129 **no one would be checking IDs at the office kegerator:** Patrick Gavin and Kiki Ryan, "*Daily Caller*, now with beer," *Politico*, last updated September 10, 2010, 5:26 p.m. EDT, www.politico.com/click/stories/1009/daily_caller_now _with_beer.html.

129 **Not long after the *Caller* launched:** Hunter Walker, "Tucker Carlson Has Some Fun at Keith Olbermann's Expense," *Observer*, November 9, 2010, observer.com/2010/11/tucker-carlson-has-some-fun-at-keith-olbermanns-expense.

129 **"WE OWN YOU":** "*Daily Caller* Buys KeithOlbermann.Com, Tells Olbermann, 'We Own You,'" *The Huffington Post*, last updated May 25, 2011, www.huffpost.com/entry/daily-caller-buys-keithol_n_647517.

130 **"Could you resist?":** Zaid Jilani, "Tucker Carlson Sent Insulting E-mails to Philadelphia Columnist While Posing as Keith Olbermann," *ThinkProgress*, November 10, 2010, archive.thinkprogress.org/tucker-carlson-sent-insulting-e-mails-to-philadelphia-columnist-while-posing-as-keith-olbermann-5f10be0c0143.

130 **Ward, who did in fact secure the *Caller* a seat in the White House briefing room:** Jon Ward, "Barack Obama's pledge to bring transparency to the White House gets an A for intention, but a lower grade for implementation," *Daily Caller*, January 13, 2010, dailycaller.com/2010/01/13/barack-obamas-pledge-to-bring-transparency-to-the-white-house-gets-a-for-intention-but-a-lower-grade-for-implementation; Jon Ward, "Dems discordant on prospects for health care," *Daily Caller*, January 28, 2010, dailycaller.com/2010/01/28/dems-discordant-on-prospects-for-health-care.

130 **Chris Moody, who'd previously worked at the libertarian Cato Institute:** Chris Moody, "Congressional Budget Office report says federal deficits and debt will soar," *Daily Caller*, July 2, 2010, dailycaller.com/2010/07/02/congressional-budget-office-report-says-federal-deficits-and-debt-will-soar; Chris Moody, "Senators trade jabs before vote to proceed on military authorization bill," *Daily Caller*, September 21, 2010, dailycaller.com/2010/09/21/senators-trade-jabs-before-vote-to-proceed-on-military-authorization-bill.

130 **And Alex Pappas, a recent Sewanee grad:** Alex Pappas, "Capitalism at the Tea Party Convention," *Daily Caller*, February 6, 2010, dailycaller.com/2010/02/06/capitalism-at-the-tea-party-convention.

130 **"There was this curiosity spike":** Mike Riggs, interview with the author.

131 **"[Curl] looked at me":** Chris Moody, host, *Finding Matt Drudge*, podcast, episode 4, "Matt Drudge's Power over the News Industry," iHeartMedia, February 6, 2024, www.iheart.com/podcast/1119-finding-matt-drudge-143594804.

132 **"'Voyeur West Hollywood' is very intriguing":** Jonathan Strong, interview with the author.

132 **"off the hook":** Ralph Z. Hallow, "Steele: GOP needs 'hip-hop' makeover," *The Washington Times*, February 19, 2009, www.washingtontimes.com/news/2009/feb/19/steele-gop-needs-hip-hop-makeover.

132 **"gutless":** "A Few Words for Michael Steele," Rush Limbaugh Show, March 2, 2009, www.rushlimbaugh.com/daily/2009/03/02/a_few_words_for_michael_steele.

132 **"chic and costly hotels":** Jonathan Strong, "High flyer: RNC Chairman Steele suggested buying private jet with GOP funds," *Daily Caller*, March 29,

2010, dailycaller.com/2010/03/29/high-flyer-rnc-chairman-steele-suggested-buying-private-jet-with-gop-funds.

132 **"You nailed him":** Strong, interview with the author.

132 **"If you're riling people up":** Chris Moody, interview with the author.

133 **Nagesh, who joined JournoList:** "Gautham Nagesh," *Daily Caller*, April 11, 2025, dailycaller.com/author/gnagesh; Sam Stein, "*Daily Caller* Fails to Report That It Too Was Part of Journolist," *The Huffington Post*, last updated May 25, 2011, www.huffpost.com/entry/daily-caller-fails-to-rep_n_654034.

133 **"He would not talk in detail":** Strong, interview with the author.

133 **"I keep hearing about how smart":** Brad DeLong, "Should You Trust Tucker Carlson's *Daily Caller* on Anything? No," *Grasping Reality*, July 22, 2010, delong.typepad.com/sdj/2010/07/should-you-trust-tucker-carlsons-daily-caller-on-anything-no.html.

134 **"It's Max Brantley":** Erik Wemple, "Fox News's Tucker Carlson has no business lecturing about journalism ethics," *The Washington Post*, December 7, 2016, www.washingtonpost.com/blogs/erik-wemple/wp/2016/12/07/fox-newss-tucker-carlson-has-no-business-lecturing-about-journalism-ethics.

134 **"I don't want to take credit":** Strong, interview with the author; a former *Daily Caller* staffer, interview with the author.

135 **"an anti-Semite":** Jonathan Strong, "E-mails reveal *Post* reporter savaging conservatives, rooting for Democrats," *Daily Caller*, June 25, 2010, dailycaller.com/2010/06/25/emails-reveal-post-reporter-savaging-conservatives-rooting-for-democrats.

135 **while Weigel apologized:** David Weigel, "How I Learned to Stop Worrying & Love Sarah Palin (Kinda)," *Esquire*, July 8, 2010, www.esquire.com/news-politics/news/a7910/dave-weigel-email-controversy-070810.

135 **would be rehired by the *Post*:** Erik Wemple, "*Washington Post* nabs Dave Weigel from *Bloomberg Politics*," *The Washington Post*, July 8, 2015, www.washingtonpost.com/blogs/erik-wemple/wp/2015/07/08/washington-post-nabs-dave-weigel-from-bloomberg-politics.

135 **the *Caller*'s website eventually crashed:** Juli Weiner, "*The Washington Post*'s Dave Weigel Resigns Following Strange Semi-Scandal," *Vanity Fair*, June 25, 2010, www.vanityfair.com/culture/2010/06/the-washington-posts-dave-weigel-resigns-following-strange-semi-scandal.

136 **"I don't really have":** Carlson, interview with the author.

136 **"People are going to hate you":** Moody, interview with the author.

136 **Strong followed up his Weigel story:** "Jonathan Strong—Page 9," *Daily Caller*, April 11, 2025, dailycaller.com/author/jonathan-strong/page/9; "Jonathan Strong—Page 8," *Daily Caller*, April 11, 2025, dailycaller.com/author/jonathan-strong/page/8.

136 **a public letter complaining:** Jonathan Chait, "Debunking the Journolist 'Conspiracy,'" *CBS News*, July 21, 2010, www.cbsnews.com/news/debunking-the-journolist-conspiracy.

137 **"We've discovered that":** "Tucker Carlson from the *Daily Caller*."

137 **"I've never dealt":** Meares, "The Great Right Hype."

137 **"When he did the CPAC speech":** Strong, interview with the author.

138 **"the man the White House wakes up to":** Mark Leibovich, "The Man the White House Wakes Up To," *The New York Times Magazine*, April 25, 2010, www.nytimes.com/2010/04/25/magazine/25allen-t.html.

138 **"couldn't have been nicer":** Carlson, interview with the author.

138 **When Strong published a subsequent scoop:** Jonathan Strong, "Stress-related condition 'incapacitates' Bachmann; heavy pill use alleged," *Daily Caller*, July 18, 2011, dailycaller.com/2011/07/18/stress-related-condition-incapacitates-bachmann-heavy-pill-use-alleged.

138 **"confirm":** Kasie Hunt and Molly Ball, "Bachmann faces more migraine questions," *Politico*, last updated July 21, 2011, 5:29 a.m. EDT, www.politico.com/story/2011/07/bachmann-faces-more-migraine-questions-059433.

138 **"a liberal publication based in suburban Virginia":** Betsy Rothstein, "The *Daily Caller* and *Politico*: It's War," *Adweek*, November 14, 2011, www.adweek.com/performance-marketing/the-daily-caller-and-politico-its-war.

138 **"left-of-center bias":** Jeff Poor, "MSNBCPOLITICO: A commanding presence for *Politico* on the left's favorite cable news channel," *Daily Caller*, November 14, 2011, dailycaller.com/2011/11/14/msnbcpolitico-a-commanding-presence-for-politico-on-the-lefts-favorite-cable-news-channel.

138 **"Tucker was just fucking":** a former *Daily Caller* staffer, interview with the author.

138 **They laughed some more:** Mike Allen, "Romney Unscathed in N.H. Debate," *Playbook*, *Politico*, January 8, 2012, www.politico.com/tipsheets/playbook/2012/01/romney-unscathed-in-nh-debate-santorum-draws-huge-crowds-gets-gary-bauer-endorsement-huntsman-claims-surge-meet-the-press-facebook-debate-this-am-anita-dunn-john-podesta-bdays-003342.

138 **And Carlson, at least, had an annual residual laugh:** Anna Palmer and Jake Sherman, "POLITICO *Playbook*: Trump is a war president now," *Playbook*, *Politico*, January 8, 2020, www.politico.com/newsletters/playbook/2020/01/08/trump-is-a-war-president-now-488014.

139 **it enjoyed its best traffic month to date:** Meares, "The Great Right Hype."

139 **"content intelligence":** Jill Lepore, "Does Journalism Have a Future?" *The New Yorker*, January 21, 2019, www.newyorker.com/magazine/2019/01/28/does-journalism-have-a-future.

139 **"The thing that Tucker valued":** Riggs, interview with the author.

139 **A graduate student at American University:** Luke Mullins, "Meet Matt Boyle, *Breitbart*'s (Other) Man in the White House," *Washingtonian*, May 21, 2017, www.washingtonian.com/2017/05/21/meet-matt-boyle-breitbarts-man-white-house; Lloyd Grove, "2016's Angry Populist Enforcer," *The Daily Beast*, November 23, 2015, www.thedailybeast.com/2016s-angry-populist-enforcer.

140 **"Whatever you want them to be":** a person familiar, interview with the author.

140 **he would threaten congressional spokespeople:** *BuzzFeed* Staff, "Democrats Accuse Conservative News Outlet of 'Blackmail,'" *BuzzFeed Politics*, March 14, 2012, www.buzzfeednews.com/article/buzzfeedpolitics/democrats-accuse-conservative-news-outlet-of-blac.

140 **"It's not an organic thing that's just happening":** Josh Gerstein, "Eric Holder to *Daily Caller*: Quit pressing me to quit," *Politico*, November 29, 2011, www.politico.com/blogs/under-the-radar/2011/11/eric-holder-to-daily-caller-quit-pressing-me-to-quit-041151.

140 **"hushed tones":** a former *Daily Caller* staffer, interview with the author.

141 **"asking for taxpayers to shoulder the burden":** Matthew Boyle, "EPA: Regulations would require 230,000 employees, $21 billion," *Daily Caller*, September 26, 2011, dailycaller.com/2011/09/26/epa-regulations-would-require-230000-new-employees-21-billion.

141 **But the article was inaccurate:** Dan Berman, "EPA $21B rumors 'comically wrong,'" September 27, 2011, www.politico.com/story/2011/09/epa-21b-rumors-comically-wrong-064582.

141 **Boyle's investigation into Democratic senator Bob Menendez:** Matthew Boyle, "Women: Sen. Bob Menendez paid us for sex in the Dominican Republic [Video]," *Daily Caller*, November 1, 2012, dailycaller.com/2012/11/01/women-sen-bob-menendez-paid-us-for-sex-in-the-dominican-republic.

142 **indeed, ABC had interviewed the same two women:** *ABC News*, "Woman Says She Was Paid to Lie About Claim of Sex with Senator Menendez," *ABC News*, March 4, 2013, abcnews.go.com/Blotter/woman-paid-lie-claim-sex-senator-menendez/story?id=18653773.

142 **"Drudge was the business":** a former *Daily Caller* staffer, interview with the author.

142 **Menendez would later be convicted:** Ryan Lucas, "Sen. Bob Menendez found guilty on all counts in bribery trial," NPR, July 16, 2024, www.npr.org/2024/07/16/g-s1-10487/menendez-jury-verdict-trial.

142 **the FBI investigated:** Carol D. Leonnig and Ernesto Londoño, "Escort says Menendez prostitution claims were made up," *The Washington Post*, March 4, 2013, www.washingtonpost.com/politics/escort-says-menendez-prostitution-claims-were-made-up/2013/03/04/31299fe2-8514-11e2-999e-5f8e0410cb9d_story.html.

142 **"credible evidence":** Carol D. Leonnig and Ernesto Londoño, "Sen. Robert Menendez seeks probe of allege Cuban plot to smear him," *The Washington Post*, July 7, 2014, www.washingtonpost.com/politics/sen-robert-menendez-seeks-probe-of-alleged-cuban-plot-to-smear-him/2014/07/07/e9ba25a0-efe8-11e3-914c-1fbd0614e2d4_story.html.

142 **"*The Daily Caller* was Tucker's menagerie":** a former *Daily Caller* staffer, interview with the author.

143 **"I felt like conservatives":** Strong, interview with the author.

143 **"The story he filed":** a former *Daily Caller* staffer, interview with the author.

143 **"There is no line":** Riggs, interview with the author.

144 **"a demarcation for the *Caller*":** Ward, interview with the author.

144 **"nose for the boring":** a person familiar, interview with the author.

144 **"high-level Republican sources":** Jon Ward, "Conservatives denounce GOP 'Pledge' as sellout, inside job," *Daily Caller*, September 24, 2010, dailycaller .com/2010/09/24/conservatives-denounce-gop-pledge-as-sellout-inside-job.

144 **"Did you just say":** a former *Daily Caller* staffer, interview with the author.

145 **"It was that time":** Ward, interview with the author.

145 **Ward resigned:** Keach Hagey, "The *Daily Caller*'s growing pains," *Politico*, November 15, 2011, www.politico.com/story/2011/11/the-daily-callers-growing-pains-068416.

146 **"Why do you favor foreign workers over Americans?":** Brian Stelter, "Reporter Interrupts Obama During Statement on Immigration," *The New York Times*, last updated June 15, 2012, 4:40 p.m., archive.nytimes.com /mediadecoder.blogs.nytimes.com/2012/06/15/reporter-interrupts-obama -during-statement-on-immigration.

146 **A representative headline from a May article:** Caroline May, "Illegal immigrants leave tons of trash in Arizona desert, devastating environment," *Daily Caller*, July 29, 2010, dailycaller.com/2010/07/29/illegal-immigrants -leave-tons-of-trash-in-arizona-desert-devastating-environmen.

146 **"Women are like Indians now":** Patrick Howley, "Liberals want to stop men from checking out women," *Daily Caller*, December 8, 2013, dailycaller .com/2013/12/08/liberals-want-to-stop-men-from-checking-out-women.

146 **the *Caller* reported that a white man:** Chuck Rudd, "Victim's sister: Mobile, Ala. black-on-white beating sparked by theft, not basketball," *Daily Caller*, April 26, 2012, dailycaller.com/2012/04/26/victims-sister-mobile-ala -black-on-white-beating-sparked-by-theft-not-basketball/.

146 **Law enforcement officials later said:** Katherine Sayre, "Judge hears testimony of Matthew Owens beating in Terry Rawls assault case," AL.com, last updated July 24, 2012, 3:37 p.m., www.al.com/live/2012/07/judge_hears_testimony_of _matth.html.

147 **In another article, the *Caller* published:** David Martosko, "The *Daily Caller* obtains Trayvon Martin's tweets," *Daily Caller*, March 26, 2012, dailycaller.com/2012/03/26/the-daily-caller-obtains-trayvon-martins-tweets.

147 **"I was struck by the immediate, uncloaked assumption":** McKay Coppins, "In Conservative Media, a 'Race War' Rages," *BuzzFeed News*, May 20, 2012, www.buzzfeednews.com/article/mckaycoppins/in-conservative -media-a-race-war-rages.

147 **After a year and a half:** Hagey, "The *Daily Caller*'s growing pains."

147 **"Subscription publications are very distant from the consumer":** "*Daily Caller* Web Site," C-SPAN, August 23, 2012, www.c-span.org/video/?307627 -5/daily-caller-web-site.

147 **"reluctant culture warrior":** "Andrew Breitbart, 'tea party' star and 'reluctant culture warrior,'" *Los Angeles Times*, April 30, 2011, www.latimes .com/archives/blogs/jacket-copy/story/2011-04-30/andrew-breitbart-tea-party -star-and-reluctant-culture-warrior.

147 **he was radicalized in his early twenties:** Lloyd Grove, "Andrew Breitbart, Mad as Hell," *The Daily Beast*, February 1, 2010, www.thedailybeast.com/andrew-breitbart-mad-as-hell.

147 **"I realized I liked being hated":** Steve Oney, "Citizen Breitbart: The Web's New Right-Wing Impresario," *Time*, March 25, 2010, content.time.com/time/subscriber/article/0,33009,1975339-1,00.html.

148 ***Breitbart News* brought down New York Democratic congressman Anthony Weiner:** David Folkenflik, "Familiar Role for Conservative Provocateur Breitbart," *All Things Considered*, NPR, June 7, 2011, www.npr.org/2011/06/07/137042268/looking-at-breitbarts-role-in-weiners-scandal.

148 **The site also posted a video of Shirley Sherrod:** *The Week* Staff, "Will Shirley Sherrod be Andrew Breitbart's downfall?" *The Week*, last updated January 8, 2015, theweek.com/articles/492542/shirley-sherrod-andrew-breitbarts-downfall.

148 **The lawsuit was settled on confidential terms:** Josh Gerstein, "Breitbart, Sherrod near libel settlement," *Politico*, July 1, 2015, www.politico.com/blogs/under-the-radar/2015/07/breitbart-sherrod-near-libel-settlement-209824; https://pdfserver.amlaw.com/nlj/Sherrod%20Breitbart%20Joint%20Statement.pdf.

148 **most of their other content:** Rebecca Mead, "Rage Machine," *The New Yorker*, May 24, 2010, www.newyorker.com/magazine/2010/05/24/rage-machine.

148 **"I've seen a lot of Congressman Weiner's body":** Maggie Haberman, "Breitbart takes over Weiner presser," *Politico*, last updated June 6, 2011, 6:15 p.m. EDT, www.politico.com/story/2011/06/breitbart-takes-over-weiner-presser-056359.

148 **Breitbart gave Carlson and Patel:** a person familiar, interview with the author.

148 **Later, Carlson and Breitbart would go quail hunting together:** x.com/AndrewBreitbart/status/128614441439870976.

148 **the *Caller* would cohost:** Moe Lane, "The *Righteous Indignation* Book Party," MoeLane.com, April 22, 2011, moelane.com/2011/04/22/the-righteous-indignation-book-party; Matthew Boyle, "Andrew Breitbart: Warrior, friend, mentor," *Daily Caller*, March 1, 2012, dailycaller.com/2012/03/01/andrew-breitbart-warrior-friend-mentor.

149 **When Carlson, as a (Breitbartesque) publicity stunt:** "Conservative wins dinner with Ayers," *Chicago Tribune*, last updated August 23, 2021, 7:33 a.m. CDT, www.chicagotribune.com/2011/12/17/conservative-wins-dinner-with-ayers.

149 **who'd been friendly with Obama:** Scott Shane, "Obama and '60s Bomber: A Look into Crossed Paths," *The New York Times*, October 4, 2008, www.nytimes.com/2008/10/04/us/politics/04ayers.html.

149 **He chose:** Bill Ayers, "My Dinner with Andrew Breitbart," *Boston Review*, March 28, 2012, www.bostonreview.net/articles/bill-ayers-tucker-carlson-andrew-breitbart-dinner; Jamie Weinstein, "Inside TheDC's dinner with former Weather Underground terrorist," *Daily Caller*, February 6, 2012,

dailycaller.com/2012/02/06/inside-thedcs-dinner-with-former-weather -underground-terrorists.

149 **"decent as hell":** Tucker Carlson, "Tucker Carlson: Andrew Breitbart, RIP," *Daily Caller*, March 1, 2012, dailycaller.com/2012/03/01/tucker-carlson -andrew-breitbart-rip.

149 **"the Leni Riefenstahl of the Tea Party movement":** Joshua Green, *Devil's Bargain: Steve Bannon, Donald Trump, and the Storming of the Presidency* (Penguin Press, 2017), 89.

149 **Shortly before Breitbart's death:** Green, *Devil's Bargain*, 130.

150 **"the *Huffington Post* of the right":** McKay Coppins, "Breitbart's Inheritors Battle Over His Legacy," *BuzzFeed News*, October 22, 2012, www.buzzfeed .com/mckaycoppins/breitbarts-inheritors-battle-over-his-legacy.

150 **"our No. 1 draft pick":** Grove, "2016's Angry Populist Enforcer."

150 ***Breitbart News* also hired Caroline May:** Nick Massella, "*Breitbart News* Snags *Daily Caller*'s Caroline May," *Adweek*, April 29, 2014, www.adweek .com/performance-marketing/breitbart-news-snags-daily-callers-caroline -may; *Breitbart News*, "Patrick Howley Joins *Breitbart News* as Investigative Reporter," *Breitbart*, August 9, 2015, www.breitbart.com/the-media/2015 /08/09/patrick-howley-joins-breitbart-news-as-investigative-reporter; Kurt Bardella, "I used to work at *Breitbart*. Here's why I think they fired that reporter over a tweet," *Vox*, last updated June 12, 2017, 11:38 a.m. EDT, www.vox.com/first-person/2017/6/7/15758376/kurt-bardella-breitbart-bannon -trump.

150 **"Where is Neil going?":** Dylan Byers, "Neil Munro, reporter who heckled Obama, out at *Daily Caller*," *Politico*, March 31, 2015, www.politico.com /blogs/media/2015/03/neil-munro-reporter-who-heckled-obama-out-at-daily -caller-204792.

150 **Shortly thereafter:** Courtney Fillmore, "Neil Munro Moves to *Breitbart*," *Adweek*, September 2, 2015, www.adweek.com/performance-marketing/neil -munro-moves-to-breitbart.

150 **who was helping Ailes run a smear campaign:** Ben Schreckinger, "The Widening Blast Radius of the Fox News Scandal," *Politico Magazine*, May 14, 2017, www.politico.com/magazine/story/2017/05/14/fox-news-scandal-impact -politics-215135.

150 **"Bannon is full of shit":** Charles Johnson, interview with the author.

151 **"troll on steroids":** David Carr, "Sowing Mayhem, One Click at a Time," *The New York Times*, December 15, 2014, www.nytimes.com/2014/12/15 /business/media/sowing-mayhem-one-click-at-a-time.html.

151 **he was later banned from Twitter:** Caitlin Dewey, "Charles Johnson one of the Internet's most infamous trolls, has finally been banned from Twitter," *The Washington Post*, May 26, 2015, www.washingtonpost.com/news/the -intersect/wp/2015/05/26/charles-johnson-one-of-the-internets-most -infamous-trolls-has-finally-been-banned-from-twitter.

151 **One of his *Caller* stories:** Charles C. Johnson, "Who funds Syrian rebel advocate O'Bagy and the Syrian Emergency Task Force? You do," *Daily Caller*,

September 9, 2013, dailycaller.com/2013/09/09/who-funds-syrian-rebel-advocate-obagy-and-the-syrian-emergency-task-force-you-do.

151 **Bannon opened up a *Breitbart News* bureau in Lubbock, Texas:** Green, *Devil's Bargain*, 108.

151 **"black crime":** Brian Beutler, "Steve Bannon Is Not Your Friend," *The New Republic*, August 22, 2017, newrepublic.com/article/144460/steve-bannon-not-friend.

151 **The site doubled its number of unique visitors:** Coppins, "Breitbart's Inheritors Battle Over His Legacy."

152 **In 2013, that agenda's top item was torpedoing bipartisan immigration-reform legislation:** Jason DeParle, "How Stephen Miller Seized the Moment to Battle Immigration," *The New York Times*, August 17, 2019, www.nytimes.com/2019/08/17/us/politics/stephen-miller-immigration-trump.html.

152 **he and the Mercers initially favored Texas senator Ted Cruz:** Jonathan Swan, "How *Breitbart* turned on Ted Cruz," *The Hill*, August 19, 2016, thehill.com/blogs/ballot-box/presidential-races/292028-how-breitbart-turned-on-ted-cruz.

152 **"the best reporter in the country":** Mullins, "Meet Matt Boyle, *Breitbart*'s (Other) Man in the White House."

153 **he had heavily edited:** a former *Daily Caller* staffer, interview with the author.

153 **"Tucker was very frustrated":** Riggs, interview with the author.

153 **"*Breitbart*'s home page":** a former *Daily Caller* staffer, interview with the author.

153 **"Links are what I'm after":** Brian Stelter, "Still a Conservative Provocateur, Carlson Angles for Clicks, Not Fights," *The New York Times*, October 8, 2012, www.nytimes.com/2012/10/08/business/media/tucker-carlson-angles-for-daily-caller-clicks-not-fights.html.

154 **One new hire was Scott Greer:** Toni Airaksinen, "'Victimhood culture' has taken over college campuses, alleges new book," *USA Today*, January 23, 2017, www.usatoday.com/story/college/2017/01/23/victimhood-culture-has-taken-over-college-campuses-alleges-new-book/37426421/ ; "Scott Greer—Page 19," *Daily Caller*, April 11, 2025, dailycaller.com/author/Scott+Greer/page/19.

154 **While in college, Greer attended gatherings:** The Lamp, "Grinding the Greer," overthrowdotcom, November 18, 2016, overthrowdotcom.com/2016/11/18/grinding-the-greer; Erik Wemple, "Tucker Carlson Says He Didn't Know About a Racist at the *Daily Caller* Again," *The Washington Post*, September 5, 2018, www.washingtonpost.com/blogs/erik-wemple/wp/2018/09/05/tucker-carlson-says-he-didnt-know-about-a-racist-at-the-daily-caller-again.

154 **Wolves of Vinland:** Betsy Swan, "Inside Virginia's Creepy White-Power Wolf Cult," *The Daily Beast*, November 12, 2015, www.thedailybeast.com/inside-virginias-creepy-white-power-wolf-cult; Rosie Gray, "'Get Out While You

Can,'" *BuzzFeed News*, May 1, 2019, www.buzzfeednews.com/article/rosiegray/katie-mchugh.

154 **"while sex laws become more draconian for White men":** Rosie Gray, "A *Daily Caller* Editor Wrote for an 'Alt-Right' Website Using a Pseudonym," *The Atlantic*, September 5, 2018, www.theatlantic.com/politics/archive/2018/09/a-daily-caller-editor-wrote-for-an-alt-right-website-using-a-pseudonym/569335.

155 **According to journalist Hannah Gais:** Hannah Gais, "Leaked Emails Show How White Nationalists Have Infiltrated Conservative Media," *Splinter*, August 29, 2019, splinternews.com/leaked-emails-show-how-white-nationalists-have-infiltra-1837681245.

155 **"When given equal opportunity":** Erik Wemple, "*Daily Caller* reporter renounces racist, misogynistic writings," *The Washington Post*, September 14, 2017, www.washingtonpost.com/blogs/erik-wemple/wp/2017/09/14/daily-caller-reporter-renounces-racist-misogynistic-writings.

156 **"I take responsibility for all my actions":** Gray, "'Get Out While You Can.'"

156 **"I think it kind of goes without saying":** Erik Wemple, "'I can't reveal my confidential sources, Mr. Wemple': The Tucker Carlson interview," *The Washington Post*, November 29, 2017, www.washingtonpost.com/blogs/erik-wemple/wp/2017/11/29/i-cant-reveal-my-confidential-sources-mr-wemple-the-tucker-carlson-interview.

156 **the Eagle's Nest:** a former *Daily Caller* staffer, interview with the author.

157 **"Jews control the media":** Matt Lewis, "I Knew Katie McHugh Was a Racist. Did I Enable Her?" *The Daily Beast*, May 10, 2019, www.thedailybeast.com/i-knew-katie-mchugh-was-a-racist-and-i-didnt-do-enough-to-stop-her.

157 **"Do any of the [*Caller*] people":** Gray, "'Get Out While You Can.'"

157 **"how supposedly bad the American justice system is for blacks":** Scott Greer, "The Selective Racial Outrage Over Police Shootings," *Daily Caller*, January 3, 2016, dailycaller.com/2016/01/03/the-selective-racial-outrage-over-police-shootings; Scott Greer, "The Familiar Narrative Crashing the McKinney Pool Party," *Daily Caller*, June 9, 2015, dailycaller.com/2015/06/09/the-familiar-narrative-crashing-the-mckinney-pool-party.

157 **"white guilt porn":** Scott Greer, "Meet the Rich Man's Malcolm X," *Daily Caller*, July 15, 2015, dailycaller.com/2015/07/15/meet-the-rich-mans-malcolm-x.

157 **"signal a black power message":** Scott Greer, "Black Power—Brought to You by These Fine Sponsors," *Daily Caller*, February 8, 2016, dailycaller.com/2016/02/08/black-power-brought-to-you-by-pepsi.

157 **He celebrated the Confederate flag:** Scott Greer, "Not Even the Dead Can Have Confederate Flags," *Daily Caller*, May 22, 2016, dailycaller.com/2016/05/22/not-even-the-dead-can-have-confederate-flags.

157 **"six suspects charged are African-American":** Scott Greer, "Horror: Pregnant woman gang-raped in vicious Wisconsin home invasion," *Daily Caller*, March 13, 2014, dailycaller.com/2014/03/13/horror-pregnant-woman-gang-raped-in-vicious-wisconsin-home-invasion.

158 **the notorious anti-Semitic evolutionary psychologist Kevin MacDonald:** David Samuels, "American Racist," *Tablet*, June 11, 2020, www.tabletmag.com/sections/news/articles/kevin-macdonald-american-anti-semitism.

158 **"as a leading intellectual":** Jonah Bennett, "Donald Trump Jr Retweets Prominent Alt-Right Psychology Professor Kevin MacDonald," *Daily Caller*, August 30, 2016, dailycaller.com/2016/08/30/donald-trump-jr-retweets-prominent-alt-right-psychology-professor-kevin-macdonald.

158 **"alt-right personality":** Jonah Bennett, "Confirmed: *Politico* Ran Laughably Fake Short Story on Voter Suppression," *Daily Caller*, November 3, 2016, dailycaller.com/2016/11/03/alt-right-group-reveals-in-depth-how-the-black-voter-suppression-plan-causing-hysteria-was-a-complete-troll.

158 **"in to the ghettos in Philly":** Ben Schreckinger, "White nationalists plot Election Day show of force," *Politico*, last updated November 4, 2016, 3:47 p.m. EDT, www.politico.com/story/2016/11/suppress-black-vote-trump-campaign-230616.

158 **hosted a neo-Nazi podcast:** Andrew Marantz, "Birth of a White Supremacist," *The New Yorker*, October 16, 2017, www.newyorker.com/magazine/2017/10/16/birth-of-a-white-supremacist.

158 **"the echo":** Amanda Hess, "For the Alt-Right, the Message Is in the Punctuaton," *The New York Times*, June 11, 2016, www.nytimes.com/2016/06/11/arts/for-the-alt-right-the-message-is-in-the-punctuation.html

159 **He frequently rewrote:** Chuck Ross, "Teens Rob, Punch Elderly Woman in the Face [VIDEO]." *Daily Caller*, May 29, 2014, dailycaller.com/2014/05/29/teens-rob-punch-elderly-woman-in-the-face-video; Chuck Ross, "Group Attacked for Being White in Cincinnati," *Daily Caller*, May 30, 2014, dailycaller.com/2014/05/30/anti-white-hate-crime-being-investigated-in-cincinnati.

159 **"a burgeoning penchant for violence":** Chuck Ross, "Judge won't allow Trayvon Martin's texts in Zimmerman trial," *Daily Caller*, July 10, 2013, dailycaller.com/2013/07/10/judge-wont-allow-trayvon-martins-texts-in-zimmerman-trial.

159 **"'What if George hadn't gotten out of his truck?'":** Chuck Ross, "George Zimmerman grabs fire extinguisher, pulls family from overturned SUV," *Daily Caller*, July 22, 2013, dailycaller.com/2013/07/22/george-zimmerman-grabs-fire-extinguisher-pulls-family-from-overturned-suv/#ixzz2Zo8CCgTf.

159 **"British settlers built the USA":** Gray, "'Get Out While You Can.'"

159 **rising to 10.2 million unique visitors by October 2016:** David Ng, "*Breitbart News*, fiery conservative outlet buoyed by Trump victories, aims to go global," *Chicago Tribune*, last updated August 22, 2019, 2:01 a.m. CDT, www.chicagotribune.com/2016/11/21/breitbart-news-fiery-conservative-outlet-buoyed-by-trump-victory-aims-to-go-global.

160 **An analysis of Twitter:** Sarah Posner, "How Steve Bannon Created an Online Haven for White Nationalists," *Mother Jones*, August 22, 2016, www.motherjones.com/politics/2016/08/stephen-bannon-donald-trump-alt-right-breitbart-news.

160 **"Neither Steve [Bannon] nor I":** Lloyd Grove, "How Breitbart Unleashes Hate Mobs to Threaten, Dox, and Troll Trump Critics," *The Daily Beast*, March 1, 2016, www.thedailybeast.com/how-breitbart-unleashes-hate-mobs-to-threaten-dox-and-troll-trump-critics.

160 **According to a study:** Yochai Benkler, Robert Faris, and Hal Roberts, *Network Propaganda: Manipulation, Disinformation, and Radicalization in American Politics* (Oxford University Press, 2018), 108–109.

160 **"Trump's personal Pravda":** Wil S. Hylton, "Down the *Breitbart* Hole," *The New York Times Magazine*, August 16, 2017, www.nytimes.com/2017/08/16/magazine/breitbart-alt-right-steve-bannon.html.

160 **"a far-left liberal":** Chris Rovzar, "Matt Lewis Abandons *Politics Daily* for *Daily Caller*," *Intelligencer*, February 8, 2011, nymag.com/intelligencer/2011/02/matt_lewis_abandons_politics_d.html.

161 **"sack up":** Matt Lewis, "Time for Rush Limbaugh to Smother Trump," *The Daily Beast*, July 22, 2015, www.thedailybeast.com/time-for-rush-limbaugh-to-smother-trump.

161 **"I have criticized both candidates for their sins":** Matt K. Lewis, "Jesus, Take the Lever," *Daily Caller*, August 15, 2016, dailycaller.com/2016/08/15/jesus-take-the-lever.

161 **"In a White House race":** Jamie Weinstein, "Hillary Is Preferable to Trump Just Like Malaria Is Preferable to Ebola," *Daily Caller*, May 3, 2016, dailycaller.com/2016/05/03/hillary-is-preferable-to-trump-just-like-malaria-is-preferable-to-ebola.

161 **"a menace to American conservatism":** Colin Campbell, "The *National Review* just dedicated an entire issue to taking down Donald Trump—here's why," *Business Insider*, January 22, 2016, www.businessinsider.com/national-review-donald-trump-issue-2016-1.

161 **"Trump at his Trumpiest":** Matt Labash, "Nine Tales of Trump at His Trumpiest," *Washington Examiner*, January 22, 2016, www.washingtonexaminer.com/magazine/2321455/nine-tales-of-trump-at-his-trumpiest.

161 **After Trump clinched the GOP nomination:** Dana Bash and Eric Bradner, "Kristol's white knight: David French," *CNN Politics*, last updated June 1, 2016, 12:41 p.m. EDT, www.cnn.com/2016/05/31/politics/bill-kristol-david-french-independent-presidential-bid/index.html.

162 **"choosing to end his campaign":** Stephen F. Hayes, "Trump Has Decided to Live in *Breitbart*'s Alternative Reality," *Washington Examiner*, August 17, 2016, www.washingtonexaminer.com/news/15337/trump-has-decided-to-live-in-breitbarts-alternative-reality.

162 **"Republican spoiler":** David Horowitz, "Bill Kristol, Republican Spoiler, Renegade Jew," *Breitbart*, May 15, 2016, www.breitbart.com/politics/2016/05/15/bill-kristol-republican-spoiler-renegade-jew.

CHAPTER SIX

163 **"I don't ignore anything":** Ken Auletta, "Vox Fox," *The New Yorker*, May 19, 2003, www.newyorker.com/magazine/2003/05/26/vox-fox.

163 **"You're a loser":** Neil Patel, interview with the author.

164 **"I'm doing whatever they want me to do":** Brian Stelter, "Tucker Carlson Turns 40, Moves to Fox News," *The New York Times*, May 15, 2009, archive .nytimes.com/mediadecoder.blogs.nytimes.com/2009/05/15/tucker-carlson -turns-40-moves-to-fox-news.

165 **"Can you build me a network that can beat CNN?":** Tom Junod, "Roger Ailes on Roger Ailes: The Interview Transcripts, Part 1," *Esquire*, January 25, 2011, www.esquire.com/news-politics/news/a9313/roger-ailes-interview -5039254.

165 **A mere five years later:** David Bauder, "Fox News Overtakes CNN in Ratings," *Midland Daily News*, January 28, 2002, www.ourmidland.com/news /article/Fox-News-Overtakes-CNN-in-Ratings-7076902.php.

165 **"audience of the disaffected":** Sherman, *The Loudest Voice in the Room*, 226.

165 **"If there was nothing happening on the screen":** Roger Ailes, *You Are the Message: Getting What You Want by Being Who You Are* (Currency, 1988), 43.

165 **"There's a sort of, like, respecting the game":** Joseph Michalitsianos, "Rachel Maddow reveals she took broadcasting tips from Roger Ailes, praises Tucker Carlson and says he's 'doing great now'—and she turned down job offer at doomed CNN+ after her agents 'balked' at $10–$15M salary,' *Daily Mail*, last updated August 9, 2022, 2:52 p.m. EDT, www.dailymail.co.uk /news/article-11095915/Rachel-Maddow-reveals-mentored-Roger-Ailes -praises-Tucker-Carlson-new-interview.html.

166 **O'Reilly, who'd been a correspondent:** Auletta, "Vox Fox."

166 **"I look for people":** Junod, "Roger Ailes on Roger Ailes."

166 **"I could have put a dead raccoon on the air this year":** Bill Carter, "Fox News Fires a Star Host Over CNN Bid," *The New York Times*, September 6, 2001, www.nytimes.com/2001/09/06/business/fox-news-fires-a-star-host-over -cnn-bid.html.

166 **"Roger liked to bring people":** a former Fox executive, interview with the author.

166 **Gretchen Carlson (no relation to Tucker):** Michael M. Grynbaum and John Koblin, "Gretchen Carlson of Fox News Files Harassment Suit Against Roger Ailes," *The New York Times*, July 7, 2016, www.nytimes.com/2016/07 /07/business/media/gretchen-carlson-fox-news-roger-ailes-sexual-harassment -lawsuit.html.

166 **21st Century Fox, Fox News's parent company:** Michael M. Grynbaum and John Koblin, "Fox Settles with Gretchen Carlson Over Roger Ailes Sex Harassment Claims," *The New York Times*, September 7, 2016, www.nytimes .com/2016/09/07/business/media/fox-news-roger-ailes-gretchen-carlson -sexual-harassment-lawsuit-settlement.html.

166 **After lawyers hired by 21st Century Fox:** Gabriel Sherman, "The Revenge of Roger's Angels," *Intelligencer*, September 2016, nymag.com/intelligencer /2016/09/how-fox-news-women-took-down-roger-ailes.html.

167 **"college boys give my dad orders":** Auletta, "Vox Fox."

167 **"They think I'm this rube from Ohio":** Jon Klein, "The dark source of Roger Ailes's power," *The Washington Post*, May 19, 2017, www

.washingtonpost.com/opinions/the-dark-source-of-roger-ailess-power /2017/05/19/8f7c29f6-3cbd-11e7-a058-ddbb23c75d82_story.html.

167 **"Roger liked the idea":** a former Fox executive, interview with the author.

167 **The original anchor of *Special Report*:** "Brit Hume," Conversations with Bill Kristol, November 25, 2014, conversationswithbillkristol.org/transcript /brit-hume-transcript.

168 **A lantern-jawed, Ken-doll reporter:** Howard Kurtz, "Respectfully, Hume Torch Is Passed," *The Washington Post*, January 6, 2009, www.washingtonpost .com/wp-dyn/content/article/2009/01/05/AR2009010503271_pf.html.

168 **One was Jonah Goldberg:** Steve Hayes and Jonah Goldberg, "Why We Are Leaving Fox News," *The Dispatch*, November 21, 2021, thedispatch.com /article/why-we-are-leaving-fox-news.

168 **Another was Stephen Hayes:** David Folkenflik, "Bret Baier: The Next Generation of Fox News Anchor," *All Things Considered*, NPR, April 6, 2011, www.npr.org/2011/04/07/135176903/bret-baier-the-next-generation-of-fox -news-anchor.

169 **Carlson, who made his Fox debut:** Stelter, "Tucker Carlson Turns 40, Moves to Fox News."

169 **"Bret's a nice guy":** a Carlson friend, interview with the author.

169 **he jumped at the opportunity:** Eric Hananoki, "*Special Report*'s 'all-star' panel is overwhelmingly conservative: 67% over last 3 months," *Media Matters for America*, July 13, 2010, www.mediamatters.org/fox-news/special-reports -all-star-panel-overwhelmingly-conservative-67-over-past-3-months.

169 **"he'd often hole up":** a former *Daily Caller* staffer, interview with the author.

169 **"a handily elastic phrase":** *Special Report with Bret Baier*, Fox News, February 10, 2010, archive.org/details/FOXNEWS_20100210_230000 _Special_Report_With_Bret_Baier/start/3240/end/3300.

169 **"Free trade actually might help the American economy":** *Fox News*, "'Special Report' Panel on U.S. Export Business and Free Trade Agreements," *Fox News*, last updated January 25, 2017, 4:07 p.m. EST, www.foxnews.com /transcript/special-report-panel-on-u-s-export-business-and-free-trade -agreements.

170 **"He felt like Kristol":** a person familiar, interview with the author.

170 **"Johnny Fontane never gets that movie":** "The Godfather | 1972 | Mr. Woltz," uploaded on April 16, 2020, by MovieResidence, YouTube, 6 min., 43 sec., www.youtube.com/watch?v=lhRfNcv_seM.

170 **"Roger loved kicking Tucker"**: a former Fox executive, interview with the author.

170 **He not only careened around the set in a go-kart:** "Best of Tucker Carlson on 'Fox & Friends Weekend,'" *Fox News*, February 4, 2017, www .foxnews.com/video/5197956334001.

170 **played the cowbell with Blue Öyster Cult:** Sanneh, "Tucker Carlson's Fighting Words."

170 **"He brought the same energy":** a former Fox executive, interview with the author.

171 **"Are you videotaping me?":** "*Fox and Friends* co-host Tucker Carlson Fly-Fishing in Central Park," uploaded on April 13, 2013, by Yosef Bootski, YouTube, 6 min., 47 sec., www.youtube.com/watch?v=ylmkVh-vCRw&t=12s.

172 **"Are you surprised":** "Hillary Clinton Goes on the *O'Reilly Factor*," uploaded on May 2, 2008, by Veracifier, YouTube, 6 min., 30 sec., www.youtube.com/watch?v=HPJ6eAEEVNg.

173 **"highly intelligent man":** Jemima Kiss, "Rupert Murdoch heaps praise on Barack Obama," *The Guardian*, May 30, 2008, www.theguardian.com/media/2008/may/30/rupertmurdoch.wallstreetjournal.

173 **That summer, Murdoch and Obama held a secret meeting:** Howard Kurtz, "Obama Met with Fox News Executives," *The Washington Post*, September 2, 2008, www.washingtonpost.com/archive/national/2008/09/03/obama-met-with-fox-news-executives/0941fcf4-43e3-4b36-aa27-e75b4659860f.

173 **In September:** James Rainey, "Obama chats with O'Reilly," *Los Angeles Times*, September 5, 2008, www.latimes.com/archives/la-xpm-2008-sep-05-na-oreilly5-story.html.

173 **"Our relationship isn't about love":** Zev Chafets, "Exclusive Excerpt: *Roger Ailes Off Camera*," *Vanity Fair*, March 6, 2013, www.vanityfair.com/culture/2013/03/roger-ailes-biography-excerpt.

173 **"People need to be reminded":** Sherman, *The Loudest Voice in the Room*, xv.

173 **As Axelrod later told *New York Magazine*:** Gabriel Sherman, "The Elephant in the Green Room," *New York Magazine*, May 20, 2011, nymag.com/news/media/roger-ailes-fox-news-2011-5.

174 **he signed Ailes to a new five-year contract:** Brian Stelter, "Ailes Agrees to Remain at Fox News 5 More Years," *The New York Times*, November 21, 2008, www.nytimes.com/2008/11/21/business/media/21fox.html.

174 **"tentative truce":** Michael Wolff, "Tuesdays with Rupert," *Vanity Fair*, September 2, 2008, www.vanityfair.com/news/2008/10/wolff200810.

174 **"The government is promoting bad behavior!":** "CNBC's Rick Santelli's Chicago Tea Party," uploaded on February 19, 2009, by The Heritage Foundation, YouTube, 4 min., 36 sec., www.youtube.com/watch?v=zp-Jw-5Kx8k

174 **"There would not have been a Tea Party without Fox":** Sherman, "The Elephant in the Green Room."

174 **"rodeo clown":** Mark Leibovich, "Being Glenn Beck," *The New York Times*, October 3, 2010, www.nytimes.com/2010/10/03/magazine/03beck-t.html.

175 **"a deep-seated hatred":** Associated Press, "Glenn Beck: Obama Is a Racist," *CBS News*, July 29, 2009, www.cbsnews.com/news/glenn-beck-obama-is-a-racist.

175 **"reparations":** Linda Feldmann, "Glenn Beck leaving Fox: his 10 most controversial statements (so far)," *The Christian Science Monitor*, April 7, 2011, www.csmonitor.com/USA/Elections/2011/0407/Glenn-Beck-leaving

-Fox-his-10-most-controversial-statements-so-far/Beck-Obama-Agenda-Based-On-Reparations-And-A-Model-That-Will-Settle-Old-Racial-Scores-Through-New-Social-Justice.

175 **"progressivism is the cancer":** *Media Matters* Staff, "Beck: 'Progressivism is the cancer in America and it is eating our Constitution,'" *Media Matters for America*, February 20, 2010, www.mediamatters.org/glenn-beck/beckprogressivism-cancer-america-and-it-eating-our-constitution.

175 **since they all supported universal health care:** Michael Calderone, "History according to Beck," *Politico*, January 22, 2010, www.politico.com/story/2010/01/history-according-to-beck-031882.

175 **"puppet master":** Brian Stelter, "Glenn Beck's Attacks on George Soros Draw Heat," *The New York Times*, November 12, 2010, www.nytimes.com/2010/11/12/us/12beck.html.

175 **His program sometimes drew:** David Folkenflik, "Glenn Beck's Show on Fox News to End," *All Things Considered*, NPR, April 6, 2011, www.npr.org/2011/04/06/135181398/glenn-beck-to-leave-daily-fox-news-show.

175 **"train wreck":** Gayle Fee, "Laura Ingraham's wilder side revealed," *The Boston Herald*, July 17, 2008. www.bostonherald.com/2008/07/17/laura-ingrahams-wilder-side-revealed/.

175 **"the most highly regarded individual":** Stanley B. Greenberg, James Carville, Jim Gerstein, Payton M. Craighill, and Kate Monninger, *Special Report on the Tea Party Movement* (Democracy Corps, 2010), democracycorps.com/wp-content/uploads/2010/07/Tea-Party-Report-FINAL.pdf.

175 **Another poll found him to be:** Andrew Marantz, "How a Liberal Scholar of Conspiracy Theories Became the Subject of a Right-Wing Conspiracy Theory," *The New Yorker*, December 27, 2017, www.newyorker.com/culture/persons-of-interest/how-a-liberal-scholar-of-conspiracy-theories-became-the-subject-of-a-right-wing-conspiracy-theory.

175 **In August 2010, Beck drew three hundred thousand people:** Kate Zernike, Carl Hulse, and Brian Knowlton, "At Lincoln Memorial, a Call for Religious Rebirth," *The New York Times*, August 29, 2020, www.nytimes.com/2010/08/29/us/politics/29beck.html.

176 **"I've got one television station":** Jennifer Dauble, "CNBC Transcript: John Harwood, CNBC's Chief Washington Correspondent, Sits Down with President Barack Obama Today, Tuesday, June 16th at 4pm ET," CNBC, last updated August 3, 2010, 11:37 a.m. EDT, www.cnbc.com/2009/06/17/cnbc-transcript-john-harwood-cnbcs-chief-washington-correspondent-sits-down-with-president-barack-obama-today-tuesday-june-16th-at-4pm-et.html.

176 **"troublesome":** Jonathan Allen and Jonathan Martin, "Obama takes on talkers," *Politico*, April 3, 2010, www.politico.com/story/2010/04/obama-takes-on-talkers-035356.

176 **Nearly three hundred companies:** Leibovich, "Being Glenn Beck."

176 **"a product of the collapse of conservatism":** Brian Stelter and Bill Carter, "Fox News's Mad, Apocalyptic, Tearful Rising Star," *The New York Times*, March 30, 2009, www.nytimes.com/2009/03/30/business/media/30beck.html.

176 **who'd go on to marry Bill Kristol's daughter:** "Anne Kristol and Matthew Continetti," *The New York Times*, February 19, 2012, www.nytimes.com/2012/02/19/fashion/weddings/anne-kristol-matthew-continetti-weddings.html.

176 **"Not even the stupidest American liberal":** Matthew Continetti, "The Two Faces of the Tea Party," *Washington Examiner*, June 28, 2010, www.washingtonexaminer.com/magazine/638009/the-two-faces-of-the-tea-party.

176 **"People like Bill Kristol":** Ben Smith, "Beck blasts Kristol: 'Do anything to keep their little fiefdom together,'" *Politico*, February 7, 2011, www.politico.com/blogs/ben-smith/2011/02/beck-blasts-kristol-do-anything-to-keep-their-little-fiefdom-together-033148.

176 **he had his own production company:** Leibovich, "Being Glenn Beck."

177 **it boasted thirty million dollars in annual revenue:** Lacey Rose, "Glenn Beck Inc," *Forbes*, April 8, 2010, www.forbes.com/forbes/2010/0426/entertainment-fox-news-simon-schuster-glenn-beck-inc.html.

177 **"The problem with predicting the end of the world":** Stirewalt, *The Hangover*, "Chapter 6: Chris Stirewalt and John Podhoretz."

177 **"Jesus, Glenn":** a former Fox executive, interview with the author.

177 **In April 2011, Beck and Ailes jointly announced:** Bill Carter and Brian Stelter, "Beck and Fox End Relationship Grown Cold," *The New York Times*, April 7, 2011, www.nytimes.com/2011/04/07/business/media/07beck.html.

177 **Beck's new streaming channel:** David Folkenflik, "Smaller Audience, Bigger Payoff for Glenn Beck," *Morning Edition*, NPR, September 21, 2012, www.npr.org/2012/09/21/161495610/smaller-audience-bigger-payoff-for-glenn-beck.

177 **"Fox News primary":** David Folkenflik, "Iowa Race Fit Many Convenient Story Lines for Media," NPR, January 4, 2012, www.npr.org/2012/01/04/144665078/iowa-race-fit-many-convenient-story-lines-for-media.

178 **He tried to recruit:** Sherman, *The Loudest Voice in the Room*, 372–373.

178 **When Mitt Romney wound up:** Sherman, *The Loudest Voice in the Room*, 381.

178 **"If Romney wins":** Sherman, *The Loudest Voice in the Room*, 383.

178 **"marginalizing itself":** Henry Barbour, Sally Bradshaw, Ari Fleischer, Zori Fonalledas, and Glenn McCall, *Growth & Opportunity Project* (Republican National Committee, 2013), www.documentcloud.org/documents/624293-republican-national-committees-growth-and.html.

179 **"The Republican Savior":** "The Republican Savior | Feb. 18, 2013," *Time*, April 11, 2025, content.time.com/time/covers/0,16641,20130218,00.html.

179 **Working with seven other senators:** David Nakamura and Ed O'Keefe, "Timeline: The rise and fall of immigration reform," *The Washington Post*, June 26, 2014, www.washingtonpost.com/news/post-politics/wp/2014/06/26/timeline-the-rise-and-fall-of-immigration-reform.

179 **"amnesty":** Mike Allen, "Talk radio helped sink immigration reform," *Politico*, August 20, 2007, www.politico.com/story/2007/08/talk-radio-helped-sink-immigration-reform-005449; Bill O'Reilly, "O'Reilly: Fixing Immigration," *MetroWest Daily News*, last updated June 17, 2007, 5:04 p.m. ET, www

.metrowestdailynews.com/story/news/2007/06/17/o-reilly-fixing-immigration/41383716007.

179 **In January, Rubio traveled to Manhattan:** Jason Horowitz, "Marco Rubio Pushed for Immigration Reform with Conservative Media," *The New York Times*, February 28, 2016, www.nytimes.com/2016/02/28/us/politics/marco-rubio-pushed-for-immigration-reform-with-conservative-media.html.

179 **"You'll have to talk to Roger about that":** David Axelrod, *Believer: My Forty Years in Politics* (Penguin Books, 2015), 424.

180 **"I like your program":** *Frontline*, "Zero Tolerance," produced by Michael Kirk, October 22, 2019, www.pbs.org/wgbh/frontline/documentary/zero-tolerance/transcript/?.

180 **"I think it's probably the most thoughtful bill":** Brett LoGiurato, "Marco Rubio Is Trying To Charm Fox News And Rush Limbaugh Into Backing His Immigration Plan," *Business Insider*, January 29, 2013, www.businessinsider.com/marco-rubio-hannity-limbaugh-mark-levin-immigration-reform-bill-plan-2013-1.

180 **After the legislation passed the Senate:** Ed O'Keefe and David Nakamura, "GOP push for immigration reform thwarted," *The Washington Post*, April 4, 2014, www.washingtonpost.com/news/post-politics/wp/2014/04/04/gop-push-for-immigration-reform-thwarted.

181 **"My father has something big to tell":** Green, *Devil's Bargain*, 179.

181 **"Mexican immigrants, as with all immigrants":** Amy Chozick and Ashley Parker, "Titans Clash as Donald Trump's Run Fuels His Feud with Rupert Murdoch," *The New York Times*, July 22, 2015, www.nytimes.com/2015/07/22/us/politics/titans-clash-as-donald-trumps-run-fuels-his-feud-with-rupert-murdoch.html.

181 **Ailes left it to O'Reilly:** Maggie Haberman, "O'Reilly slams birther Trump," *Politico*, last updated March 30, 2011, 10:05 p.m. EDT, www.politico.com/story/2011/03/oreilly-slams-birther-trump-052271.

182 **"I can assure you one thing":** *Fox News*, "Krauthammer: Trump campaign announcement 'great showmanship,'" *Fox News*, last updated December 20, 2015, 3:04 p.m. EST, www.foxnews.com/politics/krauthammer-trump-campaign-announcement-great-showmanship.

182 **"Is there anyone on stage":** *Washington Post* Staff, "Annotated transcript: The Aug. 6 GOP debate," *The Washington Post*, August 6, 2015, www.washingtonpost.com/news/post-politics/wp/2015/08/06/annotated-transcript-the-aug-6-gop-debate.

183 **"He just crashed and burned":** "Frank Luntz focus group turns on Trump during GOP Debate," uploaded on August 6, 2015, by Fox News Insider, YouTube, 2 min., 46 sec., www.youtube.com/watch?v=Rpg28vLUPlg.

183 **"You could see there was blood coming out of her eyes":** Holly Yan, "Donald Trump's 'blood' comment about Megyn Kelly draws outrage," *CNN Politics*, last updated August 8, 2015, 1:57 p.m. EDT, www.cnn.com/2015/08/08/politics/donald-trump-cnn-megyn-kelly-comment/index.html.

183 **"has been treating me very unfairly":** Nick Gass, "Trump says he won't appear on Fox News," *Politico*, last updated September 23, 2015, 5:28 p.m. EDT, www.politico.com/story/2015/09/donald-trump-fox-news-213971.

183 **"He seemed a little lost":** a former Fox employee, interview with the author.

184 **"We can't trash Fox on the site":** Dylan Byers, "Mickey Kaus quits *Daily Caller* after Tucker Carlson pulls critical Fox News column," *Politico*, March 17, 2015, www.politico.com/blogs/media/2015/03/mickey-kaus-quits-daily-caller-after-tucker-carlson-pulls-critical-fox-news-column-204135.

184 **"I'm 100 percent [Rupert Murdoch's] bitch":** Aída Chávez, "Tucker Carlson on Rupert Murdoch in 2010 Radio Segment: 'I'm 100 Percent His Bitch,'" *The Intercept*, March 12, 2019, theintercept.com/2019/03/12/tucker-carlson-tapes-rupert-murdoch.

184 **"the single most repulsive person on the planet":** Tucker Carlson, "Reckless Gossip Merchants vs. Media Hand-Wringers," *Slate*, November 29, 1999, slate.com/human-interest/1999/11/reckless-gossip-merchants-vs-media-hand-wringers.html.

184 **"It's true you have better hair than I do":** Tucker Carlson, "Donald Trump Is Shocking, Vulgar and Right," *Politico*, January 28, 2016, www.politico.com/magazine/story/2016/01/donald-trump-is-shocking-vulgar-and-right-213572.

185 **"Even among conservatives in Fox":** LaCorte, interview with the author.

185 **"The project at Fox":** a former Fox producer, interview with the author.

185 **"unexpectedly good, energetic":** *Fox News*, "Looking for room in a crowded GOP presidential field," *Fox News*, last updated January 26, 2017, 10:03 a.m. EST, www.foxnews.com/transcript/looking-for-room-in-a-crowded-gop-presidential-field.

186 **"Avert your gaze from Trump":** *Fox News*, "Will new Trump polls quell the opposition?" *Fox News*, last updated January 23, 2017, 3:58 p.m. EST, www.foxnews.com/transcript/will-new-trump-polls-quell-the-opposition.

186 **"The economy and our culture":** *Fox News*, "What Donald Trump needs to convey in his RNC speech," *Fox News*, last updated January 23, 2017, 3:09 p.m. EST, www.foxnews.com/transcript/what-donald-trump-needs-to-convey-in-his-rnc-speech.

186 **In November, five days before the election:** Michael M. Grynbaum, "Fox News Lineup Begins to Take Shape," *The New York Times*, November 4, 2016, www.nytimes.com/2016/11/04/business/media/fox-news-lineup-begins-to-take-shape.html.

CHAPTER SEVEN

187 **Approximately 3.7 million viewers:** Oliver Darcy, "Tucker Carlson's Fox News show debuts to phenomenal ratings, beats both CNN and MSNBC combined," *Business Insider*, November 15, 2016, www.businessinsider.com/tucker-carlson-fox-news-show-ratings-2016-11.

187 **Fox became the most-watched network:** Lisa de Moraes, "Fox News Channel Crowned 2016's Most Watched Basic Cable Network," *Deadline*,

December 15, 2016, deadline.com/2016/12/fox-news-channel-2016-most-watched-basic-cable-network-1201871574.

187 **In the two-and-a-half months between the election and Trump's inauguration:** Michael Wolff, "Donald Trump Didn't Want to Be President," *Intelligencer*, January 3, 2018, nymag.com/intelligencer/2018/01/michael-wolff-fire-and-fury-book-donald-trump.html; Kia Makarechi, "A Semi-Complete and Baffling List of Everyone Who Walked into Trump Tower This Week," *Vanity Fair*, November 6, 2016, www.vanityfair.com/news/2016/11/trump-tower-guest-list; Jim Pickard and Matthew Garrahan, "Rupert Murdoch secretly sat in on interview with Donald Trump," *Financial Times*, February 10, 2017, www.ft.com/content/74408ae0-eeb3-11e6-ba01-119a44939bb6.

188 **Fox News personalities:** *CBS News*, "Who's been spotted at Trump Tower?" *CBS News*, last updated on December 13, 2016, 2:02 p.m. EST, www.cbsnews.com/pictures/whos-been-spotted-at-trump-tower-nyc-post-presidential-election.

188 **Sean Hannity, meanwhile:** Robert Draper, "How Donald Trump Set Off a Civil War Within the Right-Wing Media," *The New York Times Magazine*, October 2, 2016, www.nytimes.com/2016/10/02/magazine/how-donald-trump-set-off-a-civil-war-within-the-right-wing-media.html.

188 **"natural habitat":** "Tucker Carlson previews his new prime-time show on Fox News," *Fox News*, February 4, 2017, www.foxnews.com/video/5210174517001.

189 **One was Blake Neff:** Sarah Clark, "The Right Stuff," *Dartmouth Alumni Magazine*, July–August 2020, dartmouthalumnimagazine.com/blake-neff-tucker-carlson.

189 **"the most brilliant guy":** a former *Daily Caller* staffer, interview with the author.

189 **"Tucker knew":** a former Fox producer, interview with the author.

189 **Like everyone, he'd seen the pictures:** "Why we should never forget the monstrosity that was Donald Trump's gold apartment," *House & Garden*, July 24, 2020, www.houseandgarden.co.uk/gallery/donald-trump-gold-apartment.

189 **"innkeeper's mentality":** a person familiar, interview with the author.

190 **"Vichy Republicans":** Michael Graham, "'Vichy Republicans' Prove Trump Right About Gutless Establishment," *Washington Examiner*, March 21, 2016, www.washingtonexaminer.com/news/1496696/vichy-republicans-prove-trump-right-about-gutless-establishment.

190 **"Come on, Trump's not evil":** John McCormack, "What Happened to Tucker Carlson?" *The Dispatch*, October 1, 2024, thedispatch.com/article/what-happened-tucker-carlson.

190 **"What's the show going to be about?":** www.facebook.com/watch/?v=371702426498416

191 **which saw its digital subscriptions triple:** Sara Fischer, "Trump bump: *NYT* and *WaPo* subscriptions tripled since 2016," *Axios*, November 24, 2020, www.axios.com/2020/11/24/washington-post-new-york-times-subscriptions.

191 **"Democracy Dies in Darkness":** Paul Farhi, "*The Washington Post*'s new slogan turns out to be an old saying," *The Washington Post*, February 24, 2017, www.washingtonpost.com/lifestyle/style/the-washington-posts-new-slogan-turns-out-to-be-an-old-saying/2017/02/23/cb199cda-fa02-11e6-be05-1a3817ac21a5_story.html.

192 **"After food, water, and sex":** Carlson, *Politicians, Partisans, and Parasites*, 93.

193 **a thirty-five-page dossier:** Ken Bensinger, Miriam Elder, and Mark Schoofs, "These Reports Allege Trump Has Deep Ties to Russia," *BuzzFeed News*, last updated January 10, 2017, 9:09 p.m., www.buzzfeednews.com/article/kenbensinger/these-reports-allege-trump-has-deep-ties-to-russia.

193 **for almost two years:** Erik Wemple, "Rachel Maddow rooted for the Steele dossier to be true. Then it fell apart," *The Washington Post*, December 26, 2019, www.washingtonpost.com/opinions/2019/12/26/rachel-maddow-rooted-steele-dossier-be-true-then-it-fell-apart.

193 **by the time special counsel Robert Mueller:** Special Counsel Robert S. Mueller III, *Report on the Investigation into Russian Interference in the 2016 Presidential Election* (US Department of Justice, 2019), apps.npr.org/documents/document.html?id=5955997-Muellerreport.

193 **"Let's say I had an unverified document":** "Tucker to *BuzzFeed* editor: Your agenda cloaked as journalism," uploaded on January 25, 2017, by Fox News, YouTube, 11 min., 34 sec., www.youtube.com/watch?v=Z9Yww3O5wz4; Brian Flood, "Tucker Carlson Confronts *BuzzFeed* Boss Ben Smith: 'You Just Don't Like Trump' (Video)," *The Wrap*, January 26, 2017, www.thewrap.com/tucker-carlson-takes-on-buzzfeeds-ben-smith.

194 **Boot wrote a series of influential articles:** Boot, "The Case for American Empire."

194 **"mark the moment":** Emile Doak, "The Iraq War at Twenty," *The American Conservative*, March 17, 2023, www.theamericanconservative.com/the-iraq-war-at-twenty.

194 **"I would sooner vote for Josef Stalin":** Alexander Burns, "Anti-Trump Republicans Call for a Third-Party Option," *The New York Times*, March 3, 2016, www.nytimes.com/2016/03/03/us/politics/anti-donald-trump-republicans-call-for-a-third-party-option.html.

195 **"cheerleader":** Ian Schwartz, "Fireworks: Tucker Carlson vs. Max Boot on Russia: You Dismiss Anyone Who Doesn't Share Your View as a Nazi," *RealClearPolitics*, July 13, 2017, www.realclearpolitics.com/video/2017/07/13/fireworks_tucker_carlson_vs_max_boot_on_russia_you_dismiss_anyone_who_doesnt_share_your_view_as_a_nazi.html.

195 **"political commentator":** Alex Mohajer, "The Legitimate President," *The Huffington Post*, last updated January 28, 2017, www.huffpost.com/entry/the-legitimate-president_b_587930cfe4b077a19d180d84.

195 **the section of the website:** Sydney Ember, "*HuffPost*, Breaking from Its Roots, Ends Unpaid Contributions," *The New York Times*, January 18, 2018, www.nytimes.com/2018/01/18/business/media/huffpost-unpaid-contributors.html.

195 **"How does this work exactly?":** "Trump Not Legit? Tucker Carlson & *Huffington Post* Writer Alex Mohajer," uploaded on January 20, 2017, by

Disturbing Trends, YouTube, 7 min., 48 sec., www.youtube.com/watch?v=6F-TKEPaajY.

195 **"It's not just white supremacy":** "Tucker Carlson Destroys UConn Professor Matthew Hughey Says White Supremacists Caused Trump Win," uploaded on January 24, 2017, by Ben Browski, YouTube, 7 min., 45 sec., www.youtube.com/watch?v=M9t4Uv4t2CQ.

196 **who'd refused Carlson's booker's invitations:** Ben Collins, "Tucker Carlson Couldn't Debate the Anti-Trump Organizers He Wanted, So This Actor Stepped Up," *The Daily Beast*, February 21, 2017. www.thedailybeast.com/tucker-carlson-couldnt-debate-the-anti-trump-organizer-he-wanted-so-this-actor-stepped-up/.

196 **"What's the point of it?":** "Not My President's Day Protests Across Country Shane Saunders Tucker Carlson," uploaded on February 21, 2017, by USA News Live, YouTube, 5 min., 54 sec., www.youtube.com/watch?v=zs1lTZyoJyA

196 **"You Can't Cuck The Tuck":** "You Can't Cuck the Tuck Vol. 1," uploaded on June 3, 2017, by High Energy, YouTube, 21 min., 11 sec., www.youtube.com/watch?v=GdzEpXDodUk&list=PLVX7bhAtR-yYhYzJYWF5MkfYsrEZ_H0oS.

197 **"The reason the debate era":** a former Fox producer, interview with the author.

197 **Megyn Kelly decamped to NBC News:** Jim Rutenberg, "Megyn Kelly's Jump to NBC from Fox News Will Test Her, and the Networks," *The New York Times*, January 3, 2017, www.nytimes.com/2017/01/03/business/media/megyn-kelly-nbc-fox-news.html.

197 **His ratings:** Lisa de Moraes, "Tucker Carlson's First Two Weeks in Primetime Outstrip Megyn Kelly on FNC," *Deadline*, January 24, 2017, deadline.com/2017/01/tucker-carlson-beats-megyn-kelly-ratings-first-two-weeks-1201893291.

197 **Three months later:** Emily Steel and Michael S. Schmidt, "Bill O'Reilly Thrives at Fox News, Even as Harassment Settlements Add Up," *The New York Times*, April 1, 2017, www.nytimes.com/2017/04/01/business/media/bill-oreilly-sexual-harassment-fox-news.html.

197 **Murdoch forced O'Reilly out:** Emily Steel and Michael S. Schmidt, "Bill O'Reilly Is Forced Out at Fox News," *The New York Times*, April 19, 2017, www.nytimes.com/2017/04/19/business/media/bill-oreilly-fox-news-allegations.html.

197 **made easier by the fact:** Michael M. Grynbaum and John Koblin, "For Fox News, Life After Bill O'Reilly Will Feature Tucker Carlson," *The New York Times*, April 19, 2017, www.nytimes.com/2017/04/19/business/media/life-after-bill-oreilly-for-fox-news-to-include-tucker-carlson.html.

198 **"the unofficial chief of staff":** Robert Costa, Sarah Ellison, and Josh Dawsey, "Hannity's rising role in Trump's world: 'He basically has a desk in the place,'" *The Washington Post*, April 17, 2018, www.washingtonpost.com/politics/hannitys-rising-role-in-trumps-world-he-basically-has-a-desk-in-the-place/2018/04/17/e2483018-4260-11e8-8569-26fda6b404c7_story.html.

198 **Laura Ingraham, whom Murdoch plucked from talk radio:** Michael M. Grynbaum, "Laura Ingraham Is Ready to Rev Up Fox News," *The New York*

Times, October 25, 2017, www.nytimes.com/2017/10/25/business/media/laura-ingraham-fox-news.html; Bill Powell, "How Fox News' Laura Ingraham Used Trump to Become a Political Rockstar," *Newsweek*, November 24, 2017, www.newsweek.com/2017/11/24/fox-news-laura-ingraham-used-donald-trump-support-711340.html.

198 **"I wanted to get you on":** Brian Stelter, *Hoax: Donald Trump, Fox News, and the Dangerous Distortion of Truth* (One Signal Publishers, 2020), 86.

198 **"video effect":** Abby Ohlhesier, "No, Fox News didn't get President Trump to flicker the White House lights," *The Washington Post*, January 27, 2017. www.washingtonpost.com/news/the-intersect/wp/2017/01/27/no-fox-news-didnt-get-president-trump-to-flicker-the-white-house-lights/.

198 **old friends with White House press secretary Sean Spicer:** Sean Spicer, interview with the author.

198 **"perhaps the smartest person":** a person familiar, interview with the author.

199 **Sessions allowed Carlson to accompany him:** Joe Concha, "Tucker Carlson to interview Sessions from El Salvador," *The Hill*, July 27, 2017, thehill.com/homenews/media/344112-tucker-carlson-to-interview-sessions-from-el-salvador.

199 **"Before long, some of these guys":** "'Hunting MS-13': What we learned," uploaded on July 31, 2017, by Fox News, YouTube, 4 min., 24 sec., www.youtube.com/watch?v=nsphTRgYZTg.

199 **"Tucker didn't seek it":** a former White House official, interview with the author.

199 **"The W.H. is functioning perfectly":** Donald J. Trump (@realDonaldTrump), "The W.H. is functioning perfectly, focused on HealthCare, Tax Cuts/Reform & many other things. I have very little time for watching T.V.," Twitter (now X), July 12, 2017, x.com/realDonaldTrump/status/885131482397908992.

200 **"If you heard a tape":** a former Fox colleague of Carlson's, interview with the author.

200 **"Sweden had its first terrorist, Islamic attack":** "Sweden and Migrants, Tucker Carlson Interviews Ami Hrowitz, Fox News," uploaded on February 20, 2017, by Chris Hansen, YouTube, 5 min., 25 sec., www.youtube.com/watch?app=desktop&v=Qk7V_VF8Ehs.

200 **"You look at what's happening in Germany":** *CNN Newsroom*, "President Trump addresses what he calls a Campaign rally in Melbourne, Florida. Aired 6–7 ET," CNN, February 18, 2017, transcripts.cnn.com/show/cnr/date/2017-02-18/segment/11.

200 **In fact, there hadn't been a terrorist attack in Sweden:** John F. Burns and Ravi Somaiya, "After Attack Hits Sweden, Focus Turns to Suspect," *The New York Times*, December 13, 2010, www.nytimes.com/2010/12/13/world/europe/13sweden.html.

201 **"Sweden? Terror attack?":** Carl Bildt (@carlbildt), "Sweden? Terror attack? What has he been smoking? Questions abound," Twitter (now X), February 19, 2017, x.com/carlbildt/status/833219648044855296.

201 **"My statement as to what's happening in Sweden":** Donald J. Trump (@realDonaldTrump), "My statement as to what's happening in Sweden was in reference to a story that was broadcast on @FoxNews concerning immigrants & Sweden," Twitter (now X), February 19, 2017, x.com/realdonaldtrump/status/833435244451753984.

201 **"From an Anchor's Lips to Trump's Ears":** Peter Baker and Sewell Chan, "From an Anchor's Lips to Trump's Ears to Sweden's Disbelief," *The New York Times*, February 20, 2017, www.nytimes.com/2017/02/20/world/europe/trump-pursues-his-attack-on-sweden-with-scant-evidence.html.

201 **"minute-by-minutes":** Nicholas Confessore, "How Tucker Carlson Reshaped Fox News—and Became Trump's Heir," *The New York Times*, April 30, 2022, www.nytimes.com/2022/04/30/us/tucker-carlson-fox-news.html.

202 **Carlson was particularly interested:** Doug Bandow, "Why Is Trump Abandoning the Foreign Policy That Brought Him Victory?" *The National Interest*, March 10, 2017, nationalinterest.org/blog/the-skeptics/why-trump-abandoning-the-foreign-policy-brought-him-victory-19738.

202 **When Tillerson was on the verge of appointing Elliott Abrams:** David A. Graham, "Trump's Neocon?" *The Atlantic*, February 6, 2017, www.theatlantic.com/politics/archive/2017/02/trumps-neocon-elliott-abrams/515784.

202 **Carlson had Kentucky senator Rand Paul:** Jason Zengerle, "Rex Tillerson and the Unraveling of the State Department," *The New York Times Magazine*, October 17, 2017, www.nytimes.com/2017/10/17/magazine/rex-tillerson-and-the-unraveling-of-the-state-department.html.

202 **"Powell seems like a nice person":** "Nikki Haley's possible replacement Dina Powell: Good for US?" Fox News, October 10, 2018, www.foxnews.com/video/5847198508001.

203 **"The president will have no choice":** "Did Fox's Tucker Carlson stop Trump's strike against Iran?" MSNBC, June 21, 2019, www.msnbc.com/the-beat-with-ari/watch/did-fox-s-tucker-carlson-stop-trump-s-strike-against-iran-62444613884.

203 **Trump appeared as if he was going to heed their advice:** Michael D. Shear, Eric Schmitt, Michael Crowley, and Maggie Haberman, "Strikes on Iran Approved by Trump, Then Abruptly Pulled Back," *The New York Times*, June 20, 2019, www.nytimes.com/2019/06/20/world/middleeast/iran-us-drone.html; Peter Baker, Eric Schmitt, and Michael Crowley, "An Abrupt Move That Stunned Aides: Inside Trump's Aborted Attack on Iran," *The New York Times*, June 21, 2019, www.nytimes.com/2019/09/21/us/politics/trump-iran-decision.html.

203 **"The neocons still wield enormous power":** "Tucker: US came within minutes of war with Iran," Fox News, June 21, 2019, www.foxnews.com/video/6051003481001.

204 **"America appears to be lumbering toward a new Middle East war":** Matt Gertz, "How the Fox News Cabinet is responding to Soleimani's killing," *Media Matters for America*, January 3, 2020, www.mediamatters.org/fox-news/how-fox-news-cabinet-responding-soleimanis-killing.

204 **"a huge victory":** Victor Garcia, "Sean Hannity: US forces, State Department, Trump 'on high alert' after Iranian general Soleimani's death," *Fox News*, January 2, 2020, www.foxnews.com/media/sean-hannity-on-iranian-generals-death-a-huge-victory-and-total-leadership-by-the-president.

204 **"If Iran could":** Peter Wade, "Fox News Host Is All-In on Trump's War Crimes Threats," *Rolling Stone*, January 7, 2020, www.rollingstone.com/politics/politics-news/fox-news-host-pete-hegseth-is-all-in-on-trumps-war-crimes-threats-934449.

204 **And, once again, Trump listened:** Rosie Gray and Miriam Elder, "Fox News Hosts Were Against a Ground War in Iran. Trump Listened," *BuzzFeed News*, last updated January 8, 2020, 10:03 p.m., www.buzzfeednews.com/article/rosiegray/fox-news-trump-war-iran.

205 **who'd recently written a series of articles:** "Christopher F. Rufo," *City Journal*, April 11, 2025, www.city-journal.org/person/christopher-f-rufo.

205 **"critical race theory":** Sarah Ellison, "Tucker Carlson's chief writer resigns over racist and sexist posts, the latest trouble for Fox's most controversial star," *The Washington Post*, July 11, 2020, www.washingtonpost.com/lifestyle/style/tucker-carlsons-writer-resigns-over-racist-and-sexist-posts-the-latest-trouble-for-foxs-most-controversial-star/2020/07/11/2a50dbba-c394-11ea-b178-bb7b05b94af1_story.html.

205 **The next morning, Rufo received a phone call:** Jake Lahut and Bryan Metzger, "Trump issued an executive order on Critical Race Theory after seeing a segment about it on Tucker Carlson's show: book," *Business Insider*, December 7, 2021, www.businessinsider.com/trump-critical-race-theory-found-out-from-tucker-carlson-book-2021-12.

205 **"Tucker frames the narrative":** Michael Kranish, "How Tucker Carlson became the voice of White grievance," *The Washington Post*, July 14, 2021, www.washingtonpost.com/politics/tucker-carlson/2021/07/13/398fa720-dd9f-11eb-a501-0e69b5d012e5_story.html.

205 **"Tucker was the hot girl":** a former Trump White House official, interview with the author.

206 **"You can't work in this White House":** Alyssa Farah Griffin, interview with the author.

206 **"The show itself":** a former Fox producer, interview with the author.

207 **"finance-based economy":** Tucker Carlson, "Tucker Carlson: Mitt Romney supports the status quo. But for everyone else, it's infuriating," *Fox News*, last updated January 3, 2019, 10:48 a.m. EST, www.foxnews.com/opinion/tucker-carlson-mitt-romney-supports-the-status-quo-but-for-everyone-else-its-infuriating.

208 **"vulture capitalism":** "Hedge fund forced Cabela's merger, decimated jobs in Sidney, Nebraska," uploaded on December 3, 2019, by Fox News, YouTube, 10 min., 45 sec., www.youtube.com/watch?v=UatnTSwEUoc.

209 **"a godsend":** "AEI reportedly peddled pro-oxycontin stories for Purdue," Fox News, December 6, 2019, www.foxnews.com/video/6113827111001.

209 **"defecate in public":** "Gypsies' failure to assimilate sparks uproar in Pa.," Fox News, September 12, 2017, www.foxnews.com/video/5510858469001.

210 **"we've got a moral obligation":** Tucker Carlson, "Tucker Carlson: Why no one ever makes the economic case for mass immigration," *Fox News*, December 14, 2018, www.foxnews.com/opinion/tucker-carlson-why-no-one-ever-makes-the-economic-case-for-mass-immigration.

210 **"white supremacy":** "Tucker Carlson: White Supremacy Is a 'Hoax' and 'Not a Real Problem in America,'" uploaded on August 6, 2019, by Contemptor, YouTube, 2 min., www.youtube.com/watch?v=QW-T1_Nf-pc.

210 **"Anything he's reading off the teleprompter":** Clark, "The Right Stuff."

210 **"foodie faggots":** Oliver Darcy, "Tucker Carlson's top writer resigns after secretly posting racist and sexist remarks in online forum," *CNN Business*, last updated July 11, 2020, 4:06 p.m. EDT, www.cnn.com/2020/07/10/media/tucker-carlson-writer-blake-neff/index.html.

210 **a reference to the twenty-eight-year-old Black woman:** David Montgomery, "Sandra Bland, It Turns Out, Filmed Traffic Stop Confrontation Herself," *The New York Times*, May 7, 2019, www.nytimes.com/2019/05/07/us/sandra-bland-video-brian-encinia.html.

211 **"the least racist person":** Blake Neff, interview with the author.

211 **"We don't endorse those words":** Jeremy Barr, "Tucker Carlson says there's 'no connection' between writer's hateful blog posts and his Fox News show," *The Washington Post*, July 13, 2020, www.washingtonpost.com/media/2020/07/13/tucker-carlson-says-theres-no-connection-between-writers-hateful-blog-posts-his-fox-news-show.

211 **When Scott Greer, Carlson's and Neff's old *Daily Caller* colleague:** Ian Mason, "Scott Greer Talks 'No Campus for White Men' on 'Tucker Carlson Tonight' [Video]," *Daily Caller*, February 11, 2017, dailycaller.com/2017/02/11/scott-greer-talks-no-campus-for-white-men-on-tucker-carlson-tonight-video.

211 **"the sweet treats of scholarship":** Ellison, "Tucker Carlson's chief writer resigns."

212 **"If you didn't catch the German shepherd whistles":** Frank Bruni, "Tucker Carlson Is Not Your New Best Friend," *The New York Times*, January 11, 2020, www.nytimes.com/2020/01/11/opinion/sunday/tucker-carlson.html.

212 **"Tucker FILLS Liberal Kike with LEAD":** Joseph Bernstein, "Data Shows That Tucker Carlson Is *The Daily Stormer*'s Favorite Pundit," *BuzzFeed News*, November 28, 2018, www.buzzfeednews.com/article/josephbernstein/tucker-carlson-fox-news-daily-stormers-favorite-pundit.

213 **"I've lived here for fifty years":** Tucker Carlson, "New York Times changes 'Trump urges unity vs. racism' headline after backlash," Fox News, August 6, 2019. www.foxnews.com/transcript/new-york-times-changes-trump-urges-unity-vs-racism-headline-after-backlash.

213 **Goldberg sent him a text message:** a person familiar, interview with the author.

214 **"I create monsters":** Michael Wolff, *The Fall: The End of Fox News and the Murdoch Dynasty* (Henry Holt and Company, 2023), 177.

214 **"probably too busy":** Tony Schwartz, "Wallace Taped in Ethnic Remark," *The New York Times*, January 12, 1982, www.nytimes.com/1982/01/12/arts/wallace-taped-in-ethnic-remark.html.

214 **Six years later:** "Mike Wallace apologizes for racist remark," UPI, May 3, 1987, www.upi.com/Archives/1987/05/03/Mike-Wallace-apologizes-for-racist-remark/6425547012800.

215 **Carlson decided to decorate:** a person familiar, interview with the author.

215 **Carlson, meanwhile, thought Hannity:** people familiar, interviews with the author.

215 **"People can make money":** "Tucker Snubs Hannity During Nightly Handoff 7/21/2020," uploaded on July 21, 2020, by Corona Airlines, YouTube, 4 min., 16 sec., www.youtube.com/watch?v=wAVagsy3pQQ&t=237s.

215 **Carlson's biggest enemy at Fox:** Erik Wemple, "Will Fox News's vaunted PR machine outlive Roger Ailes?" *The Washington Post*, July 20, 2016, www.washingtonpost.com/blogs/erik-wemple/wp/2016/07/20/will-fox-newss-vaunted-pr-machine-outlive-roger-ailes; Stav Ziv, "Who Is Irena Briganti? Megyn Kelly Says Fox News Flack Is 'Vindictive,' Pushes 'Negative Articles' on Sexual Harassment Accusers," *Newsweek*, last updated October 25, 2017, 8:13 a.m. EDT, www.newsweek.com/who-irena-briganti-megyn-kelly-says-fox-news-flack-vindictive-pushes-negative-691077.

216 **He became so convinced:** Wolff, *The Fall*, 96.

216 **a consulting contract to Arthur Schwartz:** person familiar, interview with the author

216 **featured spots from blue-chip brands:** Tom Kludt, "Tucker Carlson's new normal? Commercial breaks with fewer commercials," *CNN Business*, last updated April 2, 2019, 7:12 p.m. EDT, www.cnn.com/2019/04/02/media/tucker-carlson-advertisers/index.html; Tiffany Hsu, "Fox News Host Tucker Carlson Loses More Advertisers," June 12, 2020, www.nytimes.com/2020/06/12/business/media/tucker-carlson-fox-news-advertisers.html.

216 **by 2020 more than a third of the ad spending:** Hsu, "Fox News Host Tucker Carlson Loses More Advertisers."

217 **"You couldn't ask for a better relationship":** Sarah Ellison, "Fox News Host Tucker Carlson is loudly ignoring impeachment. It 'is not only dumb, it's boring,'" *The Washington Post*, November 12, 2019. www.washingtonpost.com/lifestyle/style/impeachment-is-not-only-dumb-its-boring-fox-news-host-tucker-carlson-is-covering-impeachment-by-loudly-ignoring-it/2019/11/12/93e3ac46-036a-11ea-9518-1e76abc088b6_story.html.

217 **"I'm an elitist by temperament":** Jamie Weinstein, host, *The Jamie Weinstein Show*, podcast, episode 73, "Tucker Carlson," October 15, 2018, podcasts.apple.com/us/podcast/episode-73-tucker-carlson/id1158060960?i=1000421861470.

217 **It was Lachlan, Carlson told them:** Nicholas Confessore, "How Tucker Carlson Stoked White Fear to Conquer Cable," *The New York Times*, April 30, 2022, www.nytimes.com/2022/04/30/us/tucker-carlson-gop-republican-party.html.

218 **"Tucker and I would be so grateful":** email from Susie Carlson to Hunter Biden, October 14, 2014.

218 **"totally counterproductive":** "Tucker Carlson On the Media's Deception."

218 **"He loves Washington":** Email from Tucker Carlson to Hunter Biden, November 11, 2014.

219 **"Just lost my shit":** Email from Tucker Carlson to Hunter Biden, August 27, 2015.

219 **"Are you kidding?":** Email from Tucker Carlson to Hunter Biden, August 28, 2015.

219 **A waiter at Metropolitan Club:** Michael Wolff, *Too Famous: The Rich, The Powerful, the Wishful, the Notorious, the Damned* (Henry Holt and Company, 2021), 93.

219 **"I can't really go to a lot of restaurants anymore":** Weinstein, *The Jamie Weinstein Show*, "Tucker Carlson."

220 **"promoting hate":** Allyson Chiu, "'They were threatening me and my family': Tucker Carlson's home targeted by protesters," *The Washington Post*, November 8, 2018, www.washingtonpost.com/nation/2018/11/08/they-were-threatening-me-my-family-tucker-carlsons-home-targeted-by-protesters.

220 **"I think Tucker is a terrible influence":** Max Boot (@MaxBoot), "I think Tucker is a terrible influence on modern America but that doesn't justify harassing him at home. Go high, not low," Twitter (now X), November 7, 2018, x.com/MaxBoot/status/1060367776475500544.

221 **"We're an unapologetically conservative magazine":** "New *Weekly Standard* Editor Fights Fake News with Enhanced Resources, Real Journalism," WBUR, April 10, 2017, www.wbur.org/hereandnow/2017/04/10/weekly-standard-stephen-hayes.

221 **"The pathetic and dishonest *Weekly Standard*":** Donald J. Trump (@realDonaldTrump), "The pathetic and dishonest *Weekly Standard*, run by failed prognosticator Bill Kristol (who, like many others, never had a clue), is flat broke and out of business. Too bad. May it rest in peace!" Twitter, December 15, 2018, twitter.com/realDonaldTrump/status/1073974873939169282

221 **"Washington is littered with formerly impressive people":** "Tucker: My response to my 'friend' Bill Kristol," uploaded on August 17, 2017, by *Fox News*, YouTube, 3 min. 13 sec., www.youtube.com/watch?v=g9YYZ8_HmNs.

222 **"Kristol was always encouraging me":** Tucker Carlson, *Ship of Fools*, 111.

222 **his deal with Simon & Schuster**: Associated Press, "Tucker Carlson Gets Two-Book, Eight-Figure Deal," *The Hollywood Reporter*, May 2, 2017, www.hollywoodreporter.com/lifestyle/arts/tucker-carlson-gets-two-book-eight-figure-deal-999704.

222 **But on that December evening:** former *Weekly Standard* staffers, interviews with the author.

CHAPTER EIGHT

223 **"I'm implicated":** a person familiar, interview with the author.

224 **He was angry about the way Trump had treated Jeff Sessions:** Jason Zengerle, "How Alabama's Senate Primary Became a Trump Loyalty Contest," *The New York Times Magazine*, February 10, 2020, www.nytimes.com/2020/02/10/magazine/alabama-republican-primary-senate.html.

224 **"a fucking baby":** a person familiar, interview with the author.

224 **Then Trump endorsed Tommy Tuberville:** Betsy Klein and Alex Rogers, "Trump endorses Tuberville over Jeff Sessions ahead of Alabama runoff," CNN, March 11, 2020, www.cnn.com/2020/03/10/politics/trump-endorses-tommy-tuberville-over-jeff-sessions-alabama-us-senate/index.html.

224 **They first met when Stone was raising money for Ronald Reagan's 1980 presidential campaign:** Marie Brenner, "How Donald Trump and Roy Cohn's Ruthless Symbiosis Changed America," *Vanity Fair*, June 28, 2017, www.vanityfair.com/news/2017/06/donald-trump-roy-cohn-relationship.

225 **Stone was not forthcoming, and in 2019 federal prosecutors charged him:** Mark Mazzetti, Eileen Sullivan, and Maggie Haberman, "Indicting Roger Stone, Mueller Shows Link Between Trump Campaign and WikiLeaks," *The New York Times*, January 25, 2019, www.nytimes.com/2019/01/25/us/politics/roger-stone-trump-mueller.html.

225 **Later that year he was convicted on all seven counts:** Sharon LaFraniere and Zach Montague, "Roger Stone Is Convicted of Impeding Investigators in a Bid to Protect Trump," *The New York Times*, November 15, 2019, www.nytimes.com/2019/11/15/us/politics/roger-stone-trial-guilty.html.

225 **Governor Rod Blagojevich, the former Illinois Democratic governor who'd tried to sell a senate seat:** Bobby Allyn, "Former Illinois Gov. Rod Blagojevich Released Following Trump's Commutation," NPR, February 18, 2020, www.npr.org/2020/02/18/807057090/trump-commutes-sentence-of-former-illinois-gov-rod-blagojevich.

225 **Crystal Munoz, a Texas woman who'd been sentenced to twenty years:** "Trump grants clemency to Crystal Munoz, former inmate friends with Alice Marie Johnson," NBC News, February 20, 2020, www.nbcnews.com/news/us-news/trump-grants-clemency-crystal-munoz-former-inmate-friends-alice-marie-n1139786.

225 **In a tense White House meeting:** Maggie Haberman, *Confidence Man: The Making of Donald Trump and the Breaking of America*, Penguin Press, 2022, 410.

225 **"son":** a person familiar, interview with the author.

225 **"The typical rapist":** Victor Garcia, "Tucker Carlson: Trump must 'pardon Roger Stone or commute his sentence,'" Fox News, February 12, 2020, www.foxnews.com/media/tucker-carlson-roger-stone-pardon-commute-sentence.

226 **Rupert Murdoch, who would turn eighty-nine a few days later:** Ben Smith, "As Fox News Played Down the Coronavirus, Its Chief Protected Himself," *The New York Times*, March 23, 2020, www.nytimes.com/2020/03/23/business/media/fox-news-coronavirus-rupert-murdoch.html.

226 **"This is the end of something":** a person familiar, interview with the author.

226 **"'Oh, let's bludgeon Trump with this new hoax'":** J. M. Rieger, "Sean Hannity denied calling coronavirus a hoax nine days after he called coronavirus

a hoax," *The Washington Post*, March 19, 2020, www.washingtonpost.com/politics/2020/03/19/sean-hannity-denied-calling-coronavirus-hoax-nine-days-after-he-called-coronavirus-hoax/.

227 **"And by the way, it's definitely not just the flu":** Tucker Carlson, "Tucker Carlson: The coronavirus will get worse—our leaders need to stop lying about that," Fox News, March 10, 2020, www.foxnews.com/opinion/tucker-carlson-the-coronavirus-will-get-worse-our-leaders-need-to-stop-lying-about-that.

227 **University of Chicago study later found that:** Leonardo Bursztyn, Aakaash Rao, Christopher Roth, and David Yanagizawa-Drott, "Misinformation During a Pandemic," Becker Friedman Institute, September 2020, bfi.uchicago.edu/wp-content/uploads/BFI_WP_202044.pdf.

227 **"The virus isn't just nearly as deadly as we thought it was":** "Tucker: Are coronavirus lockdowns working?" Fox News, April 27, 2020, www.youtube.com/watch?v=rBLXdKB-PjI.

227 **"In many places in this country, Americans cannot go to the park with their children":** "Tucker: Are coronavirus lockdowns working?" Fox News, April 22, 2020, www.youtube.com/watch?v=MuuA0azQRGQ.

227 **"it is definitely not about black lives":** "Tucker: Black Lives Matter is now a political party" Fox News, June 8, 2020, www.youtube.com/watch?v=l7aQ02YX7qo.

228 **triggered a number of companies, including Disney and Papa John's, to stop advertising on Carlson's show:** Tiffany Hsu, "Fox News Host Tucker Carlson Loses More Advertisers," *The New York Times*, June 12, 2020, www.nytimes.com/2020/06/12/business/media/tucker-carlson-fox-news-advertisers.html.

228 **"If you can't keep a Fox News correspondent from getting attacked directly across from your house":** Tucker Carlson, "Tucker Carlson: Our leaders have dithered and lied about the riots as the nation goes up in flames," Fox News, June 2, 2020, www.foxnews.com/opinion/tucker-carlson-nation-flames-leaders-dithered.

228 **"It's too bad":** Farah Griffin, interview with the author.

228 **"He'd say, 'Tucker's crushing us'":** Farah Griffin, interview with the author.

228 **In July, he commuted Roger Stone's prison sentence:** Peter Baker, Maggie Haberman, and Sharon LaFraniere, "Trump Commutes Sentence of Roger Stone in Case He Long Denounced," *The New York Times*, July 10, 2020, www.nytimes.com/2020/07/10/us/politics/trump-roger-stone-clemency.html.

229 **"He may be the best friend a man can have":** "Roger Stone speaks exclusively to Hannity following President Trump's commutation of his sentence," Fox News, July 13, 2020, www.foxnews.com/transcript/roger-stone-speaks-exclusively-to-hannity-following-president-trumps-commutation-of-his-sentence.

229 **"another beautiful city destroyed by the mob":** x.com/MattGertz/status/1285559476561555457

229 **Trump ignored the objections of the White House counsel and White House chief of staff:** Rhea Mahbubani, Oma Seddiq, "'I want them in jail':

Trump screamed at his aides for not doing more to quell protests in Seattle and Portland while he was 'getting killed on Tucker,' new book says," *Business Insider*, July 8, 2021, www.businessinsider.com/trump-fumed-seattle-portland-protests-want-them-in-jail-tucker-2021-7.

229 **ordered federal law enforcement officials, many of them members of the US Border Patrol's SWAT team equivalent:** Sergio Olmos, Mike Baker, and Zolan Kanno-Youngs, "Federal Officers Deployed in Portland Didn't Have Proper Training, D.H.S. Memo Said," *The New York Times*, updated July 21, 2020, www.nytimes.com/2020/07/18/us/portland-protests.html.

229 **"by far the most articulate":** "Politics With Tucker Carlson," *The Washington Post*, March 11, 2003, www.washingtonpost.com/wp-srv/liveonline/03/special/politics/sp_politics_carlson031103.html.

229 **now Carlson tried to link Biden to Antifa:** Angelica Stabile, "Tucker Carlson: Biden campaign 'surely' benefiting from Antifa, website connection," Fox News, September 2, 2020, www.foxnews.com/opinion/tucker-carlson-biden-campaign-connection-to-antifa.

229 **which he called "the armed wing of the Democratic Party":** x.com/MattGertz/status/1285559476561555457.

229 **"The leaders of today's Democratic Party . . . despise this country":** David Bauder, "Fox's Carlson criticized for saying Democrats hate America," Associated Press, July 7, 2020, apnews.com/article/donald-trump-us-news-racial-injustice-entertainment-tucker-carlson-76e2893f2397eb61f9bbe61c4941c729.

229 **Kamala Harris, who he told his viewers would actually be running the country if Trump was defeated:** Tucker Carlson, "Tucker Carlson: Presidential race coming to merciful end for Biden—and Trump still has a shot," Fox News, November 1, 2020, www.foxnews.com/opinion/tucker-carlson-2020-presidential-race-trump-biden.

229 **"A vote for Trump is a vote against them":** "Tucker Carlson: What Butler rally tells us about Trump and his support," Fox News, November 14, 2020, www.foxnews.com/transcript/tucker-carlson-what-butler-rally-tells-us-about-trump-and-his-support.

230 **including James Murdoch:** Sara Fischer, "Scoop: James and Kathryn Murdoch's next media investment," *Axios*, October 19, 2021, www.axios.com/2021/10/19/james-kathryn-murdoch-media-climate-change.

230 **he tried and failed to recruit a Republican to challenge Trump:** Mark Leibovich, "Meet the Other Resistance: The Republican One," *The New York Times Magazine*, April 24, 2019, www.nytimes.com/2019/04/24/magazine/republican-primary-trump-resistance.html.

230 **availed himself of the only option left—and endorsed Joe Biden:** William Kristol, "The Simple Answer," *The Bulwark*, March 2, 2020, www.thebulwark.com/p/the-simple-answer.

230 **who'd voted for Trump in 2016 but couldn't bring themselves to do so again:** Annie Karni, "Get Republicans to Vote Against Trump? This Group

Will Spend $10 Million to Try," *The New York Times*, May 28, 2020, www.nytimes.com/2020/05/28/us/politics/republican-voters-against-trump.html.

230 **Trump accused Chris Wallace, the debate's moderator, of asking unfair questions:** Nick Niedzwiadek, "Trump continues jabbing at moderator Wallace in debate's wake," *Politico*, September 30, 2020, www.politico.com/news/2020/09/30/donald-trump-chris-wallace-post-debate-423655.

230 **Trump's debate face-plant:** people familiar, interviews with the author.

231 **"Certainly if enthusiasm is any measure":** Tucker Carlson, "Tucker Carlson: Presidential race coming to merciful end for Biden—and Trump still has a shot."

231 **"They're fucked":** people familiar, interviews with the author.

231 **he later told multiple people that on Election Day, he voted for Kanye West:** Daniel Lippman, "Tucker Carlson told associates he voted for Kanye, not Trump," *Politico*, July 1, 2021, www.politico.com/news/2021/07/01/tucker-carlson-kanye-west-2020-vote-497654.

231 **"If Trump had run on law and order and re-opening the schools":** p. 203 of October 13, 2022, deposition of Ingraham in *Dominion Voting Systems v. Fox News Network*.

231 **"I just hate that shit":** Exhibit 519 in *Dominion Voting Systems v. Fox News Network*.

232 **claimed that the voting software made by the Dominion Voting Systems:** Linda Qiu, "How Sidney Powell inaccurately cited Venezuela's elections as evidence of U.S. fraud," *The New York Times*, November 19, 2020, www.nytimes.com/2020/11/19/technology/sidney-powell-venezuela.html.

232 **it had been a "mistake" not to cover Trump's election fraud claims:** Exhibit 519 in *Dominion Voting Systems v. Fox News Network*.

232 **"If you don't have conclusive evidence of fraud at that scale, it's a cruel and reckless thing to keep saying":** Exhibit 526 in *Dominion Voting Systems v. Fox News Network*.

232 **Then he went on his show and nuked her:** Tucker Carlson, "Tucker Carlson: Time for Sidney Powell to show us her evidence," Fox News, November 19, 2020, www.foxnews.com/opinion/tucker-carlson-rudy-giuliani-sidney-powell-election-fraud.

232 **"not a member":** Rosalind S. Helderman and Josh Dawsey, "Ex-Trump aide at Fox wrestled with election claims, network's interests," *The Washington Post*, March 12, 2023, www.washingtonpost.com/politics/2023/03/12/raj-shah-fox-trump/.

233 **The "irrational reaction" to his Powell segment:** Exhibit 528 in *Dominion Voting Systems v. Fox News Network*.

233 **"Like negotiating with terrorists," he added, "but especially dumb ones":** Sebastian Murdock, "Tucker Carlson's Ex-Producer Called Election Deniers 'Terrorists... Cousin F**king Types,'" *Huffpost*, March 14, 2023, sg.news.yahoo.com/tucker-carlson-ex-producer-called-182140041.html.

233 **"The Newsmax surge is a bit troubling":** Exhibit 223 in *Dominion Voting Systems v. Fox News Network*; Sarah Ellison, Paul Farhi, and Jeremy Barr, "Fox News feared losing viewers by airing truth about election, documents show," *The Washington Post*, February 17, 2023, www.washingtonpost.com/media/2023/02/17/fox-news-dominion-ratings-fear/.

233 **"News guys have to be careful how they cover this rally":** Mary Yang, "Fox Corp CEO praises Fox News leader as network faces $1.6 billion lawsuit," NPR, March 10, 2023, www.npr.org/2023/03/10/1162367271/fox-news-suzanne-scott-lachlan-murdoch.

234 **"[W]e will highlight our stars":** Exhibit 214 of *Dominion Voting Systems v. Fox News Network*.

234 **"We are screwed," Ingraham wrote:** Exhibit 555 of *Dominion Voting Systems v. Fox News Network*.

234 **"In one week and one debate they destroyed a brand that took twenty-five years to build":** Exhibit 230 of *Dominion Voting Systems v. Fox News Network*.

234 **"I hate him passionately," Carlson wrote of Trump:** Derek Hawkins, Sarah Ellison, and Blair Guild, "What Tucker Carlson said about Trump in private texts vs. on Fox News," *The Washington Post*, updated April 24, 2023, www.washingtonpost.com/media/2023/03/09/tucker-carlson-trump-texts-fox-news/.

235 **Trump's biggest cheerleaders at Fox sent desperate text messages to Mark Meadows:** Jeremy Barr, "Fox News hosts urged Meadows to have Trump stop Jan. 6 violence, texts show," *The Washington Post*, December 13, 2021, www.washingtonpost.com/media/2021/12/13/fox-ingraham-hannity-kilmeade-jan-6-trump-texts/.

235 **his son, Buckley, who was in the Capitol:** Alisha Rahaman Sarkar, "Tucker Carlson reveals his son was in Capitol building on 6 January," *The Independent*, December 10, 2021, www.the-independent.com/news/world/americas/us-politics/tucker-carlson-son-capitol-building-riot-b1973389.html.

235 **"Trump has two weeks left":** Derek Hawkins, Sarah Ellison, and Blair Guild, "What Tucker Carlson said about Trump in private texts vs. on Fox News."

236 **"a huge inflection point to keep Trump down and move on for the future of the conservative movement":** "Dominion's Combined Opposition to Fox News Network, LLC's and Fox Corporation's Rule 56 Motions for Summary Judgment" in *Dominion Voting Systems v. Fox News Network*, February 27, 2023, int.nyt.com/data/documenttools/dominion-opp-brief/823d0af7d1f7174b/full.pdf.

236 **"We want to make Trump a non person":** David Folkenflik, "Rupert Murdoch says Fox stars 'endorsed' lies about 2020. He chose not to stop them," NPR, February 28, 2023, www.npr.org/2023/02/28/1159819849/fox-news-dominion-voting-rupert-murdoch-2020-election-fraud.

236 **It was his numerous appearances:** Karen Zraick, "Ron DeSantis, the Republican Trump Wants to Be Florida's Governor," *The New York Times*,

August 29, 2018, www.nytimes.com/2018/08/29/us/politics/ron-desantis-bio-facts.html

236 **DeSantis appeared on Fox 113 times, almost once a day:** Steve Contorno, "Inside Fox News, DeSantis is 'the future of the party.' And he's taking advantage," *Tampa Bay Times*, August 13, 2021, www.tampabay.com/news/florida-politics/2021/08/13/inside-fox-news-desantis-is-the-future-of-the-party-and-hes-taking-advantage/

237 **cast doubt on the new COVID vaccines:** Aaron Blake, "The dangerous game Tucker Carlson is playing on vaccines," *The Washington Post*, March 16, 2021, www.washingtonpost.com/politics/2021/03/16/dangerous-game-tucker-carlson-is-playing-vaccines/.

237 **"than all vaccines":** Michael Luciano, "RFK Jr. Makes Nutso Claim to Tucker Carlson That Vaccine 'Appears to Be Killing More People Than All Vaccines Combined,'" *Mediate*, November 15, 2021, www.mediaite.com/media/tv/rfk-jr-tells-tucker-carlson-covid-vaccine-is-most-deadly/.

237 **"gentle people waving American flags":** Martin Pengelly, "Fox News host Tucker Carlson calls QAnon followers 'gentle' Patriots," *The Guardian*, March 6, 2021, www.theguardian.com/us-news/2021/mar/06/fox-news-host-tucker-carlson-qanon-followers.

237 **"feminizing":** Meghann Myers, "Senior leaders dunk on Tucker Carlson's misogynistic comments about maternity flight suits," *Military Times*, March 11, 2021, www.militarytimes.com/news/your-military/2021/03/11/senior-leaders-dunk-on-tucker-carlsons-misogynistic-comments-about-maternity-flight-suits/.

237 **"turn our country":** Tulsi Gabbard, "Tucker Carlson Tonight," Fox News, January 26, 2021, www.foxnews.com/transcript/gabbard-democrats-trying-to-turn-america-into-police-state.

237 **"He's not just a pig":** Brendan Cole, "Tucker Carlson Doubles Down on Mark Milley Criticism, Brands Comments 'Race Attack,'" *Newsweek*, January 26, 2021, www.newsweek.com/fox-news-tucker-carlson-critical-race-theory-racist-1604389.

237 **introduced his more than 4 million viewers . . . to "replacement theory":** Tucker Carlson, "Tucker Carlson: The truth about demographic change and why Democrats want it," Fox News, April 12, 2021, www.foxnews.com/opinion/tucker-carlson-immigration-demographic-change-democrats-elections.

238 **"legacy Americans":** Confessore, "How Tucker Carlson Stoked White Fear to Conquer Cable."

238 **Carlson complained about Wyoming Republican congresswoman Liz Cheney:** Exhibit 526 in *Dominion Voting Systems v. Fox News Network*.

238 **He revealed that Republican leader Kevin McCarthy:** Tucker Carlson, "Tucker Carlson: Why Republicans no longer recognize their own party," Fox News, May 1, 2021, www.foxnews.com/opinion/tucker-carlson-frank-luntz-republicans-kevin-mccarthy.

239 **highlighted South Carolina senator Lindsey Graham's long track record of being wrong:** Tucker Carlson, "Tucker: Lindsey Graham has long been a mouthpiece for Afghanistan lies," Fox News, September 1, 2021, www.foxnews.com/video/6270546838001.

239 **"hating Putin":** Tucker Carlson, "Tucker Carlson: Americans have been trained to hate Putin, and will suffer because of it," Fox News, February 23, 2022, www.foxnews.com/opinion/tucker-carlson-hate-putin-americans-suffer.

240 **Carlson making his trademark facial expressions as he watched the speech:** Erik Wemple, "President Biden heals America by muting Tucker Carlson," *The Washington Post*, March 12, 2021, www.washingtonpost.com/opinions/2021/03/12/president-biden-heals-america-by-muting-tucker-carlson/.

240 **"illiberal state":** Zsuzsanna Szelenyi, "How Viktor Orban Built His Illiberal State," *The New Republic*, April 5, 2022.

241 **NatCon Epcot:** John Ganz, "Anti-Democratic Vistas, Part I: The Right Goes to Hungary," *Unpopular Front*, August 10, 2021, www.unpopularfront.news/p/anti-democratic-vistas-part-i.

241 **"I've rarely thought we could learn":** Tucker Carlson, "Hungary Foreign Minister: Having another kid must not be an ecomomic decision anymore," Fox News, February 13, 2019, www.foxnews.com/video/6001934644001#sp=show-clips.

241 **"Trump fights like a drunk":** Benjamin Wallace-Wells, "What American Conservatives See in Hungary's Leader," *The New Yorker*, September 13, 2021, www.newyorker.com/news/annals-of-inquiry/what-rod-dreher-sees-in-viktor-orban.

241 **Dreher would leave the United States:** Rod Dreher, "Being Happy and Making Plans in Budapest," *The American Conservative*, October 6, 2022, www.theamericanconservative.com/being-happy-and-making-plans-in-budapest/.

242 **"It's a place we're going to be telling you a lot about":** Tucker Carlson, "The mainstream media's job is to defend the ruling class," Fox News, August 3, 2021, www.foxnews.com/transcript/tucker-the-mainstream-medias-job-is-to-defend-the-ruling-class.

242 **"the small country with a lot of lessons":** Tucker Carlson, "Making someone pay to live on your property is now a federal crime," Fox News, August 5, 2021, www.foxnews.com/transcript/tucker-making-someone-pay-to-live-on-your-property-is-now-a-federal-crime.

242 **"There are not tent cities":** Rosa Schwartzburg and Imre Szijarto, "Tucker Carlson Is Touting Hungary's Viktor Orban as a Competent Trump," *Jacobin*, August 17, 2021, jacobin.com/2021/08/tucker-carlson-viktor-orban-hungary-trump.

242 **"perfectly clean and orderly":** Carlson, "Making someone pay to live on your property is now a federal crime."

243 **He then pivoted to leadership:** Tucker Carlson, "'Tucker Carlson Tonight' on vaccines, Hungary Prime Minister interview," Fox News, August 5, 2021,

www.foxnews.com/transcript/tucker-carlson-tonight-on-vaccines-hungary-prime-minister-interview.

243 **On one of his last nights in Budapest:** Rod Dreher (@roddreher), "@TuckerCarlson giving an inspirational talk at dinner at the Prime Minister's office, talking about why #Hungary is a great place, and what we in the West have to learn from it," Twitter (now X), August 4, 2021, x.com/roddreher/status/1422999780133728256.

244 **Mike Pence went:** Jacob Knutson, "Pence says he hopes Supreme Court will overturn abortion rights," *Axios*, September 2, 2021, www.axios.com/2021/09/23/pence-texas-abortion-ban-hungary-forum.

244 **Jeff Sessions showed up:** David Nagy, "A Message to Hungary: 'We Need You!'" *Hungarian Conservative*, September 9, 2021, www.hungarianconservative.com/articles/current/a-message-to-hungary-we-need-you/.

244 **"represents Christian conservative values":** David Gilbert, "Why the Hell Is CPAC in Hungary This Year?" *Vice*, May 18, 2022, www.vice.com/en/article/cpac-hungary-orban/.

244 **another CPAC was held in Dallas:** Natalie Allison and Lamar Johnson, "Orban gets warm CPAC reception after 'mixed race' speech blowback," *Politico*, August 4, 2022, www.politico.com/news/2022/08/04/viktor-orban-cpac-00049935.

244 **Trump hosted Orbán:** Marton Losonczi, "PM Orban Meets with Trump, Musk at Mar-a-Lago: Alliance Still Strong," December 10, 2024, www.hungarianconservative.com/articles/current/viktor-orban-donald-trump-elon-musk-mar-a-lago-visit/.

244 **"the week that changed American conservatism":** Rod Dreher, "Budapest, City of Conservatives," *Hungarian Conservative*, January 16, 2023, www.hungarianconservative.com/articles/politics/budapest-city-of-conservatives/.

245 **"Whatever you thought about what happened yesterday, what was racist about it?":** "Tucker Carlson Tonight 1721 FULL Fox Trump Breaking News January 7 2021," Daily Motion, www.dailymotion.com/video/x7yjqnc.

245 **"In her eyes you can see that she knows she's about to die":** "Tucker Carlson Tonight 1-6-21 - Breaking Fox News January 06, 2021," Daily Motion, www.dailymotion.com/video/x7yixq7.

246 **"a mob of older people from unfashionable zip codes":** Tucker Carlson, "Tucker Carlson: Why are Jan. 6 protesters still in jail while murderers walk free?" Fox News, April 6, 2021, www.foxnews.com/opinion/tucker-carlson-jan-6-protesters-jailed-murderers-walk-free.

246 **"the vast majority of people inside the Capitol on January 6 were peaceful":** Tucker Carlson, "Tucker: What really happened on Jan 6," Fox News, September 23, 2021, www.foxnews.com/transcript/tucker-carlson-tonight-on-biden-late-night-hosts.

246 **"I believe it would be wise, and reassuring to our viewers":** Exhibit 211 in *Dominion Voting Systems v. Fox News Network*.

247 **TCO's early efforts featured Carlson's familiar hobbyhorses:** www.imdb.com/title/tt15676222/?ref_=ttep_ep_5

247 **Directed by Scooter Downey, a filmmaker who previously worked with the far-right conspiracy theorist Mike Cernovich:** Will Sommer, "He's Writing Tucker's Deranged Jan. 6 Movie—After Directing a Pizzagater's Opus," *The Daily Beast*, October 28, 2021, www.thedailybeast.com/tucker-carlsons-deranged-jan-6-movie-writer-scooter-downey-also-made-film-for-pizzagater-mike-cernovich/.

248 **"the only politician with zero interest in controlling other people":** Ryan Grim, "Gustav doesn't sidetrack Paulites," *Politico*, September 3, 2008, www.politico.com/story/2008/09/gustav-doesnt-sidetrack-paulites-013091.

248 **written about his longshot presidential bid for** The New Republic: Tucker Carlson, "Pimp My Ride," *The New Republic*, December 31, 2007, newrepublic.com/article/61255/representative-ron-paul-2008-republican-primary-president.

248 **"This is crazy," he told Labash. "I've got to get out of here.":** Matt Labash, "Among the Paultards," *Washington Examiner*, September 15, 2008, www.washingtonexaminer.com/magazine/780207/among-the-paultards/.

248 **for the sole purpose of humiliating him in a combative hour-long interview:** "Dangerous Conversation with Scott Ledger and Tucker Carlson on the phone," Part 1 of 4, February 6, 2012, www.youtube.com/watch?v=rOxBQnnK_Ms.

249 **Privately, Chris Wallace and Bret Baier both protested:** David Folkenflik, "2 Fox News commentators resign over Tucker Carlson series on the Jan. 6 siege," NPR, November 22, 2021, www.npr.org/2021/11/21/1052837157/fox-resignations-tucker-carlson-patriot-purge-documentary.

249 **Wallace had Liz Cheney . . . essentially rebut Carlson's claims:** "'Fox News Sunday' on November 7, 2021," Fox News, November 7, 2021, www.foxnews.com/transcript/fox-news-sunday-on-november-7-2021.

249 **a segment on Special Report . . . debunking false flag theories about January 6:** "Congress continues to investigate January 6 riot," Fox News, October 29, 2021, www.foxnews.com/video/6279428246001#sp=show-clips.

250 **in a letter posted on *The Dispatch*'s site, they explained that:** Steve Hayes and Jonah Goldberg, "Why We Are Leaving Fox News," *The Dispatch*, November 21, 2021, thedispatch.com/article/why-we-are-leaving-fox-news/.

250 **"Our viewers will be grateful," he taunted his erstwhile friends:** Ben Smith, "Two Fox News Contributors Quit in Protest of Tucker Carlson's Jan. 6 Special," *The New York Times*, November 21, 2021, www.nytimes.com/2021/11/21/business/jonah-goldberg-steve-hayes-quit-fox-tucker-carlson.html.

250 **He set out to do a "detailed examination" of** *Patriot Purge's claims*: Jon Ward, "Does Tucker Carlson's Jan. 6 documentary hold up under scrutiny?" *Yahoo! News*, January 5, 2022, www.yahoo.com/news/does-tucker-carlsons-jan-6-documentary-hold-up-under-scrutiny-013315104.html.

250 **Ward thanked Carlson for the correction:** Jon Ward, "Why Tucker Carlson attacked me on TV," *Medium*, January 5, 2022, jonward11.medium.com/why-tucker-carlson-attacked-me-on-tv-2b55490a468c

251 **On his show, alongside an unflattering photo of Ward:** x.com/AKA_RealDirty/status/1478903621962117128.

251 **"I was quite an idealist":** Ward, email to the author.

252 **Joe Kent was running in a Washington State congressional district:** Blake Hounshell, "A Trump-Backed Veteran Ran Hard to the Right, Only to Be Outflanked," *The New York Times*, July 25, 2022, www.nytimes.com/2022/07/25/us/politics/joe-kent-house-trump.html.

252 **"I was up against a Republican who was backed by the full weight of the Republican establishment":** Charles Homans, "Without Tucker Carlson, Far Right Loses a Foothold in the Mainstream," *The New York Times*, May 16, 2023, www.nytimes.com/2023/05/16/us/politics/tucker-carlson-far-right.html.

252 **Blake Masters, who was running for the US Senate in Arizona:** Jason Zengerle, "The Rise of the Tucker Carlson Politician," *The New York Times Magazine*, March 22, 2022, www.nytimes.com/2022/03/22/magazine/tucker-carlson-politician.html.

252 **"no longer believe[d] that freedom and democracy are compatible":** Peter Thiel, "The Education of a Libertarian," *Cato Unbound*, April 13, 2009, www.cato-unbound.org/2009/04/13/peter-thiel/education-libertarian/.

253 **Masters won the GOP primary in a rout:** "Senate: Arizona Primary Results (R)," CNN, April 19, 2023, www.cnn.com/election/2022/results/arizona/republican-primaries/senate.

254 **"a compassionate, discerning sociological analysis of the white underclass":** Jennifer Senior, "Review: In 'Hillbilly Elegy,' a Tough Love Analysis of the Poor Who Back Trump," *The New York Times*, August 10, 2016, www.nytimes.com/2016/08/11/books/review-in-hillbilly-elegy-a-compassionate-analysis-of-the-poor-who-love-trump.html

254 **gracing the stages of the Aspen Institute:** "Book Talk with JD Vance on 'Hillbilly Elegy,'" The Aspen Institute, September 20, 2017, www.youtube.com/watch?v=lKU9nlR-cQI.

254 **the 92nd Street Y, and other highbrow forums:** "JD Vance, author of Hillbilly Elegy, with General (Ret.) David H. Petraeus," The 92nd Street Y, October 10, 2017, www.youtube.com/watch?v=s3w5unMsjEM.

254 **calling him, in an essay for *The Atlantic*, "cultural heroin":** JD Vance, "Opioid of the Masses," *The Atlantic*, July 2016, www.theatlantic.com/politics/archive/2016/07/opioid-of-the-masses/489911/.

254 **in private, "a moral disaster" and "America's Hitler":** Andrew Kaczynski and Em Steck, "JD Vance, Trump's VP pick, once called him a 'moral disaster,' and possibly 'America's Hitler,'" CNN, July 15, 2024, www.cnn.com/2024/07/15/politics/kfile-jd-vance-comments-trump/index.html.

254 **As he later recounted:** a Vance friend, interview with the author.

255 **"Dominant elite society is boring, it is completely unreflective, and it is increasingly wrong":** Simon van Zuylen-Wood, "The Radicalization of JD Vance," *The Washington Post Magazine*, January 4, 2022, www.washingtonpost.com/magazine/2022/01/04/jd-vance-hillbilly-elegy-radicalization/

255 **When Mitch McConnell tried to recruit Vance to run for the US Senate:** Seung Min Kim and Kevin Robillard, "'Hillbilly Elegy' author Vance urged to run for Senate," *Politico*, January 8, 2018, www.politico.com/story/2018/01/08/ohio-senate-vance-brown-328565.

255 **he appeared fifteen times on** Tucker Carlson Tonight: Matt Gertz, "How Tucker Carlson helped JD Vance to victory in the Ohio Senate primary," *Media Matters*, May 4, 2022, www.mediamatters.org/fox-news/how-tucker-carlson-helped-jd-vance-victory-ohio-senate-primary.

255 **"the most-watched news program":** a Fox News producer, interview with the author.

255 **promoted replacement theory, warning of an immigrant "invasion":** "Republican Senate candidates promote 'replacement' theory," PBS News, May 17, 2022, www.pbs.org/newshour/politics/republican-senate-candidates-promote-replacement-theory

256 **"I don't really care what happens to Ukraine one way or another":** Kelsey Vlamis, "GOP Senate candidate JD Vance said he doesn't 'really care what happens to Ukraine,'" *Business Insider*, February 20, 2022, www.businessinsider.com/gop-candidate-jd-vance-i-dont-care-what-happens-ukraine-2022-2.

256 **"Silicon Valley technology companies as the enemies of western civilization":** Josh Feldman, "JD Vance Calls Silicon Valley Companies 'The Enemies of Western Civilization': It's 'Time to Destroy Them,'" Mediaite, November 19, 2021, www.mediaite.com/tv/j-d-vance-calls-silicon-valley-companies-the-enemies-of-western-civilization-its-time-to-destroy-them/.

256 **delivering the closing speech at their second annual conference:** JD Vance, "The Universities Are the Enemy," National Conservatism conference, October 31–November 2, 2021, nationalconservatism.org/natcon-2-2021/presenters/jd-vance/.

256 **releasing a TV ad that began: *"Are you a racist? Do you hate Mexicans?":*** www.youtube.com/watch?v=K3qYJoSV0lI

256 **"I think Tucker":** a Vance adviser, interview with the author.

256 **slowly brought Trump around on the elegiac hillbilly:** Alex Isenstadt, "Trump gives Vance coveted endorsement in Ohio Senate race," *Politico*, April 15, 2022, www.politico.com/news/2022/04/15/trump-vance-endorsement-ohio-senate-race-00025667.

256 **Vance made sure to thank both Trump and Carlson for their support:** "JD Vance U.S. Senate Republican Primary Victory Speech," C-SPAN, May 3, 2022, www.c-span.org/program/campaign-2022/jd-vance-us-senate-republican-primary-victory-speech/611870.

257 **Republican politicians and Fox hosts gleefully predicted a "red wave":** "How Fox News hyped a 'red wave' for weeks," *The Washington Post* video, November 10, 2022, www.youtube.com/watch?v=rEg2eXO4-kg.

257 **"The conventional view among people who follow politics is that the Democratic Party is about to suffer":** Tucker Carlson, "TUCKER CARLSON: Transparency restores faith in institutions," Fox News,

November 2, 2022, www.foxnews.com/opinion/tucker-carlson-transparency-restores-faith-institutions.

257 **was the fifth-smallest margin of control in modern history:** Drew DeSilver, "Narrow majorities in U.S. House have become more common but haven't always led to gridlock," Pew Research, May 5, 2023, www.pewresearch.org/short-reads/2023/05/05/narrow-majorities-in-u-s-house-have-become-more-common-but-havent-always-led-to-gridlock/.

257 **a group he once hailed as "surging outsiders":** "Voters are tired of the 'same old establishment talking points': Joe Kent," Fox News, October 22, 2022, www.foxnews.com/video/6314161492112.

257 **"I've never gotten anything wronger in my life":** Rob Crilly, "'I've never gotten anything wronger in my life': Tucker Carlson says he's getting out of the prediction game after the 'humiliation' of seeing his midterm picks flop and the red wave fail," *Daily Mail*, December 18, 2022, www.dailymail.co.uk/news/article-11550301/Tucker-Carlson-says-hes-getting-prediction-game-midterm-humiliation.html.

257 **"Occasionally, you run into somebody who could actually change things":** Shane Goldmacher and Maggie Haberman, "Tucker, Thiel and Trump: How JD Vance Won in Ohio," *The New York Times*, May 4, 2022, www.nytimes.com/2022/05/04/us/politics/jd-vance-trump-ohio-fox-news.html.

CHAPTER NINE

258 **delivered the keynote speech to more than two thousand people at the Heritage Foundation's fiftieth-anniversary gala:** "Tucker Carlson to Keynote Speech at Heritage's 50th Anniversary Gala," The Heritage Foundation, February 16, 2023, www.heritage.org/press/tucker-carlson-keynote-speech-heritages-50th-anniversary-gala.

258 **sued Fox for $1.6 billion for defaming it by repeatedly broadcasting Powell's bogus claims:** Karl Baker and David Folkenflik, "Meet the judge deciding the $1.6 billion defamation case against Fox News," NPR, February 15, 2023, www.npr.org/2023/02/15/1156610403/dominion-voting-vs-fox-news-judge-smartmatic-newsmax.

258 **obtained thousands of emails and text messages from Carlson and other Fox employees:** Stuart A. Thompson, Karen Yourish, and Jeremy W. Peters, "What Fox News Hosts Said Privately vs. Publicly About Voter Fraud," *The New York Times*, February 25, 2023, www.nytimes.com/interactive/2023/02/25/business/media/fox-news-dominion-tucker-carlson.html.

259 **the first draft of his monologue for that evening's show:** "EXCLUSIVE: Tucker Carlson's final, unaired Fox News monologue," Chadwick Moore, April 24, 2024, www.chadwickmoore.com/p/exclusive-tucker-carlsons-final-unaired.

260 **speculation, both inside and outside of Fox, about the reasons behind it:** Jason Zengerle, "Fox News Gambled, but Tucker Can Still Take Down the House," *The New York Times*, April 28, 2023, www.nytimes.com/2023/04/28/opinion/tucker-carlson-fox.html.

260 **Smith, who believed Carlson was "a messenger from God":** Gabriel Sherman, "Tucker Carlson's Prayer Talk May Have Led to Fox News Ouster: 'That Stuff Freaks Rupert Out,'" *Vanity Fair*, April 25, 2023, www.vanityfair.com/news/2023/04/tucker-carlson-fox-news-rupert-murdoch.

261 **that his firing was part of Fox's settlement with Dominion:** Michael Wolff, *The Fall*, 266–267.

262 **So did Omeed Malik, who together with Rebekah Mercer ran 1789 Capital:** Keach Hagey, "Tucker Carlson's Media Company Secures Investment Led by New 'Anti-Woke' Firm 1789 Capital," *The Wall Street Journal*, October 17, 2023, www.wsj.com/business/media/tucker-carlsons-media-company-secures-investment-led-by-new-anti-woke-firm-1789-capital-a47d20dd.

262 **"The world is his oyster":** a Carlson associate, interview with the author.

262 **cities he once derided as "chintzy" and "prefab":** Tucker Carlson, "Tucker: US came within minutes of war with Iran," Fox News, June 21, 2019, www.foxnews.com/video/6051003481001.

262 **buy out their investors:** Sara Fischer, "Scoop: Tucker Carlson buys out investors in his media company," *Axios*, June 13, 2025, www.axios.com/2025/06/13/tucker-carlson-investors.

262 **Finally, in July 2022:** Zengerle, "Fox News Gambled, but Tucker Can Still Take Down the House."

263 **"No, I'm sorry":** person familiar, interview with the author.

263 **"Nikki Haley believes":** Zengerle, "Fox News Gambled, but Tucker Can Still Take Down the House."

263 **DeSantis and his wife visited Carlson and Susie at their home:** Michael Wolff, *The Fall*, 245–246.

263 **"For a man who is caricatured":** Philip Bump, "Tucker Carlson gives Donald Trump an hour to say what he wants," *The Washington Post*, April 12, 2023, www.washingtonpost.com/politics/2023/04/12/trump-tucker-carlson-fox-news/.

264 **He accused Fox of having gone to the "dark side":** truthsocial.com/@realDonaldTrump/posts/108707942896549589

264 **Trump strung them along for months:** Jonathan Swan, Jeremy W. Peters, and Maggie Haberman, "Inside Trump's Decision to Skip the G.O.P. Debate," *The New York Times*, August 19, 2023, www.nytimes.com/2023/08/19/us/politics/trump-fox-debate.html.

264 **a pre-taped interview between the two that would be posted on X at the same time Fox was hosting the debate:** "Tucker on X Debate Night Interview with Donald Trump Transcript," Rev, www.rev.com/transcripts/tucker-on-x-debate-night-interview-with-donald-trump-transcript.

264 **"They started with protests":** Philip Bump, "Tucker did his best to drag Trump into his political violence fantasies," *The Washington Post*, August 24, 2023, www.washingtonpost.com/politics/2023/08/24/tucker-did-his-best-drag-trump-into-his-political-violence-fantasies/.

265 **Wells's cameras were about fifteen feet away . . . when Trump was shot:** "Justin Wells, Producer of "Art of the Surge" Takes Us Inside Trump World," The Clay Travis and Buck Sexton Show, November 1, 2024, at 0:44/12:08, www.youtube.com/watch?v=4VIHuMgKadg.

265 **made a long-since debunked claim that he smoked crack and had sex with Barack Obama:** x.com/tuckercarlson/status/1699142858844864846.

266 **Carlson traveled to Romania:** x.com/TuckerCarlson/status/1678873144201818115.

266 **"obviously a setup":** Alisha Rahaman Sarkar, "Tucker Carlson defends 'really smart' Andrew Tate yet again," *The Independent*, March 14, 2023, www.aol.com/tucker-carlson-defends-really-smart-082602064.html.

266 **Tate was eventually charged:** Isabella Kwai, "What to Know About the Accusations Against Andrew Tate," *The New York Times*, May 30, 2025, www.nytimes.com/article/andrew-tate-arrests-explained.html.

266 **"ratlike" and "a persecutor of Christians":** Justin Baragona, "ADL Warns Twitter Against Working With 'Obvious Antisemite' Tucker Carlson," *The Daily Beast*, June 8, 2023, www.thedailybeast.com/adl-warns-twitter-against-working-with-obvious-antisemite-tucker-carlson/.

266 **"blowing up churches and killing Christians":** Zack Beauchamp, "Tucker Carlson went after Israel—and his fellow conservatives are furious," *Vox*, April 16, 2024, www.vox.com/2024/4/16/24131384/tucker-carlson-interview-israel-palestine-munther-isaac.

266 **"focused on a conflict":** Jerusalem Post Staff, "Tucker Carlson: Ben Shapiro, pro-Israel voices don't care about America," *The Jerusalem Post*, December 31, 2023, www.jpost.com/diaspora/antisemitism/article-780172.

267 **hosted Darryl Cooper, a Nazi apologist historian:** Jason Zengerle, "The Strange Afterlife of Tucker Carlson," *The New York Times*, September 20, 2024, www.nytimes.com/2024/09/20/opinion/vance-tucker-carlson-interview.html.

267 **"He's what's called a useful idiot," Hillary Clinton told MSNBC:** "Hillary Clinton on Tucker Carlson: 'He's a useful idiot,'" MSNBC, February 7, 2024, www.youtube.com/watch?v=uFnsRbapyb4.

267 **After the interview was broadcast, Clinton seemed to have had a point:** "Tucker Carlson Interviews Vladimir Putin Transcript," Rev, www.rev.com/transcripts/tucker-carlson-interviews-vladimir-putin-transcript.

267 **Carlson had gone to Moscow with the goal of freeing Evan Gershkovich:** Joe Parkinson, Drew Hinshaw, Bojan Pancevski, and Aruna Viswanatha, "Inside the Secret Negotiations to Free Evan Gershkovich," *The Wall Street Journal*, August 1, 2024, www.wsj.com/world/europe/evan-gershkovich-prisoner-exchange-ccb39ad3.

268 **Vadim Krasikov, a Russian hitman:** "Putin called him a patriot. But who is Vadim Krasikov, a Russian released in the mass prisoner swap?" Associated Press, August 1, 2024, apnews.com/article/russia-us-prisoner-swap-gershkovich-krasikov-a48a143c9e6336738745e559adacffaf.

268 **Six months later, as part of a prisoner swap negotiated by the US and Russian governments:** Bojan Pancevski, "The Dark Figure at the Center of

Putin's Prisoner-Swap Demands," *The Wall Street Journal*, updated August 1, 2024, www.wsj.com/world/vadim-krasikov-putin-evan-gershkovich-prisoner-swap-f28e7b6d.

269 **Trump told reporters he was entertaining the idea of tapping Carlson as his veep:** Dominick Mastrangelo, "Trump says he'd consider Tucker Carlson as running mate," *The Hill*, November 9, 2023, thehill.com/homenews/campaign/4301977-trump-tucker-carlson-running-mate/.

269 **"God would have to yell at me very loud":** Dominick Mastrangelo, "Tucker Carlson: 'God would have to yell at me very loud' to be Trump running mate," *The Hill*, December 8, 2023, thehill.com/homenews/media/4349451-tucker-carlson-donald-trump-2024-running-mate-god-would-have-to-yell-at-me-very-loud/.

269 **Pfeiffer dug up Kamala Harris's 2019 candidate interview with the American Civil Liberties Union:** Jonathan Larsen, "It Wasn't Fox That Made Transgender Issues an Issue," The Fucking News, November 30, 2024, thefuckingnews.substack.com/p/it-wasnt-fox-that-made-transgender.

270 **"Kamala is for they/them. President Trump is for you.":** Shane Goldmacher, "Trump and Republicans Bet Big on Anti-Trans Ads Across the Country," *The New York Times*, October 8, 2024, www.nytimes.com/2024/10/08/us/politics/trump-republican-transgender-ads.html.

270 **invited Carlson to sit in his private box on the first night:** Michael M. Grynbaum and Jim Rutenberg, "Tucker Carlson, Ousted by Fox, Roars Into Milwaukee as a Top Trump Ally," *The New York Times*, July 18, 2024, www.nytimes.com/2024/07/18/business/media/tucker-carlson-trump-rnc.html.

270 **gave him a prime-time speaking slot on its final, most watched night:** "Tucker Carlson Speaks at RNC 2024 Night Four," Rev, www.rev.com/transcripts/tucker-carlson-speaks-at-rnc-2024-night-four.

270 **he had returned to the nation's capital like de Gaulle returning to Paris:** x.com/FrontlinesTPUSA/status/1881425939529449533.

271 **"Not one person was rude to me":** Piers Morgan, "Shut The F*ck Up!" Tucker Carlson vs Piers Morgan," *Piers Morgan Uncensored*, January 29, 2025, www.youtube.com/watch?v=qRO2NvIWCEY.

271 **"Trump wanted Tucker's opinion":** a Trump adviser, interview with the author.

271 **"so handsome":** Jesse McKinley, "The President-Elect Comments Often on the Men Around Him," *The New York Times*, December 27, 2024, www.nytimes.com/2024/12/27/style/donald-trump-compliments-looks-men.html.

271 **launched a furious lobbying campaign:** Vivian Salama, "How Tucker Carlson Killed Mike Pompeo's Hopes of Joining the Trump Administration," *The Wall Street Journal*, December 18, 2024, www.wsj.com/politics/trump-tucker-carlson-cabinet-pompeo-683d9150?mod=Searchresults_pos3&page=1.

271 **"warmonger"; "criminal":** people familiar, interviews with the author.

272 **revoked the security detail:** Maggie Haberman, "Trump Revokes Security Detail for Pompeo and Others, Despite Threats From Iran," *The New York*

Times, January 23, 2025, www.nytimes.com/2025/01/23/us/politics/trump-pompeo-security-iran.html.

272 **Howard Lutnick, Trump's transition-team cochair, had promised:** Xavier Martinez, "RFK Jr. Won't Be Health and Human Services Secretary if Trump Is Elected, Transition Leader Says," *The Wall Street Journal*, November 1, 2024, www.wsj.com/livecoverage/harris-trump-election-10-31-24/card/rfk-jr-won-t-be-health-and-human-services-secretary-if-trump-is-elected-transition-leader-says-ZlqEk7p0yqxK8A0aLvU7.

272 **Apple's most-shared episode:** "Apple shares the most popular podcasts of 2024," www.apple.com/newsroom/2024/11/apple-shares-the-most-popular-podcasts-of-2024/.

273 **"an enemy of the United States":** Clay Walker, "Tucker Carlson: Every GOP Sen Must Support Tulsi," *The Daily Beast*, December 22, 2024, www.yahoo.com/news/tucker-carlson-every-gop-sen-051830854.html.

273 **She was confirmed:** Amy MacKinnon, "Tulsi Gabbard confirmed as director of national intelligence," *Politico*, www.politico.com/news/2025/02/12/tulsi-gabbard-confirmed-as-director-of-national-intelligence-00203829.

273 **became a leading "realist" voice:** Jacob Heilbrunn, "Elbridge Colby Wants to Finish What Donald Trump Started," *Politico*, April 11, 2023, www.politico.com/news/magazine/2023/04/11/tucker-carlson-eldridge-colby-00090211.

273 **"one of the very few":** Tucker Carlson (@TuckerCarlson) "Elbridge Colby is one of the very few experienced national security officials who actually agrees with Donald Trump. He's likely to play a big role in the new administration," X, November 10, 2024, x.com/TuckerCarlson/status/1855675378637090883.

273 **"play a large and meaningful":** Tucker Carlson, "National Security Expert Elbridge Colby's Advice to Trump on How to Avoid WWIII & Handle the CIA," *The Tucker Carlson Show*, November 10, 2024, www.youtube.com/watch?v=PtsGqGc-Iuw.

273 **over the objections:** Matthew Kassel, "Rumored for a Trump posting, Elbridge Colby's dovish views on Iran stand out," *Jewish Insider*, November 13, 2024, jewishinsider.com/2024/11/elbridge-colby-trump-administration-iran/.

273 **Trump tapped Colby:** Greg Jaffe, "A Pentagon Nomination Fight Reveals the New Rules of Trump's Washington," *The New York Times*, March 17, 2025, www.nytimes.com/2025/03/17/us/politics/elbridge-colby-pentagon-trump.html.

273 **Darren Beattie:** Alex Demas, "Controversial Posts by State Department Appointee Are Genuine," *The Dispatch*, February 5, 2025, thedispatch.com/article/fact-check-darren-beattie-tweets-white-men/.

273 **Alex Pfeiffer:** The White House, "President Trump Announces Appointments to White House Offices of Communications, Public Liaison, and Cabinet Affairs," January 24, 2025, www.whitehouse.gov/briefings-statements/2025/01/president-trump-announces-appointments-to-the-white-house-offices-of-communications-public-liaison-and-cabinet-affairs/.

274 **deport more than two hundred Venezuelan immigrants:** Julie Turkewitz, Jazmine Ulloa, Isayen Herrera, Hamed Aleaziz, and Zolan Kanno-Youngs,

"'Alien Enemies' or Innocent Men? Inside Trump's Rushed Effort to Deport 238 Migrants," *The New York Times*, April 15, 2025, www.nytimes.com/2025/04/15/world/americas/trump-migrants-deportations.html.

274 **It was Carlson who:** "Tucker Carlson Originals: Hunting MS13," Fox Nation, June 10, 2021.

274 **Noem later released:** Julie Turkewitz, Jazmine Ulloa, Isayen Herrera, Hamed Aleaziz, and Zolan Kanno-Youngs, "'Alien Enemies' or Innocent Men? Inside Trump's Rushed Effort to Deport 238 Migrants."

274 **Vance's remarkable dressing-down:** Adriana Gomez Licon, "What They Said: Trump, Zelenskyy and Vance's Heated Argument in the Oval Office," Associated Press, updated February 28, 2025, apnews.com/article/trump-zelenskyy-vance-transcript-oval-office-80685f5727628c64065da81525f8f0cf.

274 **white South African landowners:** Tyler Pager, John Eligon, Hamed Aleaziz, and Aishvarya Kavi, "White South Africans Granted Refugee Status by Trump Arrive in the U.S.," *The New York Times*, May 12, 2025, www.nytimes.com/2025/05/12/us/politics/white-south-africans-refugees.html.

275 **Trump's landmark speech in Riyadh:** "Full text of Trump's speech in Riyadh: 'Dawn of the bright new day for the great people of the Middle East,'" *The Times of Israel*, May 16, 2025, www.timesofisrael.com/full-text-of-trumps-speech-in-riyadh-dawn-of-the-bright-new-day-for-the-great-people-of-the-middle-east/.

275 **competitive authoritarianism:** Andrew Marantz, "Is It Happening Here?" *The New Yorker*, April 28, 2025, www.newyorker.com/magazine/2025/05/05/is-the-us-becoming-an-autocracy.

275 **TC's dire predictions about Iran war:** x.com/TuckerCarlson/status/1930430114602402183.

276 **TC on Fox's "propaganda hose":** Sonam Sheth, "Tucker Carlson and Steve Bannon Lead MAGA Resistance to Iran War," *Newsweek*, June 16, 2025, www.newsweek.com/tucker-carlson-steve-bannon-maga-trump-iran-israel-war-2086346.

276 **Trump calling TC "kooky" and taunting him for not having a TV show:** Tess Patton, "Trump Mocks 'Kooky' Tucker Carlson for Getting Fired From Fox After Disagreeing on Iran-Israel Conflict | Video," Yahoo! News, June 16, 2025, www.yahoo.com/news/trump-mocks-kooky-tucker-carlson-005427572.html.

277 ***Ceasefire*:** Michael M. Grynbaum, "Can C-SPAN Pull Off 'Crossfire,' but With Civility?" *The New York Times*, May 15, 2025, www.nytimes.com/2025/05/15/business/media/cspan-ceasefire.html.

277 ***The Atlantic*'s "accountability journalism":** Benjamin Mullin, "The Atlantic Beefs Up Politics Coverage Under Trump" *The New York Times*, December 31, 2024, www.nytimes.com/2024/12/31/business/media/atlantic-politics-parker-scherer.html.

277 **Decline of WaPo:** Clare Malone, "Is Jeff Bezos Selling Out the Washington Post?" *The New Yorker*, May 12, 2025, www.newyorker.com/magazine/2025/05/26/is-jeff-bezos-selling-out-the-washington-post.

277 ***The Dispatch* Hayes quote:** Steve Hayes, "Thank You," *The Dispatch*, October 8, 2024, thedispatch.com/article/thank-you-five-years-2/.

277 ***The Dispatch* having 50k paid subscribers and 700k free ones:** Goldberg, interview with the author.

277 ***The Dispatch* eight staffers:** Laura Hazard Owen, "Substack's first media company is The Dispatch, a center-right site founded by former Weekly Standard and National Review editors," NiemanLab, October 8, 2019, www.niemanlab.org/2019/10/substacks-first-media-company-is-the-dispatch-a-center-right-site-founded-by-former-weekly-standard-and-national-review-editors/.

277 ***The Dispatch* more than twenty staffers:** thedispatch.com/staff/.

278 **Bulwark sub numbers:** Natalie Korach, "'People Feel Like They Are Friends With Us': How The Bulwark Is Thriving in a New Trump Era," *Vanity Fair*, May 7, 2025, www.vanityfair.com/news/story/the-bulwark-is-thriving-in-trump-era?srsltid=AfmBOop3EGoPlaNz81VBJpA72VvvC5X3Jw2khd1-N4bgOAVGaKm26_s9.

278 **Kristol "former conservative":** Jesús Rodríguez, "The Bulwark: How Could It Be Wrong When It Feels So Center-Right?" *The Washington Post*, May 28, 2024, www.washingtonpost.com/style/power/2024/05/28/the-bulwark-podcasts-newsletters/.

278 **"Anti Semite filth":** x.com/jpodhoretz/status/1777827087417573674.

278 **"Trump bombed Iran":** x.com/jpodhoretz/status/1941185424174821558.

278 **"to keep the lines of communication open":** Ferguson, interview with the author.

278 **Labash and Carlson ceased contact altogether:** Labash, interview with the author.

279 **Demon attack:** www.youtube.com/watch?v=LDIqoPKNhgo.

INDEX

ABOUT THE AUTHOR

JASON ZENGERLE is a contributing writer for *The New York Times Magazine*. He is a winner of the Toner Prize for Excellence in Political Reporting and the recipient of a New America fellowship. He lives with his family in Chapel Hill, North Carolina.